DISCOVERING AUTOCAD® RELEASE 12

MARK DIX and PAUL RILEY
CAD Support Associates

PRENTICE HALL, Englewood Cliffs, New Jersey 07632

Library of Congress Cataloging-in-Publication Data

Dix, Mark.
    Discovering AutoCAD release 12 / Mark Dix & Paul Riley.
       p. cm.
    Includes bibliographical references and index.
    ISBN 0-13-042904-X
    1. Computer graphics. 2. AutoCAD (Computer file) I. Riley,
Paul. II. Title.
T385.D63 1994
620′.0042′02855369—dc20   93-4820
                                              CIP

Acquisitions Editor: Linda Ratts
Production Editor: Irwin Zucker
Copy Editor: Dan Mausner
Production Coordinator: Linda Behrens
Cover Design: Design Solutions
Supplements Editor: Alice Dworkin

The author and publisher of this book have used their best efforts in preparing this book. These efforts include the development, research, and testing of the theories and programs to determine their effectiveness. The author and publisher make no warranty of any kind, expressed or implied, with regard to these programs or the documentation contained in this book. The author and publisher shall not be liable in any event for incidental or consequential damages in connnection with, or arising out of, the furnishing, performance, or use of these programs.

ISBN 0-13-042904-X

Prentice-Hall International (UK) Limited, *London*
Prentice-Hall of Australia Pty. Limited, *Sydney*
Prentice-Hall Canada Inc., *Toronto*
Prentice-Hall Hispanoamericana, S.A., *Mexico*
Prentice-Hall of India Private Limited, *New Delhi*
Prentice-Hall of Japan, Inc., *Tokyo*
Simon & Schuster Asia Pte. Ltd., *Singapore*
Editora Prentice-Hall do Brasil, Ltda., *Rio De Janeiro*

For Sylvia and Peggy

CONTENTS

CHAPTER 3   **52**

CHAPTER 4   **80**

CHAPTER 5   **106**

CHAPTER 6   *132*

PART II   **Text, Dimensions, and Other Complex Entities**   *164*

CHAPTER 7   *164*

CHAPTER 8   *196*

CHAPTER 9

Commands: DONUT, FILL, MSLIDE, OFFSET, PEDIT, PLINE, POINT, POLYGON, SKETCH, SOLID, VSLIDE

CHAPTER 10

Commands: ATTDEF, ATTDISP, ATTEDIT, ATTEXT, BLOCK, DDATTE, DDATTDEF, INSERT, WBLOCK, XBIND, XREF

CHAPTER 11

Commands: ELLIPSE, ISOPLANE, SNAP (isometric), VIEW, ZOOM (dynamic)

PART III   **Three-Dimensional Modeling**   ***320***

CHAPTER **12**   ***320***

Commands: DDVPOINT, RULESURF, UCS, UCSICON, VPOINT

CHAPTER **13**   ***354***

Commands: 3DMESH, EDGESURF, HIDE, REVSURF, REDRAWALL,
REGENALL, RULESURF, TABSURF, VPORTS

CHAPTER **14**   ***386***

Commands: DDSOLPRM, SOLBOX, SOLCUT, SOLCHP, SOLFEAT,
SOLMASSP, SOLLIST, SOLMAT, SOLMOVE, SOLSECT, SOLSUB,
SOLUNION, SOLWEDGE

PREFACE

Drawing on a CAD system is a skill that can be learned only through many hours of practice. Like driving a car or playing a musical instrument, it cannot be learned by reading about it or watching someone else do it.

Accordingly, this book takes a very active approach to teaching AutoCAD. It is designed as a teaching tool and a self-study guide and assumes that readers will have access to a personal computer CAD workstation. It is organized around drawing exercises or tasks that offer the reader a demonstration of the commands and techniques being taught at every point, with illustrations that show exactly what to expect on the computer screen when steps are correctly completed. While the focus is on the beginning AutoCAD user, we have found over the years that experienced CAD operators also look to our books for tips, suggestions, and clear explanations of AutoCAD commands and principles.

The AutoCAD world is full of books, many of which do little more than duplicate the function of the *AutoCAD Reference Manual*. In this text we strive to present an optimal learning sequence. Topics are carefully grouped so that readers will progress logically through the AutoCAD command set. Explanations are straightforward and focus on what is relevant to actual drawing procedures. Most important, drawing exercises are included at the end of every chapter so that newly learned techniques are applied to practical drawing situations immediately. The level of difficulty increases steadily as skills are acquired through experience and practice.

All figures and working drawings have been prepared using AutoCAD. Drawing exercises at the end of all chapters are reproduced in a large, clearly dimensioned format on each right-hand page with accompanying tips and suggestions on the left-hand page. Drawing suggestions offer time-saving tips and explanations on how to use new techniques in actual applications. The book is not a drafting manual, yet the drawings include a wide range of applications, and anyone completing them all will be well equipped to move on to more advanced and specialized applications.

We would like to thank the many people who have helped us in the preparation of this book. To begin with, thanks to Doug Humphrey, our editor at Prentice Hall, for his encouragement and support, to Irwin Zucker, for his expert production editing; and to Russ Ryden, our friend and colleague at CAD Support Associates for his enthusiasm and technical expertise.

    We are grateful to a number of people at Autodesk, Inc., including Gloria Bastides
for her help, Mark Sturges and Joe Oakley for the use of software, Nancy Angell and
Wayne Hodgins for their help in establishing an authorized AutoCAD Teacher Training
Center.

    Thanks to Houston Instruments for the use of DMP-62 plotters and the supply of
pens and plotter paper used in preparing illustrations and to Summagraphics for the use
of Microgrid digitizers.

    We are grateful to Mike Pillarella for technical advice and support; and to Clifton
Boyle and Louis D'Abrosca at Johnson and Wales University Graduate School, for their
interest in this project and commitment to CAD education.

    Finally, thanks to Stanley Hopkins, Maria Hull, and Donald Wendt, for their
thoughtful reviews and suggestions, and to Dave Sumner and Jim Marshall for classroom testing the manuscript.

Mark Dix and Paul Riley

INTRODUCTION TO RELEASE 12

Release 12 provides a richer, friendlier, more flexible drawing environment than any previous AutoCAD release. From the moment you enter the drawing editor to the time you are ready to plot your drawing, you will be working with dramatic enhancements in the way this powerful software package supports drafting and design procedures.

This book will take you through a broad range of essential AutoCAD drawing techniques. In Part I (Chapters 1–6) you will learn 2D drawing and editing procedures using lines, arcs, and circles, with multiple layers, linetypes, and colors. In Part II (Chapters 7–11) you will add text and dimensions to your drawings and work with blocks, polylines, and other complex 2D entities. Part III (Chapters 12–14) will lead you into the exciting world of 3D, including wire frame, surface, and solid modeling. Part IV (Chapter 15) is devoted to the mechanics of getting your drawing out on paper.

Drawing and Plotting: Using Part IV

We have maintained a clear separation between drawing and plotting procedures throughout this book. This is consistent with AutoCAD's separation of "model space" and "paper space," and will help you to develop good CAD technique. All major plotting issues are saved for separate treatment in Part IV. However, it is certainly not our intention that you should put off plotting until you have completed everything else. Part IV is accessible from any point in the book. Whenever you are ready to plot your first drawing, turn to this section and work through Task 1, which covers basic 2D plotting. Later, as you need more elaborate plotting procedures involving multiple viewports, you will find what you need in Tasks 2–6.

Varieties of CAD

AutoCAD has become the industry standard software for computer-aided drafting and design. It is widely used for the preparation of all types of drawings that previously would have been created on a drafting board.

Its "open architecture" allows companies and third-party developers to customize it for specific applications, so that productivity is further enhanced.

AutoCAD is a full 3D package capable of a tremendous range of both 2D and 3D applications. As you learn, it will be useful to begin to think in terms of a hierarchy of complexity in the use of CAD.

On the first level is 2D drafting. This is the world for which AutoCAD was originally developed. Two-dimensional drawings in AutoCAD can be stored, edited, and plotted to any scale or paper size. The windowing, layering, and multiple viewport capabilities of AutoCAD allow a single drawing to produce a variety of different plots, depending on the type of information required. Through the process of attribute extraction, 2D drawings also can be used in conjunction with database programs to produce numerical data for cost estimates and bills of materials (see Chapter 10). 2D drawing techniques are the subject of Chapters 1–11. However, everything you learn in the 2D chapters will be useful when you get to 3D, and nothing will need to be relearned.

The second level in this hierarchy is 3D wireframe modeling. This is the focus of Chapter 12. Wireframe models share with 2D drawings an emphasis on precise dimensioning, which can be used in communicating design specifications for manufacturing, as well as for cost estimates and bills of materials. There is no attempt in either 2D drafting or wire frame modeling to represent the physical qualities of the object being drawn. Rather, the emphasis is on a precise mathematical description of outlines, boundaries, and edges. A wire frame model may be viewed from any angle and may be used to produce 2D orthographic projections, which may be plotted simultaneously.

Surface modeling is the third level. A surface model not only shows the outline of objects, but it also attempts to fill in between the lines. Surface models are explored in Chapter 13. One of the primary uses of surface modeling is to produce realistic shaded renderings that simulate the effect of light and shadow on real surfaces. This is accomplished by linking AutoCAD surface models with software such as AutoSHADE, AutoAnimator, RenderMan, and 3D Studio.

Finally, solid modeling is the fourth level of CAD. In solid modeling the goal is to represent not only the shapes but also interior characteristics of solid objects. Solid modeling is used by engineering firms to perform finite element analysis (FEA). FEA allows designers and engineers to simulate and predict the behavior of 3D objects based on mathematical representations of their interior physical properties. AME (the Advanced Modeling Extension) is AutoCAD's powerful add-on solid modeling program. In Chapter 14 we offer a substantial introduction to AME for those who have the software.

Using This Book with Earlier Versions of AutoCAD

The first 11 chapters of this book can be used effectively with any version of AutoCAD. You will notice significant differences, but you can work around them. Chapters 12 and 13 can be used with Release 10 or later versions only. Chapter 14 requires Release 11 or 12 and the AME programs. Chapter 15 requires Release 12.

ROAD MAP

You will notice that all the chapters in this book follow the same layout. We have included this road map to help you find your way around. Following is a description of each of the major sections of the chapter format along with sample entries.

COMMANDS (sample)

INQUIRY	EDIT
HELP	ERASE
	MOVE
	COPY

The COMMANDS section lists the commands and topics that are introduced in the chapter. Headings are taken from the AutoCAD standard screen menu. For example, you will see HELP under INQUIRY; and ERASE, MOVE, and COPY under EDIT, just as they are located in the standard screen menu. See the primary screen menu hierarchy in Appendix A for more information on where to find commands in the screen menu system.

OVERVIEW

Each chapter begins with a brief overview that gives you an idea of what you will be able to do with the new commands in that chapter.

TASKS (sample)

1. Read about introductory tasks.
2. Read about drawing projects.
3. Begin Chapter 1.

All the tasks that make up a chapter are listed at the beginning of the chapter. This tells you at a glance exactly what you will be required to do to complete the chapter.

Each chapter consists of two types of tasks. The body of the text includes step-by-step exercises in which new commands are introduced. Then, at the end of the chapter, you will find drawing projects, which require the use of the new commands and techniques. By completing the exercises in the chapter you will learn the skills needed to complete the drawings at the end of the chapter.

TASK 1: Introductory tasks

Procedure. (sample)

1. Type or select "HELP".
2. Type a command name or pick "Index..." to see a list of commands for which help is available.

A procedure list is placed at the beginning of many of the introductory exercises. It is intended as a reference and a quick overview of the command sequence you will be learning. The instructions in the list are general and are not sufficient to give the specific results that are required to complete the task. *The procedure list is not the exercise itself, and we do not recommend that you try to learn the command by following the list.* The actual instructions in the Discussion section are much more specific and are always preceded by an arrow ">".

Discussion.   The Discussion section includes specific instructions along with explanations, illustrations, and feedback about what will happen on your monitor when you carry out the instructions. Typically, there will be an instruction followed by AutoCAD's response and any information we feel is necessary or helpful.

The HELP command

The following sample instructions show how to use AutoCAD's HELP command. It is included here for reference and as an example and is not intended for actual execution at this time. The HELP feature is useful, and you are encouraged to try it out at any point as you progress through the book.

(sample instructions)

> Type or select "HELP" or press enter at the "Command:" prompt.

In Release 12 this will call the Help dialogue box shown in *Figure 1*.

NOTE: We have chosen to use the term "enter" to refer to what AutoCAD commonly calls the "Return" key. This is because "enter" is more common on newer keyboards.

> Type the name of a command, LINE for example, and press enter, or move the arrow over "Index..." and press the pick button.

If you pick "Index...", AutoCAD will open a second dialogue box with a list of commands. You can move up and down in the list by clicking on the arrows in the scroll bar at the right. Then click on the item you want and click on "OK" to exit the index dialogue.

Typing the name of a command or selecting from the index will call up information on the chosen command. This information will be displayed in the dialogue box. You can move on to the next page of information by clicking on "Next", or you can move back a page by clicking on "Previous".

> Click on "OK" to exit the Help dialogue box.

(end of sample)

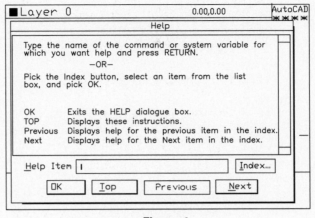

Figure 1

Notice that all instructions are highlighted with an arrow (>). This will make it easy for you to know exactly what you are expected to do. The comments that accompany instructions are important for your understanding of what is happening and will help you to avoid confusion.

> NOTE: You will find the *AutoCAD Reference Manual* cited in numerous places along the way. When you need additional information on a command or topic, this is the best place to go. The reference manual is an indispensable tool, and any experienced AutoCAD user consults it frequently. We encourage you to become familiar with it.

TASK 2: Drawing projects

There are three to six drawing projects at the end of each chapter. These are progressive, making use of previously learned commands as well as new ones. You will find the drawing itself on the right-hand page and drawing suggestions on the left-hand page.

Remember that any drawing may be executed in a number of ways. Our suggestions are not written in stone. Unlike the instructions in the introductory exercises, drawing instructions will not take you through the complete project. Besides the suggestions themselves, there is information on the drawing page that may assist you. In earlier chapters, this includes a list of commands you will need to use, a list of function keys and their functions, and, of course, the dimensions of the drawing itself. Later on you will see only the dimensions.

TASK 3: Chapter 1

You are now ready to begin Chapter 1.

CHAPTER

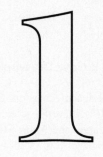

1

DRAW	EDIT	UTILITY	DISPLAY
LINE	U	END	REDRAW
	REDO	NEW	UCSICON
		QUIT	
		QSAVE	
		SAVE	
		SAVEAS	

OVERVIEW

This chapter will introduce you to some of the tools you will use whenever you draw in AutoCAD. You will learn to control basic elements of the drawing editor using five function keys. You will produce drawings involving straight lines and learn to undo your last command with the U command. Your drawings will be saved, if you wish, using the END, SAVE, QSAVE, or SAVEAS commands.

Look over the following tasks to get an idea of where we are going, and then begin Task 1.

TASKS

1. Begin a new drawing.
2. Explore the drawing editor and the F keys.
3. Draw a line. Undo it.
4. Review.
5. Draw a square. Use REDRAW to remove blips.

6. Save a drawing.
7. Do Drawing 1-1 ("Grate").
8. Do Drawing 1-2 ("Design").
9. Do Drawing 1-3 ("Shim").

TASK 1: Beginning a New Drawing

Discussion. Release 12 differs from all previous AutoCAD releases in the way that you begin drawings. In earlier releases the first thing you encounter when you load AutoCAD is a menu called the Main Menu. Before you can do any actual drawing or editing you have to name a new or an existing drawing. By contrast, Release 12 puts you immediately into the drawing editor, which is where you do most of your work with AutoCAD. You can begin drawing immediately and name your drawing file later, or you can open a new or previously saved file. In this task you will begin a new drawing in Release 12 and ensure that your drawing editor shows the "No Prototype" default settings we have used in preparing this chapter.

> Load AutoCAD.

This is done by going into the directory or subdirectory where ACAD.exe resides and typing "ACAD" <enter>. Your system probably has a simpler method, utilizing a batch file to automate the loading process. If so, we assume that there is someone around who can show you how.

> Wait....

Assuming you are in Release 12, you will see the AutoCAD drawing editor, as shown in *Figure 1-1*. When you see the "Command:" prompt at the bottom of the screen you are ready to proceed.

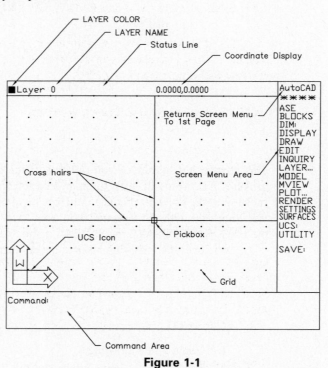

Figure 1-1

At this point you could begin drawing immediately. However, for our purposes it will be a good idea to use the NEW command to ensure that your drawing editor shows the same default settings as are used in this chapter.

> Type "new" and press enter.

After you press enter a dialogue box will appear, as shown in *Figure 1-2*. Dialogue boxes are used extensively in Release 12 and are discussed throughout this book. For now, simply notice the flashing vertical line in the rectangle at the bottom right. This indicates that AutoCAD is ready to accept typed input.

You will also see a small arrow somewhere on your screen. If you do not see it, move your pointing device to the middle of your drawing area or digitizer. When you see the arrow, you are ready to proceed.

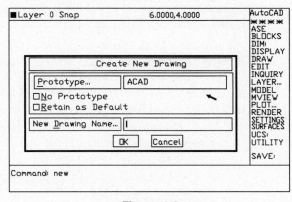

Figure 1-2

> Move your pointing device until the arrow is in the box labelled "No Prototype" and press the pick button.

An X will appear in the box indicating that "No Prototype" has been selected.

> Move the arrow down to "OK" and click there.

The dialogue box will disappear and you will see the AutoCAD logo for a few moments. Then your screen should resemble *Figure 1-1* again, but without the dots. You are now ready to proceed to Task 2.

TASK 2: Exploring the Drawing Editor

Discussion. You are looking at the AutoCAD drawing editor. There are many ways that you can alter it to suit a particular drawing application. To begin with, there are a number of features that can be turned on and off using the F-keys on your keyboard, or an equivalent using the control (Ctrl) key along with a letter. The F-keys are more efficient, since a single key does not require you to take your drawing hand off the pointing device. The Ctrl key alternatives are presented in this chapter for reference and are not used elsewhere in this book. Note that the five function keys and their functions are listed at the bottom of every drawing through Chapter 8 of this book, so it is not necessary to memorize them now. You will learn them best through repeated use. Also note that if you are using something other than an IBM-style keyboard, these important functions may be assigned to different keys. If you need more information, refer to the *AutoCAD Interface, Installation, and Performance Guide*.

The Screen

When you have entered the drawing editor, your screen should appear much like *Figure 1-1*. One major difference is that there will be no grid (dots) on your screen initially. One of the first things you will do is turn the grid on.

On the left side of the status line (at the top of the screen) you will see this: "Layer 0". You don't have to worry about layers until Chapter 3. For now, simply be aware that you are drawing on a layer called "0", and that it uses white, continuous lines. The small white box next to the word "Layer" indicates the color of the current layer. It will remain white until you change layers in Chapter 3.

On the right of the screen, in the Screen Menu Area, you will see a screen menu. Probably, but not necessarily, it will be the AutoCAD standard screen menu shown here. The AutoCAD standard menu is discussed in Appendix B. If you have some other menu, we assume that there is someone around who can get you started on it. Also, the general discussion of menus in Appendix B will help. In any case, you can do everything in this book without ever using the screen menu or a tablet menu if you wish.

Switching Screens

>Press F1 (there is no ctrl key equivalent for F1).

Oops! What happened to the screen?

What you see now is a text screen. You can switch back and forth between text and graphics using F1, the flip screen key.

>Press F1 again.

This brings back the graphics screen. Any text that does not fit in the command area is not visible.

NOTE: Sometimes AutoCAD switches to the text screen automatically when there is not enough room in the command area for prompts or messages. If this happens, use F1 when you are ready to return to the graphics screen.

Cross Hairs and Pickbox

You should see two lines at right angles horizontally and vertically, intersecting somewhere in the display area of your screen. These are the cross hairs, or screen cursor, that tell you where your pointing device (puck, mouse, cursor, stylus, whatever) is located on your digitizer or drawing pad. (If there are no cross hairs on your screen, make sure your pointing device is placed within the digitizing area.)

At the intersection of the cross hairs you will also see a small box. This is called the "pickbox" and is used to select objects for editing. You will learn more about the pickbox later.

Move the pointer and see how the cross hairs move in coordination with your hand movements.

Status Line and Pull Down Menus

> Move the pointer so that the cross hairs move to the top of the screen, into the status line.

When you reach the status line, your cross hairs will change into a pointing arrow, and the pull down menu bar will replace the status line.

Your screen should resemble *Figure 1-3*.

This is the pull down bar from which you can open up pull down menus that contain a set of the most often used commands. Pull downs are discussed at the beginning of Task 3.

NOTE: Here and throughout this book we show the Release 12 versions of AutoCAD screens in our illustrations. If you are working with another version, your screen may show significant variations.

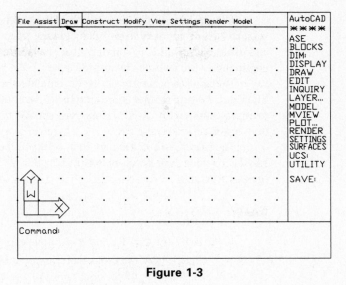

Figure 1-3

> Move the cursor back into the display area and the pull down bar will disappear.

The Coordinate Display

The coordinate display on the upper right side of the screen keeps track of coordinates as you move the pointer. The coordinate display is controlled using the F6 key or Ctrl-D.

Move the cursor around slowly and keep your eye on the line of numbers and text at the top of the screen. Watch the coordinate display. It is probably moving very rapidly through four-place decimal numbers. When you stop moving, the numbers will be showing coordinates for the location of the pointer. These coordinates are standard ordered pairs in a coordinate system originating from (0,0) at the lower left corner. The first value is the x value, showing the horizontal position of the cross hairs, measuring left to right. The second value is y, or the vertical position of the cross hairs, measured from bottom to top. Points also have a z value, but it will always be 0 in two dimensional drawing and can be ignored until you begin to draw in 3D (Chapter 12).

> Press F6 (or Ctrl-D) to turn the coordinate display off, and move the cross hairs slowly.

Now when you move the cross hairs you will see that the coordinate display does not change.

> Press F6 to turn the coordinate display on again.

F6 is actually a three-way switch, but this will not be apparent until you enter a drawing command such as LINE (Task 3). For now, F6 will simply turn the display on and off.

NOTE: The units AutoCAD uses for coordinates, dimensions, and for measuring distances and angles can be changed at any time using the UNITS command (Chapter 2). For now we will accept the AutoCAD default values, including the four-place decimals. In the next chapter we will be changing to two-place decimals. *The F-keys are switches only, they cannot be used to change settings.*

The Grid

> Press F7 (or Ctrl-G) to turn the grid on.

The grid is simply a matrix of dots that helps you find your way around on the screen. It will not appear on your drawing when it is plotted, and it may be turned on and off at will using F7. You may also change the spacing between dots, using the GRID command as we will be doing in Chapter 2.

The grid is presently set up to emulate the shape of an "A"-size piece of paper. There are 10 grid points from bottom to top, numbered 0 to 9, and 13 points from left to right, numbered 0 to 12. This corresponds to a standard 9 x 12 or 8 1/2 x 11 inch drawing sheet.

The AutoCAD command that controls the outer size and shape of the grid is LIMITS, which will be discussed in Chapter 4. Until then we will continue to use the present format.

Snap

> Press F9 (or Ctrl-B) and then move the cursor slowly around the drawing area.

Notice how the cross hairs jump from point to point. If your grid is on, you will see that it is impossible to make the cross hairs touch a point that is not on the grid. Try it.

You will also see that the coordinate display shows only integer values, and that the word "Snap" is displayed on the status line next to "Layer 0".

> Press F9 again.

Snap should now be off and the word no longer displayed on the status line.

If you move the cursor in a circle now you will see that the cross hairs move smoothly, without jumping. You will also observe that the coordinate display moves rapidly through a series of four-place decimal values.

F9 turns snap on and off. With snap off you can, theoretically, touch every point on the screen. With snap on you can move only in predetermined increments. By default the snap is set to a value of 1.0000. In the next chapter you will learn how to change this setting using the SNAP command. For now we will leave it alone. A snap setting of 1 will be convenient for the drawings at the end of this chapter.

Using an appropriate snap increment is a tremendous timesaver. It allows for a degree of accuracy that is not possible otherwise. If all the dimensions in a drawing fall into one-inch increments, for example, there is no reason to deal with points that are not on a one-inch grid. You can find the points you want much more quickly and accurately if all those in between are temporarily eliminated. F9 and the snap setting allow you to do that.

Ortho

F8 (or Ctrl-O) turns ortho mode on and off. You will not observe the ortho mode in action until you have entered the LINE command, however. We will try it out at the end of Task 3.

The User Coordinate System Icon

At the lower left of the screen you will see the User Coordinate System (UCS) icon. These two arrows clearly indicate the directions of the X and Y axes, which are currently aligned with the sides of your screen. In Chapter 12, when you begin to do 3D drawings you will be defining your own coordinate systems that can be turned at any angle and originate at any point in space. At that time you will find that the icon is a very useful visual aid. However, it is hardly necessary in two-dimensional drawing and may be distracting. For this reason you may want to turn it off now and keep it turned off until you actually need it.

> Type "ucsicon" and press enter.

AutoCAD will show the following prompt in the command area:

ON/OFF/All/Noorigin/ORigin <ON>:

As you explore AutoCAD commands you will become familiar with many prompts like this one. It is simply a series of options separated by slashes (/). For now we only need to know about "on" and "off".

> Type "off" and press enter.

The UCS icon will disappear from your screen. Anytime you want to see it again, type in "ucsicon" and then type "on".

TASK 3: Drawing a LINE

Procedure.

(Remember, procedure lists are provided at the beginning of some tasks as an overview and a reference. *Do not try to complete the task using the procedure list alone.*)

1. Type "L" or select "LINE".
2. Pick a start point.
3. Pick an end point.
4. Pick another end point to continue in the LINE command, or press enter to stop.

Discussion.   You can communicate drawing instructions to AutoCAD in one of four ways: by typing; or by selecting items from a screen menu, a pull down menu, or a tablet menu. Each has its advantages and disadvantages depending on the situation. Often a combination of two or more methods is the most efficient way to carry out a complete command sequence. The instructions in this book are not specific about which to use, except when necessary. This is because we have no way of knowing what kind of system you may be working with, and because all operators develop their own preferences. Consider the phrase "type or select" to include all four possibilities.

Each method is described briefly. You do not have to try them all out at this time. Read them over to get a feel for the possibilities and then proceed to the LINE command. As a rule, we suggest learning the keyboard procedure first. It is the most basic, the most comprehensive, and changes the least from release to release. But do not limit yourself by typing everything. As soon as you know the keyboard sequence, try out the other methods to see how they vary and how you can use them to save time. Ultimately, you will want to type as little as possible and use the differences between the menu systems to your advantage.

The Keyboard

The keyboard is the most primitive and fundamental method of interacting with Auto-CAD. Screen menus, pull down menus, and tablet menus all function by automating basic command sequences as they would be typed on the keyboard. It is therefore useful to be familiar with the keyboard procedures even if the other methods are sometimes faster.

As you type commands and responses to prompts, the characters you are typing will appear in the command area after the colon (see *Figure 1-4*). Remember that you must press enter to complete your commands and responses.

COMMAND ALIAS CHART		
LETTER + ENTER		= COMMAND
A	⏎	ARC
C	⏎	CIRCLE
E	⏎	ERASE
L	⏎	LINE
M	⏎	MOVE
P	⏎	PAN
R	⏎	REDRAW
U	⏎	UNDO
Z	⏎	ZOOM

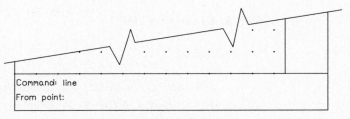

Command: line
From point:

Figure 1-4

Some of the most often used commands, such as LINE, ERASE, and CIRCLE have "aliases." These one- or two-letter abbreviations are very handy. A few of the most commonly used aliases are shown in *Figure 1-4*.

The Screen Menu

All of the menu systems have the advantage that instead of typing a complete command, you can simply "point and shoot" to select an item. The screen menu and pull down menus also have the advantage of proximity to your drawing area. You can make selections without taking your eyes off the screen. The major disadvantage of the screen menu is that you will often need to search through two or more submenus before locating the command you want. If you are using the AutoCAD standard menu, see the Primary Screen Menu Hierarchy in Appendix A. This chart will show you where all basic commands are located in the standard menu system. It may be useful to make a copy and keep it handy, so that you do not have to turn to the back of the book to find a command.

To select an item from a screen menu, move the cross hairs to the right side of the screen until a highlight appears in the screen menu area. Then move the highlight up or down until the item you want is highlighted. Press the pick button on your pointing device to select the item. You may have to move through one or more submenus to get to the item you want (see *Figure 1-5*).

The Pull Down Menu

The pull down menu contains only a subset of the AutoCAD commands, but it is a useful subset and it is often quicker to find what you want on a pull down than on a screen menu. The key is to become familiar with what is there and what is not there.

To use the pull down menu, move the cross hairs up into the status line area until the pull down bar appears. Then move left or right to highlight the menu heading you want. Select it with the pick button. A menu will appear. Run down the list of items until the one you want is highlighted. Press the pick button again to select the item (see *Figure 1–6*). In Release 12 items followed by a triangle have "cascading" submenus.

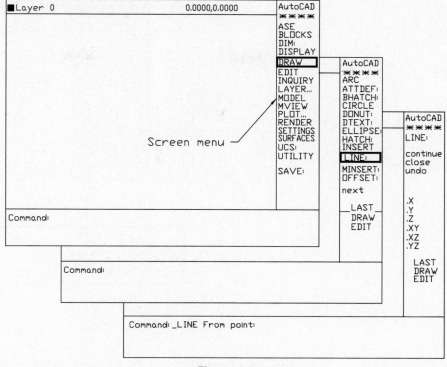

Figure 1-5

When these items are highlighted, moving the arrow to the right will cause a submenu to appear, partially overlaying the pull down menu. Picking an item that is followed by an ellipsis (. . .) will call up a dialogue box (see *Figure 1-7*).

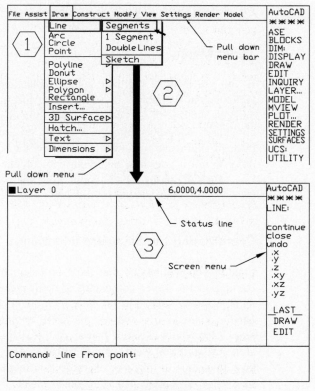

Figure 1-6

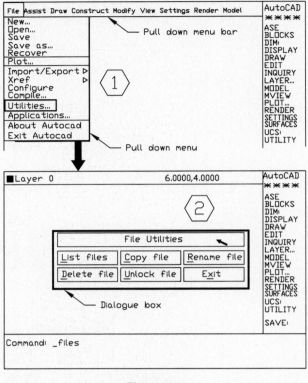

Figure 1-7

Dialogue boxes (see Task 6) are familiar features in many Windows and Macintosh programs. They require a combination of pointing and typing that is fairly intuitive. We will discuss many dialogue boxes in detail as we go along.

Tablet Menus

If you are using a digitizer with a tablet (as opposed to a mouse) you may have a tablet menu available. In some ways, locating a command on a tablet menu is the quickest method of all. With any good menu system there should be a large number of commands and subcommands available on the tablet, and you will not have to search through submenus to find them. The major disadvantage of the tablet menu is that in order to use it you must take your eyes off the screen.

On a digitizing tablet simply move the pointing device over the item you want and press the pick button (see *Figure 1-8*).

Coordinating the Keyboard and Menus

Finally, you will notice that there is a degree of automated coordination between the menu systems. Typed commands or items picked from the tablet or the pull downs bring up appropriate submenus on the screen menu. For example, if you type "L" to enter the LINE command you will see the LINE command submenu appear in the screen menu area. Also, you will notice that all of the menu systems call up prompts in the command area, just as if you were typing. To become an efficient AutoCAD user you will want to take advantage of this. For example, you might enter a command by typing an alias and then select an option from the screen menu. The subject of menus and how they work is treated in more depth in Appendix B.

Now let's get started.

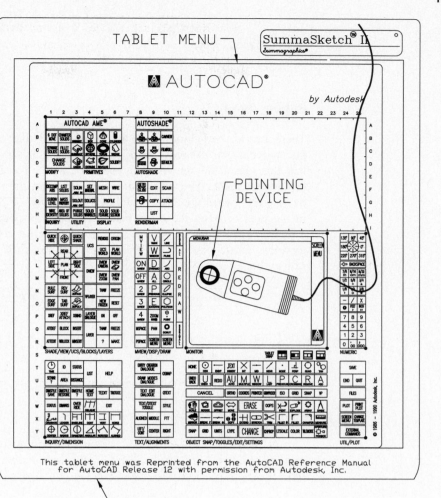

DIGITIZING TABLET

Figure 1-8

The LINE Command

> Type "L" or select "LINE" (remember to press enter if you are typing). LINE is under "Draw" on either the screen or pull down menu. If you are using the pull down menu, highlight "Line" under "Draw" and then pick the "Segments" option on the cascading submenu.

Look at the command area. You should see this, regardless of how you enter the command:

From point:

This is AutoCAD's way of asking for a start point.

Also, notice that the pickbox disappears from the cross hairs when you have entered a drawing command.

> Type "1,1" and press enter, or point to (1.0000,1.0000) as a start point.

Most of the time when you are drawing you will want to point rather than type. In order to do this you need to pay attention to the grid and the coordinate display. If snap is off switch it on (F9 or Ctrl-B). Move the cursor until the display reads "1.0000,1.0000". Then press the pick button.

Now AutoCAD will ask for a second point. You should see this in the command area:

To point:

Rubber Band

There are two new things to be aware of. One is the "rubber band" that extends from the start point to the cross hairs on the screen. If you move the cursor, you will see that this visual aid stretches, shrinks, or rotates like a tether keeping you connected to the start point. You will also notice that when the rubber band and the cross hairs overlap (i.e., when the rubber band is at 0, 90, 180, or 270 degrees) they both disappear in the area between the cross hairs and the start point, as illustrated in *Figure 1-9*. This may seem odd at first, but it is actually a great convenience. You will find many instances where you will need to know that the cross hairs and the rubber band are exactly lined up.

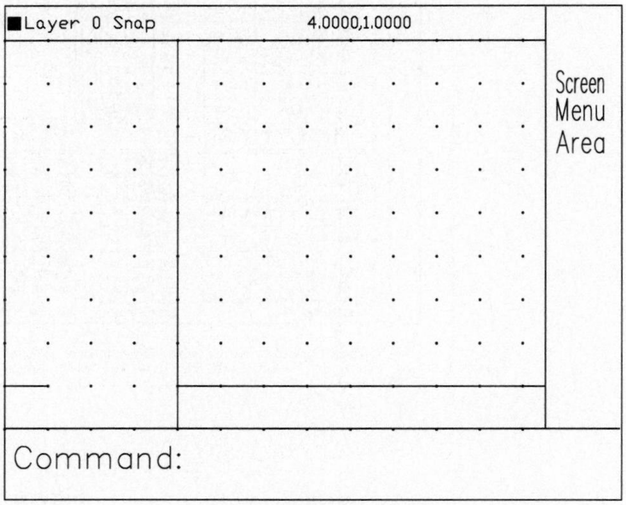

Figure 1-9

XY and Polar Coordinates

The other thing to watch is the coordinate display. If it is off (no change in coordinates when the cursor moves), press F6 to turn it on. Once it is on it will show either *xy* coordinates or polar coordinates. *xy* coordinates are the familiar ordered pairs discussed previously. They are lengths measured from the origin (0,0) of the coordinate system at the lower left corner of the grid. If your display shows two four-digit numbers, then these are the *xy* coordinates.

If your display shows something like "4.5555<45", it is set on polar coordinates.

> Press F6 and move your cursor.

Which type of coordinates is displayed?

> Press F6 and move your cursor again.

Observe the coordinate display.

You will see that there are three coordinate display modes: off (no change), *xy* (*x* and *y* values separated by a comma), and polar (length<angle).

> Press F6 once or twice until it shows polar coordinates.

Polar coordinates are in a length, angle format and are given relative to the starting point of your line. They look something like this: 4.0000<0 or 5.6569<45. The first number is the distance from the starting point of the line and the second is an angle of rotation, with 0 degrees being straight out to the right. In LINE, as well as most other draw commands, the polar coordinates are very useful because they give you the length of the segment you are currently drawing.

> Press F6 to read *xy* coordinates.
> Pick the point (8.0000,8.0000).

Your screen should now resemble *Figure 1-10*. AutoCAD has drawn a line between (1,1) and (8,8) and is asking for another point.

To point:

This will allow you to stay in the LINE command to draw a whole series of connected lines if you wish. You can draw a single line from point to point, or a series of lines from point to point to point to point. In either case, you must tell AutoCAD when you are finished with a set of lines by pressing enter or the enter equivalent button on the cursor, if you have one, or the space bar.

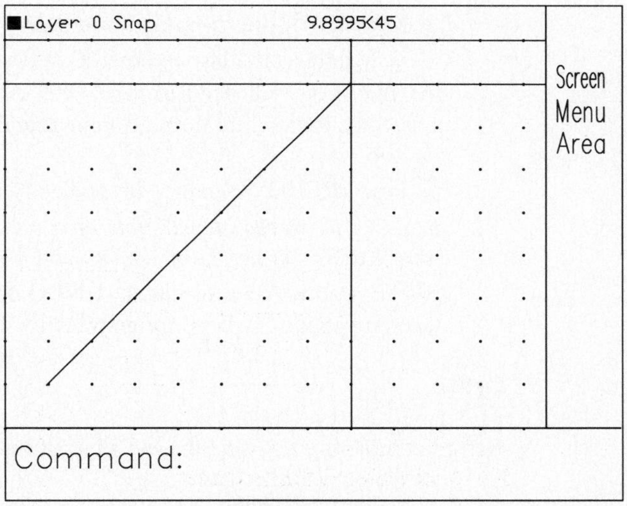

Figure 1-10

There is one exception to this sequence. If you are using the Release 12 pull down you have a choice between "Segments" and "1 Segment" (leave "Double Lines" and "Sketch" alone for now). Segments works like the regular LINE command, while 1 Segment will not ask for another second point.

NOTE: When you are drawing a continuous series of lines, the polar coordinates on the display are given relative to the most recent point, not the original starting point.

> Press enter or the space bar to end the LINE command.

You should be back to the "Command:" prompt again, and the pickbox has reappeared at the intersection of the cross hairs.

Space Bar and Enter Key

In most cases AutoCAD allows you to use the space bar as a substitute for the enter or return key. This is a major convenience, since the space bar is easy to locate with one hand while the other hand is on the pointing device. For example, the LINE command can be entered without removing your right hand from your pointing device by typing the "L" on the keyboard and then hitting the space bar, both with the left hand. The major exception to the use of the space bar as an enter key is when you are entering text in the TEXT command (Chapter 7). Since a space may be part of a text string, the space bar must have its usual significance there.

> NOTE: Hitting either the space bar or the enter key at the command prompt will repeat the last command entered, another major convenience.

Relative Coordinates and "@"

Besides typing or showing absolute *xy* coordinates, AutoCAD allows you to enter points using coordinates relative to the last point selected. To do this, use the "@" symbol. For example, after picking the point (1,1) in the last exercise you could have specified the point (8,8) by typing "@7,7", since the second point is over 7 and up 7 from the first point. Or, using polar coordinates relative to (1,1), you could type "@9.8995 < 45". All of these methods would give the same results.

Undoing a Line Using U

> Type "U" <enter> to undo the line you just drew.

U undoes the last command, so if you have done anything else since drawing the line, you will need to type "U" <enter> more than once. In this way you can walk backwards through your drawing session undoing your commands one by one.

> Type "REDO" <enter> immediately to bring the line back.

REDO only works immediately after U, and it only works once! That is, you can only REDO the last U or UNDO and only if it was the last command executed.

NOTE: AutoCAD also has an UNDO command, which is more elaborate than U (see Appendix C). U is *not* an alias for UNDO.

Ortho

Before completing this section, we suggest that you try the ortho mode.

> Type "L" <enter> or select "Line" to enter the LINE command.
> Pick a starting point. Any point near the center of the screen will do.
> Press F8 (or Ctrl-O) and move the cursor in slow circles.

Notice how the rubber band jumps between horizontal and vertical without sweeping through any of the angles between. Ortho forces the pointing device to pick up points only along the horizontal and vertical quadrant lines from a given starting point. With ortho on you can select points at 0, 90, 180, and 270 degrees of rotation from your starting point only (see *Figure 1-10*).

The advantages of ortho are similar to the advantages of snap mode, except that it limits angular rather than linear increments. It ensures that you will get precise and true right angles and perpendiculars easily when that is your intent. Ortho will become more important as drawings grow more complex. In this chapter it is hardly necessary, though it will be convenient in drawings 1 and 3.

Cancel

> Hold down the <control> button (ctrl) and press "c". This will abort the LINE command and bring back the "Command:" prompt.

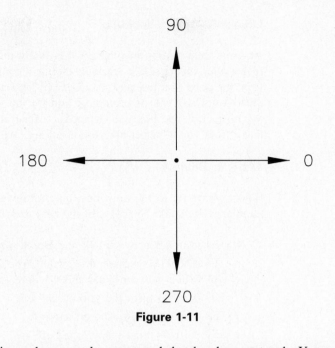

Figure 1-11

Ctrl-C is used to cancel a command that has been entered. You may also have a CANCEL button on your cursor and a CANCEL box on your tablet menu. On the Release 12 pull down, you will find "Cancel" under "Assist". Any of these will perform the same function.

Arrow Keys

Finally, there is one other way to control point selection that you should be aware of. Using the arrow keys in lieu of the cursor can be useful when you are working with very small increments, when you want to move an exact number of snap points, or when you want to lock the cross hairs onto a point so that slight movements of the pointer will not affect point selection. An important limitation of the arrow keys is that you cannot use them to move diagonally.

> Press any of the arrow keys to initiate arrow key control of the cross hairs.

By pressing any of the arrow keys once, you lock in the arrow key system and lock out the pointing device.

> Now try moving the cross hairs up, down, left, and right with the appropriate arrow keys.

One press will move the cross hairs one snap point if snap is on and one pixel (the smallest unit your monitor can display) if snap is off. Try it with snap on and off (press F9) to see what happens.

Holding down an arrow key will give you fast, continuous motion, much as it would on a word processor.

You can change the size of a single jump by using the page up and page down keys, but it is usually faster to get the cursor near the point you want using the pointing device in the usual manner, and then use the arrow keys close up.

When the cross hairs have reached the desired point, you can select that point by pressing enter. This will also end arrow key control and reactivate the cursor.

If you want to reactivate the cursor without selecting a point, simply press the end key.

> Press "end" to reactivate the cursor.

Object Selection Window

At some time during this chapter it is likely that you will accidentally or intentionally pick a point on the screen without entering a command. If you then drag the cursor away from the point you just picked, a box will appear and stretch as you move. At the same time, AutoCAD will be prompting you for the "Other corner:" of the box. But as soon as you pick it, the box will disappear. What is this? It's the object selection window that allows you to select objects for editing. We will begin using it in Chapter 2.

TASK 4: Review

Before going on to the drawings, quickly review the following items. If it all seems familiar, you should be ready for the next drawing task.

- F1 switches between text and graphics screens.
- F6 (Ctrl-D) is a three-way switch. Use it to turn the coordinate display off and to switch between polar and *xy* coordinates.
- F7 (Ctrl-G) turns the grid on and off.
- F8 (Ctrl-O) turns ortho on and off.
- F9 (Ctrl-B) turns snap on and off.
- Commands may be entered by typing, or by selecting from a screen menu, pull down menu, or tablet menu.
- Points may be selected by pointing or by typing coordinates.
- Once inside the LINE command you can draw a single line or a whole series of connected lines.
- Press enter or the space bar to end working in the LINE command.
- U will undo your most recent command.
- REDO will redo a U.
- Ctrl-C will cancel a command.
- The arrow keys may be used as an alternative way to control the cross hairs.

TASK 5: Drawing and REDRAWing a Square

To practice what you have learned so far, reproduce the square in *Figure 1-12* on your screen. Then erase it using the U command as many times as necessary. The coordinates of the four corner points are (2, 2), (7, 2), (7, 7), and (2, 7).

CLOSEing a Set of Lines

For drawing an enclosed figure like this one using the LINE command, AutoCAD provides a convenient "Close" option. "Close" will connect the last in a continuous series of lines back to the starting point of the series. In drawing the square, for instance, you would simply type "c" <enter> or select "Close" in lieu of drawing the last of the four lines. In order for this to work, the whole square must be drawn without leaving the LINE command.

REDRAW—Cleaning Up Your Act

You may have noticed that every time you select a point AutoCAD puts a "blip" on the screen in the form of a small cross. These are only temporary; they are not part of your drawing file database and will not appear on your drawing when it is plotted or printed. However, you will want to get rid of them from time to time to clean up the screen and avoid confusion.

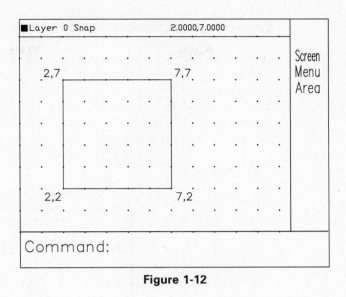

Figure 1-12

> Type "r" <enter> or select "Redraw" (under "View" on the pull down, "DIS-PLAY" on the screen menu).

The display will be redrawn without the blips.

TASK 6: Saving Your Drawings

Discussion.   AutoCAD Release 12 has several commands that allow you to save drawings. Your choice of which to use will depend on whether you want to exit AutoCAD as you save or stay in the drawing editor, and whether you want to give the saved drawing a new name or keep it under the current drawing name. In all cases, a .dwg extension is added to file names to identify them as AutoCAD files. This is automatic when you name a file.

Before Release 12 it was always necessary to name a drawing in order to enter the drawing editor. With Release 12 it is possible to complete a drawing session without ever giving your file a name. This makes for some significant differences between Release 12 commands and previous releases. In addition, Release 12 uses many more dialogue boxes than earlier versions.

The END Command

To save your drawing and leave the drawing editor at the same time, type "end" <enter> or select "END" from the screen menu, under "UTILITY".

If you are working on a previously named drawing, AutoCAD will save your drawing under that name and will return you to your operating system prompt. If you have not yet named your drawing, a Create Drawing File dialogue box will appear. The dialogue box cursor will be blinking in the area labeled "File:" (see *Figure 1-13*). Type in the name of the file, such as "1-1", and press enter or click on OK.

Include a drive designation, (i.e., "A:1-1") if you are saving your work on a floppy disk. AutoCAD will add the .dwg extension automatically.

The SAVE and SAVEAS Commands

To save your drawing without leaving the editor, type "save" <enter>, or select "Save as..." from the pull down menu, under FILE.

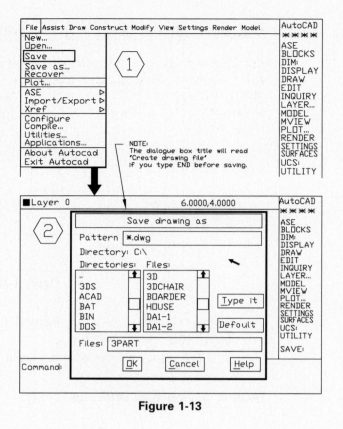

Figure 1-13

In Release 12 you will see a Save drawing as a dialogue box with the cursor blinking in the area labelled "Files". This is exactly the same dialogue box as the one called up by the END command, except for the title of the box (see *Figure 1-13*). However, in this case you will stay in the drawing editor after you type in the name of the file, rather than exiting to the operating system prompt.

The SAVE and SAVEAS commands allow you to save different versions of the same drawing under different names while continuing to edit.

The QSAVE Command—Release 12 Only

To save your work under the current drawing name without leaving the drawing editor, type "qsave" <enter> or select "Save" from the pull down, under File, or SAVE: on the screen menu.

In addition to SAVE, Release 12 has a "quick save" command. If your drawing is already named and you are saving it under the current name, the QSAVE command will do this quickly without intervening dialogue. This command allows you to save your work frequently as you go along to protect it from system failures. Note that "Save" on the pull down and screen menus actually executes the QSAVE command, not the SAVE command.

The QUIT Command

To leave the drawing editor without saving changes to your drawing, type "quit" <enter>, or select "Exit AutoCAD" from the pull down menu, under "File".

In Release 12 a small dialogue box will appear. Pick "Save Changes...", "Discard Changes", or "Cancel Command" as you wish.

TASKS 7, 8, AND 9: Three Simple Drawings

You are now ready to complete this chapter by creating Drawings 1-1, 1-2, and 1-3. If you wish to save your drawings, use END, SAVE, SAVEAS, or QSAVE. Whenever you wish to start a new drawing, type "new" and enter a file name as we did at the beginning of the chapter. *Remember to use a drive designation if you are saving your work on a floppy disk.*

DRAWING 1–1: GRATE

Before beginning, look over the drawing page. Notice the F-key reminders and other drawing information at the bottom. The commands on the right are the new commands you will need to do this drawing. They are listed with their screen menu headings in parentheses on the left and alias on the right.

The first two drawings in this chapter are given without dimensions. Instead, we have drawn them as you will see them on the screen, against the background of a one-unit grid. Remember that all of these drawings were done using a one-unit snap, and that all points will be found on one-unit increments.

DRAWING SUGGESTIONS

> Remember to watch the coordinate display when searching for a point.

> Be sure that grid, snap, and the coordinate display are all turned on.

> Draw the outer rectangle first. It is 6 units wide and 7 units high, and its lower left-hand corner is at the point (3.0000, 1.0000). The three smaller rectangles inside are 4 × 1.

If You Make A Mistake

The U command works nicely within the LINE command to undo the last line you drew, or the last two or three if you have drawn a series.

> Type "U" <enter>. The last line you drew will be gone or replaced by the rubber band awaiting a new end point. If you want to go back more than one line, type "U" <enter> again, as many times as you need.

> If you have already left the LINE command, U will still work, but instead of undoing the last line, it will undo the last continuous series of lines. In "Grate" this could be the whole outside rectangle, for instance.

> Remember, if you have mistakenly undone something, you can get it back by typing "REDO" <enter>. You cannot perform other commands between U and REDO.

U is quick, easy to use, and efficient as long as you always spot your mistakes immediately after making them. Most of us, however, are more spontaneous in our blundering. We may make mistakes at any time and not notice them until the middle of next week. For us, AutoCAD provides more flexible editing tools, like ERASE, which is introduced in the next chapter.

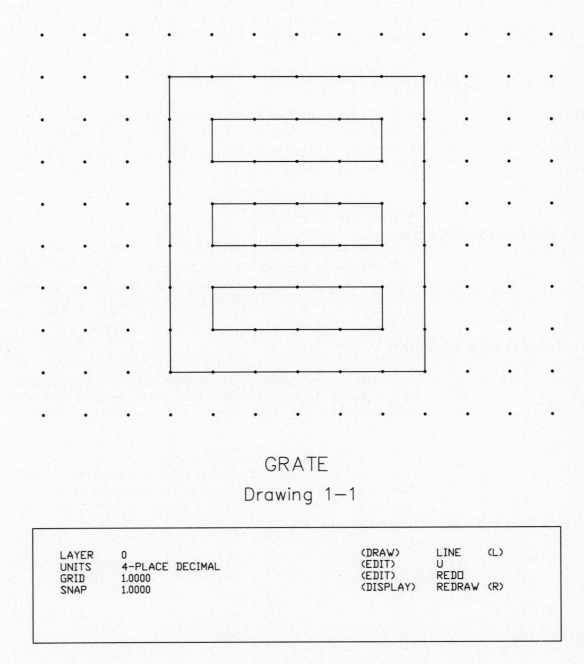

GRATE

Drawing 1-1

LAYER	0		(DRAW)	LINE	(L)
UNITS	4-PLACE DECIMAL		(EDIT)	U	
GRID	1.0000		(EDIT)	REDO	
SNAP	1.0000		(DISPLAY)	REDRAW	(R)

F1   F6   F7   F8   F9

ON/OFF   ABSOLUTE/OFF/POLAR   ON/OFF   ON/OFF   ON/OFF
SCREEN   COORDS   GRID   ORTHO   SNAP

DRAWING 1–2: DESIGN

This design will give you further practice with the LINE command.

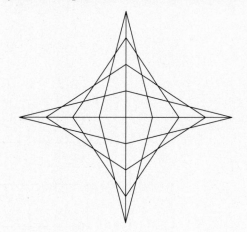

DRAWING SUGGESTIONS

> Draw the horizontal and vertical lines first. Each is eight units long.

> Notice how the rest of the lines work—outside point on horizontal to inside point on vertical, then working in, or vice-versa.

REPEATING A COMMAND

Remember, you can repeat a command by pressing enter or the space bar at the "Command:" prompt. This will be useful in this drawing, since you have several sets of lines to draw.

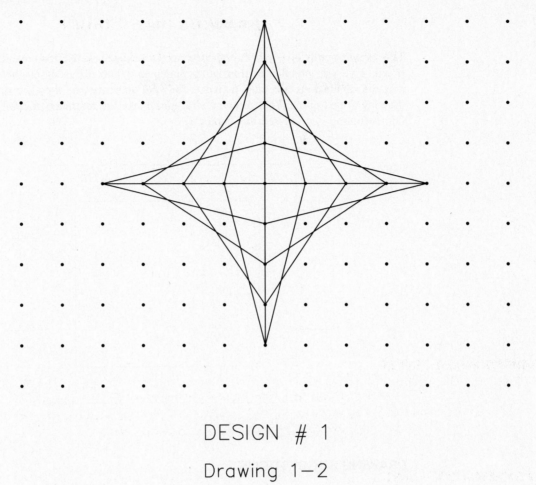

DESIGN # 1

Drawing 1-2

LAYER	0	(DRAW)	LINE	(L)
UNITS	4-PLACE DECIMAL	(EDIT)	U	
GRID	1.0000	(EDIT)	REDO	
SNAP	1.0000	(DISPLAY)	REDRAW	(R)

F1	F6	F7	F8	F9
ON/OFF	ABSOLUTE/OFF/POLAR	ON/OFF	ON/OFF	ON/OFF
SCREEN	COORDS	GRID	ORTHO	SNAP

DRAWING 1-3: SHIM

This drawing will give you further practice in using the LINE command. In addition, it will give you practice in translating dimensions into distances on the screen. Note that the dimensions are only included for your information; they are not part of the drawing at this point. Your drawing will appear like the reference drawing that follows. Dimensioning is discussed in Chapter 8.

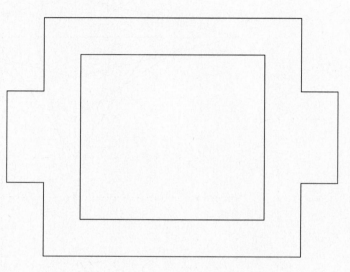

DRAWING SUGGESTIONS

> It is most important that you choose a starting point that will position the drawing so that it fits on your screen. If you begin with the bottom left-hand corner of the outside figure at the point (3,1), you should have no trouble.

> Read the dimensions carefully to see how the geometry of the drawing works. It is good practice to look over the dimensions before you begin drawing. Often the dimension for a particular line may be located on another side of the figure or may have to be extrapolated from other dimensions. It is not uncommon to misread, misinterpret, or miscalculate a dimension, so take your time.

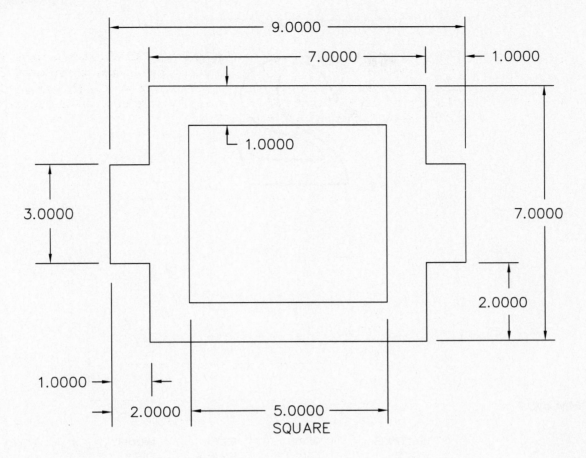

SHIM
Drawing 1–3

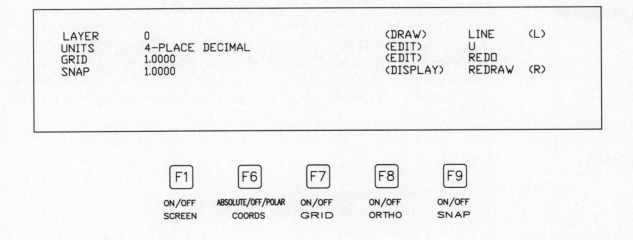

LAYER	0		(DRAW)	LINE	(L)
UNITS	4-PLACE DECIMAL		(EDIT)	U	
GRID	1.0000		(EDIT)	REDO	
SNAP	1.0000		(DISPLAY)	REDRAW	(R)

F1	F6	F7	F8	F9
ON/OFF	ABSOLUTE/OFF/POLAR	ON/OFF	ON/OFF	ON/OFF
SCREEN	COORDS	GRID	ORTHO	SNAP

CHAPTER

COMMANDS

SETTINGS	DRAW	EDIT	INQUIRY
GRID	CIRCLE	ERASE	DIST
SNAP		OOPS	
DDRMODES			
		UTILITIES	
		UNITS	

OVERVIEW

In this chapter you will learn to change the spacing of the grid and the snap. You will also change the units in which coordinates are displayed. You will produce drawings containing straight lines and circles and learn to delete them selectively using the ERASE command. Also, you will learn to measure and mark distances on the screen using the DIST command.

TASKS

1. Change the SNAP spacing.
2. Change the GRID spacing.
3. Change UNITS.
4. Draw three concentric circles using the center point, radius method.
5. Draw three more concentric circles using the center point, diameter method.
6. ERASE the circles, using four selection methods.
7. Mark distances with DIST.
8. Do Drawing 2-1 ("Aperture Wheel").

9. Do Drawing 2-2 ("Roller").
10. Do Drawing 2-3 ("Fan Bezel").
11. Do Drawing 2-4 ("Switch Plate").

TASK 1: Changing the SNAP

Procedure.

1. Type or select "SNAP".
2. Enter a value.

Discussion.   When you begin a new drawing using no prototype (prototypes are discussed in Chapter 4), the grid and snap are set with a spacing of 1. Moreover, they are linked so that changing the snap will also change the grid to the same value. In Task 2 we will set the grid independently. For now we will leave them linked.

In Chapter 1 all drawings were done without altering the grid and snap spacings from the prototype value of 1. Frequently you will want to change this, depending on your application. You may want a 10-foot snap for a building layout, or a 0.010-inch snap for a printed circuit diagram.

> To begin, type "new" or select "New" from the pull down menu under "File".

This will open the Create New Drawing dialogue box used in Chapter 1.

> Click on "No Prototype" to ensure that your drawing editor uses the default settings shown in this chapter.

> Using F7 and F9, be sure that grid and snap are both on.

> Type or select "snap" (we will no longer remind you to press enter after typing a command or response to a prompt).

The prompt will appear like this, with options separated by slashes (/):

Snap spacing or ON/OFF/Aspect/Rotate/Style <1.0000>:

You can ignore most of these options for now. The number <1.0000> shows the present setting. AutoCAD uses this format (<default>) in many command sequences to show you a present value or default setting. It usually comes at the end of a series of options. Pressing the enter key or space bar at this point will give you the default setting.

> In answer to the prompt, type ".5" and watch what happens (of course you remembered to press enter).

Because the grid is set to change with the snap, you will see the grid redrawn to a .5 increment.

> Move the cursor around to observe the effects of the new snap setting.

> Try other snap settings. Try 2, .25, and .125.

How small a snap will AutoCAD accept? Notice that when you get smaller than .065, the grid becomes too dense to display, but the snap can still be set smaller.

Using the Drawing Aids Dialogue Box

You can also change snap and grid settings using a dialogue box. The procedure is somewhat different, but the result is the same. Select "Settings" from the pull down bar or screen menu and then "Drawing Aids" from the pull down menu or "DDRMODES" from the screen menu. DDRMODES is the command that calls up this dialogue box, so you can actually open it from the keyboard as well. Most dialogue boxes are called by a command name beginning with DD, which stands for "Dynamic Dialogue".

Any of these methods will bring up the dialogue box shown in *Figure 2-1*. This dialogue box contains some typical features, including check boxes, edit boxes, and radio buttons.

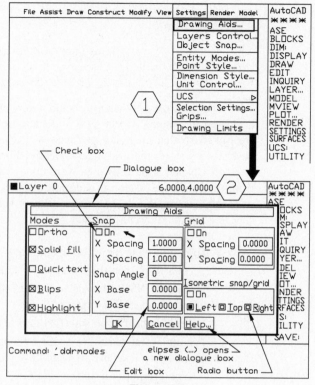

Figure 2-1

You can turn ortho, snap, and grid on and off by moving the arrow inside the appropriate check box and pressing the pick button. A check box with an "x" is on, while an empty check box is off. Notice that there are four other check boxes in the area on the left under "Modes". We will only have use for the snap and grid settings at this point, but for reference, "Solid fill" is discussed in Chapter 9 and "Quick text" in Chapter 7. If "Blips" is turned off, AutoCAD will not show blips on the screen as you draw. If "Highlight" is turned off, AutoCAD will not highlight selected entities. We will get to highlighting at the end of this chapter when we discuss the ERASE command.

On the right you will see a box for isometric snap and grid control. We will have no use for these until Chapter 11. But notice the boxes in the lower line of the isometric snap/grid area labelled "Left", "Top", and "Right". These are examples of radio buttons, which are discussed in Task 3.

Also notice the "Help..." box at the bottom right. Again, any box with an ellipsis (...) calls another dialogue box that will overlay the current one. Picking this box would activate the HELP command. Then when you exit the HELP dialogue you would return to this Drawing Aids dialogue box.

The snap and grid settings are shown in edit boxes. Edit boxes contain text or numerical information that can be edited as you would in a text editor. You can highlight the entire box to replace the text, or point anywhere inside to do partial editing.

To change the grid or snap setting, use the following procedure:

1. Move the arrow into the box in the table where the change is to be made ("X Spacing" under "Snap" or "Grid").

2. Double click to highlight the entire number.

3. Type a new value and press enter. Notice that the Y spacing changes automatically when you change the X spacing (see note following).

4. Click on the OK box at the bottom to confirm changes, or "Cancel" to cancel changes.

NOTE: The dialogue box has places to set both X and Y spacing. It is unlikely that you will want to have a grid or snap matrix with different horizontal and vertical increments, but the capacity is there if you do. Also notice that you can change the snap angle. Setting the snap angle to 45, for example, would turn your snap and grid at a 45 degree angle.

TASK 2: Changing the GRID

1. Type or select "Grid", or activate the Drawing Aids dialogue box.

2. Enter a value.

Discussion. Whether you are typing or using one of your menus, the process for changing the grid setting is the same as changing the snap. In fact the two are similar enough to cause confusion. The grid is only a visual reference. It has no effect on selection of points. Snap is invisible, but it dramatically affects point selection. Grid and snap may or may not have the same setting.

> Using F7, be sure the grid is turned on.

> Type or select "Grid", or use the dialogue box, as discussed previously.

The prompt will appear like this, with options separated by slashes (/):

Grid spacing(X) or ON/OFF/Snap/Aspect <1.0000>:

> Type ".5".

> Try other grid settings. Try 2, .25, and .125. What happens when you try .0625?

> Now try setting snap to 1 and the grid spacing to .25. Notice how you cannot touch many of the dots. This is because the visible grid matrix is set to a smaller spacing than the invisible snap matrix.

In practice this relationship is likely to be reversed. Since the grid is merely a visual aid, it will often be set "coarser" than the snap.

> Try setting the grid to .5 and the snap to .25.

With this type of arrangement you can still pick exact points easily, but the grid is not so dense as to be distracting.

If you wish to keep snap and grid the same, you can respond with an "s" or a "0" when you set the grid (or select "grd=snap" from the screen menu). The grid will then change to match the snap and will continue to change any time you reset the snap. To free the grid, just give it its own value again using the GRID command or the dialogue box.

TASK 3: Changing UNITS

Procedure.

1. Type or select "UNITS", or activate the Units Control dialogue box.
2. Answer the prompts.
3. Press F1, if necessary.

Discussion.

> Type or select "UNITS".

Presto! No more graphics. We told you this would happen. The command area is too small to display the complete UNITS sequence, so it has disappeared temporarily. What function key will bring it back?

What you now see looks like this:

REPORT FORMATS	EXAMPLES
1. Scientific	1.55E+01
2. Decimal	15.50
3. Engineering	1' — 3.50"
4. Architectural	1' — 3 1/2"
5. Fractional	15 1/2

With the exception of Engineering and Architectural formats, these formats can be used with any basic unit of measurement. For example, decimal mode is perfect for metric units as well as English units.

Enter choice, 1 to 5 <2>:

> Type "2" or simply press enter, since the default system, and the one we will use, is decimal units.

Through most of this book we will stick to decimal units. Obviously, if you are designing a house you will want architectural units. If you are building a bridge you may want engineering-style units. You might want scientific units if you are doing research.

Whatever your application, once you know how to change units, you can do so easily and at any time. However, as a drawing practice you will want to choose appropriate units when you first begin work on a new drawing. Not only will co-ordinates be displayed in the units you select, but later, when you use AutoCAD's dimensioning features (see Chapter 8), your drawing will be dimensioned in these units.

AutoCAD should now be showing the following prompt:

Number of digits to right of decimal point, (0 to 8) <4>:

We will use two-place decimals because they are practical and more common than any other choice.

> Type "2" in answer to the prompt for the number of decimal places you wish to use.

AutoCAD now gives you the opportunity to change the units in which angles are measured. In this book we will use all of the default settings for angle measure, since they are by far the most common. If your application requires something different, the UNITS command is the place to change it.

The default system is standard degrees without decimals, measured counterclockwise, with 0 being straight out to the right (3 o'clock); 90, straight up (12 o'clock); 180, to the left (9 o'clock); and 270, straight down (6 o'clock).

> Press enter four times, or until the "Command:" prompt reappears. Be careful not to press enter again, or the UNITS command sequence will be repeated.

> Press F1 to return to the graphics screen. Did you remember?

Looking at the coordinate display, you should now see values with only two digits to the right of the decimal. This setting will be standard in this book.

We suggest, as always, that you experiment with other choices in order to get a feel for the options that are available to you. If you are using Release 12 you should experiment using the Units Control dialogue box described next.

The Units Control Dialogue Box

Activate the Units Control dialogue box by picking "Settings" and then "Units Control..." from the pull down menu. You will see the command DDUNITS entered on the command line, and the dialogue box shown in *Figure 2-2* will appear. This box shows all of the settings that are also available through the UNITS command sequence. There are two dialogue box features here that we have not discussed previously. First are the radio buttons in the columns labelled "Units" and "Angles". Radio buttons are used with lists of settings that are mutually exclusive. You should see that the Decimal button is shaded in the format column. All other buttons in this column are not shaded. You can switch settings by simply picking another button, but you can have only one button on at a time. Radio buttons are used here because you can use only one format at a time.

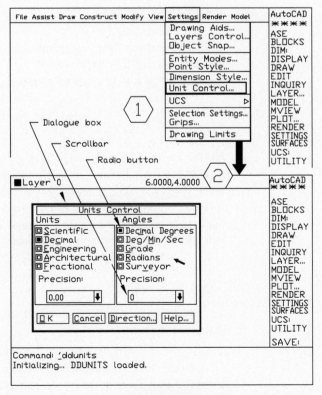

Figure 2-2

The second new feature is the pop down lists at the bottom of the units and angles columns. You should try these out to see how they function. You can change the precision (number of place values shown) by picking the arrow at the right of the box and then picking a setting, such as ".000" for three place decimals, from the list that appears.

Experiment as much as you like with the dialogue box. None of your changes will be reflected in the drawing editor until you click on the OK button or press enter on the keyboard. When you are through be sure to leave your units set for two-place decimals, your angle measure set for zero-place decimal degrees, and your angle zero direction set to East.

NOTE: All dialogue boxes can be moved on the screen. This is done by clicking and dragging in the gray title area at the top of the dialogue box. Click once and hold down the pick button as you move the dialogue box to any part of the screen.

TASK 4: Drawing CIRCLES Giving Center Point and Radius

Procedure.

1. Type "c" or select "CIRCLE".
2. Pick a center point.
3. Enter or drag a radius value.

Discussion. Circles can be drawn by giving AutoCAD either three points on the circle's circumference, two points that determine a diameter, two tangents and a radius, a center point and a radius, or a center point and a diameter. In this chapter we will use the latter two options.

We will begin by drawing a circle with radius 3 and center at the point (6,5). Then we will draw two smaller circles centered at the same point. Later we will erase them using the ERASE command.

> Using what you have just learned, set grid and snap to .5 and units to two-place decimal.

> Type "c" or select "CIRCLE". The prompt that follows will look like this:

3P/2P/TTR/<Center point>:

NOTE: On the pull down menu pick "Draw", highlight "Circle", then move to the right to see the submenu. Pick "Center, Radius" from the submenu. On the screen menu pick "DRAW", then "CIRCLE", and then "CEN,RAD:".

> Type coordinates or point to the center point of the circle you want to draw. In our case it will be the point (6,5). AutoCAD will assume that a radius or diameter will follow and will show the following prompt:

Diameter/<Radius>:

If we type or point to a value now, AutoCAD will take it as a radius, since that is the default.

> Type "3" or show by pointing that the circle has a radius of 3.

Notice how the rubber band works to drag out your circle as you move the cursor. Remember, if your coordinate display is not showing polar coordinates, press F6 once or twice until you see something like "3.00<0".

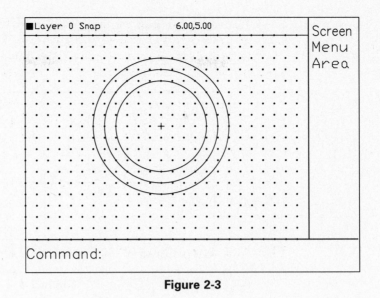

Figure 2-3

You should now have your first circle complete. Next, draw two more circles using the same center point, radius method. They will be centered at (6,5) and have radii of 2.50 and 2.00. The results are illustrated in *Figure 2-3*.

Remember that you can repeat a command, in this case the CIRCLE command, by pressing enter or the space bar.

TASK 5: Drawing CIRCLES Giving Center Point and Diameter

Procedure.

1. Type "c" or select "CIRCLE".
2. Pick a center point.
3. Respond to the prompt with a "d".
4. Type or drag a diameter length.

Discussion. We will draw three more circles centered on (6,5) having diameters of 2, 1.5, and 1. Drawing circles this way is almost the same as the radius method, except you will not use the default, and you will see that the rubber band works differently.

> If necessary, press enter to repeat the CIRCLE command. (Type "c" or select "CIRCLE" if you have done something else, such as a redraw, since drawing the first three circles.)

> Indicate the center point (6,5) by typing coordinates or pointing.

> Answer the prompt with a "d", for diameter. (This step will be done automatically if you have chosen "CEN,DIA" from the screen menu or "Center, Diameter" from the pull down.)

Notice that the cross hairs are now outside the circle you are dragging on the screen (see *Figure 2-4*). This is because AutoCAD is looking for a diameter, but the last point you gave was a center point. So the diameter is being measured from the center point out, twice the radius. Move the cursor around, in and out from the center point, to get a feel for this.

> Point to a diameter of 2.00, or type "2".

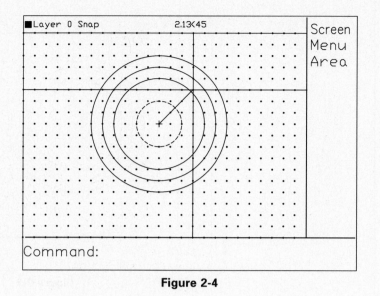

Figure 2-4

You should now have four circles. Repeat the instructions for using diameter twice more to complete the drawing, giving diameters of 1.5 and 1. When you are done, your screen should look like *Figure 2-5*.

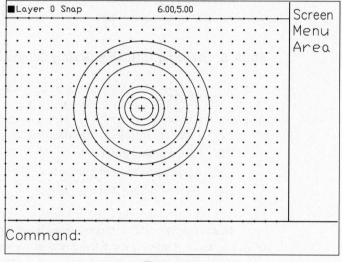

Figure 2-5

Sit back and admire your work, because we are about to erase it. In the meantime, studying *Figure 2-6* will give you a good introduction to the remaining options in the CIRCLE command. None of these is necessary to complete the drawings in this chapter. See the *AutoCAD Reference Manual* for additional information.

TASK 6: Using the ERASE Command

Procedure.

1. Type "e" or select "ERASE".
2. Select objects.
3. Press enter.

–or–

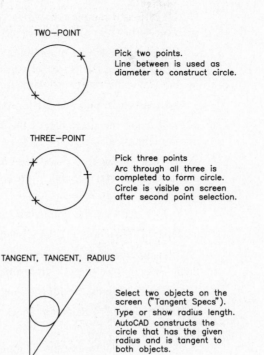

TWO—POINT

Pick two points.
Line between is used as
diameter to construct circle.

THREE—POINT

Pick three points
Arc through all three is
completed to form circle.
Circle is visible on screen
after second point selection.

TANGENT, TANGENT, RADIUS

Select two objects on the
screen ("Tangent Specs").
Type or show radius length.
AutoCAD constructs the
circle that has the given
radius and is tangent to
both objects.

Figure 2-6

1. Select objects.
2. Type "e" or select "ERASE".

Discussion.   AutoCAD Release 12 allows for many different methods of editing
and even allows you to alter some of the basics of how edit commands work. Fundamentally, there are two different sequences for using most edit commands. These are
called the Noun/Verb and the Verb/Noun methods.

Prior to Release 12, most editing was carried out in a verb/noun sequence. That is,
you would enter a command, such as ERASE (the verb), then select objects (the nouns),
and finally press enter to carry out the command. This method is still perfectly reasonable
and effective, but AutoCAD now allows you to reverse the verb/noun sequence. You
can use either method as long as "Noun/Verb" selection is enabled in your drawing.

In this task we will explore the traditional verb/noun sequence and then introduce
the new noun/verb or "pick first" method along with some of the many methods for
selecting objects.

> To begin this task you should have the six circles on your screen, as shown in
Figure 2-5.

We will use verb/noun editing to erase the two outer circles.

> Type "e" or select "Erase".

The cross hairs will disappear, but the pickbox will still be on the screen and
will move when you move your cursor.

Also notice the command area. It should be showing this:

Select objects:

This is a very common prompt. You will find it in all edit commands and
many other commands as well.

> Move your cursor so that the outer circle crosses the pickbox.

> Press the pick button.

NOTE: In more complex drawings you may find it convenient or necessary to turn snap off (F9) while selecting objects.

The circle will be highlighted (dotted). This is how AutoCAD indicates that an object has been selected for editing. It is not yet erased, however. You can go on and add more objects to the selection set and they, too, will become dotted.

> Use the box to pick the second circle. It too should now be dotted.

> Press enter, the space bar, or the enter equivalent button on your cursor to carry out the command.

This is typical of most edit commands. Once a command has been entered and a selection set defined, a press of the enter key is required to complete the command.

Now let's try the noun/verb sequence.

> Type "u" to undo the ERASE and bring back the circles.

> To ensure that noun/verb editing is enabled in your drawing, pick "Settings" and then "Selection Settings..." from the pull down menu.

This will open the Entity Selection Settings dialogue box.

> If the Noun/Verb Selection check box is not checked, click in the box to check it.

> Click on "OK" to exit the dialogue.

You are now ready to use pick first editing.

> Use the pickbox to select the outer circle.

The circle will be highlighted, and your screen should now resemble *Figure 2-7*. Those little blue boxes are called "grips". They are part of the Release 12 autoediting system, which we will begin exploring in Chapter 3. For now you can ignore them.

> Pick the second circle in the same fashion.

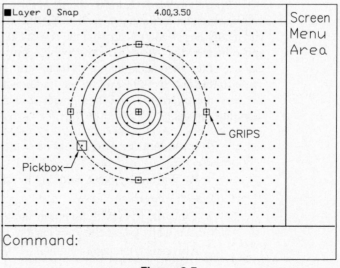

Figure 2-7

The second circle will also become dotted and more grips will appear.

> Type "e" or select "ERASE".

Your two outer circles will disappear as soon as you press enter.

The two outer circles should now be gone. As you can see there is not a lot of difference between the two sequences. One difference that is not immediately apparent is that there are a number of selection methods available in the older verb/noun system that cannot be activated when you pick objects first. We will get to other object select methods momentarily, but first try out the OOPS command.

OOPS!

> Type or select "OOPS" and watch the screen.

If you have made a mistake in your erasure, you can get your selection set back by typing (or selecting) "OOPS". OOPS is to ERASE as REDO is to UNDO. You can use OOPS to undo an ERASE command, as long as you have not done another ERASE in the meantime. In other words, AutoCAD only saves your most recent ERASE selection set.

You can also use U to undo an ERASE, but notice the difference: U simply undoes the last command, whatever it might be; OOPS works specifically with ERASE to recall the last set of erased objects. If you have drawn other objects in the meantime, you can still use OOPS to recall a previously erased set. But if you tried to use U, you would have to backtrack, undoing any newly drawn objects along the way.

Other Object Selection Methods

You can select individual entities on the screen by pointing to them one by one, as we have done above, but in complex drawings this will often be inefficient. AutoCAD offers a variety of other methods, all of which have application in specific drawing circumstances. In this exercise we will select circles by the "windowing" and "crossing" methods, by indicating "last" or "L", meaning the last entity drawn, and by indicating "previous" or "P" for the previously defined set.

In addition, we suggest that you study *Figure 2-8* to learn about other methods. The number of selection options available may seem a bit overwhelming at first, but the time you spend learning them will be well spent. These same options will appear in numerous AutoCAD editing commands (MOVE, COPY, ARRAY, ROTATE, MIRROR) and should become part of your CAD vocabulary.

Selection by "Window"

In Release 12, window and crossing selections, like pointing to individual objects, can be initiated without entering a command. In other words, they are available for noun/verb selection. Also, whether you select objects first or enter a command first, you can force a window or crossing selection simply by picking points on the screen that are not on objects. AutoCAD will assume you want to select by windowing and will ask for a second point.

Let's try it. We will show AutoCAD that we want to erase all of the inner circles by throwing a temporary selection window around them. The window will be defined by two points moving left to right that serve as opposite corners of a rectangle. Only entities that lie completely within the window will be selected. See *Figure 2-9*.

> Pick point 1 at the lower left of the screen, as shown. Any point in the neighborhood of (3.5,1) will do.

AutoCAD will prompt for another corner:

Other corner:

OBJECT SELECTION METHOD	DESCRIPTION	ITEMS SELECTED
(W) WINDOW	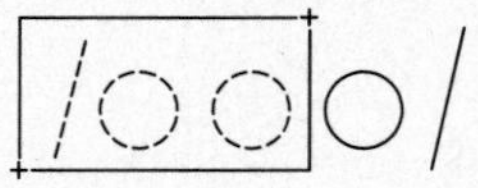	THE ENTITIES WITHIN THE BOX
(C) CROSSING	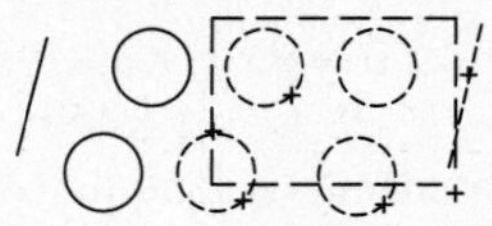	THE ENTITIES CROSSED BY OR WITHIN THE BOX
(P) PREVIOUS	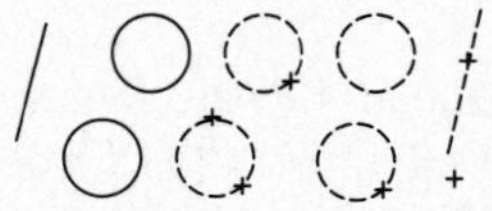	THE ENTITIES THAT WERE PREVIOUSLY PICKED
(L) LAST	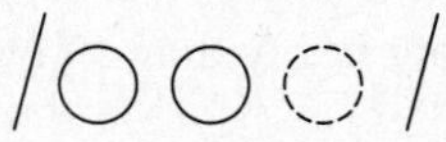	THE ENTITY THAT WAS DRAWN LAST
(R) REMOVE	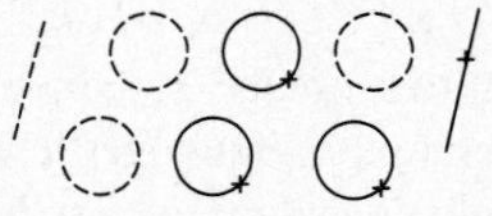	REMOVES ENTITIES FROM THE ITEMS SELECTED SO THEY WILL NOT BE PART OF THE SELECTED GROUP
(A) ADD	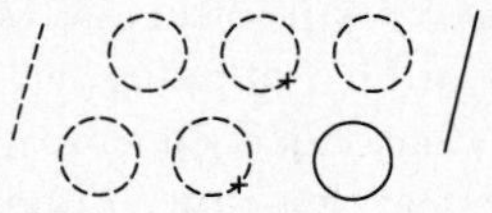	ADDS ENTITIES THAT WERE REMOVED AND ALLOWS FOR MORE SELECTION AFTER THE USE OF REMOVE
ALL	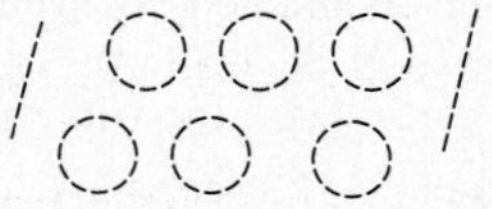	ALL ENTITIES CURRENTLY VISIBLE ON THE DRAWING
(F) FENCE	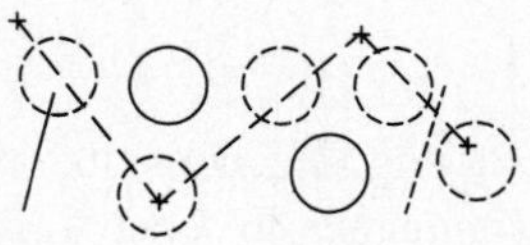	THE ENTITIES CROSSED BY THE FENCE
(WP) WPOLYGON	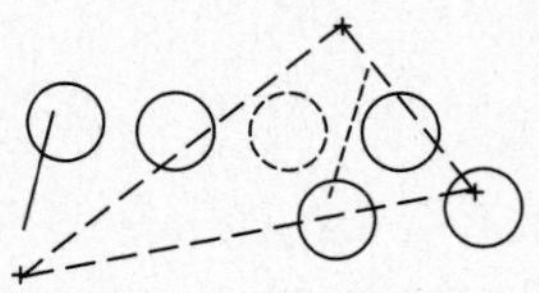	THE ENTITIES WITHIN THE THE POLYGON
(CP) CPOLYGON	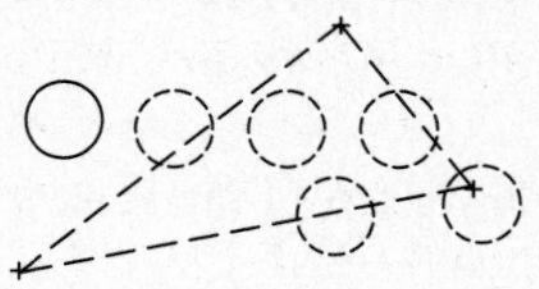	THE ENTITIES CROSSED BY OR WITHIN THE PLOYGON

Figure 2-8

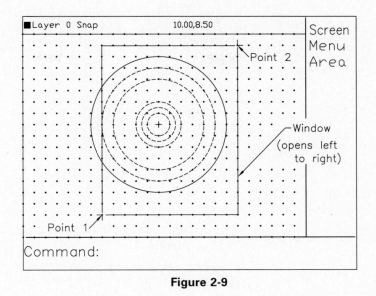

Figure 2-9

> Pick point 2 at the upper right of the screen, as shown. Any point in the neighborhood of (9.5,8.5) will do. To see the effect of the window, be sure that it crosses the outside circle as in *Figure 2-9*.

> Type "e" or select "ERASE".

The inner circles should now be erased.

> Type or select "OOPS" to retrieve the circles once more. Since ERASE was the last command, typing "U" will work equally well.

Selection by Crossing

Crossing is an alternative to windowing that is useful in many cases where a standard window selection could not be performed. The selection procedure is the same, but a crossing box opens to the left instead of to the right, and all objects that cross the box will be chosen, not just those that lie completely inside the box.

We will use crossing to select the inside circles.

> Pick point 1 close to (8.0,3.0) as in *Figure 2-10*.

AutoCAD prompts:

Other corner:

> Pick a point near (4.0,7.0). This point selection must be done carefully in order to demonstrate a crossing selection. Notice that the crossing box is shown with dotted lines, whereas the window box was shown with solid lines.

Also, notice how the circles are selected: those that cross and those that are completely contained within the box, but not those that lie outside.

At this point we could enter the ERASE command to erase the circles, but instead we will demonstrate how to use Ctrl-C to cancel a selection set.

> Hold down the Ctrl key and type "c" or select "Cancel" under "Assist" on the pull down menu. This will cancel the selection set. The circles will no longer be highlighted, but you will see that the grips are still visible. To get rid of the grips you will need another cancel.

> Type Ctrl-C or select "Cancel" again.

The grips should now be gone as well.

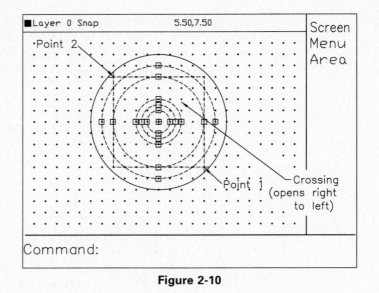

Figure 2-10

Selecting the "Last" Entity

AutoCAD remembers the order in which new objects have been drawn during the course of a single drawing session. As long as you do not leave the drawing editor, you can select the last-drawn entity using the "last" option. If you leave the drawing editor and return later, this information will no longer be available.

> Type or select "ERASE".

Notice that there is no way to specify "last" before you enter a command. This option is only available as part of a command procedure. In other words, it only works in a verb/noun sequence.

> Type or select "L" or "last".

The inner circle should be highlighted.

> Press enter to carry out the command.

The inner circle should be erased.

Selecting the "Previous" Selection Set

The P or previous option works with the same procedure, but it selects the previous selection set rather than the last-drawn entity. If the difference is not obvious to you now, don't worry: It will become clear as you work more with edit commands and selection sets.

Remove and Add

Together, the remove and add options form a switch in the object selection process. Under ordinary circumstances, whatever you select using any of the options above will be added to your selection set. By typing "r" or selecting "Remove" at the "Select objects:" prompt you can switch over to a mode in which everything you pick is deselected or removed from the selection set. Then by typing "a" or selecting "add" you can return to the usual mode of adding objects to the set.

Undo

The ERASE command and other edit commands have an internal undo feature, similar to that found in the LINE command. By typing "u" at the "Select objects:" prompt you can undo your last selection without leaving the edit command you are in and without undoing previous selections. You can also type "u" several times to undo your most recent selections one by one. This allows you to back up one step at a time without having to cancel the command and start all over again.

ALL

"All" is one of several new options for selecting objects in Release 12. By typing "all" at the Select objects: prompt you can select all objects currently visible in your drawing.

Fence

In Release 12, type "f" or select "fence" at the "Select objects:" prompt, and AutoCAD will prompt for a series of "fence points". These points will define a series of line segments called a fence. Any entity that the fence crosses or touches will be selected. This is a very useful option in tight, complex areas.

WPolygon and CPolygon

These are also new in Release 12. Type "wp" for "window polygon" or "cp" for "crossing polygon" at the "Select objects:" prompt. AutoCAD will ask for a series of polygon points. These will become the vertices of an irregular polygon of as many sides as you like. Objects will be selected as in window and crossing selections. That is, a window polygon will select only objects that lie completely within the window. A crossing polygon will select objects inside and objects that cross the polygon.

Other Options

If you hit any key other than the ones AutoCAD recognizes, at the "Select objects:" you will see the following prompt:

```
Expects a point or
Window/Last/Crossing/Box/All/Fence/WPolygon/Cpolygon/
Add/Remove/Multiple/Previous/Undo/AUto/SIngle/Implied
Select objects:
```

Along with the options already discussed, you will see Box, Multiple, AUto, SIngle, and Implied. These options mostly are used in programming customized applications. See the Release 12 *AutoCAD Reference Manual* for additional information.

TASK 7: Using the DIST command

Procedure.

1. Type or select "DIST".
2. Pick first point.
3. Pick second point.
4. Read information in command area or use blips as guide points.

Discussion. The DIST command is one of AutoCAD's most useful inquiry commands. Inquiry commands give you information about your drawing. DIST works like a simple LINE command procedure, but gives you distances instead of actually drawing a line.

There are two principal uses of the DIST command. The most obvious is that it may be used to measure distances or the lengths of linear objects on the screen. The second use may be less obvious, but may be more common. Like other commands that ask you to select points, DIST places blips on the screen. These can be very handy when used as guide points for drawing lines, circles, or other entities. This "guide" method is introduced in the drawing suggestions for Drawing 2-4, "Switch Plate."

The following exercise will introduce you to the DIST command procedure.

> Type or select "DIST".

AutoCAD will prompt you to pick a point:

First point:

> Pick a point anywhere near the middle of the screen.

Notice that AutoCAD gives you a blip at the first point and a rubber band, just as if you were drawing a line. You are also prompted for a second point:

Second point:

> Pick any other point on the screen.

A blip is placed at the second point as well, but no line is drawn between the two points. Instead, you should see something like this in the command area:

Distance = 5.00,   Angle in XY Plane = 53,   Angle from XY Plane = 0
Delta X = 3.00,   Delta Y = 4.00,   Delta Z = 0.00

All of this information can be useful, depending on the situation. "Distance" gives the straight-line distance between the two selected points. "Angle in XY Plane" gives the angle that a line between the two points would make within the coordinate system in which 0 degrees represents a horizontal line out to the right. "Angle from XY Plane" is a 3D feature and will always be 0 in 2D drawings. "Delta X" is the horizontal displacement, which may be either positive or negative. Similarly, "Delta Y" is the vertical displacement. "Delta Z" is the displacement in the Z direction. It will always be 0 until we begin to explore AutoCAD's 3D drawing capabilities in Chapter 12.

Compare what is on your screen with *Figure 2-11*.

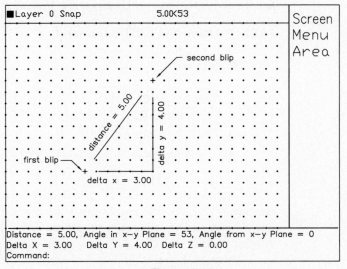

Figure 2-11

TASKS 8, 9, 10, and 11

You are now ready to complete Drawings 2-1 through 2-4. Remember to set grid, snap, and units before you begin each drawing. Use either ERASE or U if you make a mistake, depending on the situation. Use whichever form of the CIRCLE command seems most appropriate or efficient to you. Be sure to try out DIST in Drawing 2-4.

Good luck!

DRAWING 2-1: APERTURE WHEEL

This drawing will give you practice drawing circles using the center point, radius method. Refer to the table below the drawing for radius sizes. With snap set at .25, some of the circles can be drawn by dragging and pointing. Other circles have radii that are not on a snap point. These circles can be drawn easily by typing in the radius.

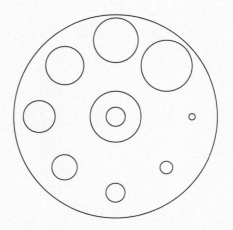

DRAWING SUGGESTIONS

GRID = .50

SNAP = .25

> A good sequence for doing this drawing would be to draw the outer circle first, followed by the two inner circles (h and c). These are all centered on the point (6.00,5.00). Then begin at circle a and work around clockwise, being sure to center each circle correctly.

> Notice that there are two circles c and two h. This simply indicates that the two circles having the same letter are the same size.

> Remember, you may type any value you like and AutoCAD will give you a precise graphic image, but you cannot always show the exact point you want with a pointing device. Often it is more efficient to type a few values than to turn snap off or change its setting for a small number of objects.

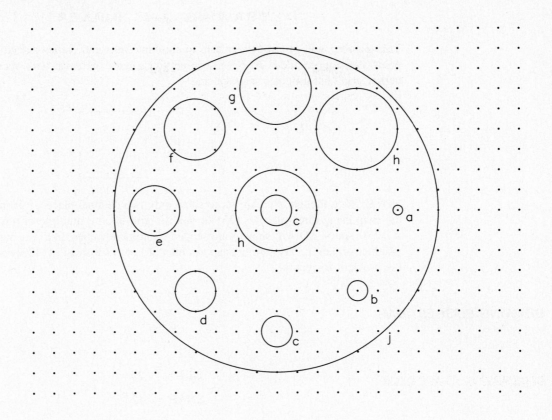

LETTER	a	b	c	d	e	f	g	h	j
RADIUS	.12	.25	.38	.50	.62	.75	.88	1.00	4.00

APERTURE WHEEL

Drawing 2-1

LAYER	0	(DRAW)	CIRCLE	(C)
UNITS	2-PLACE DECIMAL	(EDIT)	ERASE	(E)
GRID	.50	(EDIT)	OOPS	
SNAP	.25	(DISPLAY)	REDRAW	(R)

F1	F6	F7	F8	F9
ON/OFF	ABSOLUTE/OFF/POLAR	ON/OFF	ON/OFF	ON/OFF
SCREEN	COORDS	GRID	ORTHO	SNAP

DRAWING 2–2: ROLLER

This drawing will give you a chance to combine lines and circles and to use the center point, diameter method. It will also give you some experience with smaller objects, a denser grid, and a tighter snap spacing.

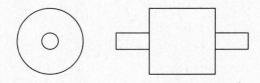

NOTE: Even though units are set to show only two decimal places, it is important to set the snap using three places (.125) so that the grid is on a multiple of the snap (.25 = 2 x .125). AutoCAD will show you rounded coordinate values, like .13, but will keep the graphics on target. Try setting snap to either .13 or .12 instead of .125, and you will see the problem for yourself.

DRAWING SUGGESTIONS

GRID = .25

SNAP = .125

> The two views of the roller will appear fairly small on your screen, making the snap setting essential. Watch the coordinate display as you work and get used to the smaller range of motion.

> Choosing an efficient sequence will make this drawing much easier to do. Since the two views must line up properly, we suggest that you draw the front view first, with circles of diameter .25 and 1.00, and then use these circles to position the lines in the right side view.

> The circles in the front view should be centered in the neighborhood of (2.00,6.00). This will put the upper left-hand corner of the 1 × 1 square at around (5.50,6.50).

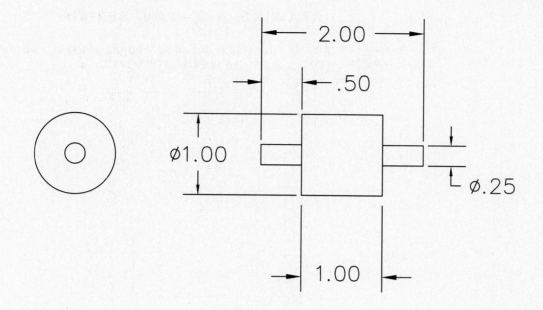

ROLLER
Drawing 2–2

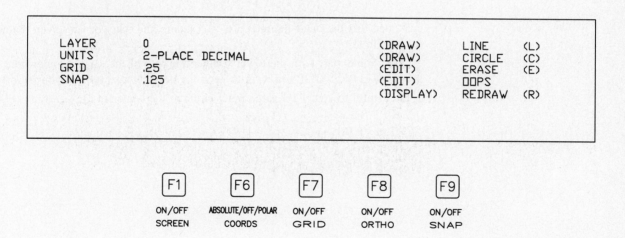

LAYER	0	(DRAW)	LINE	(L)
UNITS	2-PLACE DECIMAL	(DRAW)	CIRCLE	(C)
GRID	.25	(EDIT)	ERASE	(E)
SNAP	.125	(EDIT)	OOPS	
		(DISPLAY)	REDRAW	(R)

F1	F6	F7	F8	F9
ON/OFF	ABSOLUTE/OFF/POLAR	ON/OFF	ON/OFF	ON/OFF
SCREEN	COORDS	GRID	ORTHO	SNAP

DRAWING 2-3: FAN BEZEL

This drawing should be easy for you at this point. Set grid to .50 and snap to .25 as suggested, and everything will fall into place nicely.

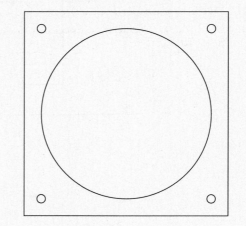

DRAWING SUGGESTIONS

GRID = .50

SNAP = .25

> Notice that the outer figure is a 6 × 6 square and that you are given diameters for the circles.

> You should start with the lower left-hand corner of the square somewhere near the point (3.00,2.00) if you want to keep the drawing centered on your screen.

> Be careful to center the large inner circle at the center of the square.

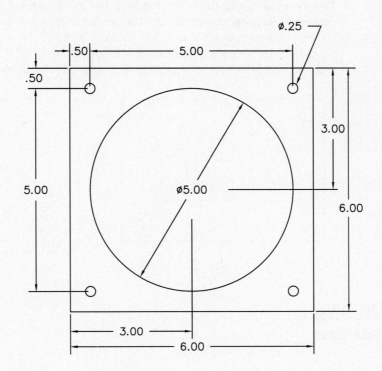

Ø.25

.50

5.00

.50

.50

3.00

Ø5.00

6.00

5.00

3.00

6.00

FAN BEZEL

Drawing 2–3

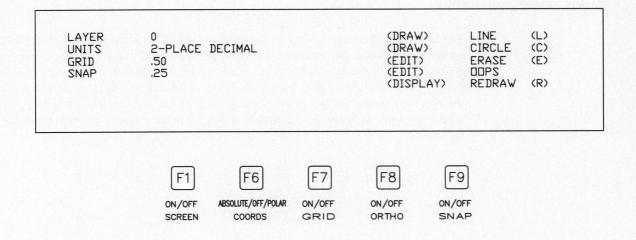

LAYER	0	(DRAW)	LINE	(L)
UNITS	2-PLACE DECIMAL	(DRAW)	CIRCLE	(C)
GRID	.50	(EDIT)	ERASE	(E)
SNAP	.25	(EDIT)	OOPS	
		(DISPLAY)	REDRAW	(R)

F1	F6	F7	F8	F9
ON/OFF	ABSOLUTE/OFF/POLAR	ON/OFF	ON/OFF	ON/OFF
SCREEN	COORDS	GRID	ORTHO	SNAP

DRAWING 2-4: SWITCH PLATE

This drawing is similar to the last one, but the dimensions are more difficult, and a number of important points do not fall on the grid. It will give you practice using grid and snap points and the coordinate display. Refer to the table below the drawing for dimensions of the circles, squares, and rectangles inside the 7×10 outer rectangle. The placement of these smaller figures is shown by the dimensions on the drawing itself.

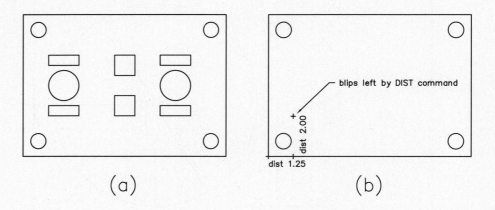

(a)   (b)

DRAWING SUGGESTIONS

GRID = .50

SNAP = .25

> Turn ortho on to do this drawing.

> A starting point in the neighborhood of (1,1) will keep you well positioned on the screen.

GUIDE POINTS WITH DIST

The squares, rectangles, and circles in this drawing can be located easily using DIST to set up guide points. For example, set a first point at the lower left corner of the outer rectangle as in Reference 2-4b. Then set the second point at 1.25 to the right along the bottom of the rectangle. Now repeat the DIST command and use this second point as the new first point. Set the new second point 2.00 up, and you will have a blip right where you want to begin the c rectangle. Look for other places to use this technique in this drawing.

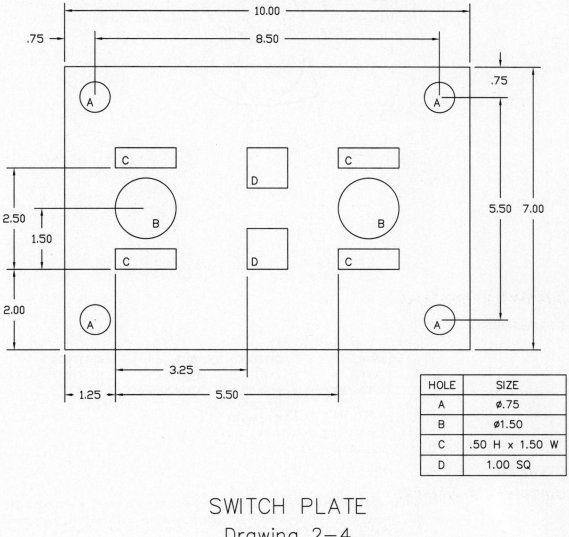

HOLE	SIZE
A	⌀.75
B	⌀1.50
C	.50 H x 1.50 W
D	1.00 SQ

SWITCH PLATE
Drawing 2-4

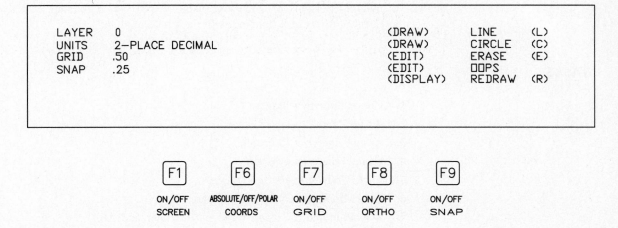

LAYER	0	(DRAW)	LINE	(L)
UNITS	2-PLACE DECIMAL	(DRAW)	CIRCLE	(C)
GRID	.50	(EDIT)	ERASE	(E)
SNAP	.25	(EDIT)	OOPS	
		(DISPLAY)	REDRAW	(R)

F1	F6	F7	F8	F9
ON/OFF	ABSOLUTE/OFF/POLAR	ON/OFF	ON/OFF	ON/OFF
SCREEN	COORDS	GRID	ORTHO	SNAP

CHAPTER

COMMANDS

LAYERS	DISPLAY	EDIT	SETTINGS
LAYER	ZOOM	FILLET	LTSCALE
DDLMODES	PAN	CHAMFER	
	REGEN		
	VPORTS		

OVERVIEW

So far all the drawings you have done have been on a single white layer called "0". In this chapter you will create and use three new layers, each with its own associated color and linetype.

You will also learn to FILLET and CHAMFER the corners of previously drawn objects, to magnify portions of a drawing using the ZOOM command, and to move between adjacent portions of a drawing with the PAN command.

TASKS

1. Create three new layers.
2. Assign colors to layers.
3. Assign linetypes to layers.
4. Change the current layer.
5. FILLET the corners of a square.
6. CHAMFER the corners of a square.
7. ZOOM in and out using Window, Previous, and All.
8. PAN to display another area of a drawing.

9. Create multiple viewports (optional).
10. Do Drawing 3-1 ("Mounting Plate").
11. Do Drawing 3-2 ("Stepped Shaft").
12. Do Drawing 3-3 ("Base Plate").
13. Do Drawing 3-4 ("Bushing").
14. Do Drawing 3-5 ("Half Block").

TASK 1: Creating New LAYERS

Procedure.

1. Type "la" or select "LAYER".
2. Type "n" or select "New".
3. Enter the names of new layers.
4. Press enter to leave LAYER command.

Discussion. Layers allow you to treat specialized groups of entities on your drawing separately from other groups. For example, all of the dimensions in this book were drawn on a special dimension layer so that we could turn them on and off at will. We turned off the dimension layer in order to prepare the reference drawings for chapters 1 through 7, which are shown without dimensions. When a layer is turned off, all the objects on that layer become invisible, though they are still part of the drawing database and can be recalled at any time.

It is common to put dimensions on a separate layer, and there are many other uses of layers as well. Fundamentally, layers are used to separate colors and linetypes, and these in turn take on special significance depending on the drawing application. It is standard drafting practice, for example, to use small, evenly spaced dashes to represent objects or edges that would in reality be hidden from view. On a CAD system with a color monitor, these hidden lines can also be given their own color to make it easy for the operator to remember what layer he or she is working on.

In this book we will use a simple and practical layering system, most of which will be presented in this chapter. You should remember that there are many other systems in use, and many other possibilities. AutoCAD allows as many as 256 different colors and as many layers as you like.

You should also be aware that linetypes and colors are not restricted to being associated with layers. It is possible to mix linetypes and colors on a single layer. But while this may be useful for certain applications, we do not recommend it at this point.

> Begin a new drawing and use the No Prototype check box to ensure that you are using the same defaults as those used in this chapter.

> Type "la" or select "LAYER".

AutoCAD will respond with the following options:

?/Make/Set/New/ON/OFF/Color/Ltype/Freeze/Thaw/Lock/Unlock:

In this chapter we will be concerned with ?, Make, Set, New, Color, and Ltype.

> Type "n" to select the New option.

You will now see this prompt:

New layer name(s):

Notice that you can create more than one layer at a time. Many of the options work this way, allowing you to change the characteristics of a number of different layers at the same time.

> Type "1,2,3" <enter>.

The commas are necessary for this to be read as a list of three names.

Layer names may be up to thirty-one characters long. We have chosen single-digit numbers because they are easy to type and because we can match them to AutoCAD's color numbering sequence.

At this point the three layers have been created. To exit from the LAYER command now, we would simply press the enter key again. Instead, we will ask AutoCAD to show us a list of defined layers and see if the new ones are there.

> Type or select "?".

This option asks AutoCAD to list layers presently defined in a drawing. It is followed by a prompt that allows you to specify the layer or group of layers you want listed:

Layer name(s) for listing < * >:

The <*> default tells you that you can use wild card characters to specify layers. The wild card characters * and ? are used as they are in MS-DOS. The * represents any string of characters, the ? represents any single character. If you accept the default, all defined layers will be listed, since the * can represent any layer name.

> Press enter to list all layers.

You can see by the list that the three new layers "1", "2", and "3" are now defined.

LAYER NAME	STATE	COLOR	LINETYPE
0	On	7 (white)	CONTINUOUS
1	On	7 (white)	CONTINUOUS
2	On	7 (white)	CONTINUOUS
3	On	7 (white)	CONTINUOUS

TASK 2: Assigning Colors to LAYERS

Procedure.

1. Type "la" or select LAYER if not already in the LAYER command.
2. Type "c" or select "Color".
3. Type or select a color name or number.
4. Type the name of a layer or layers.

Discussion. We now have four layers, but they are all pretty much the same. Obviously we have more changes to make before our new layers will have useful identities.

Layer 0 has some special features, which will be discussed in Chapter 10. Because of these it is common practice to leave it defined the way it is. We will begin our changes on layer 1.

> (If for any reason you have left the LAYER command you will need to reenter it by typing "la" or selecting "LAYER", or by pressing enter to repeat the command).

> Type "c" or select "Color".

You will see this prompt:

Color:

> Type "1" or select "red". (Typing "red" will also work.)

AutoCAD has assigned numbers to seven colors (1 through 7). These are standard for all color monitors. Numbers from 8 to 255 specify colors and shades that will vary from one machine to another. The seven standard colors are:

1–Red   5–Blue
2–Yellow   6–Magenta
3–Green   7–White
4–Cyan

Since the color red is number 1 on AutoCAD's color list, a response of either "red" or "1" will have the same effect.

AutoCAD will now want to know which layer(s) are to be red:

Layer name(s) for color 1 (red) <0>:

Layer 0 is the default because it is the currently active layer, the one you have been drawing on. In Task 4 you will see how to make a different layer current.

> Type "1" and press enter.

If you look at the layer list now (type "?"), you will see that layer 1 is assigned the color red.

> Type "c" again and assign the color yellow (color #2) to layer 2.

> Type "c" again and assign the color green (color #3) to layer 3.

Look at the layer list ("?"). It should look like this:

LAYER NAME	STATE	COLOR	LINETYPE
0	On	7 (white)	CONTINUOUS
1	On	1 (red)	CONTINUOUS
2	On	2 (yellow)	CONTINUOUS
3	On	3 (green)	CONTINUOUS

TASK 3: Assigning Linetypes

Procedure.

1. Type "la" or select "LAYER".
2. Type "L" or select "Ltype".
3. Type the name of a linetype.
4. Type the name of a layer or layer(s).
5. Press enter to exit the LAYER command.

Discussion. AutoCAD has a standard library of linetypes that can be assigned easily to layers. There are twenty-four standard types in addition to continuous lines. If you do not assign a linetype AutoCAD will assume you want continuous lines. In addition to continuous lines we will be using hidden and center lines. We will put hidden lines in yellow on layer 2 and center lines in green on layer 3.

> (If for any reason you have left the LAYER command you will need to reenter it by typing "la" or selecting "LAYER", or by pressing enter to repeat the command.)

> Type "L" or select "Ltype".

You will see the following prompt:

Linetype (or ?) <CONTINUOUS>:

If you respond with a ?, AutoCAD will show you a list of linetypes in use in the present drawing. If you press enter you will get the default, which is continuous lines.

> Type or select "Hidden".

As in the color sequence, AutoCAD will ask which layer(s) are to use hidden lines:

Layer name(s) for linetype hidden <0>:

Layer 0 is the default because it is the current layer.

> Type "2".

Now anything drawn on layer 2 will have the hidden linetype.

> Type "L" or select "Ltype" again and assign the "center" linetype to layer 3.

> Now, type "?" once more and examine your layer list. It should look like the one following. If not, use the LAYER command to fix it.

LAYER NAME	STATE	COLOR	LINETYPE
0	On	7 (white)	CONTINUOUS
1	On	1 (red)	CONTINUOUS
2	On	2 (yellow)	HIDDEN
3	On	3 (green)	CENTER

TASK 4: Changing the Current LAYER

Procedure.

1. Type "la" or select "LAYER".
2. Type "s" or select "set".
3. Enter a new current layer.
4. Press enter to exit the LAYER command.

Discussion. In order to draw new entities on a layer, you must make it the currently active layer. Previously drawn objects on other layers also will be visible and will be plotted if that layer is turned on, but new objects will go on the current layer.

> (If for any reason you have left the LAYER command, you will need to reenter it by typing "la" or selecting "LAYER", or by pressing enter to repeat the command.)

> Type "s" or select "set".

You will be prompted for a layer name:

New current layer <0>:

Layer 0 has been current up until now, so it is the default.

> Type "1" and press enter.

At this point you should still be in the LAYER command, with the usual options showing. Though you have completed the set option sequence, the current layer will not show on the status line until you have left the LAYER command and returned to the "Command:" prompt. To do this, simply press enter again.

> Press enter to exit the LAYER command.

You have made layer 1 current. If you go over to the graphics screen (press F1) you will see "Layer 1" in the upper left-hand corner.

NOTE: The "make" option works like the "new" option, except that it makes the newly defined layer current. Of course, this means you can define only one layer at a time with "make".

At this point we suggest that you try drawing some lines to see that you are, in fact, on layer 1 and drawing in red, continuous lines. If you have a monochrome monitor this effect will not be visible. You will see the effect, however, when you switch to layer 2 and draw hidden lines. Even if you are working in monochrome it is good practice to use color settings, because they can be used when you plot your drawings if you have colored pens in your plotter.

When you are satisfied with the red lines you have drawn, go into the LAYER command again and set the current layer to 2. Now draw more lines and see that they are "hidden" yellow lines. (Remember to press enter to exit the LAYER command before entering the LINE command).

Finally, set layer 3 as the current layer and draw some green center lines.

The Layer Control Dialogue Box (DDLMODES)

Selecting "Layer Control..." under "Settings" on the pull down or under "LAYER..." on the screen menu will open up the Layer Control dialogue box, illustrated in *Figure 3-1*. The command that activates this dialogue box is "DDLMODES".

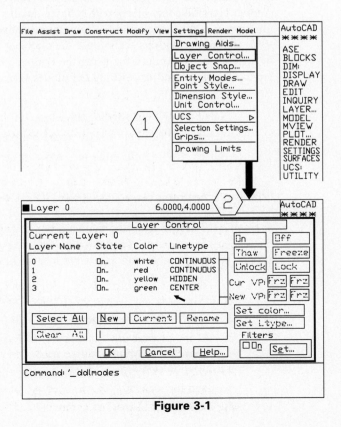

Figure 3-1

The main advantage of this system is that the table of layers is displayed in front of you as you make changes, and you can make several changes at once. The major disadvantage is that you cannot load new linetypes through the dialogue box. That is, you can set a layer to a previously loaded linetype, but if you want to load a new linetype, you will have to leave the dialogue box and go back to the basic LAYER command "Ltype" option, as discussed in Task 3. You can get around this limitation, however, if you load all the standard linetypes at once, using the LINETYPE command. This procedure is presented at the end of this task.

In the upper right-hand corner you will see three pairs of layer mode settings. These settings probably will not be useful to you until later on, but we introduce them briefly here for your information. On and Off affect only the visibility of objects on a layer. Objects on layers that are off are not visible or plotted, but are still in the drawing and are considered when the drawing is "regenerated". Regeneration is the process by which AutoCAD translates the very precise numerical data that make up a drawing file database into the less-precise values of screen graphics. Although Release 12 performs far fewer "regens" than previous releases and does them faster, regeneration can be a slow process in large, complex drawings. As a result it may be useful not to regenerate all the time. This is where "Freeze" comes in. Frozen layers are not only invisible but are ignored in regeneration. "Thaw", of course, reverses this setting. "Lock" and "Unlock" are new in Release 12. Objects on locked layers are visible but cannot be edited. "Unlock" reverses this setting.

Notice that there are four boxes with ellipses in this dialogue box. As you recall, boxes like these will always call other dialogue boxes. Here there are additional dialogues for setting color and linetype, and for using the HELP command. You may want to explore these on your own.

Finally, in the lower right corner of the box you will see a "Filters" section. By selecting "Set..." you call a dialogue box that allows you to limit the layers listed in the Layer Name box. This is an important feature in large drawings where it is not unusual to have thirty or more layers. Using filters you could, for example, list only the green colored layers, or only layers with red, continuous lines. The On box allows you to turn filtering on and off once filtering criteria are defined.

Before leaving this section use the dialogue box to set the current layer to layer 1. In general, the procedure for using the dialogue box involves first selecting a layer or group of layers, and then picking the modes you wish to set for those layers.

> Select layer 1 by clicking anywhere on the layer 1 line.

> Select the "Current" square in the bottom center.

> Select "OK" to close the box and execute the change.

Loading Linetypes Using the LINETYPE Command

Assigning a linetype from the dialogue box is convenient but cannot be done until the linetype has been loaded. The following simple procedure will load all standard linetypes at once so that they become accessible in your drawing.

1. Type or select "Linetype" (under "Settings" on the screen menu).
2. Type "L" or select "Load".
3. At the prompt for "Linetype(s) to load", type or select "*". This wild card character will represent the names of all linetypes.
4. Click on "OK" in the Select Linetype File dialogue box. This procedure will load the standard ACAD linetype file.
5. Press enter to exit the command.

After the linetypes have been loaded you will find a list of 25 linetypes when you select "Set Ltype..." in the Layer Control dialogue box (DDLMODES).

TASK 5: Editing Corners Using FILLET

Procedure.

1. Type or select "FILLET".
2. Type "r" or select "radius".
3. Enter a radius value.
4. Press enter to repeat the FILLET command.
5. Select two lines that meet at a corner.

Discussion.   Now that you have a variety of linetypes to use, you can begin to do some more realistic mechanical drawings. All you will need is the ability to create filleted (rounded) and chamfered (cut) corners. The two work similarly, and AutoCAD makes them easy.

> Erase any lines left on the screen from the last exercise.
> If you have not already done so, set layer 1 as the current layer.
> Draw a 5 × 5 square on your screen, as in *Figure 3-2*.

We will use this figure to practice fillets and chamfers. Exact coordinates and lengths are not significant.

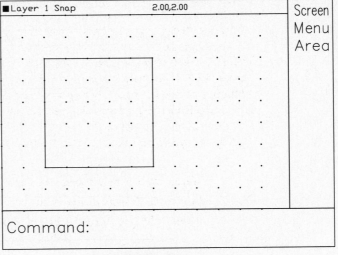

Figure 3-2

> Type or select "FILLET".
The following prompt will appear:

Polyline/Radius/<Select first object>:

Polylines are discussed in Chapter 8.
The first thing you must do is determine the degree of rounding you want. Since fillets are really arcs, they can be defined by a radius.
> Type "r" or select "radius".
AutoCAD prompts:

Enter fillet radius <0.00>:

The default is 0 because no fillet radius has been defined for this drawing yet. You can use a 0 fillet radius to connect two lines at a corner or, more commonly, you can define a fillet radius by typing a value or showing two points that define the radius length.

> Type ".5" or show two points .5 units apart.

You have set .5 as the standard fillet radius for this drawing. You can change it at any time, but it will not affect previously drawn fillets.

There is a slight variation in the menus and the command line here. If you have selected "radius" from the screen menu, the FILLET command will repeat automatically after you type in a radius value. If you have typed the "r", FILLET will not repeat.

> If necessary, press enter to repeat FILLET.

The prompt is the same as before:

Polyline/Radius/<Select first object>:

You will notice that you have the pickbox on the screen now. Use it to select two lines that meet at any corner of your square.

Behold! A fillet! You did not even have to press enter. AutoCAD knows that you are done after selecting two lines.

> Press enter to repeat FILLET. Then fillet another corner.

We suggest that you proceed to fillet all four corners of the square. When you are done your screen should resemble *Figure 3-3*.

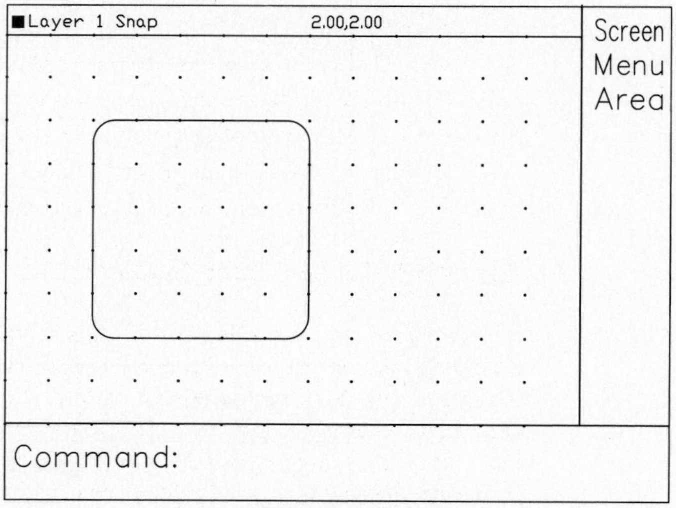

Figure 3-3

TASK 6: Editing Corners with CHAMFER

Procedure.

1. Type or select "CHAMFER".
2. Type "d" or select "distances".
3. Enter a chamfer distance.
4. Press enter to repeat the CHAMFER command.
5. Select two lines that meet at a corner.

Discussion. The CHAMFER command sequence is almost identical to the FIL-LET command, with the exception that chamfers may be uneven. That is, you may cut back farther on one side of a corner than the other. To do this you must give AutoCAD two distances instead of one.

> Prepare for this exercise by undoing all your fillets with the U command.
> Type or select "CHAMFER". (CHAMFER is under "Construct" on the pull down and under "EDIT" on the screen menu.)
   AutoCAD prompts:

Polyline/Distances/<Select first line>:

> Type "d" or select "distances".
   The next prompt will be:

Enter first chamfer distance <0.00>:

The present default is 0 because we have yet to define a chamfer distance for this drawing.
> Type ".25".
   AutoCAD asks for another distance with a prompt like this:

Enter second chamfer distance <0.25>:

The first distance has become the default and most of the time it will be used. If you want an asymmetric chamfer, enter a different value for the second distance.
> Press enter to accept the default, making the chamfer distances symmetrical.
> If necessary, press enter to repeat the CHAMFER command.
> Answer the prompt by pointing to a line this time.
> Point to a second line, perpendicular to the first.
   You should now have a neat chamfer on your square.

The MULTIPLE Command Modifier

If you are creating many fillets or chamfers at once you might want to use the MULTIPLE command modifier to force automatic repetition of the command. At the "Command:" prompt simply type the command modifier "MULTIPLE" before the command itself, with a space between, like this: "multiple chamfer". Then you can proceed to chamfer one corner after another without having to reenter the command. MULTIPLE can be used with other drawing and editing commands as well. When you are ready to move on to another command, press Ctrl-C or "Cancel" to return to the "Command:" prompt. We suggest that you continue this exercise by chamfering the other three corners of your square, using multiple chamfer if you wish. When you are done, your screen should resemble *Figure 3-4*.

TASK 7: ZOOMing Window, Previous, and All

Procedure.

1. Type "z" or select "ZOOM".
2. Enter a ZOOM method or magnification value.
3. Enter values or points if necessary, depending on choice of method.

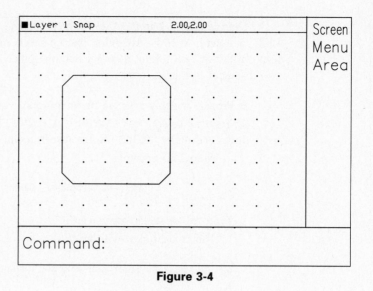

Figure 3-4

Discussion. The capacity to zoom in and out of a drawing is one of the more impressive benefits of working on a CAD system. When drawings get complex it often becomes necessary to work in detail on small portions of the drawing space. Especially with a small monitor, the only way to do this is by making the detailed area larger on the screen. This is easily done with the "ZOOM" command. You should have a square with chamfered corners on your screen from the previous exercise. If not, a simple square will do just as well, and you should draw one now.

> Type "z" or select "ZOOM". (ZOOM is under "View" on the pull down and under "Display" on the screen menu).

The prompt that follows looks like this:

All/Center/Dynamic/Extents/Left/Previous/Vmax/Window/<Scale(X/XP)>:

We are interested, for now, in All, Previous, and Window, which we will explore in reverse order. See the *AutoCAD Reference Manual* for further information.

As in ERASE and other edit commands, you can force a window selection by typing "w" or selecting "window". However, in Release 12 this is unnecessary. The windowing action is automatically initiated if you pick a point on the screen after entering "ZOOM".

> Pick a point just below and to the left of the lower left-hand corner of your square (point 1 in *Figure 3-5*).

AutoCAD asks for another point:

Other corner:

You are being asked to define a window, just as in the ERASE command. This window will be the basis for what AutoCAD displays next. Since you are not going to make a window that exactly conforms to the screen size and shape, AutoCAD will interpret the window this way: Everything in the window will be shown, plus whatever additional area is needed to fill the screen. The center of the window will become the center of the new display.

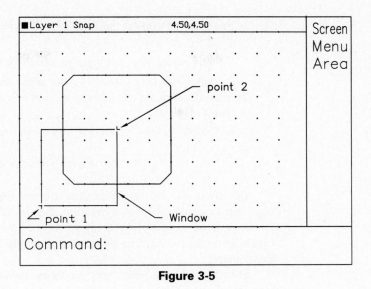

Figure 3-5

> Pick a second point near the center of your square (point 2 in the figure).

The lower left corner of the square should now appear enlarged on your screen, as shown in *Figure 3-6*.

> Using the same method, try zooming up further on the chamfered corner of the square.

Remember that you can repeat the ZOOM command by pressing enter.

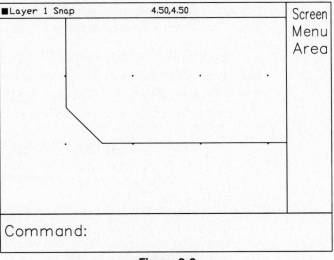

Figure 3-6

At this point, most people cannot resist seeing how much magnification they can get by zooming repeatedly on the same corner or angle of a chamfer. Go ahead. After a couple of zooms the angle will not appear to change. An angle is the same angle no matter how close you get to it. But what happens to the spacing of the grid and snap as you move in? You may have to turn snap off (F9) in order to continue defining windows.

When you are through experimenting with window zooming, try zooming out to the previous display.

> Press enter to repeat the ZOOM command.

> Type "p" or select "Previous".

You should now see your previous display.

AutoCAD keeps track of your most recent displays. The exact number of displays it stores depends on the version you are using. Release 12 remembers ten previous displays.

> ZOOM "Previous" as many times as you can until you get a message that says:

No previous display saved.

One more ZOOM type you should know right now is ZOOM All. ZOOM All zooms out to display the whole drawing. It is useful when you have been working on a number of small areas and are ready to view the whole scene. You do not want to have to wade through previous displays to find your way back. ZOOM All will take you there in one jump.

In order to see it work, you should be zoomed in on a portion of your display before executing ZOOM All.

> Press enter to repeat the ZOOM command.

> Type "a" or select "all".

There you have it.

TASK 8: Moving the Display Area with PAN

Procedure.

1. Type "p" or select "PAN".
2. Pick a displacement base point.
3. Pick a second point to show displacement.

Discussion. As soon as you start to use ZOOM you are likely to need PAN as well. While ZOOM allows you to magnify portions of your drawing, PAN allows you to shift the area you are viewing in any direction.

> Type "p" or select "PAN".

AutoCAD will prompt you to show a displacement:

Displacement:

Imagine that your complete drawing is hidden somewhere behind your monitor, and that the display area is now functioning like a microscope with the lens focused on one portion. If the ZOOM command increases the magnification of the lens, then PAN moves the drawing like a slide under the lens, in any direction you want.

To move the drawing you will indicate a displacement by picking two points on the screen. The line between them will serve as a vector, showing the distance and direction you want to PAN. Notice that the objects on your screen will move in the direction you indicate; if your vector moves to the right, so will the objects.

> Pick point 1 to begin your displacement vector, as shown in *Figure 3-7*.

You will be prompted for another point:

Second point:

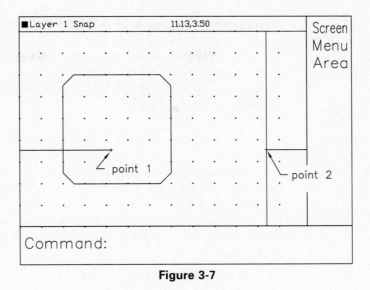

Figure 3-7

> Pick point 2 to the right of your first point.

As soon as you have shown AutoCAD the second point, objects on the screen will shift to the right, as in *Figure 3-8*.

> Press enter to repeat the PAN command.

> Indicate a displacement to the left, moving objects back near their previous positions.

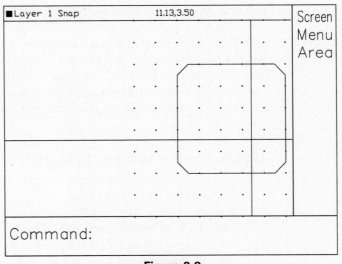

Figure 3-8

Experiment with the PAN command, moving objects up, down, left, right, and diagonally. What function key would make it impossible to PAN diagonally? Hint: The name of the function begins and ends with an "o" and the F-key that turns it on and off begins with an "F" and ends with an "8".

Transparent Commands

If you have used any of the menus to enter the ZOOM and PAN commands you may have noticed that they place an apostrophe before the name of the command. If you select PAN from the AutoCAD standard screen menu, for example, you will see the following in the command area:

Command: '_pan

The apostrophe is a command modifier that makes the command transparent. This means that you can enter it in the middle of another command sequence, and when you are done you will still be in that sequence. For example, you can pan while drawing a line. This is a major convenience if you already have selected the first point and then realize that the second point will be off the screen. A sample procedure using transparent PAN would be as follows:

1. Type or select "LINE".
2. Pick a first point.
3. Type "'p" (notice the apostrophe) or select "PAN".
4. Show a displacement vector.
5. Pick a second point to complete the line.

The major limitation in the use of transparency is that a command cannot be used transparently if its use would require a regeneration of the drawing. This would happen, for example, if you tried to pan beyond the limits of a drawing (see Section on LIMITS in Chapter 4). Then AutoCAD would give you this message in the command area:

** Requires a regen, cannot be transparent **

and your previous command sequence would be resumed without change.

NOTE: By now you probably are wondering about the underline character (_) you see before the apostrophe and before many commands that AutoCAD sends to the command line. It is added to commands in menu systems to ensure that AutoCAD interprets the commands in English. Foreign language versions of AutoCAD have their own command names, but can still use menus developed in English, as long as the underline is there as a flag.

TASK 9: Creating Multiple Viewports in 2D (Optional)

Procedure.

1. Type "VPORTS" or select "Layout" and then "Tiled Viewports..." under "View" on the pull down menu.
2. Type or select the number of viewports (2, 3, or 4).
3. Specify horizontal and vertical arrangement of windows.

Discussion. Assuming you are working in Release 10 or higher, you have the ability to create multiple viewports, or windows, on your screen. In Release 11 and 12 you have the additional capability of positioning viewports anywhere on the screen, varying their size, and plotting any configuration of viewports. These features are most useful in 3D drawings and will be discussed in depth in Chapters 13 and 15.

Multiple viewports also may be used in 2D to allow you to view different parts of a drawing or a complete drawing and a zoomed portion simultaneously. With multiple viewports you have the advantage of switching views less frequently, but this must be weighed against the disadvantage of working in smaller viewing windows.

In Release 11 and 12 there are two types of viewports: tiled and non-tiled. Tiled viewports cover the whole screen and do not overlap. They must be plotted one at a time. Non-tiled viewports can be placed in any configuration on the screen and can be plotted as they appear on the screen. They must be created in paper space: See Chapter 15 on plotting and paper space. If you are interested you can access the first two tasks in Chapter 15 at any time.

In this exercise we will create a simple tiled two-viewport configuration with a full view in one window and a zoomed view in the other.

> To begin this exercise, you should have a full view of the chamfered square, as shown previously in *Figure 3-4*.

> Type "vports" or select "Layout" and then "Tiled Viewports..." under "View" on the pull down menu.

If you are typing, AutoCAD will prompt:

Save/Restore/Delete/Join/SIngle/?/2/<3>/4:

"Save", "Restore", and "Delete" allow you to keep viewport configurations in memory once they have been created. "Join" will reduce the number of viewports by joining two adjacent windows. "SIngle" returns you to a single window. "?" will give you a list of viewport configurations you have previously saved. The numbers 2, 3, and 4 specify numbers of windows. We will use two windows in this exercise.

If you are using the pull down you will see a dialogue box with twelve standard viewport configurations on the right. These are named on the left.

> Type "2" or select "Two: Vertical" from the dialogue box and then click on "OK".

If you are typing, AutoCAD still needs to know which way to split the screen:

Horizontal/<Vertical>:

> Type "v" or press enter (since vertical is the default).

Your screen will be redrawn as shown in *Figure 3-9*.

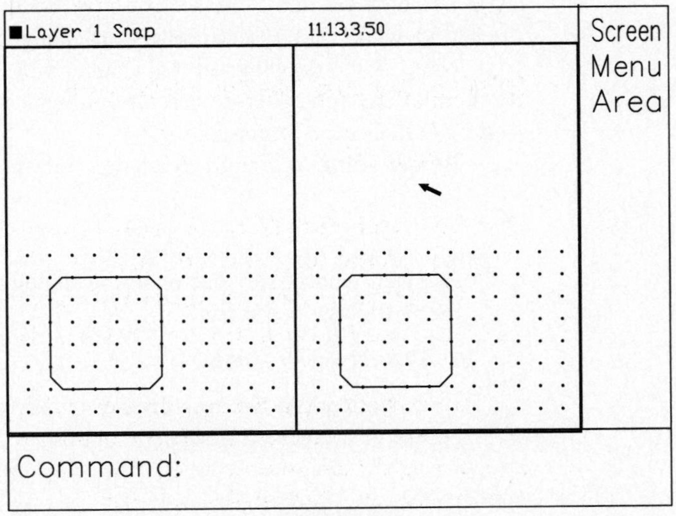

Figure 3-9

> Now move your cursor back and forth between the two windows.

You will see the cross hairs whenever you are in the right viewport and an arrow when you are in the left viewport. This indicates that the right viewport is currently active. You can perform drawing or editing in the current viewport only. However, any changes you make will be immediately reflected in all viewports.

> Move the cursor to the left viewport and press the pick button.

The cross hairs will appear on the left. The left viewport is now active. If you move back to the right you will see the arrow. Often you can switch viewports while you are in the middle of a command sequence. With some commands, such as ZOOM and PAN, this will not work.

> With the left viewport active, enter the ZOOM command and zoom in on a window around the lower left corner of the square.

Your screen should now resemble *Figure 3-10*.

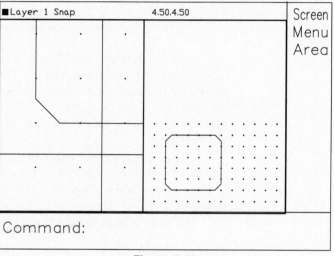

Figure 3-10

To complete this exercise, you may want to do some simple drawing and editing in each viewport and observe how your changes appear in both viewports.

None of the drawings in this chapter will require multiple viewports, but you may try them at any time if you wish. If you want more information, see Chapter 15 or the *AutoCAD Reference Manual*.

Before going on, return to a single viewport by using the Single option.

> Type "vports" or reactivate the dialogue box by clicking twice on "View" on the pull down menu bar.

> Type or select "Single".

Notice that the new display is derived from whichever viewport was active before you executed the Single option.

TASKS 10, 11, 12, 13, and 14

With layers, colors, linetypes, fillets, chamfers, zooming, and panning you are ready to do the drawings for Chapter 3.

Remember to set grid, snap, and units and to define layers before you begin each drawing. Use the ZOOM and PAN commands whenever you think they would help you to draw more efficiently.

DRAWING 3-1: MOUNTING PLATE

This drawing will give you experience using center lines and chamfers. Since there are no hidden lines, you will have no need for layer 2, but we will continue to use the same numbering system for consistency. Draw the continuous lines in red on layer 1 and the center lines in green on layer 3.

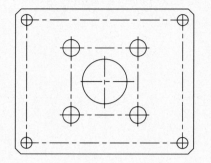

DRAWING SUGGESTIONS

GRID = .5

SNAP = .25

LTSCALE = .5

LTSCALE

The size of the individual dashes and spaces that make up center lines, hidden lines, and other linetypes is determined by a global setting called "LTSCALE". By default it is set to a factor of 1.00. In smaller drawings this setting will be too large and cause some of the shorter lines to appear continuous regardless of what layer they are on.

To remedy this, change LTSCALE as follows:

1. Type or select "LTSCALE".
2. Enter a value.

For the drawings in this chapter use a setting of .50. See *Figure 3-11* for some examples of the effect of changing LTSCALE.

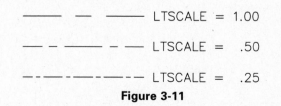

Figure 3-11

> Draw the chamfered rectangle and the nine circles on layer 1 first. Then set current layer to 3 and draw the center lines.

NOTE: In manual drafting it would be more common to draw the center lines first and use them to position the circles. Either order is fine, but be aware that what is standard practice in pencil and paper drafting may not be efficient or necessary on a CAD system.

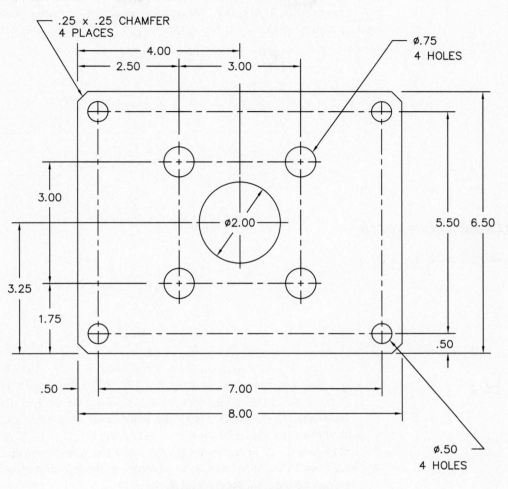

.25 x .25 CHAMFER
4 PLACES

ø.75
4 HOLES

4.00

2.50

3.00

3.00

ø2.00

3.25

1.75

5.50 6.50

.50

.50

7.00

8.00

ø.50
4 HOLES

MOUNTING PLATE
Drawing 3–1

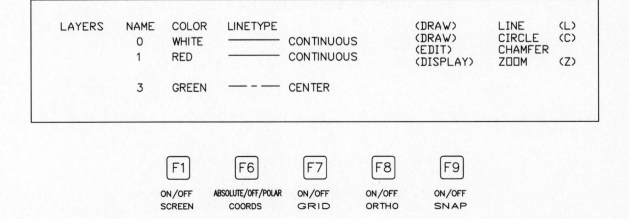

LAYERS	NAME	COLOR	LINETYPE		(DRAW)	LINE	(L)
	0	WHITE	————	CONTINUOUS	(DRAW)	CIRCLE	(C)
	1	RED	————	CONTINUOUS	(EDIT)	CHAMFER	
					(DISPLAY)	ZOOM	(Z)
	3	GREEN	— — —	CENTER			

F1	F6	F7	F8	F9
ON/OFF	ABSOLUTE/OFF/POLAR	ON/OFF	ON/OFF	ON/OFF
SCREEN	COORDS	GRID	ORTHO	SNAP

DRAWING 3–2: STEPPED SHAFT

This two-view drawing uses continuous lines, center lines, chamfers, and fillets. You may want to zoom in to enlarge the drawing space you are actually working in, and pan right and left to work on the two views.

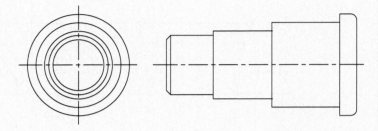

DRAWING SUGGESTIONS

GRID = .25

SNAP = .125

LTSCALE = .5

> Center the front view in the neighborhood of (2,5). Then the right side view will have a starting point at about (5,4.12), before the chamfer cuts this corner off.

> Draw the circles in the front view first, using the vertical dimensions from the side view for diameters. Save the inner circle until after you have drawn and chamfered the right side view.

> Draw a series of rectangles for the side view, lining them up with the circles of the front view. Then chamfer two corners of the left-most rectangle and fillet two corners of the right-most rectangle.

> Use the chamfer on the side view to line up the radius of the inner circle.

> Remember to set current layer to 3 before drawing the center line through the side view.

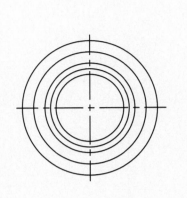

.12 X .12
CHAMFER

.12 FILLET

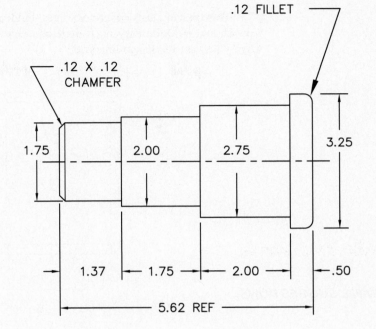

1.75   2.00   2.75   3.25

1.37   1.75   2.00   .50

5.62 REF

STEPPED SHAFT
Drawing 3–2

LAYERS	NAME	COLOR	LINETYPE			
	0	WHITE	———— CONTINUOUS	(DRAW)	LINE	(L)
	1	RED	——— CONTINUOUS	(DRAW)	CIRCLE	(C)
				(EDIT)	CHAMFER	
				(EDIT)	FILLET	
	3	GREEN	— – — CENTER	(DISPLAY)	ZOOM	(Z)

F1	F6	F7	F8	F9
ON/OFF	ABSOLUTE/OFF/POLAR	ON/OFF	ON/OFF	ON/OFF
SCREEN	COORDS	GRID	ORTHO	SNAP

DRAWING 3-3: BASE PLATE

This drawing uses continuous lines, hidden lines, center lines, and fillets. The side view should be quite easy once the front view is drawn. Remember to change layers when you want to change linetypes.

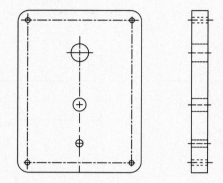

DRAWING SUGGESTIONS

GRID = .25

SNAP = .125

LTSCALE = .5

> Study the dimensions carefully and remember that every grid increment is .25, while snap points not on the grid are exactly halfway between grid points. The four circles at the corners are .38 (actually .375 rounded off) over and in from the corner points. This is three snap spaces (.375 = 3 x .125).

> Position the three circles along the center line of the rectangle carefully. Notice that dimensions are given from the center of the screw holes at top and bottom.

> Use the circle perimeters to line up the hidden lines on the side view, and the centers to line up the center lines.

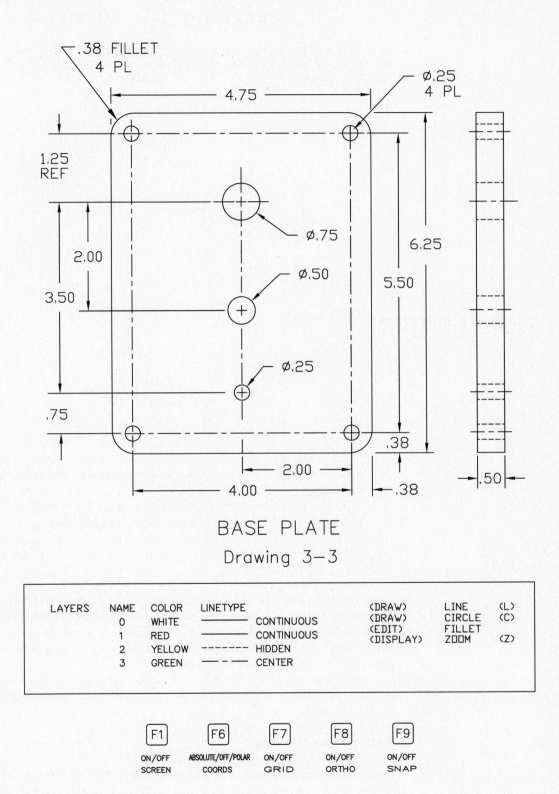

BASE PLATE
Drawing 3–3

LAYERS	NAME	COLOR	LINETYPE			
	0	WHITE	———— CONTINUOUS	(DRAW)	LINE	(L)
	1	RED	——— CONTINUOUS	(DRAW)	CIRCLE	(C)
	2	YELLOW	------- HIDDEN	(EDIT)	FILLET	
	3	GREEN	— — — CENTER	(DISPLAY)	ZOOM	(Z)

F1	F6	F7	F8	F9
ON/OFF	ABSOLUTE/OFF/POLAR	ON/OFF	ON/OFF	ON/OFF
SCREEN	COORDS	GRID	ORTHO	SNAP

DRAWING 3-4: BUSHING

This drawing will give you practice with chamfers, layers, and zooming. Notice that because of the smaller dimensions here, we have recommended a smaller LTSCALE setting.

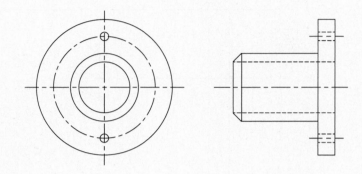

DRAWING SUGGESTIONS

GRID = .25

SNAP = .125

LTSCALE = .5

> Since this drawing will appear quite small on your screen, it would be a good idea to ZOOM in on the actual drawing space you are using, and use PAN if necessary.

> Notice that the two .25-diameter screw holes are 1.50 apart. This puts them squarely on grid points that you will have no trouble finding.

REGEN

When you zoom you may find that your circles turn into many sided polygons. AutoCAD does this to save time. These time savings are not noticeable now, but when you get into larger drawings they become very significant. If you want to see a proper circle, type or select "REGEN". This command will cause your drawing to be regenerated more precisely from the data you have given.

Also you may notice that REGENs happen automatically when certain operations are performed, such as adding new layers, or changing the LTSCALE setting after objects are already on the screen.

Plotting Your Drawings

Plotting drawings is an important and sometimes complicated process. In this book we have adhered to a rule of treating plot procedures separately from drawing procedures. Everything you need to know to get started with printing and plotting is presented in Chapter 15. The first two tasks in Chapter 15 are accessible as you progress through Part I, Chapters 1-6 of this book. The drawing on this page is used to illustrate basic 2D plotting in Task 1 of Chapter 15. You may want to turn to it when you have completed the drawing.

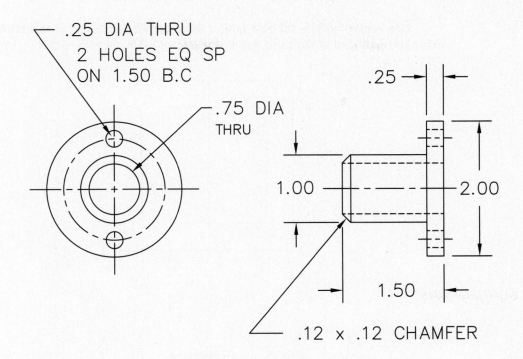

.25 DIA THRU
2 HOLES EQ SP
ON 1.50 B.C

.75 DIA
THRU

.25

1.00

2.00

1.50

.12 x .12 CHAMFER

BUSHING
Drawing 3–4

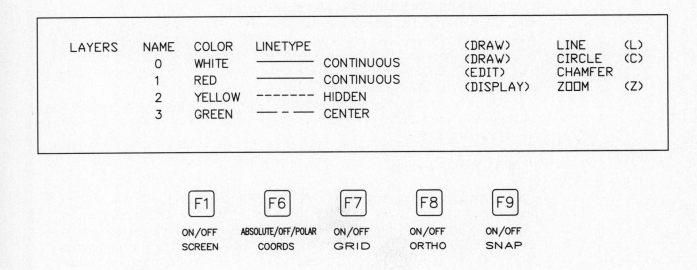

LAYERS	NAME	COLOR	LINETYPE	
	0	WHITE	———————	CONTINUOUS
	1	RED	———————	CONTINUOUS
	2	YELLOW	- - - - - - -	HIDDEN
	3	GREEN	—— – ——	CENTER

(DRAW) LINE (L)
(DRAW) CIRCLE (C)
(EDIT) CHAMFER
(DISPLAY) ZOOM (Z)

F1
ON/OFF
SCREEN

F6
ABSOLUTE/OFF/POLAR
COORDS

F7
ON/OFF
GRID

F8
ON/OFF
ORTHO

F9
ON/OFF
SNAP

DRAWING 3-5: HALF BLOCK

This cinder block is the first project using architectural units in this book. Set units, grid, and snap as indicated, and everything will fall into place nicely.

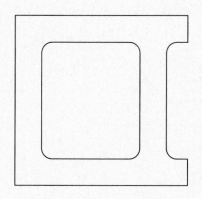

DRAWING SUGGESTIONS

UNITS = Architectural

smallest fraction = 4 (1/4")

GRID = 1/4"

SNAP = 1/4"

> Start with the lower left corner of the block at the point (0'-1",0'-1") to keep the drawing well placed on the display.

> After drawing the outside of the block with the 5 1/2" indentation on the right, use the DIST command to locate the inner rectangle 1 1/4" in from each side.

> Set the FILLET radius to 1/2" or .5. Notice that you can use decimal versions of fractions. The advantage is that they are easier to type.

> Use MULTIPLE FILLET to fillet the six corners.

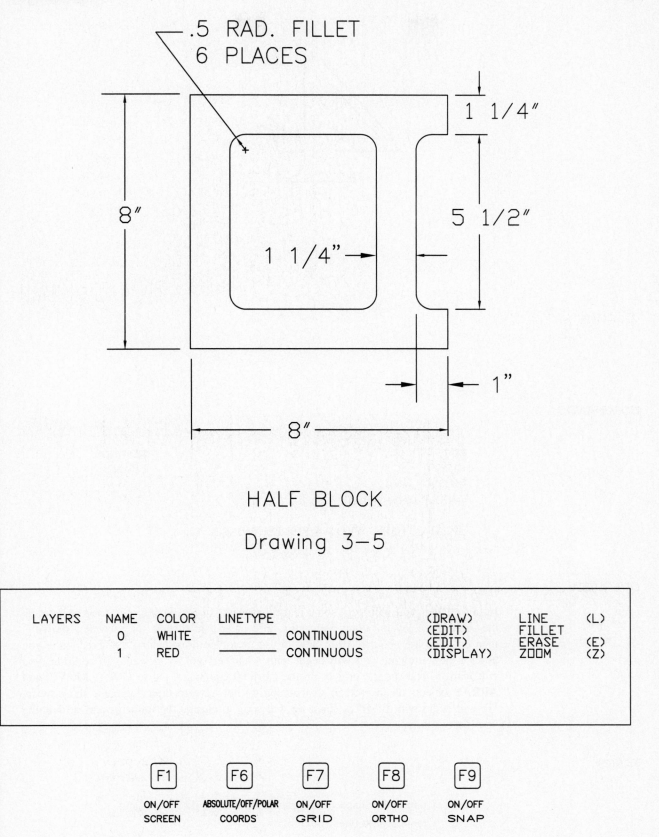

.5 RAD. FILLET
6 PLACES

1 1/4"

8"

5 1/2"

1 1/4"

1"

8"

HALF BLOCK

Drawing 3–5

LAYERS	NAME	COLOR	LINETYPE				
	0	WHITE	———— CONTINUOUS	(DRAW)	LINE	(L)
	1	RED	———— CONTINUOUS	(EDIT)	FILLET	
				(EDIT)	ERASE	(E)
				(DISPLAY)	ZOOM	(Z)

F1	F6	F7	F8	F9
ON/OFF	ABSOLUTE/OFF/POLAR	ON/OFF	ON/OFF	ON/OFF
SCREEN	COORDS	GRID	ORTHO	SNAP

CHAPTER

COMMANDS

EDIT
COPY
MOVE
ARRAY (rectangular)

SETTINGS
LIMITS

SPECIAL TOPIC: PROTOTYPE DRAWINGS

OVERVIEW

In this chapter you will learn some real timesavers. If you have grown tired of defining the same three layers, along with units, grid, snap, and ltscale for each new drawing, read on. You are about to learn how to use prototype drawings so that every time you begin a new drawing you will begin with whatever setup you want. In addition, you will learn to reshape the grid using the LIMITS command and to COPY, MOVE, and ARRAY objects on the screen so that you do not have to draw the same thing twice. We will begin with LIMITS, since we will want to change the limits as part of defining your first prototype.

TASKS

1. Change the shape of the grid using the LIMITS command.
2. Create a prototype drawing.
3. Select your drawing as the prototype.
4. MOVE an object in a drawing.
5. COPY an object in a drawing.

6. Create a rectangular ARRAY.
7. Do Drawing 4-1 ("Pattern").
8. Do Drawing 4-2 ("Grill").
9. Do Drawing 4-3 ("Weave").
10. Do Drawing 4-4 ("Test Bracket").
11. Do Drawing 4-5 ("Floor Framing").

TASK 1: Setting LIMITS

Procedure.

1. Type or select "LIMITS".
2. Enter lower left-hand coordinates.
3. Enter upper right-hand coordinates.
4. ZOOM All.

Discussion.   You have changed the density of the screen grid many times, but always within the same 12 × 9 space, which basically represents an A-size sheet of paper. Now you will learn how to change the shape, by setting new limits to emulate other sheet sizes or any other space you want to represent. But first, a word about model space and paper space.

Model Space and Paper Space

Model space is an AutoCAD concept that refers to the imaginary space in which we create and edit objects. In model space objects are always drawn full scale (1 screen unit = 1 unit of length in the real world). The alternative to model space is paper space, in which screen units represent units of length on a piece of drawing paper. Paper space is most useful in plotting multiple views of 3D drawings. In this book we will keep the discussion of plotting separate from the discussion of drawing techniques. Plotting and paper space are presented in Chapter 15. If you wish to explore multiple viewports and paper space you can look into this chapter any time along the way. Meanwhile, we will continue working in model space.

In this exercise we will reshape our model space to emulate different drawing sheet sizes. You should be aware, however, that this is by no means a necessary practice. With AutoCAD you will be able to scale your drawing to fit any drawing sheet size when it comes time to plot. Model space limits should be determined by the size and shapes of objects in your drawing, not by the paper you are going to use when you plot. However, setting limits in paper space is done in exactly the same way, and paper space limits generally will be set to emulate sheet sizes. Therefore, what you learn here will translate very easily when you begin using paper space.

> Begin a new drawing using "No Prototype".

After we are finished exploring the LIMITS command, we will create the new settings we want and save this drawing as your B-size prototype.

> Use F7 to turn the grid on.

> Type or select "LIMITS".

AutoCAD will prompt you as follows:

```
Reset Model Space limits
ON/OFF/<lower left corner>  <0.0000,0.0000>:
```

The ON and OFF options determine what happens when you attempt to draw outside the limits of the grid. With LIMITS off, nothing will happen. With LIMITS on, you will get a message that says "Attempt to draw outside of limits". Also, with LIMITS on, AutoCAD will not accept any attempt to begin an entity outside of limits, but will allow you to extend objects beyond the limits as long as they were started within them. By default, LIMITS is off, and we will leave it that way.

> Press enter.

This will enter the default values for the lower left corner (0,0). Another common practice is to move the point (0,0) in slightly from the corner of the screen by using something like (−1,−1) as your lower left limit. This will put the (0,0) point over 1 and up 1. If you do this, remember that you also may have to adjust the upper right corner.

For now we will leave the lower left corner at (0,0). AutoCAD will give you a second prompt:

                        Upper right corner <12.0000,9.0000>:

Notice the default coordinates. These determine the size and shape of the grid you have been working with. We will set the limits to emulate a B-size sheet of paper.

> Type "18,12".

The grid will be regenerated, but you will not see any change. Under the new limits the complete grid has become larger than the present display, but you are only seeing part of it. Whenever you set limits larger or smaller than the current display, you will have to do a ZOOM All to see the display defined according to the new limits.

> Type or select "ZOOM".
> Type "A" or select "All".

You should have an 18 × 12 grid on your screen. Place the cursor on the upper right-hand grid point to check its coordinates. This is the grid you will use for a B-size prototype.

We suggest that you continue to experiment with setting limits, and that you try some of the possibilities listed in *Figure 4-1*, which is a table of sheet sizes.

Notice that there are two sets of standards commonly in use. Sometimes the standard you use will be determined by your plotter. This is particularly true for the larger sheet sizes. Some plotters that plot on C-size paper, for example, will take a 24 × 18 inch sheet but not a 22 × 17.

> When you are done experimenting, return LIMITS to (0,0) and (18,12), using the LIMITS command, and then ZOOM All.

You are now in the drawing that we will use for your prototype, so it is not necessary to begin a new one for the next section.

TASK 2: Creating a Prototype

Procedure.

1. Define layers and change settings (grid, snap, units, limits, ltscale, etc.) as desired.
2. Save the drawing, giving it an appropriate name for a prototype.

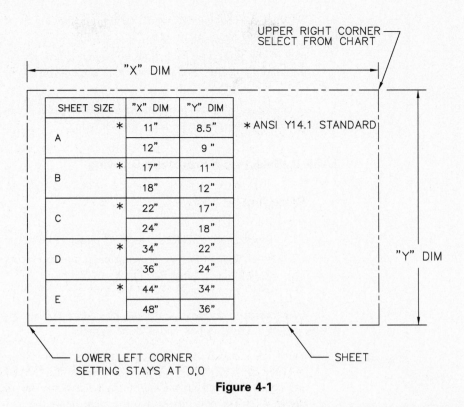

Figure 4-1

Discussion. To make your own prototype, so that new drawings will begin with the settings you want, all you have to do is create a drawing that has those settings and then tell AutoCAD that this is the drawing you want to use to define your initial drawing setup. The first part should be easy for you now, since you have been doing your own drawing setup for each new drawing in this book.

> Make changes to the present drawing as follows:

GRID	1.00 ON (F7)	COORD	ON (F6)
SNAP	.25 ON (F9)	LTSCALE	.5
UNITS	2-place decimal	LIMITS	(0,0) (18,12)

> Enter the LINETYPE command and load all linetypes in the standard ACAD linetype file.

> Create the following layers and associated colors and linetypes.

Remember that you can make changes to your prototype at any time. The layers called "text", "hatch", and "dim" will not be used until Chapters 7 and 8, in which we introduce text, hatch patterns, and dimensions to your drawings. Creating them now will save time and avoid confusion later on.

Layer 0 is already defined.

LAYER name	STATE	COLOR	LINETYPE
0	On	7 (white)	CONTINUOUS
1	On	1 (red)	CONTINUOUS
2	On	2 (yellow)	HIDDEN
3	On	3 (green)	CENTER
TEXT	On	4 (cyan)	CONTINUOUS
HATCH	On	5 (blue)	CONTINUOUS
DIM	On	6 (magenta)	CONTINUOUS

> When all changes are made, save your drawing as "B".

NOTE: Do not leave anything drawn on your screen or it will come up as part of the prototype each time you open a new drawing. For some applications this may be useful. For now we want a blank prototype.

If you have followed instructions up to this point, B.dwg should be on file. Now we will use it as the prototype for a new drawing.

TASK 3: Selecting a Prototype Drawing

Procedure.

1. Type "new" or select "New..." under "File" on the pull down menu.
2. Enter your prototype drawing name in the Prototype drawing edit box.
3. Press enter or click on "OK".

Discussion. In Release 12 the procedure for designating a prototype drawing makes use of a dialogue box and is quite simple.

> Type "new" or select "New..." from the pull down menu under "File".

This will call up the familiar Create New Drawing dialogue box shown in *Figure 4-2*. The edit box on the top right holds the name of the current prototype drawing. In effect, the drawing named in this box will appear when a new drawing is created, unless you specifically tell AutoCAD to do otherwise. If there is no name in the box, then AutoCAD will use its own ACAD.dwg.

The simplest way to change the prototype is to type the name of a new prototype drawing in this box.

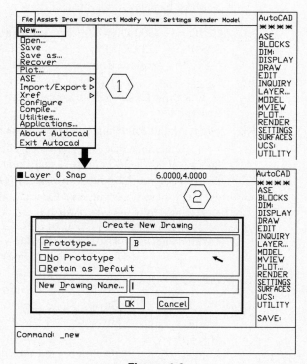

Figure 4-2

> To change the prototype drawing, double click inside the Prototype drawing name box.

If there is already a name in the box, it will become highlighted.

If the box is grayed out, you will notice that the box next to "No Prototype" is checked. Clicking in this box will remove the "x" and make the Prototype name box accessible.

If you prefer to select from a list, you can pick the "Prototype..." box, which will call up a Standard file list box. You can select any file in the list to become the prototype for your new drawing.

> Type "B" to make B.dwg the current prototype.

If your prototype is to be found in a directory other than the one in which ACAD.exe, the AutoCAD program, is found, you will need to include a drive designation. For example "A:B" means B.dwg is on a floppy disk in drive A.

Your B drawing is now designated as the prototype for the new drawing you are about to open. If you also want to retain B as the default prototype, so that it comes up every time you open any new drawing, you will need to click in the Retain as Default check box. If you are using this book in a course, ask your instructor about setting up a default prototype. Since other people probably use your workstation, your instructor will want to manage your use of a prototype carefully.

> Click inside the New Drawing Name edit box, and then type "4-1" or "A:4-1".

> Click on "OK" to exit the edit box and begin the new drawing.

You will find that the new drawing includes all the changes made to B.dwg.

NOTE: There are other ways to control your initial drawing setup. Suppose you have created three or four different prototypes that you want to use at different times for different projects. You might, for example, have C-, D-, and E-size prototypes as well as a B size. With B as the default prototype it is still easy to begin a drawing using some other drawing file for the initial setup.

To open a new drawing called GIZMO.dwg and use the setup from C.dwg, for example, you would use the following procedure:

1. Type "New" or select "New...".
2. In the edit box next to "New Drawing Name" type "GIZMO=C" or "GIZMO=A:C".

The format for this response, then, is:

<new drawing name>=<alternate prototype>

This is the equivalent of typing "Gizmo" in the Prototype box in place of your default prototype, but without clicking on "Retain as Default".

Finally, if you wanted to return to the AutoCAD prototype settings that you have been using up until now, you could simply drop the second name, like this:

<new drawing name>=

This is the equivalent of clicking on "No Prototype".

TASK 4: Using the MOVE Command

Procedure.

1. Type "m" or select "MOVE".

2. Define a selection set. (If noun/verb selection is enabled, you can reverse steps 1 and 2.)

3. Choose the base point of a displacement vector.

4. Choose a second point.

Discussion.   The ability to copy and move objects on the screen is one of the great advantages of working on a CAD system. It can be said that CAD is to drafting as word processing is to typing. Nowhere is this analogy more appropriate than in the "cut and paste" capacities that the COPY and MOVE commands give you.

> Draw a circle with a radius of 1 somewhere near the center of the screen (9,6), as shown in *Figure 4-3*.

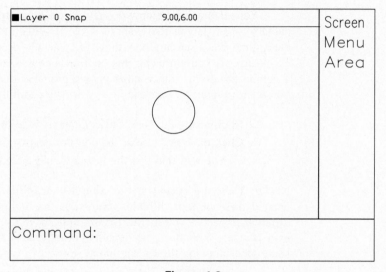

Figure 4-3

As discussed in Chapter 2, Release 12 allows you to pick objects before or after entering an edit command. In this exercise we will use MOVE both ways, beginning with the noun/verb or "pickfirst" method. We will pick the circle you have just drawn, but be aware that the selection set could include as many entities as you like, and that a group of entities can be selected with a window or crossing box.

> Type "m" or select "Move". (MOVE is under "Modify" on the pull down menu and under "EDIT" on the screen menu.)

> Point to the circle.

As in the ERASE command, your circle will become dotted.

On the command line, AutoCAD will tell you how many objects have been selected and ask where you want to move them. Most often you will show the movement by defining a vector that gives the distance and direction you want the object to be moved. The prompt will be this:

Base point or displacement:

We will answer by showing AutoCAD the base point of a vector.

NOTE: In order to define movement with a vector, all AutoCAD needs is a distance and a direction. Therefore, the base point does not have to be on or near the object you are moving. Any point will do, as long as you can use it to show how you want your objects moved. This may seem strange at first, but it will soon become quite natural. Of course, you may choose a point on the object if you wish. With a circle, the center point may be convenient.

> Point to any location not too near the right edge of the screen.

AutoCAD will give you a rubber band from the point you have indicated and will ask for a second point:

Second point of displacement:

As soon as you begin to move the cursor, you will see that AutoCAD also gives you a circle to drag so you can immediately see the effect of the movement you are indicating. Let's say you want to move the circle 3.00 to the right. Watch the coordinate display and stretch the rubber band out until the display reads "3.00<0" (press F6 to get polar coordinates), as in *Figure 4-4*.

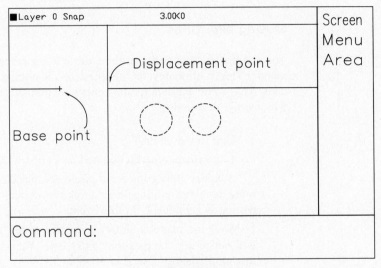

Figure 4-4

> Pick a point 3.00 to the right of your base point.

The rubber band and your original circle disappear, leaving you a circle in the new location.

Now, if ortho is on, turn it off (F8) and try a diagonal move. This time we will use the previous option to select the circle.

> Type "m" or select "MOVE", or press enter to repeat the command.

AutoCAD follows with the "Select objects:" prompt.

> Reselect the circle by typing "p" for previous.

> Press enter to end the object selection process.

> Select a base point.

> Move the circle diagonally in any direction you like.

Figure 4-5 is an example of how this might look.

Try moving the circle back to the center of the screen. It may help to choose the center point of the circle as a base point this time, and choose a point at or near the center of the grid for your second point.

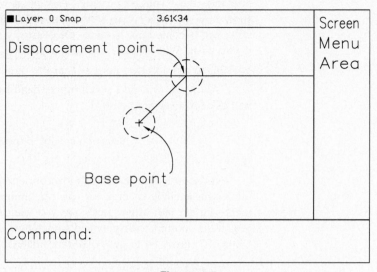

Figure 4-5

Moving with Grips

You can use grips to perform numerous editing procedures without ever entering a command. This is probably the simplest of all editing methods, called "autoediting". It does have some limitations, however. In particular, you can only select by pointing, windowing, or crossing.

> Point to the circle.

It will become highlighted and grips will appear.

Notice that grips for a circle are placed at quadrants and at the center. In more involved editing procedures the choice of which grip or grips to use for editing is significant. In this exercise you will do fine with any of the grips.

> Move the pickbox slowly over one of the grips. If you do this carefully you will notice that the pickbox "locks onto" the grip as it moves over it. You will see this more clearly if snap is off (F9).

> When the pickbox is locked on a grip, press the pick button.

The selected grip will become filled and change colors (from blue to red).

In the command area you will see this:

```
** STRETCH **
<Stretch to point>/Base point/Copy/Undo/eXit:
```

Stretching is the first of a series of five autoediting modes that you can activate by selecting grips on objects. The word "stretch" has many meanings in AutoCAD and they are not always what you expect. We will explore the stretch autoediting mode and the STRETCH command in Chapter 6. For now we will bypass stretch and use the MOVE mode.

> Press enter, the enter button on your cursor, or the space bar to bring up the MOVE autoedit mode.

You should see the following in the command area:

```
** MOVE **
<Move to point>/Base point/Copy/Undo/eXit:
```

Move the cursor now and you will see a rubber band from the selected grip to the same grip on a dragged circle, as illustrated in *Figure 4-6*.

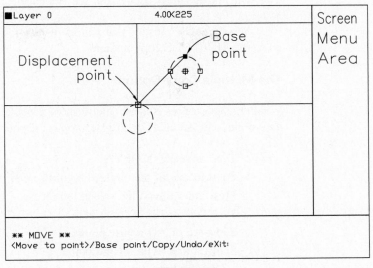

Figure 4-6

> Pick a point anywhere on the screen.

The circle will move where you have pointed.

Moving by Typing a Displacement

Before you proceed to the COPY command there is one more way to use the MOVE command, which is also convenient in many cases. Instead of showing AutoCAD a distance and direction, you can type a horizontal and vertical displacement. For example, to move the circle 3 units to the right and 2 units up you would follow this procedure. There is no autoediting equivalent for this procedure.

1. Pick the circle.
2. Type "m" or select "MOVE".
3. Type "3,2" in response to the prompt for base point or displacement.
4. Press enter in response to the prompt for a second point.

TASK 5: Using the COPY Command

Procedure.

1. Type or select "COPY".
2. Define a selection set (steps 1 and 2 can be reversed if noun/verb selection is enabled).
3. Choose a base point.
4. Choose a second point.

Discussion. The COPY command works so much like the MOVE command that you should find it quite easy to learn at this point. The main difference is that the original object will not disappear when the second point of the displacement vector is given. Also there is an additional option, to make multiple copies of the same object, which we will explore in a moment.

But first, we suggest that you try making several copies of the circle in various positions on the screen. Try using both noun/verb and verb/noun sequences. Notice that "c" is *not* an alias for COPY and that COPY is not on the Release 12 pull down menu. You will find it under "EDIT" on the screen menu. For reference, use the procedure above.

When you are satisfied that you know how to use the basic COPY command, move on to the MULTIPLE copy option.

The Multiple Copy Option

What this option does is allow you to show a whole series of vectors starting at the same base point, and AutoCAD will place copies of your selection set accordingly.

> Type or select "COPY".
> Point to one of the circles on your screen.
> Press enter to end the selection process.
> Type "m" or select "multiple".
> Show AutoCAD a base point.
> Show AutoCAD a second point.

You will see a new copy of the circle, and notice also that the prompt for a "Second point of displacement" has returned in the command area. AutoCAD is waiting for another vector, using the same base point as before.

> Show AutoCAD another second point.
> Show AutoCAD another second point.

Repeat as many times as you wish. If you get into this you may begin to feel like a magician pulling ring after ring out of thin air and scattering them across the screen. The results will appear something like *Figure 4-7*.

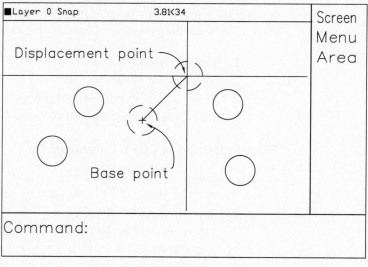

Figure 4-7

Copying with Grips

The grip editing system includes a variety of special techniques for creating multiple copies in all five modes. For now we will stick with the copy option in the MOVE mode, which provides a short cut method for creating the same kind of process you just went through with the COPY command.

Since you should have several circles on your screen now, we will take the opportunity to demonstrate how you can use grips on more than one object at a time.

> Pick any two circles.

The circles you pick should become highlighted and grips should appear on
both, as illustrated in *Figure 4-8*.

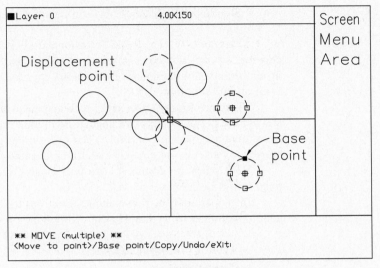

Figure 4-8

> Pick any grip on either of the two highlighted circles.

The grip should change colors.

> Press enter, the enter button on your cursor, or the space bar.

This should bring you into MOVE mode. Notice the prompt:

    ** MOVE **
    <Move to point>/Base point/Copy/Undo/eXit:

> Type "c" to initiate copying. The prompt will change to:

    ** MOVE (multiple) **
    <Move to point>/Base point/Copy/Undo/eXit:

You will find that all copying in the grip editing system is multiple copying.
Once in this mode AutoCAD will continue to create copies wherever you press the
pick button until you exit by typing "x" or pressing enter.

> Move the cursor and observe the two dragged circles.

> Pick a point to create copies of the two highlighted circles.

> Pick another point to create two more copies.

> When you are through, press enter to exit the grip editing system.

TASK 6: Using the ARRAY Command—Rectangular Arrays

Procedure.

   1.   Type or select "ARRAY".

2. Define a selection set. (Steps 1 and 2 can be reversed if noun/verb editing is enabled.)
3. Press enter to end selection.
4. Type "r" or select "rectangular".
5. Enter the number of rows in the array.
6. Enter the number of columns.
7. Enter the distance between rows.
8. Enter the distance between columns.

Discussion.   The ARRAY command gives you a powerful alternative to simple copying. It takes an object or group of objects and copies it a specific number of times in mathematically defined, evenly spaced, locations. An array is a repetition in matrix form of the same figure.

There are two types of arrays. Rectangular arrays are linear and defined by rows and columns. Polar arrays are angular and based on the repetition of objects around the circumference of an arc or circle. The dots on the grid are an example of a rectangular array; the lines on any circular dial are an example of a polar array.

Both types are common. We will explore rectangular arrays in this chapter and polar arrays in the next.

In preparation for this exercise, erase all the circles from your screen. This is a good opportunity to try the ERASE All option.

> Type "e" or select "ERASE".

> Type "all".

> Press enter.

> Now draw a single circle, radius .5, centered at the point (2,2).

> Type or select "ARRAY". (ARRAY is under "Construct" on the pull down and under "EDIT" on the screen menu.)

You will see the "Select objects" prompt.

> Point to the circle.

> Press enter to end the selection process.

AutoCAD will ask which type of array you want:

Rectangular or Polar array (R/P) <R>:

> Type "r" or select "rectangular". Or, you can press enter if R is the default.

AutoCAD will prompt you for the number of rows in the array.

Number of rows (---) <1>:

The (---) is to remind you of what a row looks like, i.e., it is horizontal.

The default is 1. So if you press enter you will get a single row of circles. The number of circles in the row will depend, then, on the number of columns you specify. We will ask for three rows instead of just one.

> Type "3".

AutoCAD now asks for the number of columns in the array:

Number of columns (|||) <1>:

Using the same format (|||), AutoCAD reminds you that columns are vertical. The default is 1 again. What would an array with three rows and only one column look like?

We will construct a five column array.

> Type "5".

Now AutoCAD needs to know how far apart to place all these circles. There will be 15 of them in this example—three rows with five circles in each row. AutoCAD prompts:

Unit cell or distance between rows (---):

"Unit cell" means that you can respond by showing two corners of a window. The horizontal side of this window would give the space between columns; the vertical side would give the space between rows. You could do this exercise by showing a 1 × 1 window. We will use the more basic method of typing values for these distances. The distance between rows will be a vertical measure.

> Type "1".

AutoCAD now asks for the horizontal distance between columns:

Distance between columns (||||):

> Type "1" again.

You should have a 3 × 5 array of circles, as shown in *Figure 4-9*.

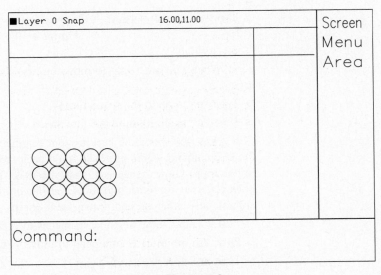

Figure 4-9

Notice that AutoCAD builds arrays up and to the right. This is consistent with the coordinate system, which puts positive values to the right on the horizontal x axis, and upwards on the vertical y axis. Negative values can be used to create arrays in other directions.

We will use the array now on your screen as the selection set to create another array. We will specify an array that has three rows and three columns, with 3.00 between rows and 5.00 between columns. This will keep our circles touching without overlapping.

> Type or select "ARRAY" or press enter to repeat the ARRAY command.

> Using a window, select the whole array of 15 circles.

> Press enter to end the selection process.

> Type "r" or select "rectangular".

> Type "3" for the number of rows.
> Type "3" for the number of columns.
> Type "3" for the distance between rows.
> Type "5" for the distance between columns.

You should have a screen full of circles, as in *Figure 4-10*.

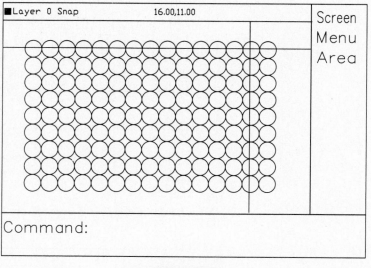

Figure 4-10

When you are ready to move on, use the U command to undo the last two arrays.

> Type "u" to undo the second array.
> Type "u" again to undo the first array.

Now you should be back to your original circle centered at (2,2). Notice that the U command works nicely to undo an incorrectly drawn array quickly. This is important to know, because it is easy to make mistakes creating arrays. Be aware, however, that for other purposes the objects in an array are treated as separate entities, just as if you had drawn them one by one.

Try using some negative distances to create an array down and to the left.

> First, use the MOVE command to move your circle to the middle of the screen.
> Type or select "ARRAY".
> Select the circle by pointing or typing "L" for last.
> Press enter to end the selection process.
> Type "r" or select "rectangular".
> Type "3" for the number of rows.
> Type "3" for the number of columns.
> Type "−2" for the distance between rows.
> Type "−2" for the distance between columns.

Your array should be built down and to the left. The −2 distance between rows causes the array to be built going down. The −2 distance between columns causes the array to be built across to the left.

NOTE: After an array has been drawn, the last drawn entity is the last object in the array to appear on the screen. A "last" selection will select this object. If you want to reselect the selection set used to create the array (in this case the original circle in the center of the screen), use a "previous" selection. "Last", then, refers to the last drawn entity, while "previous" refers to the previous selection set.

TASKS 7, 8, 9, 10, AND 11

All the drawings in this chapter will use your new prototype. Whether you have defined a prototype in the Create New Drawing dialogue box or use the equal sign to load your prototype, the settings and layers should be as you have defined them. Do not expect, however, that you will never need to change them. Layers will stay the same throughout this book, but limits will change from time to time, and grid and snap will change frequently.

The main thing you should be focused on in doing these drawings is to become increasingly familiar with the COPY and ARRAY commands.

DRAWING 4–1: PATTERN

This drawing will give you practice using the COPY command. There are numerous ways in which the drawing can be done. The key is to try to take advantage of the repetition in the pattern by copying in an efficient manner. The following figures suggest one way it can be done.

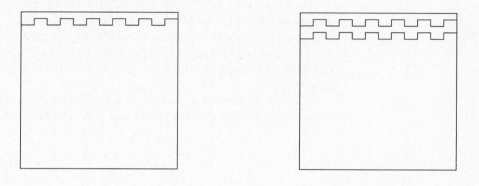

(a)   (b)

DRAWING SUGGESTIONS

GRID = .5

SNAP = .25

> Begin with a 6 × 6 square. Then draw the first set of lines as in *Reference 4-1a*.

> Copy the first set down .5 to produce *Reference 4-1b*.

> Draw the first set of v-shaped lines. Then use a multiple copy to produce *Reference 4-1c*.

> Finally, make a single copy of all the lines you have so far, using a window for selection. (Be careful not to select the outside lines.) Watch the displacement carefully and you will produce *Reference 4-1d*, the completed drawing.

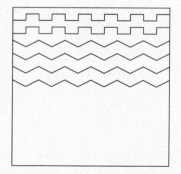

(c)

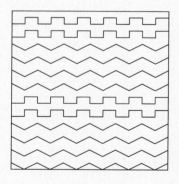

(d)

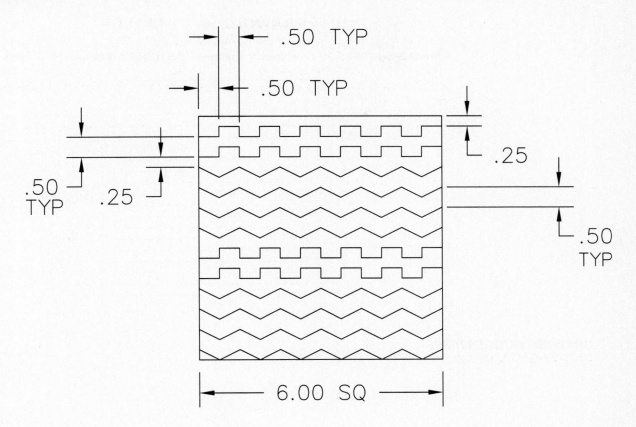

PATTERN

Drawing 4-1

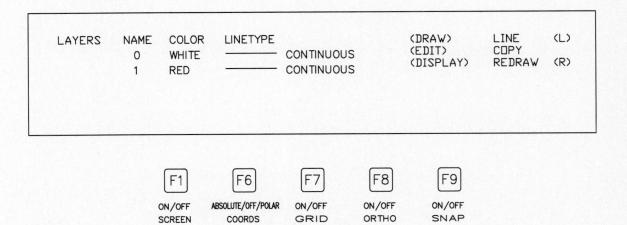

LAYERS	NAME	COLOR	LINETYPE		(DRAW)	LINE	(L)
	0	WHITE	———— CONTINUOUS		(EDIT)	COPY	
	1	RED	———— CONTINUOUS		(DISPLAY)	REDRAW	(R)

F1	F6	F7	F8	F9
ON/OFF	ABSOLUTE/OFF/POLAR	ON/OFF	ON/OFF	ON/OFF
SCREEN	COORDS	GRID	ORTHO	SNAP

DRAWING 4-2: GRILL

This drawing should go very quickly if you use the ARRAY command.

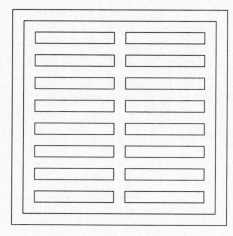

DRAWING SUGGESTIONS

GRID = .5

SNAP = .25

> Begin with a 4.75 × 4.75 square.
> Move in .25 all around to do the inside square.
> Draw the rectangle in the lower left-hand corner first, then use the ARRAY command to create the rest.
> Also remember that you can undo a misplaced array using the U command.

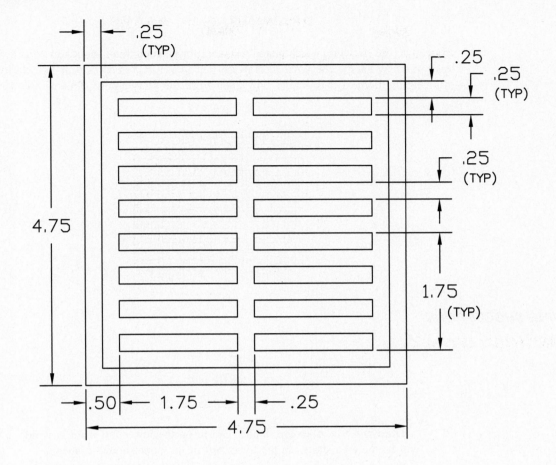

GRILL
Drawing 4–2

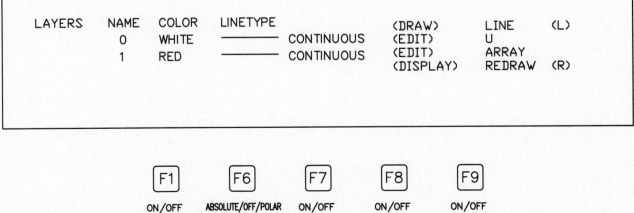

LAYERS	NAME	COLOR	LINETYPE		(DRAW)	LINE	(L)
	0	WHITE	————	CONTINUOUS	(EDIT)	U	
	1	RED	————	CONTINUOUS	(EDIT)	ARRAY	
					(DISPLAY)	REDRAW	(R)

F1	F6	F7	F8	F9
ON/OFF	ABSOLUTE/OFF/POLAR	ON/OFF	ON/OFF	ON/OFF
SCREEN	COORDS	GRID	ORTHO	SNAP

DRAWING 4–3: WEAVE

As you do this drawing, watch AutoCAD work for you and think about how long it would take to do by hand! The finished drawing will look like *Reference 4-3*. For clarity, the drawing on the next page shows only one cell of the array and its dimensions.

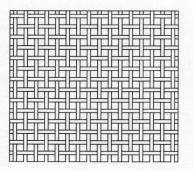

DRAWING SUGGESTIONS

GRID = .5

SNAP = .12

> Draw the 6 × 6 square, then zoom in on the lower left using a window. This will be the area shown in the lower left of the dimensioned drawing.

> Observe the dimensions and draw the line patterns for the lower left corner of the weave. You could use the COPY command in several places if you like, but the time gained will be minimal. Don't worry if you have to fuss with this a little to get it correct; once you've got it right the rest will be easy.

> Use ARRAY to repeat the lower left-hand cell in an 8 × 8 matrix.

> If you get it wrong, use U and try again.

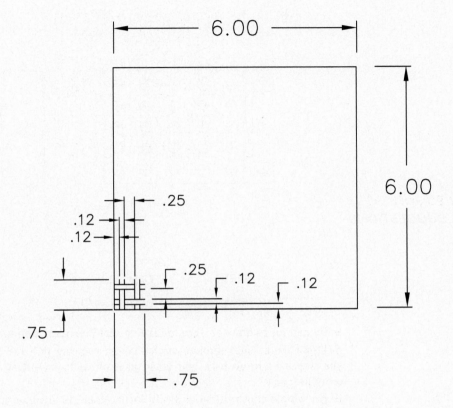

6.00

6.00

.25

.12
.12

.25

.12

.12

.75

.75

WEAVE

Drawing 4–3

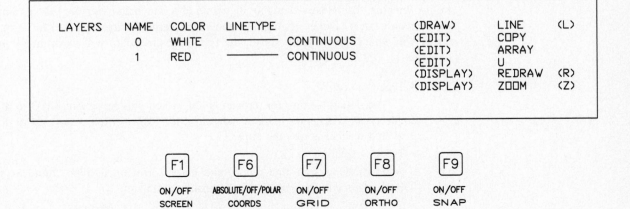

LAYERS	NAME	COLOR	LINETYPE				
	0	WHITE	——— CONTINUOUS		(DRAW)	LINE	(L)
	1	RED	——— CONTINUOUS		(EDIT)	COPY	
					(EDIT)	ARRAY	
					(EDIT)	U	
					(DISPLAY)	REDRAW	(R)
					(DISPLAY)	ZOOM	(Z)

F1	F6	F7	F8	F9
ON/OFF	ABSOLUTE/OFF/POLAR	ON/OFF	ON/OFF	ON/OFF
SCREEN	COORDS	GRID	ORTHO	SNAP

DRAWING 4–4: TEST BRACKET

This is a great drawing for practicing much of what you have learned up to this point. Notice the suggested snap, grid, ltscale, and limit settings, and use the ARRAY command to draw the 25 circles on the front view.

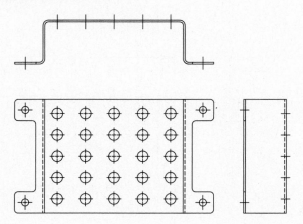

DRAWING SUGGESTIONS

GRID = .5   LTSCALE = .50

SNAP = .25   LIMITS = (0, 0)(24, 18)

> Be careful to draw all lines on the correct layers, according to their linetypes.

> Draw center lines through circles before copying or arraying them; otherwise you will have to go back and draw them on each individual circle or repeat the array process.

> A multiple copy will work nicely for the four .50 diameter holes. A rectangular array is definitely desirable for the twenty-five .75 diameter holes.

CREATING CENTER MARKS WITH THE DIMCEN SYSTEM VARIABLE

There is a simple way to create the center marks and center lines shown on all the circles in this drawing. It involves changing the value of a dimension variable called "dimcen" (dimension center). Dimensioning and dimension variables are discussed in Chapter 8, but if you would like to jump ahead, the following procedure will work nicely in this drawing.

> Type "dimcen".

The default setting for dimcen is .09, which will cause AutoCAD to draw a simple cross as a center mark. Changing it to −.09 will tell AutoCAD to draw a cross that reaches across the circle.

> Type "−.09".

> After drawing your first circle, and before arraying it, type "dim" or select "DIM:". This will put you in the dimension command.

> Type "cen", indicating that you want to draw a center mark. This is a very simple dimension feature.

> Point to the circle.

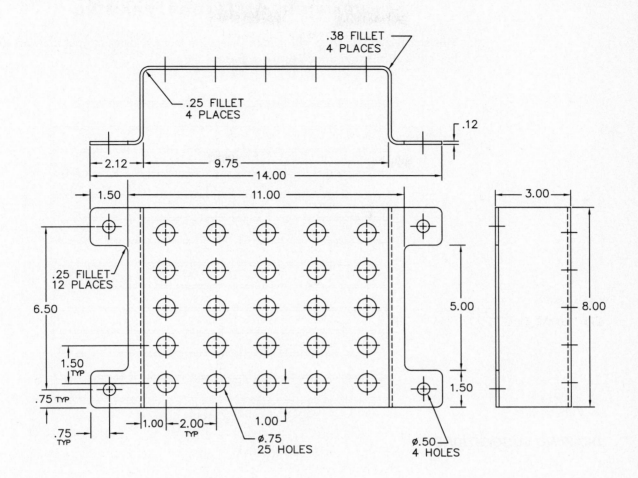

.38 FILLET
4 PLACES

.25 FILLET
4 PLACES

.12

2.12   9.75   14.00

1.50   11.00   3.00

.25 FILLET
12 PLACES

6.50   5.00   8.00

1.50
TYP

1.50

.75 TYP

.75
TYP   1.00   2.00
TYP   1.00

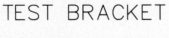

Ø.75
25 HOLES

Ø.50
4 HOLES

TEST BRACKET
Drawing 4–4

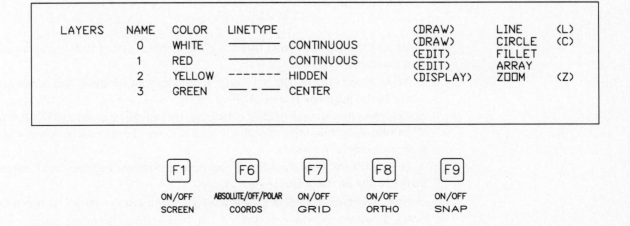

LAYERS	NAME	COLOR	LINETYPE			
	0	WHITE	————	CONTINUOUS	(DRAW)	LINE (L)
	1	RED	———	CONTINUOUS	(DRAW)	CIRCLE (C)
	2	YELLOW	-------	HIDDEN	(EDIT)	FILLET
	3	GREEN	— – —	CENTER	(EDIT)	ARRAY
					(DISPLAY)	ZOOM (Z)

F1	F6	F7	F8	F9
ON/OFF	ABSOLUTE/OFF/POLAR	ON/OFF	ON/OFF	ON/OFF
SCREEN	COORDS	GRID	ORTHO	SNAP

DRAWING 4–5: FLOOR FRAMING

This architectural drawing will require changes in many features of your drawing setup. Pay close attention to the suggested settings.

DRAWING SUGGESTIONS

UNITS = Architectural,

smallest fraction = 1″

LIMITS = 36′, 24′

GRID = 1′

SNAP = 2″

LTSCALE = 12

> Be sure to use foot (′) and inch (″) symbols when setting limits, grid, and snap (but not ltscale).

> Begin by drawing the 20′ × 17′–10″ rectangle, with the lower left corner somewhere in the neighborhood of (4′,4′).

> Complete the left and right 2 × 10 joists by copying the vertical 17′–10″ lines 2″ in from each side. You may find it helpful to use the arrow keys when working with such small increments.

> Draw a 19′–8″ horizontal line 2″ up from the bottom and copy it 2″ higher to complete the double joists.

> Array the inner 2 × 10 in a 14-row by 1-column array, with 16" between rows.

> Set to layer 2 and draw the three 17′–4″ hidden lines down the center.

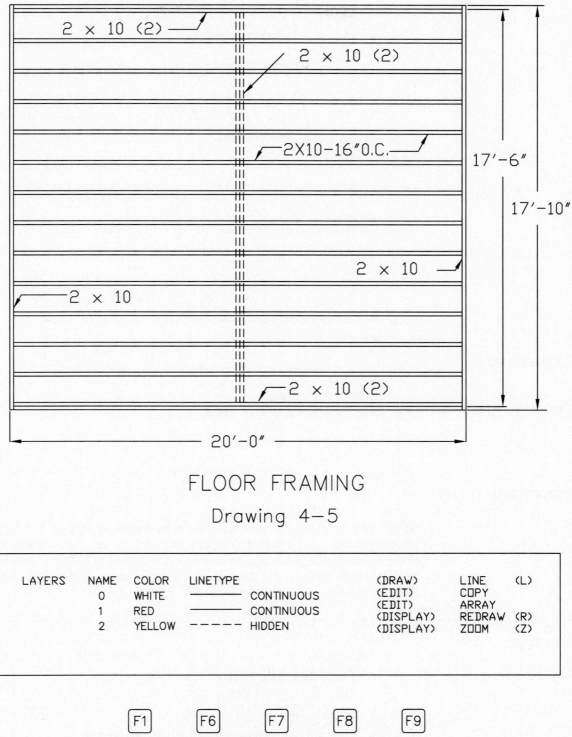

FLOOR FRAMING
Drawing 4–5

LAYERS	NAME	COLOR	LINETYPE				
	0	WHITE	——————— CONTINUOUS		(DRAW)	LINE	(L)
	1	RED	——————— CONTINUOUS		(EDIT)	COPY	
	2	YELLOW	– – – – – HIDDEN		(EDIT)	ARRAY	
					(DISPLAY)	REDRAW	(R)
					(DISPLAY)	ZOOM	(Z)

F1	F6	F7	F8	F9
ON/OFF	ABSOLUTE/OFF/POLAR	ON/OFF	ON/OFF	ON/OFF
SCREEN	COORDS	GRID	ORTHO	SNAP

CHAPTER

COMMANDS

DRAW	EDIT
ARC	ARRAY (polar)
	ROTATE
	MIRROR

OVERVIEW

So far, every drawing you have done has been composed of lines and circles. In this chapter you will learn a third major entity, the ARC. In addition, you will expand your ability to manipulate objects on the screen. You will learn to ROTATE objects and create their MIRROR images. But first, we will pick up where we left off in Chapter 4 by showing you how to create polar arrays.

TASKS

1. Create three polar arrays.
2. Draw arcs in eight different ways.
3. Rotate a previously drawn object.
4. Create mirror images of previously drawn objects.
5. Do Drawing 5-1 ("Flanged Bushing").
6. Do Drawing 5-2 ("Guide").
7. Do Drawing 5-3 ("Dials").
8. Do Drawing 5-4 ("Alignment Wheel").
9. Do Drawing 5-5 ("Hearth").

TASK 1: Creating Polar Arrays

Procedure.

1. Type or select "ARRAY."
2. Define a selection set. (Steps 1 and 2 can be reversed if noun/verb selection is enabled.)
3. Type "p" or select "polar".
4. Pick a center point.
5. Enter the number of items to be in the array (or press enter).
6. Enter the angle to fill (or 0).
7. Enter the angle between items.
8. Tell whether or not to rotate items.

Discussion.   The procedure for creating polar arrays is lengthy and requires some explanation. The first two steps are the same as in rectangular arrays. Step 3 is also the same, except that you respond with "polar" or "p" instead of "rectangular" or "r". From here on the steps will be new. First you will pick a center point, and then you will have several options for defining the array.

There are three qualities that define a polar array, but any two are sufficient. A polar array is defined by two of the following: 1) a certain number of items, 2) an angle that these items span, and 3) an angle between each item and the next. However you define your polar array, you will have to tell AutoCAD whether or not to rotate the newly created objects as they are copied.

> Begin a new drawing using the B prototype.

> In preparation for this exercise, draw a vertical 1.00 line at the bottom center of the screen, near (9.00,2.00), as shown in *Figure 5-1*. We will use a 360 degree polar array to create *Figure 5-2*.

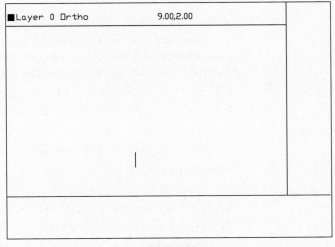

Figure 5-1

> Type or select "ARRAY".
> Select the line.
> Type "p" or select "polar".

So far, so good. Nothing new up to this point. Now you have a prompt that looks like this:

Center point of array:

Rectangular arrays are not determined by a center, so we did not encounter this prompt before. Polar arrays, however, are built by copying objects around the circumferences of circles or arcs, so we need a center to define one of these.
> Pick a point directly above the line and somewhat below the center of the screen. Something in the neighborhood of (9.00,4.50) will do. The next prompt is:

Number of items:

Remember that we have a choice of two out of three among number of items, angle to fill, and angle between items. This time we will give AutoCAD the first two.
> Type "12".
Now that AutoCAD knows that we want 12 items, all it needs is either the angle to fill with these, or the angle between the items. It will ask first for the angle to fill:

Angle to fill (+=ccw,−=cw) <360>:

The symbols in parentheses tell us that if we give a positive angle the array will be constructed counterclockwise; if we give a negative angle, it will be constructed clockwise. Get used to this; it will come up frequently.
The default is 360 degrees, meaning an array that fills a complete circle.
If we did not give AutoCAD an angle (that is, if we responded with a "0"), we would be prompted for the angle between. This time around we will give 360 as the angle to fill.
> Press enter to accept the default, a complete circle.
AutoCAD now has everything it needs, except that it doesn't know whether we want our lines to retain their vertical orientation or to be rotated along with the angular displacement as they are copied. AutoCAD asks:

Rotate objects as they are copied? <Y>:

Notice the default, which we will accept.
> Press enter or type "y".

Your screen should resemble *Figure 5-2*. Now let's try some of the other options. We will define an array that has 20 items placed 15 degrees apart and not rotated.

> Type "U" to undo the first array.
> Type or select "ARRAY".
> Select the line again.
> Type "p" or select "polar".
> Pick the same center point as before.

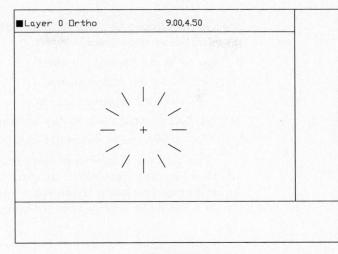

Figure 5-2

> Type "20" for the number of items.

> Type "0" for the angle to fill.

As mentioned, this response tells AutoCAD to issue a prompt for the angle between items:

The symbols in parentheses are familiar from the "Angle to fill" prompt. Notice that there is no default angle here.

> Type "15" for the angle between items.

All that remains is to tell AutoCAD not to rotate the lines as they are copied.

> Type "n".

Your screen should now resemble *Figure 5-3*.

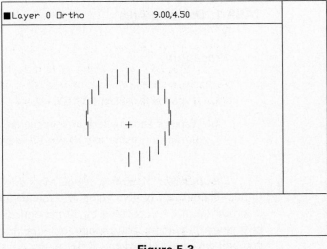

Figure 5-3

Try one more and then you will be on your own with polar arrays. For this one, define an array that fills 270 degrees and has -30 degrees between each angle, as in *Figure 5-4*.

> Undo the last array.

> Repeat the first four steps, up to the "number of items" prompt.

> Press enter to skip the "Number of items" prompt. This tells AutoCAD to issue the other two prompts instead.

> Type "-270" for the angle to fill.

> Type "30" for the angle between.

What will the negative angle do?

> Press enter to rotate items as they are copied.

Your screen should resemble *Figure 5-4*.

This ends our discussion of polar arrays. With the options AutoCAD gives you there are many possibilities that you may want to try out. As always, we encourage experimentation. When you are satisfied, erase everything on the screen and do a REDRAW in preparation for learning the ARC command.

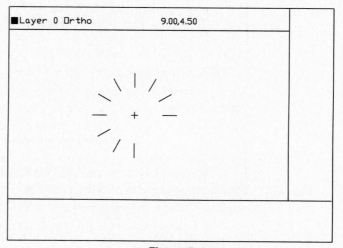

Figure 5-4

TASK 2: Drawing Arcs

Procedure.

1. Type "a" or select "ARC".

2. Type or show where to start the arc, where to end it, and what circle it is a portion of, using any of the 11 available methods.

Discussion. Learning AutoCAD's ARC command is an exercise in geometry. In this section we will give you a firm foundation for understanding and drawing arcs so that you will not be confused by all the options that are available. The information we give you will be more than enough to do the drawings in this chapter and most drawings you will encounter elsewhere. Refer to the *AutoCAD Reference Manual* and the chart at the end of this section (*Figure 5-5*) if you need additional information.

AutoCAD gives you eight distinct ways to draw arcs, and if you count variations in order, 11. With this much to work with, some generalizations will be helpful.

First, notice that every option requires you to specify three pieces of information: where to begin the arc, where to end it, and what circle it is theoretically a part of. To get a handle on the range of options, look at the following standard screen menu abbreviations and meanings.

Screen Menu	Information needed
1 3-point:	Three points on arc
2 S,C,E:	Start,Center,End
3 S,C,A:	Start,Center,Angle
4 S,C,L:	Start,Center,Length of chord
5 S,E,A:	Start,End,Angle
6 S,E,R:	Start,End,Radius
7 S,E,D:	Start,End,Starting direction
8 C,S,E:	Center,Start,End
9 C,S,A:	Center,Start,Angle
10 C,S,L:	Center,Start,Length of chord
11 Contin:	Start given as end point of previous line or arc; Circle tangent to previous line or arc; End required

Notice that options 8, 9, and 10 are simply reordered versions of 2, 3, and 4. This is how we end up with 11 options instead of 8.

Notice, also, that "start" is always included. In every option, a starting point must be specified, though it does not have to be the first point given.

The options arise from the different ways you can specify the end and the circle that the arc is cut from. The end may be shown as an actual point (all E options) or inferred from a specified angle or length of chord (all A and L options).

The circle that the arc is part of may be specified directly by its center point (all C options) or inferred from other information, such as a radius length (R options), an angle between two given points (A options), or a tangent direction (S,E,D and Contin).

With this framework in mind, we will begin by drawing an arc using the simplest method, which is also the default, the 3-point option. The geometric key to this method is that any three points not on the same line determine a circle or an arc of a circle. AutoCAD uses this in the CIRCLE command (the 3P option) as well as in the ARC command.

> Type "a" or select "ARC".

AutoCAD's response will be this prompt:

Center/<Start point>:

Accepting the default by specifying a point will leave you open to all those options in which the start point is specified first.

If you type a "C", AutoCAD will prompt for a center point and follow with those options that begin with a center.

> Select a starting point near the center of the screen. AutoCAD prompts:

Center/End/<Second point>:

We will continue to follow the default, three-point, sequence by specifying a second point. You may want to refer to the chart (*Figure 5-5*) as you draw this arc.

> Select any point one or two units away from the previous point. Exact coordinates are not important.

Once AutoCAD has two points, it gives you an arc to drag. By moving the cursor slowly in a circle and in and out you can see the range of what the third point will produce.

AutoCAD also knows now that you have to provide an end point to complete the arc, so the prompt has only one option:

End point:

Any point you select will do, as long as it produces an arc that fits on the screen.

> Pick an end point.

As you can see, three-point arcs are easy to draw. It is much like drawing a line, except that you have to specify three points instead of two. In practice, however, you do not always have three points to use this way. This necessitates the broad range of options in the ARC command. The dimensions you are given and the objects already drawn will determine what options are available to you.

Next, we will create an arc using the start, center, end method, the second option illustrated in *Figure 5-5*.

> Type "U" to undo the three-point arc.
> Type "a" or select "ARC".

If you are using the AutoCAD menu, you can select the "S,C,E" option from the screen or the pull down. If you do, you will be able to skip the step of specifying "center" as noted following.

> Select a point near the center of the screen as a start point.

The prompt that follows is the same as for the three-point option, but we will not use the default this time:

Center/End/<Second point>:

We will choose the Center option.

NOTE: If you selected "S,C,E" from the screen menu or "Start, Cen, End" from the pull down, you will be able to skip the next step. Briefly, this is because the menu is a system of "macros" that automate some of your keystrokes. The "c" that we type next will be provided automatically by the screen or pull down macro if you have selected the option there.

> If not using the screen menu, type "c".

This tells AutoCAD that we want to specify a center point next, so we see this prompt:

Center:

> Select any point roughly one to three units away from the start point.

The circle from which the arc is to be cut is now clearly determined. All that is left is to specify how much of the circle to take, which can be done in one of three ways, as the prompt indicates:

Angle/Length of chord/<End point>:

We will simply specify an end point by typing coordinates or pointing. But first, move the cursor slowly in a circle and in and out to see how the method works (snap should be off—press F9). As before, there is an arc to drag, and now there is a radial direction rubber band as well. If you pick a point anywhere along this rubber band, AutoCAD will assume you want the point where it crosses the circumference of the circle.

NOTE: Here, as in the polar arrays in this chapter, AutoCAD is building arcs *counterclockwise*, consistent with its coordinate system.

> Select an end point to complete the arc.

We will draw one more arc, using the start, center, angle method, before going on. This method has some peculiarities in the use of the rubber band that are typical of the ARC command and can be confusing. An example of how the S,C,A method may look is shown in *Figure 5-5*.

> Type "U" to undo the last arc.
> Pick the S,C,A option from the screen menu, assuming it is still showing.

   AutoCAD will ask for a center or start point:

Center/<Start Point>:

> Pick a start point near the center of the screen.
> Pick a center point one to three units below the start point.

   AutoCAD will prompt as before:

Angle/Length of chord/<End point>:

> Type "a" to indicate that you will specify an angle.

   If you have selected S,C,A from a menu, this step will be automated. Auto-CAD will ask for the included angle.

   You can type an angle specification or show an angle on the screen. Notice that the rubber band now shows an angle only; its length is insignificant. The angle is being measured from the horizontal, but the arc begins at the start point and continues counterclockwise, as illustrated in *Figure 5-5*.

> Type "45" or show an angle of 45 degrees.

Now that you have tried three of the basic methods for constructing an arc, we strongly suggest that you study the chart and then try out the other options. The notes in the right-hand column will serve as a guide to what to look for.

The differences in the use of the rubber band from one option to the next can be confusing. You should understand, for instance, that in some cases the linear rubber band is only significant as a distance indicator; its angle is of no importance and is ignored by AutoCAD. In other cases it is just the reverse. The length of the rubber band is irrelevant, while its angle of rotation is important.

NOTE: One additional trick you should try out as you experiment with arcs is as follows: If you press enter or the space bar at the "Center/<Start point>" prompt, AutoCAD will use the end point of the last line or arc you drew as the new starting point and construct an arc tangent to it. This is the same as the Contin option on the screen menu.

This completes the present discussion of the ARC command. Constructing arcs, as you may have realized, can be tricky. Another option that is available and often useful

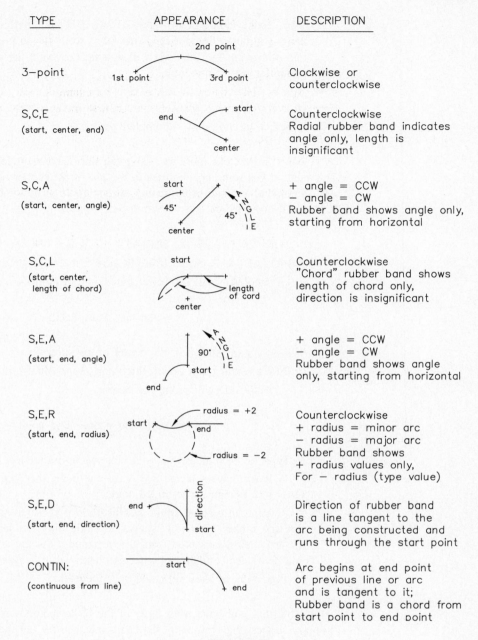

TYPE	APPEARANCE	DESCRIPTION

3–point — Clockwise or counterclockwise

S,C,E (start, center, end) — Counterclockwise Radial rubber band indicates angle only, length is insignificant

S,C,A (start, center, angle) — + angle = CCW − angle = CW Rubber band shows angle only, starting from horizontal

S,C,L (start, center, length of chord) — Counterclockwise "Chord" rubber band shows length of chord only, direction is insignificant

S,E,A (start, end, angle) — + angle = CCW − angle = CW Rubber band shows angle only, starting from horizontal

S,E,R (start, end, radius) — Counterclockwise + radius = minor arc − radius = major arc Rubber band shows + radius values only, For − radius (type value)

S,E,D (start, end, direction) — Direction of rubber band is a line tangent to the arc being constructed and runs through the start point

CONTIN: (continuous from line) — Arc begins at end point of previous line or arc and is tangent to it; Rubber band is a chord from start point to end point

Figure 5-5

is to draw a complete circle and then use the TRIM or BREAK commands to cut out the arc you want. BREAK and TRIM are introduced in the next chapter.

TASK 3: Using the ROTATE Command

Procedure.

1. Type or select "ROTATE".

2. Define the selection set. (Steps 1 and 2 can be reversed if noun/verb selection is enabled.)

3. Pick a base point.

4. Indicate an angle of rotation.

Discussion. ROTATE is a fairly straightforward command, and it has some uses that might not be apparent immediately. For example, it frequently is easier to draw an object in a horizontal or vertical position first and then ROTATE it than it would be to draw it diagonally.

In addition to the ROTATE command there is also a rotate mode in the grip edit system, which we will introduce at the end of the exercise.

> In preparation for this exercise clear your screen and draw a horizontally oriented arc near the center of your screen, as in *Figure 5-6*. Exact coordinates and locations are not important.

We will begin by rotating the arc to the position shown in *Figure 5-7*.

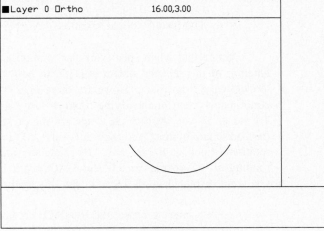

Figure 5-6

> Select the arc.

> Type or select "ROTATE".

You will be prompted for a base point.

Base point:

This will be the point around which the object is rotated. The results of the rotation, therefore, are dramatically affected by your choice of base point. We will choose a point at the left tip of the arc.

> Point to the left tip of the arc.

The prompt that follows looks like this:

<Rotation angle>/Reference:

The default method is to indicate a rotation angle directly. The object will be rotated through the angle specified and the original object deleted.

Move the cursor in a circle and you will see that you have a copy of the object to drag into place visually. If ortho or snap are on, turn them off to see the complete range of rotation.

> Type "90" or point to a rotation of 90 degrees (remember to use F6 if your coordinate display is not showing polar coordinates).

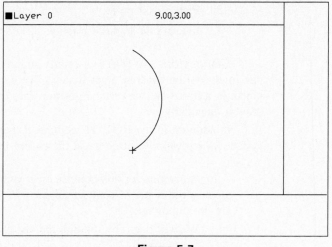

Figure 5-7

The results should resemble *Figure 5-7*.

Notice that when specifying the rotation angle directly like this, the original orientation of the selected object is taken to be 0 degrees. The rotation is figured counterclockwise from there. However, there may be times when you want to refer to the coordinate system in specifying rotation. This is the purpose of the "reference" option. To use it, all you need to do is specify the present orientation of the object relative to the coordinate system, and then tell AutoCAD the orientation you want it to have after rotation. Look at *Figure 5-8*. To rotate the arc as shown, you either can indicate a rotation of -45 degrees or tell AutoCAD that it is presently oriented to 90 degrees and you want it rotated to 45 degrees. Try this method for practice.

> Press enter to repeat the ROTATE command.
> Select the arc.
> Press enter to end selection.
> Choose a base point at the lower tip of the arc.
> Type "r" or select "Reference".
    AutoCAD will prompt for a reference angle:

                    Reference angle <0>:

> Type "90".
    AutoCAD prompts for an angle of rotation:

                    Rotation angle:

> Type "45".
    Your arc should now resemble the solid arc in *Figure 5-8*.

Rotating with Grips

Rotating with grips is simple and there is a very useful option for copying, but your choice of object selection methods is limited, as always, to pointing and windowing. Try this:

> Pick the arc.

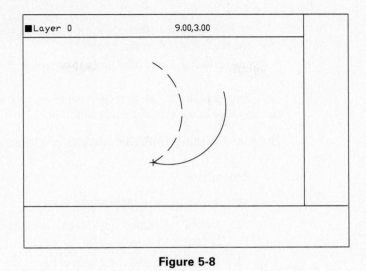

Figure 5-8

The arc will become highlighted and grips will appear.
> Pick the center grip.

Notice that as soon as you pick a grip, a Grip edit mode menu appears in the screen menu area. You can pick "rotate" from the menu or press enter twice to bypass Stretch and Move.
> Select "ROtate" from the screen menu.

Move your cursor in a circle and you will see the arc rotating around the grip at the center of the arc.
> Now, select "Base pt" from the screen menu.

This will allow you to pick a base point other than the selected grip.
> Pick a base point above and to the left of the grip, as shown in *Figure 5-9*.

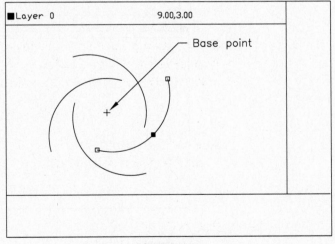

Figure 5-9

Move your cursor in circles again. You will see the arc rotating around the new base point.
> Select "Copy" from the menu.

Notice the Command area prompt, which indicates you are now in a rotate and multiple copy mode.
> Pick a point showing a rotation angle of 90 degrees, as illustrated by the top arc in Figure 5-9.

> Pick a second point showing a rotation angle of 180 degrees, as illustrated by the arc at the left in the figure.

> Pick point 3 at 270 degrees to complete the design shown in *Figure 5-9*.

This capacity to create rotated copies is very useful, as you will find when you do the drawings at the end of the chapter.

TASK 4: Creating MIRROR Images of Objects on the Screen

Procedure.

1. Type or select "MIRROR".

2. Define a selection set. (Steps 1 and 2 can be reversed if noun/verb selection is enabled.)

3. Point to two ends of a mirror line.

4. Indicate whether or not to delete original object.

Discussion.   There are two main differences between the command procedures for MIRROR and ROTATE. First, in order to mirror an object you will have to define a mirror line, and second you will have an opportunity to indicate whether you want to retain the original object or delete it. In the ROTATE sequence the original is always deleted.

There is also a mirror mode in the grip edit system, which we will explore at the end of the task.

> To begin this exercise, undo the rotate copy process so that you are left with a single arc. Rotate it and move it to the left so that you have a bowl-shaped arc placed left of the center of your screen, as in *Figure 5-10*.

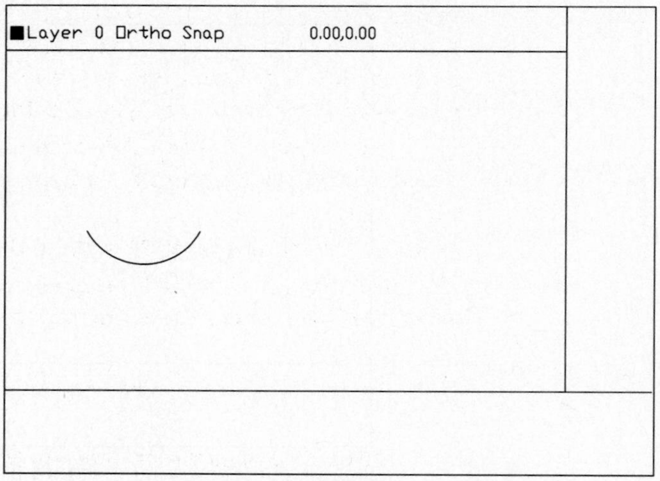

```
■Layer 0 Ortho Snap          0.00,0.00
```

Figure 5-10

Except where noted, you should have snap and ortho on to do this exercise.

> Select the arc.

> Type or select "MIRROR".

Now AutoCAD will ask you for the first point of a mirror line.

First point of mirror line:

A mirror line is just what you would expect; all points on your object will be mirrored across the line at a distance equal and opposite to their distance away from it.

We will show a mirror line even with the top of the arc, so that the end points of the mirror images will be touching.

> Select a point even with the left end point of the arc, as in *Figure 5-11*.

You are prompted to show the other end point of the mirror line:

Second point:

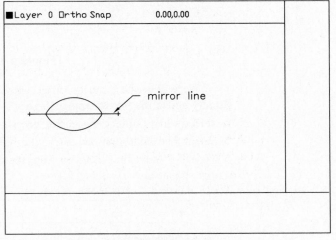

Figure 5-11

The length of the mirror line is not important. All that matters is its orientation. Move the cursor slowly in a circle, and you will see an inverted copy of the arc moving with you to show the different mirror images that are possible, given the first point you have specified. Turn ortho off to see the whole range of possibilities, then turn it on again to complete the exercise.

We will select a point at 0 degrees from the first point, so that the mirror image will be directly above the original arc, and touching at the end points as in *Figure 5-11*.

> Select a point directly to the right (0 degrees) of the first point.

The dragged object will disappear until you answer the next prompt, which asks if you want to delete the original object or not.

Delete old objects? <N>:

This time around we will not delete the original.

> Press enter to retain the old object. Your screen will look like *Figure 5-11*, without the mirror line in the middle.

Now let's repeat the process, deleting the original this time, and using a different mirror line, to produce *Figure 5-13*.

> Press enter to repeat the MIRROR command.
> Select the original (lower) arc.
> Press enter to end selection.

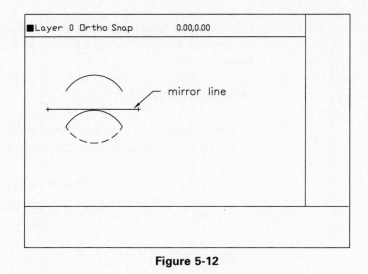

Figure 5-12

We will create a mirror image above the last one by choosing a mirror line slightly above the two arcs as in *Figure 5-12*.

> Select a first point of the mirror line slightly above and to the left of the figure.

> Select a second point directly to the right of the first point.

> Type "y" indicating that you want the old object, the lower arc, deleted. Your screen should now resemble *Figure 5-13*.

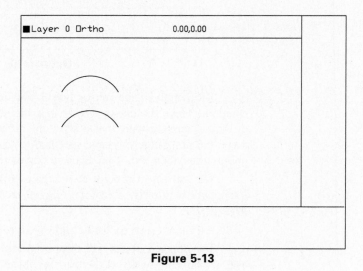

Figure 5-13

Mirroring with Grips

Mirror is the fifth grip mode, after stretch, move, rotate, and scale. It works exactly like the rotate mode, except that the rubber band will show you a mirror line instead of a rotation angle. The option to retain or delete the original is obtained through the copy option, just as in the rotate mode. Try it.

> Select the two arcs on your screen by pointing or windowing.

The arcs will be highlighted and grips will be showing.

> Pick any of the grips.

> Pass to the MIRROR mode by pressing enter four times, or by selecting "MIrror" from the screen menu.

Move the cursor and observe the dragged mirror images of the arcs. Notice that the rubber band operates as a mirror line, just as in the MIRROR command.

> Type "b" or select "Base pt".

This frees you from the selected grip and allows you to create a mirror line from any point on the screen. Notice the "Base point:" prompt in the command area.

> Type "c" or select "Copy".

As in the rotate mode, this is how you retain the original in a grip edit mirroring sequence.

> Pick a base point below the arcs.

> Pick a second point to the right of the first.

Your screen should resemble *Figure 5-14*.

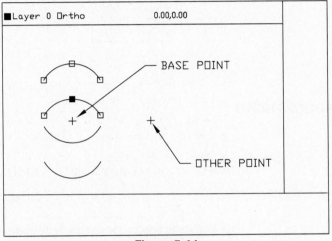

Figure 5-14

We suggest that you complete this exercise by using the MIRROR grip edit mode with the copy option to create *Figure 5-15*.

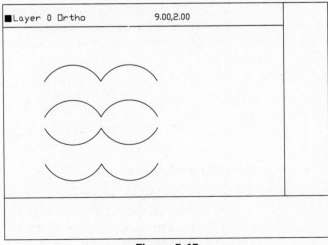

Figure 5-15

TASKS 5, 6, 7, 8, and 9

You have learned some complex sequences in this chapter, especially in the ARC and polar ARRAY commands, so take your time doing the next five drawings, and be sure that you understand the commands involved. Your knowledge of AutoCAD and CAD operation is increasing rapidly at this point, and it will be important that you practice what you have learned carefully.

DRAWING 5-1: FLANGED BUSHING

This drawing makes use of a polar array to draw eight screw holes in a circle. It will also review the use of layers and linetypes.

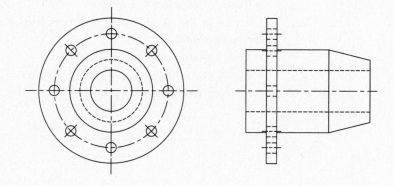

DRAWING SUGGESTIONS

> GRID = .25   LTSCALE = .50
>
> SNAP = .25   LIMITS = (0, 0)(18, 12)

> Draw the concentric circles first, using dimensions from both views. Remember to change layers as needed.

> Once you have drawn the 2.75 diameter bolt circle, use it to locate one of the bolt holes. Any of the circles at a quadrant point (0, 90, 180, or 270 degrees) will do.

> Draw a center line across the bolt hole, and then array the hole and the center line 360 degrees. Be sure to rotate the objects as they are copied, otherwise you will get strange results from your center lines.

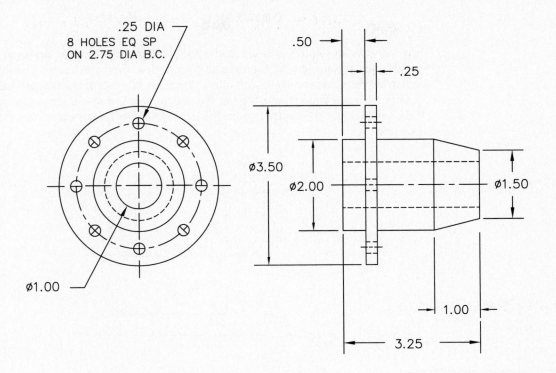

.25 DIA
8 HOLES EQ SP
ON 2.75 DIA B.C.

Ø1.00

.50

.25

Ø3.50

Ø2.00

Ø1.50

1.00

3.25

FLANGED BUSHING

Drawing 5–1

LAYERS	NAME	COLOR	LINETYPE		
	0	WHITE	——————— CONTINUOUS		
	1	RED	——————— CONTINUOUS		
	2	YELLOW	- - - - - - - HIDDEN		
	3	GREEN	— — — CENTER		

(DRAW)	LINE	(L)
(DRAW)	CIRCLE	(C)
(EDIT)	ARRAY	
(EDIT)	MIRROR	
(DISPLAY)	ZOOM	(Z)

F1	F6	F7	F8	F9
ON/OFF	ABSOLUTE/OFF/POLAR	ON/OFF	ON/OFF	ON/OFF
SCREEN	COORDS	GRID	ORTHO	SNAP

DRAWING 5-2: GUIDE

There are six arcs in this drawing, and while some of them could be drawn as fillets, we suggest that you use the ARC command for practice. Furthermore, by drawing arcs you will avoid a common problem with fillets. Since fillets are designed to round intersections at corners, when you create a fillet in the middle of a line it will erase part of that line. This would affect the center line on the left side of the front view of this drawing, for example.

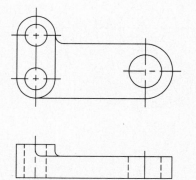

DRAWING SUGGESTIONS

GRID = .25   LTSCALE = .50

SNAP = .125   LIMITS = (0, 0)(12, 9)

> The three large arcs in the top view all can be drawn easily using Start, Center, End.

> The smaller .375 arc in the top view could be drawn by filleting the top arc with the horizontal line to its right. However, we suggest you try an arc giving start, center, end or start, center, angle. Note that you can easily locate the center by moving .375 to the right of the end point of the upper arc.

> The same method will work to draw the .25 arc in the front view. Begin by dropping a line down .25 from the horizontal line. Start your arc at the end of this line, and move .25 to the right to locate its center. Then the end will simply be .25 down from the center (or you could specify an angle of 90 degrees).

> Similarly, the arc at the center line can be drawn from a start point .25 up from the horizontal. It will have a radius of .25 and make an angle of 90 degrees.

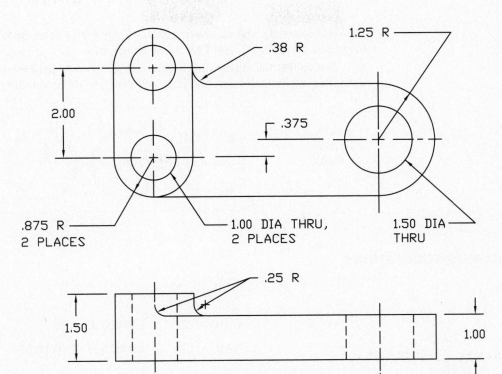

.38 R

1.25 R

2.00

.375

.875 R
2 PLACES

1.00 DIA THRU,
2 PLACES

1.50 DIA
THRU

.25 R

1.50

1.00

5.00

GUIDE
Drawing 5–2

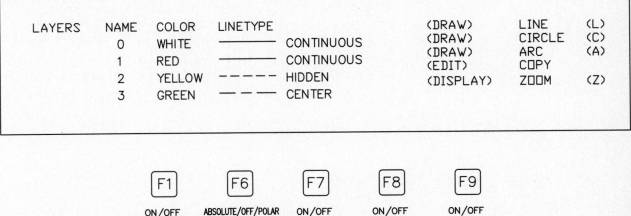

LAYERS	NAME	COLOR	LINETYPE			
	0	WHITE	———— CONTINUOUS	(DRAW)	LINE	(L)
	1	RED	———— CONTINUOUS	(DRAW)	CIRCLE	(C)
	2	YELLOW	– – – – HIDDEN	(DRAW)	ARC	(A)
	3	GREEN	— — — CENTER	(EDIT)	COPY	
				(DISPLAY)	ZOOM	(Z)

F1	F6	F7	F8	F9
ON/OFF	ABSOLUTE/OFF/POLAR	ON/OFF	ON/OFF	ON/OFF
SCREEN	COORDS	GRID	ORTHO	SNAP

DRAWING 5-3: DIALS

This is a relatively simple drawing that will give you some good practice with polar arrays and the ROTATE and COPY commands.

    Notice that the needle drawn at the top of the next page is only for reference; the actual drawing includes only the plate and the three dials with their needles.

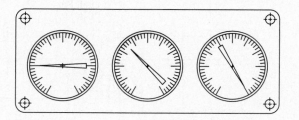

DRAWING SUGGESTIONS

         GRID = .25   LTSCALE = .50

         SNAP = .125   LIMITS = (0, 0)(18, 12)

> After drawing the outer rectangle and screw holes, draw the left-most dial, including the needle. Draw a .50 vertical line at the top and array it to the left (counterclockwise—a positive angle) and to the right (negative) to create the 11 larger lines on the dial. Use the same operation to create the 40 small (.25) markings.

> Complete the first dial and then use a multiple copy to produce two more dials at the center and right of your screen. Be sure to use a window to select the entire dial.

> Finally, use the ROTATE command to rotate the needles as indicated on the new dials. Use a window to select the needle, and rotate it around the center of the dial.

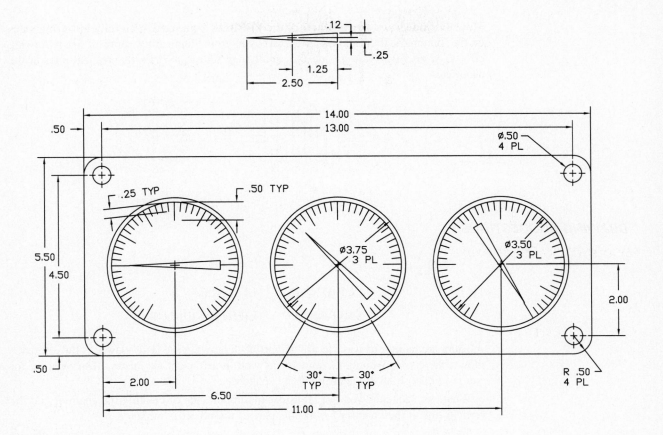

DIALS
Drawing 5-3

LAYERS	NAME	COLOR	LINETYPE			
	0	WHITE	———— CONTINUOUS		(DRAW)	LINE (L)
					(DRAW)	CIRCLE (C)
	1	RED	———— CONTINUOUS		(EDIT)	ARRAY
					(EDIT)	COPY
					(EDIT)	FILLET
	3	GREEN	—·—·— CENTER		(EDIT)	ROTATE
					(DISPLAY)	ZOOM (Z)

F1	F6	F7	F8	F9
ON/OFF	ABSOLUTE/OFF/POLAR	ON/OFF	ON/OFF	ON/OFF
SCREEN	COORDS	GRID	ORTHO	SNAP

DRAWING 5–4: ALIGNMENT WHEEL

This drawing shows a typical use of the MIRROR command. Carefully mirroring sides of the symmetrical front view will save you from duplicating some of your drawing efforts. Notice that you will need a small snap setting to draw the vertical lines at the chamfer.

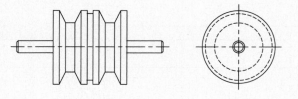

DRAWING SUGGESTIONS

GRID = .25   LTSCALE = .50

SNAP = .125   LIMITS = (0, 0)(12, 9)

> There are numerous ways to use MIRROR in drawing the front view. As the reference shows, there is top–bottom symmetry as well as left–right symmetry. The exercise for you is to choose an efficient mirroring sequence.

> Whatever sequence you use, consider the importance of creating the chamfer and the vertical line at the chamfer *before* this part of the object is mirrored.

> Once the front view is drawn, the right side view will be easy. Remember to change layers for center and hidden lines and to line up the small inner circle with the chamfer.

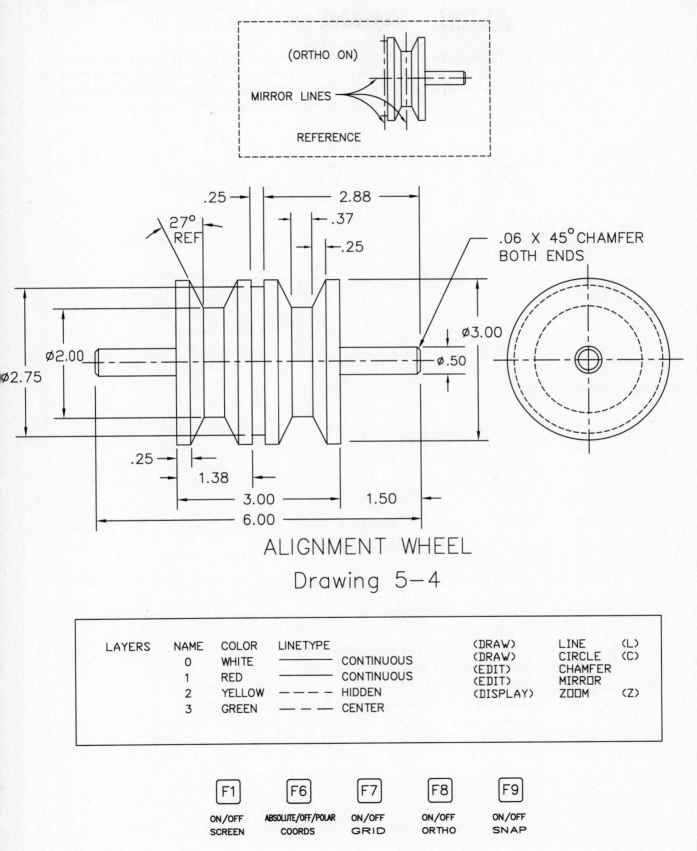

(ORTHO ON)

MIRROR LINES

REFERENCE

.25

2.88

27°
REF

.37

.25

.06 X 45°CHAMFER
BOTH ENDS

Ø2.00

Ø2.75

Ø3.00

Ø.50

.25

1.38

3.00

1.50

6.00

ALIGNMENT WHEEL
Drawing 5-4

LAYERS	NAME	COLOR	LINETYPE				
	0	WHITE	——————— CONTINUOUS	(DRAW)	LINE	(L)	
	1	RED	——————— CONTINUOUS	(DRAW)	CIRCLE	(C)	
	2	YELLOW	– – – – HIDDEN	(EDIT)	CHAMFER		
	3	GREEN	— – — CENTER	(EDIT)	MIRROR		
				(DISPLAY)	ZOOM	(Z)	

F1	F6	F7	F8	F9
ON/OFF	ABSOLUTE/OFF/POLAR	ON/OFF	ON/OFF	ON/OFF
SCREEN	COORDS	GRID	ORTHO	SNAP

DRAWING 5-5: HEARTH

Once you have completed this architectural drawing as it is shown, you might want to experiment with filling in a pattern of firebrick in the center of the hearth. The drawing itself is not complicated, but little errors will become very noticeable when you try to make the row of 4 x 8 bricks across the bottom fit with the arc of bricks across the top, so work carefully.

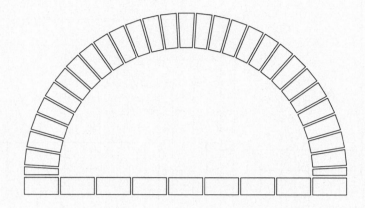

DRAWING SUGGESTIONS

UNITS = Architectural

smallest fraction = 8(1/8″)

LIMITS = (0, 0)(12′, 9′)

GRID = 1′

SNAP = 1/8″

> Zoom in to draw the wedge-shaped brick indicated by the arrow on the right of the dimensioned drawing. Draw half of the brick only and mirror it across the centerline as shown. (Notice that the centerline is for reference only.) It is very important that you use MIRROR so that you can erase half of the brick later.

> Array the brick in a 29 item, 180 degree polar array.

> Erase the bottom halves of the end bricks at each end.

> Draw a new horizontal bottom line on each of the two end bricks.

> Draw a 4 × 8 brick directly below the half brick at the left end.

> Array the 4 × 8 brick in a 1 row, 9 column array, with 8.5″ between columns.

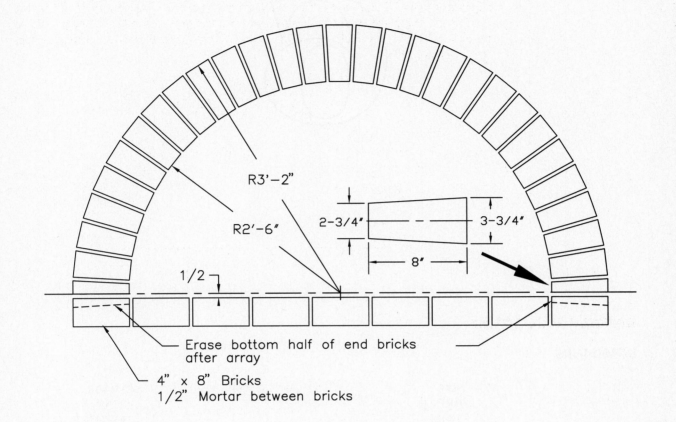

R3'–2"

R2'–6"

2-3/4"

3-3/4"

8"

1/2

— Erase bottom half of end bricks
  after array

— 4" x 8" Bricks
  1/2" Mortar between bricks

HEARTH
Drawing 5–5

Drawing Compliments of Thomas Casey

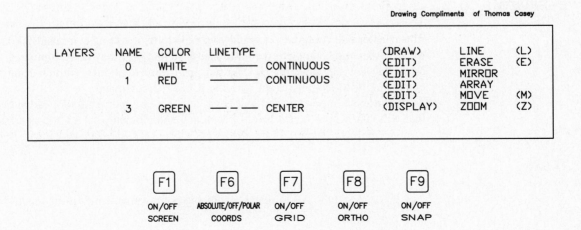

LAYERS	NAME	COLOR	LINETYPE				
	0	WHITE	———— CONTINUOUS	(DRAW)	LINE	(L)
				(EDIT)	ERASE	(E)
	1	RED	———— CONTINUOUS	(EDIT)	MIRROR	
				(EDIT)	ARRAY	
	3	GREEN	— · — · CENTER	(EDIT)	MOVE	(M)
				(DISPLAY)	ZOOM	(Z)

F1	F6	F7	F8	F9
ON/OFF	ABSOLUTE/OFF/POLAR	ON/OFF	ON/OFF	ON/OFF
SCREEN	COORDS	GRID	ORTHO	SNAP

CHAPTER

COMMANDS

EDIT
BREAK
TRIM
EXTEND
STRETCH
SPECIAL TOPIC: Object Snap (OSNAP)

SETTINGS
OSNAP
APERTURE

OVERVIEW

This chapter will continue to expand your repertoire of editing commands. You will learn to BREAK entities on the screen into pieces so that they may be manipulated separately, or so that you can erase parts. You will also learn to shorten entities using the TRIM command, or to lengthen them with the EXTEND command.

But most important, you will begin to use a very powerful tool called Object Snap that will take you to a new level of accuracy and efficiency as a CAD operator.

TASKS

1. Use OSNAP to select specifiable points on an entity using single-point overrides.
2. Select points with OSNAP using running modes.
3. Use BREAK to break a previously drawn entity into two separate entities.
4. Use TRIM to shorten entities.
5. Use EXTEND to lengthen entities.

6. Use STRETCH to move selected objects while retaining their connections to other objects.
7. Do Drawing 6-1 ("Bike Tire").
8. Do Drawing 6-2 ("Archimedes Spiral").
9. Do Drawing 6-3 ("Spiral Designs").
10. Do Drawing 6- 4 ("Grooved Hub").
11. Do Drawing 6-5 ("Cap Iron").
12. Do Drawing 6- 6 ("Deck Framing").

TASK 1: Selecting Points with OSNAP (Single-point Override)

Procedure.

1. Enter a drawing command, such as LINE, CIRCLE, or ARC.
2. Type or select the name of an OSNAP mode.
3. Point to a previously drawn object.

Discussion. Some of the drawings in the last two chapters have pushed the limits of what you can accomplish accurately on a CAD system with incremental snap alone. Object snap is a related tool that works in a very different manner. Instead of snapping to points defined by the coordinate system, it snaps to geometrically specifiable points on objects that you already have drawn.

Let's say you want to begin a new line at the end point of one that is already on the screen. If you are lucky it may be on a snap point, but it is just as likely not to be. Turning snap off and using the arrow keys may appear to work, but chances are that when you zoom in you will find that you have actually missed the point. Using object snap is the only precise way, and it is as precise as you could want. Let's try it.

> To prepare for this exercise, draw a 6 × 6 box with a circle inside, as in *Figure 6-1*. Exact sizes and locations are not important; however, the circle should be centered within the square.

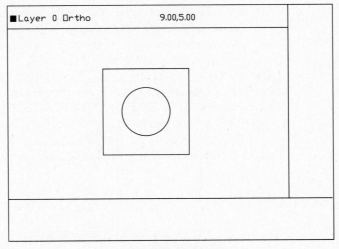

Figure 6-1

> Now enter the LINE command.

We are going to draw a line from the lower left corner of the square to a point on a line tangent to the circle, as shown in *Figure 6-2*. Notice that this task would be extremely difficult without osnap. The corner is easy to locate, since you probably have drawn it on snap, but the tangent may not be.

We will use an "end point" object snap to locate the corner and a "tangent" object snap to locate the tangent point.

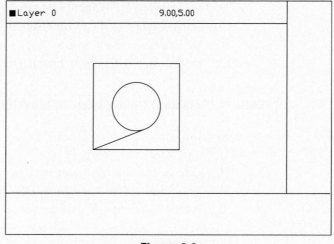

Figure 6-2

> At the "From point:" prompt, type "end" or select "ENDpoint" instead of specifying a point.

If you want to use the screen menu, select the row of asterisks at the top (* * * *), then select "ENDpoint". You may also have an object snap button on your cursor that will open up a floating pop-up menu. If so, it will be the quickest and most convenient way to enter an object snap mode. Do not select from the pull down for now, we will get to it in Task 2.

Entering "ENDpoint" by any of these methods tells AutoCAD that you are going to select the start point of the line by using an end point object snap rather than direct pointing or entering coordinates.

Now that AutoCAD knows that we want to begin at the end point of a previously drawn entity, it needs to know which one.

The pickbox at the intersection of the cross hairs is now a target box. Its size can be set separately from the size of the pickbox using the APERTURE command, as discussed later. To be selected, a point or an entity containing the point must be within the aperture, as in *Figure 6-3*.

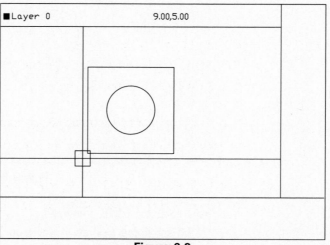

Figure 6-3

> Position the cursor so that the lower left corner of the square is within the target box, then press the pick button.

Now we will draw the tangent.

> At the "To point:" prompt, type "tan" or select "Tangent".

> Move the cursor to the right and position the cross hairs so that the circle crosses the target box. Press the pick button. AutoCAD will locate the tangent point and draw the line.

> Press enter to exit the LINE command. Your screen should now resemble *Figure 6-2*.

NOTE: In more complex drawings it is quite possible that there will be more than one point that fits the definition of the osnap mode you have selected (for example, two or more distinct end points or objects with end points within the box, as in *Figure 6-4*). In this case AutoCAD first will search for all possible candidates and then will select the one nearest the intersection of the cross hairs. An exception to this can be made using the "quick" mode described on the chart at the end of this discussion of OSNAP (see *Figure 6-8*).

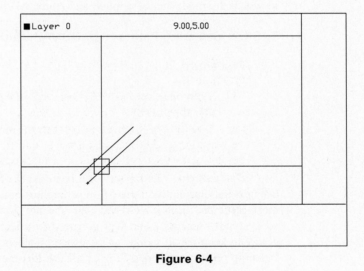

Figure 6-4

We will repeat the process now, but start from the midpoint of the bottom side of the square instead of its end point.

> Repeat the LINE command.

> At the prompt for a point, type "mid" or select "Midpoint".

> Position the aperture anywhere along to the bottom side of the square and press the pick button.

> At the prompt for a second point, type "tan" or select "tangent".

> Position the aperture along the lower right side of the circle and press the pick button.

> Press enter or the space bar to exit the LINE command.

At this point your screen should resemble *Figure 6-5*.

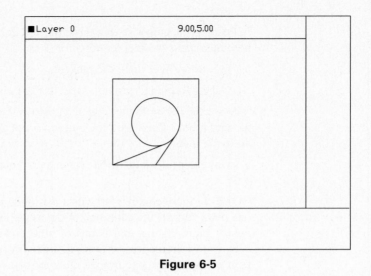

Figure 6-5

That's all there is to it. Remember the steps: 1) enter a command; 2) when AutoCAD asks for a point, type or select an OSNAP mode instead; 3) select an object to which the mode can be applied and AutoCAD will find the point.

TASK 2: Selecting Points with OSNAP (Running Mode)

Procedure.

1. Type or select "OSNAP" or pick "Object Snap..." under "Settings" on the pull down menu.
2. Type or select one or more OSNAP modes.
3. Enter drawing commands.

Discussion. So far we have been using object snap one point at a time. Since osnap is not constantly in use for most applications, this single point method is probably most common. But if you find that you are going to be using one or a number of osnap types repeatedly and will not need to select many points without them, there is a way to keep osnap modes on so that they affect all point selection. These are called "running object snap modes". We will use this method to complete the drawing shown in *Figure 6-6*. Notice how the lines are drawn from midpoints and corners to tangents to the circle. This is easily done with object snap.

In order to turn on a running osnap mode you can enter the OSNAP command at the command line or through the screen menu, or use the dialogue box from the pull down menu, under "Settings". We recommend the dialogue box because it is quick, easy, and also gives you the chance to change the aperture size.

> Select "Settings" and then "Object Snap..." from the pull down.

You will see the dialogue box illustrated in *Figure 6-7*. This box can also be called by the DDOSNAP command. At the top is a list of object snap modes with check boxes. At the bottom is a box with a scroll bar where you can change the object snap aperture size.

You will find a description of all of the osnap modes on the chart (*Figure 6-8*) at the end of this task, but for now we will be using three: midpoint, tangent, and intersect. Midpoint and tangent you already know. Intersect snaps to the point where two entities meet or cross. We will use intersect instead of end point to select the remaining three corners of the square.

> Type "mid,tan,int" or click on the check boxes next to "Midpoint", "Tangent", and "Intersection".

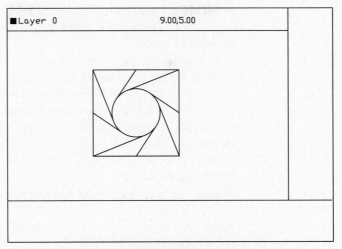

Figure 6-6

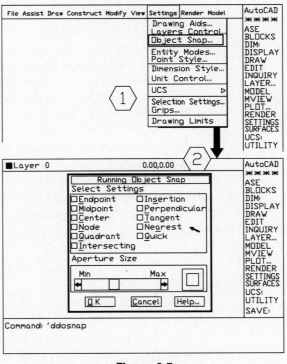

Figure 6-7

Before you leave the dialogue box, try changing the aperture size.

Changing the Size of the Aperture

The aperture can be changed visually using the scroll bar in the usual manner, or by entering the APERTURE command and typing a number. If you type the command you will be asked to specify the aperture size in pixels (from 1 to 50, one pixel being the smallest unit your monitor can display).

> Click on the box in the middle of the scroll bar and drag it to the right, or click on the right arrow.

Watch the aperture in the black box on the right growing larger.

> Set the aperture by moving the scroll bar box to the left of center, as shown in *Figure 6-7*. The aperture itself should be somewhat larger than the pickbox you are used to seeing.

Remember, the aperture is distinct from the pickbox. Changing the osnap aperture has no effect on the size of the object selection pickbox. The size of this box is controlled by another system variable called PICKBOX.

The best size for your aperture depends on your drawing. If you are doing a lot of point selection in tight spaces, and especially if you are using multiple osnap modes, you may want a smaller aperture to avoid confusion. If you have plenty of room to work in, you may want a larger aperture to make the selection process looser and faster.

> Click on "OK" to exit the dialogue box.

AutoCAD returns you to the "Command:" prompt and you are ready to draw with the running osnap modes in effect. We will draw tangent lines from the corners of the square and from the midpoints of their sides to produce *Figure 6-6*.

Now back to our drawing.

> Enter the LINE command.

Notice the size of the aperture on the cross hairs. The change in size tells you that you are looking at the osnap aperture instead of the pickbox and that there are osnap modes in effect. When you select points now, AutoCAD will look for the point nearest the center of the aperture that fulfills the geometric requirements of one of the three running osnap modes you have chosen. If there is more than one point, it will select the one nearest the intersection of the cross hairs.

> Position the aperture so that the lower right corner is within the box and press the pick button.

AutoCAD will select the intersection of the bottom and the right sides and give you the rubber band and the prompt for a second point.

Notice that the osnap aperture is still on the cross hairs.

> Move the cross hairs up and along the right side of the circle and press the pick button.

Be sure that the intersection of the previous tangent and the circle is not within the aperture.

AutoCAD will construct a new tangent from the lower right corner to the circle.

> Press enter to complete the command sequence.

> Press enter again to repeat LINE so you can begin with a new start point.

We will continue to move counterclockwise around the circle. This should begin to be easy now.

> Position the aperture along the right side of the square and press the pick button. Be sure the corner is not within the aperture.

AutoCAD snaps to the midpoint of the side.

> Move up along the upper right side of the circle and press the pick button.

> Press enter to exit LINE.

> Press enter again to repeat LINE and continue around the circle drawing tangents like this: upper right corner to top of circle, top side midpoint to top left of circle, upper left corner to left side, left side midpoint to lower left side.

Remember that running osnap modes should give you both speed and accuracy, so push yourself a little to see how quickly you can complete the figure.

Your screen should now resemble *Figure 6-6*.

Before going on we need to turn off the running osnap modes.

> Click twice on "Settings" on the pull down menu bar.

Notice that AutoCAD remembers your pull down menu selections. You can re-open a dialogue box by clicking twice on the heading at the top of the menu.

> Click in all the check boxes that are showing x's.

> Click on "OK" to exit the dialogue box.

AutoCAD will return you to the "command" prompt, and when you begin drawing again, you will see that the aperture is gone.

NOTE: You can also turn off all running osnap modes by typing "osnap" and then pressing enter when asked for osnap modes.

Now we will move on to four very useful and important new editing commands, BREAK, TRIM, EXTEND, and STRETCH. Before leaving OSNAP, be sure to study the chart, *Figure 6-8*.

TASK 3: BREAKing Previously Drawn Objects

Procedure.

1. Type or select "BREAK".
2. Select an object to be broken.
3. Show the first point of the break.
4. Show the second point of the break.

Discussion. The BREAK command allows you to break an object on the screen into two entities, or to cut a segment out of the middle or off the end. The command sequence is similar for all options. The action taken will depend on the points you select for breaking. BREAK works on lines, circles, arcs, traces, and polylines (traces and polylines are discussed in Chapter 9).

> In preparation for this section, clear your screen of any objects left over from Task 2 and draw a 5.0 horizontal line across the middle of your screen, as in *Figure 6-9*. Exact lengths and coordinates are not important. Also, turn off any running osnap modes that may be on from the last exercise.

We begin by breaking the line you have just drawn into two independent lines. This procedure is the same as the "At Selected Point" option on the pull down menu.

> Type or select "BREAK". (BREAK is under "MODIFY" on the pull down and under "EDIT" on the screen menu.)

Be aware that the noun/verb or pick first sequence does not work with BREAK.

AutoCAD will prompt you to select an object to break:

Select object:

You may select an object in any of the usual ways, but notice that you can only break one object at a time. If you try to select more, with a window, for

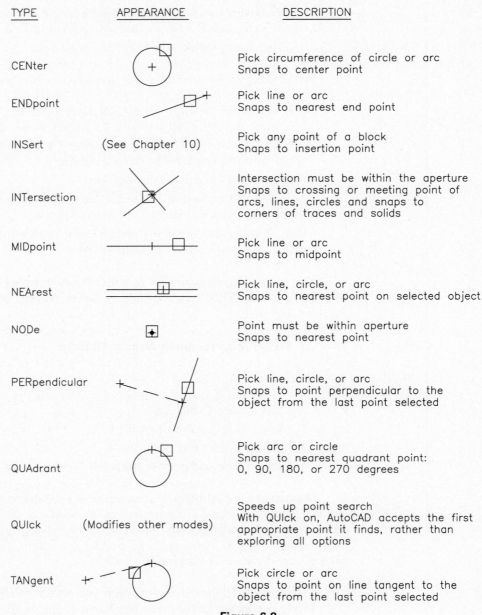

TYPE	APPEARANCE	DESCRIPTION
CENter		Pick circumference of circle or arc Snaps to center point
ENDpoint		Pick line or arc Snaps to nearest end point
INSert	(See Chapter 10)	Pick any point of a block Snaps to insertion point
INTersection		Intersection must be within the aperture Snaps to crossing or meeting point of arcs, lines, circles and snaps to corners of traces and solids
MIDpoint		Pick line or arc Snaps to midpoint
NEArest		Pick line, circle, or arc Snaps to nearest point on selected object
NODe		Point must be within aperture Snaps to nearest point
PERpendicular		Pick line, circle, or arc Snaps to point perpendicular to the object from the last point selected
QUAdrant		Pick arc or circle Snaps to nearest quadrant point: 0, 90, 180, or 270 degrees
QUIck	(Modifies other modes)	Speeds up point search With QUIck on, AutoCAD accepts the first appropriate point it finds, rather than exploring all options
TANgent		Pick circle or arc Snaps to point on line tangent to the object from the last point selected

Figure 6-8

example, AutoCAD will give you only one. Because of this you will best indicate the object you want to break by pointing to it.

NOTE: Osnap modes work well in edit commands like BREAK. If you wish to break a line at its midpoint, for example, you can use the osnap to midpoint mode to select the line and the break point.

> Select the line by picking any point near its middle. (The exact point is not critical; if it were, we could use a midpoint osnap.)

The line has now been selected for breaking, and since there can be only one object, you do not have to press enter to end the selection process as you often do in other editing commands. AutoCAD will prompt as follows:

Enter second point (or F for first point):

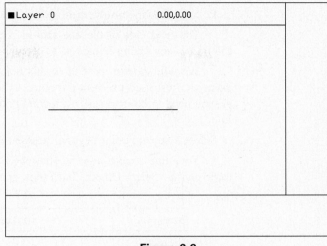

Figure 6-9

When you are selecting an object by pointing, AutoCAD will assume that the point you use for selection is also the first point of the break. It will be most efficient, therefore, if you do select the object with a break point. Then you can proceed by selecting the second point immediately. If not, type "f" and you will be prompted for the first break point, as the parentheses tell you. The f is typed automatically if you have entered BREAK by picking "Select Object, Two Points" from the pull down.

What we want to do now is to select a point that will break the object in two without erasing anything. To do this, simply pick the same point again. If you have used the pull down "At Selected Point" option, this step will be done automatically.

> Point to the same point that you just used to select the line, or type "@".

The "@" symbol is shorthand for the last point entered. If you are using the pull down, notice that the @ is entered automatically.

The break is complete. In order to demonstrate that the line is really two lines now, we will select the right half of it for our next break.

> Press enter or the space bar to repeat the BREAK command.

Figure 6-10

> Point to the line on the right side of the last break.

The right side of the line should become dotted, as in *Figure 6-10*. Clearly the line is now being treated as two separate entities.

We will shorten the end of this dotted section of the line. Assume that the point you just used to select the object is the point where you want it to end; now all you need to do is to select a second point anywhere beyond the right end of the line.

> Select a second point beyond the right end of the line.

Your line should now be shortened, as in *Figure 6-11*. This method is the same as the "Select Object, 2nd Point" method on the pull down.

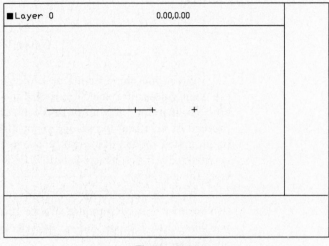

Figure 6-11

Next we will cut a piece out of the middle of the left side.

> Press enter or the space bar to repeat BREAK.

> Select the left side of the original line with a point toward the left end.

We want to cut a piece out of the middle of the left side, so the second point needs to be to the right of the first point, but still toward the middle of the left hand line.

NOTE: It is actually not necessary that the second point be on the line at all. It could be above or below it, as in *Figure 6-12*. AutoCAD will break the line along a perpendicular between the point we choose and the line we are breaking. The same system would apply if we were breaking a polyline or a trace. An arc or a circle would be broken along a line between the selected point and the center of the arc or circle.

> Select a second point on or off the line, somewhat to the right of the first point.

Your line should now have a piece cut out, as in *Figure 6-12*. Notice that there are now three distinct lines on the screen.

BREAK is a very useful command, but there are times when it is cumbersome to shorten objects one at a time. The TRIM command has some limitations that BREAK does not have, but it is much more efficient in situations where you want to shorten objects at intersections.

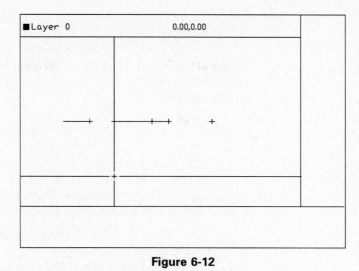

Figure 6-12

TASK 4: Using the TRIM Command

Procedure.

1. Type or select "TRIM".
2. Select a cutting edge, or edges.
3. Press enter to end the cutting edge selection process.
4. Select object to trim.
5. Select other objects to trim.
6. Press enter to return to "command" prompt.

Discussion.   The TRIM command works wonders in many situations where you want to shorten objects at their intersections with other objects. It will work with lines, circles, arcs, and polylines (see Chapter 9). The only limitation is that you must have at least two objects and they must cross or meet. If you are not trimming to an intersection, use BREAK.

> In preparation for exploring TRIM, clear your screen and then draw two horizontal lines crossing a circle, as in *Figure 6-13*. Exact locations are not important.

First we will use the TRIM command to go from *Figure 6-13* to *Figure 6-14*.

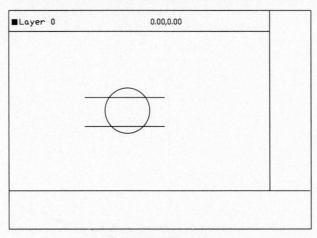

Figure 6-13

> Type or select "TRIM".

The first thing AutoCAD will want you to specify is at least one cutting edge. A cutting edge is an entity you want to use to trim another entity. That is, you want the trimmed entity to end at its intersection with the cutting edge. The prompt looks like this:

Select cutting edge(s)...
Select objects:

The first line reminds you that you are selecting edges first—the objects you want to trim will be selected later. The option of selecting more than one edge is a useful one, which we will get to shortly.

For now we will select the circle as an edge and use it to trim the two lines.
> Point to the circle.

The circle becomes dotted and will remain so until you leave the TRIM command. AutoCAD will prompt for more objects until you indicate that you are through selecting edges.
> Press enter or the space bar to end the selection of cutting edges.

You will be prompted for an object to trim:

<Select object to trim>/Undo:

We will trim off the segment of the upper line that lies outside the circle on the left. The important thing is to point to the part of the object you want to remove, as shown by the blips in *Figure 6-14*.
> Point to the upper line to the left of where it crosses the circle.

The line is trimmed immediately, but the circle is still dotted, and AutoCAD continues to prompt for more objects to trim. Note how this differs from the BREAK command, in which you could only break one object at a time.

Also notice that you have an undo option, so that if the trim does not turn out the way you wanted, you can back up without having to leave the command and start over.
> Point to the lower line to the left of where it crosses the circle.

Now you have trimmed both lines.
> Press enter or the space bar to end the TRIM operation.

Your screen should resemble *Figure 6-14*.

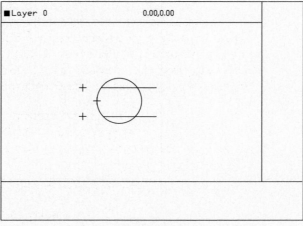

Figure 6-14

This has been a very simple trimming process, but more complex trimming is just as easy. The key is that you can select as many edges as you like and that an entity may be selected as both an edge and an object to trim, as we will demonstrate.

> Repeat the TRIM command.
> Select both lines and the circle as cutting edges.

   This can be done with a window or with a crossing box.

> Press enter to end the selection of edges.
> Point to each of the remaining two line segments that lie outside the circle on the right, and to the top and bottom arcs of the circle to produce the band-aid shaped object in *Figure 6-15*.
> Press enter to exit the TRIM command.

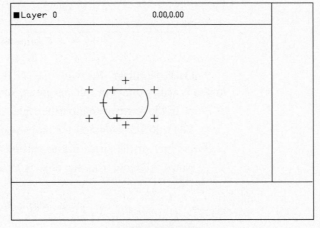

Figure 6-15

TASK 5: Using the EXTEND Command

Procedure.

1. Type or select "EXTEND".
2. Select a boundary, or boundaries.
3. Press enter to end the boundary selection process.
3. Select object to extend.
4. Select other objects to extend.
5. Press enter to return to "command" prompt.

Discussion.   If you compare the procedures of the EXTEND command and the TRIM command you will notice a remarkable similarity. Just substitute the word "boundary" for "cutting edge" and the word "extend" for "trim" and you've got it. These two commands are so quick to use that it is sometimes efficient to draw a cutting edge or boundary on your screen and erase it afterwards if it is not really part of your drawing.

> Leave *Figure 6-15*, the "band-aid," on your screen and draw a vertical line to the right of it, as in *Figure 6-16*. We will use this line as a boundary to which to extend the two horizontal lines, as in *Figure 6-17*.
> Type or select "EXTEND".

   You will be prompted for objects to serve as boundaries:

                    Select boundary edge(s)...
                    Select objects:

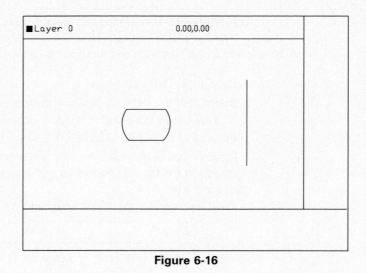

Figure 6-16

Look familiar? As with the TRIM command, any of the usual selection methods will work. For our purposes, simply point to the vertical line.

> Point to the vertical line on the right.

You will be prompted for more boundary objects until you press enter.

> Press enter or the space bar to end the selection of boundaries.

AutoCAD now asks for objects to extend:

<Select objects to extend>/Undo:

> Point to the right half of one of the two horizontal lines.

Notice that you have to point to the line on the side closer to the selected boundary. Otherwise AutoCAD will look to the left instead of the right and give you the following message:

Entity does not intersect an edge

Note also that you can only select objects to extend by pointing. Windowing, crossing, or last selections will not work.

> Point to the right half of the other horizontal line. Both lines should be extended to the vertical line.

Your screen should resemble *Figure 6-17*.

> Press enter to exit the EXTEND command.

TASK 6: Using the STRETCH Command

Procedure.

1. Type or select "STRETCH".
2. Select objects to stretch, using at least one window or crossing selection.
3. Press enter to end selection.
4. Show first point of stretch displacement.
5. Show second point of stretch displacement.

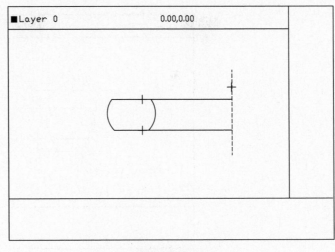

Figure 6-17

Discussion. The STRETCH command is a phenomenal timesaver in special circumstances in which you want to move objects without disrupting their connections to other objects. Often STRETCH can take the place of a whole series of moves, trims, breaks, and extends. It is commonly used in such applications as moving doors or windows within walls without having to redraw the walls.

The term "stretch" must be understood to have a special meaning in AutoCAD. When a typical stretch is performed some objects are lengthened, while others are shortened, and others are simply moved.

There is also a stretch mode in the grip edit system, as we have seen previously. We will take a look at it at the end of the exercise.

First, we will do a simple stretch on the objects you have already drawn on your screen. This will give you a good basic understanding of the STRETCH command. Further experimentation on your own is also recommended.

> Type or select "STRETCH".

AutoCAD will prompt for objects to stretch in the following manner:

> Select objects to stretch by window or polygon...
> Select objects:

The first line of this prompt reminds you of a unique quality of the STRETCH command procedure. You must include at least one window, window polygon, crossing, or crossing polygon selection in your selection set. Beyond that you can include other selection types as well.

This restriction should not cause any trouble, because if you are using the command correctly you will most often use a crossing selection.

> Point to the first corner of a crossing box, as shown by point 1 in *Figure 6-18*.

AutoCAD will prompt for a second corner:

> Other corner:

> Point to a second corner, as shown by point 2 in the figure.

AutoCAD will continue to prompt for objects, so we need to show that we are through selecting.

> Press enter or the space bar to end the selection process.

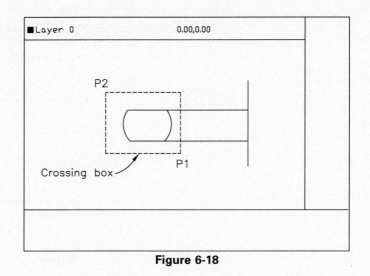

Figure 6-18

Now you will need to show the degree of stretch you want. In effect, you will be showing AutoCAD how far to move the objects that are completely within the box. Objects that cross the box will be extended or shrunk so that they remain connected to the objects that move.

The prompt sequence for this action is the same as the sequence for a move:

Base point or displacement:

> Pick any point near the middle of the screen, leaving room to indicate a horizontal displacement to the right, as illustrated in *Figure 6-19*.

AutoCAD prompts:

Second point of displacement:

> Pick a second point to the right of the first, as shown in *Figure 6-19*.

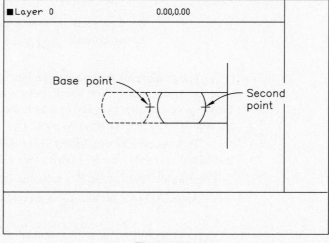

Figure 6-19

The arcs will be moved to the right and the horizontal lines will be shrunk as shown. Notice that nothing here is literally being stretched. The arcs are being moved and the lines are being compressed. This is one of the ways STRETCH can be used.

Try performing another stretch like the one illustrated in *Figures 6-20* and *6-21*. Here the lines are being lengthened, while one arc moves and the other stays put, so that the original "band aid" is indeed stretched.

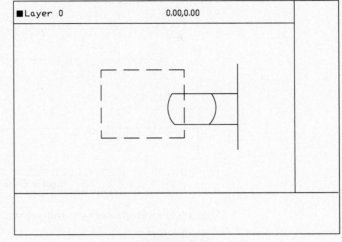

Figure 6-20

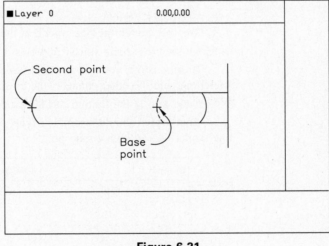

Figure 6-21

Stretching with Grips

Stretching with grips is a simple operation and is best reserved for simple stretches. Stretches like the ones you have just performed with the STRETCH command are possible in grip editing, but they require very careful selection of multiple grips. The results are not always what you expect and it takes more time to complete the process. The type of stretch that works best is illustrated in the following exercise.

> Pick the lower horizontal line.

The line will be highlighted and grips will appear.

> Pick the vertical line.

Now both lines should appear with grips, as in *Figure 6-22*. We will use one grip on the horizontal line and one on the vertical line to create *Figure 6-23*.

> Pick the grip at the right end of the horizontal line.

As soon as you press the pick button, the autoedit system puts you into STRETCH mode and the grip will change color.

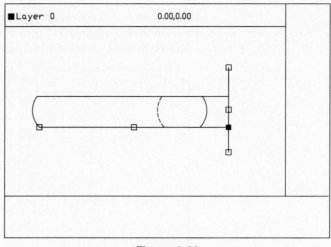

Figure 6-22

In the command area you will see the following:

                              ** STRETCH **
                              <Stretch to point>/Base point/Copy/Undo/eXit:

We will stretch the line to end at the lower end point of the vertical line.
> Move the cross hairs slowly downward and observe the screen.

If ortho is off, you will see two rubber bands. One represents the line you are stretching, and the other connects the cross hairs to the grip you are manipulating.
> Pick the grip at the bottom of the vertical line.

Your screen should resemble *Figure 6-23*. Notice how the grip on the vertical line works like an object snap point.

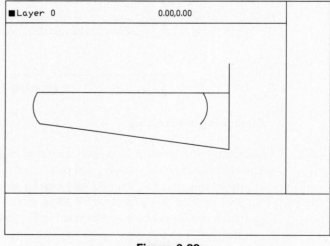

Figure 6-23

Try one more grip stretch to create *Figure 6-24*. You will move the end point of the upper line just as you did the lower.

TASKS 7, 8, 9, 10, 11, and 12

The drawings that follow will bring you to the end of Part I of this book. With OSNAP and the new editing commands you have learned in this chapter, you have reached a significant plateau. Most of the fundamental drawing, editing, and setting tools are now in your repertoire of CAD skills. The six drawings that follow will give you the opportunity to practice what you have learned. Notice that BREAK and TRIM often are used deliberately as part of a planned drawing sequence, whereas EXTEND and STRETCH tend to appear more frequently as "quick fixes" when something needs to be moved or changed.

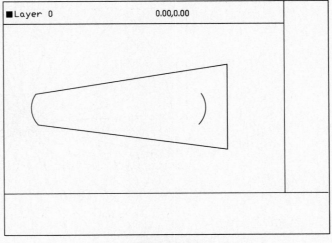

Figure 6-24

DRAWING 6-1: BIKE TIRE

This drawing can be done very quickly with the tools you now have. It makes use of one osnap, three trims, and a polar array. Be sure to set the limits large, as suggested.

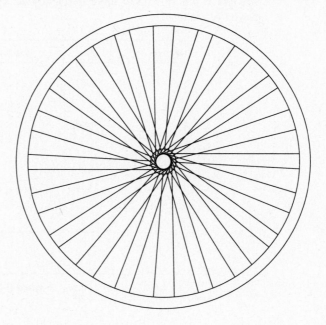

DRAWING SUGGESTIONS

GRID = 1.00   LIMITS = (0, 0)(48, 36)

SNAP = .25

> Begin by drawing the 1.25″, 2.50″, 24.00″, and 26.00″ diameter circles centered on the same point near the middle of your display.

> Draw line (a) using a QUADrant osnap to find the first point on the inside circle. The second point can be anywhere outside the 24″ circle at 0 degrees from the first point. The exact length of the line is insignificant since we will be trimming it back to the circle.

> Draw line (b) from the center of the circles to a second point anywhere outside the 24″ circle at an angle of 14 degrees. Remember to use the coordinate display to construct this angle. This line will also be trimmed.

> Trim lines (a) and (b) using the 24″ circle as a cutting edge.

> Trim the other end of line (b) using the 1.25″ circle as a cutting edge.

> Construct a polar array, selecting lines (a) and (b). There are 20 items in the array, and they are rotated as they are copied.

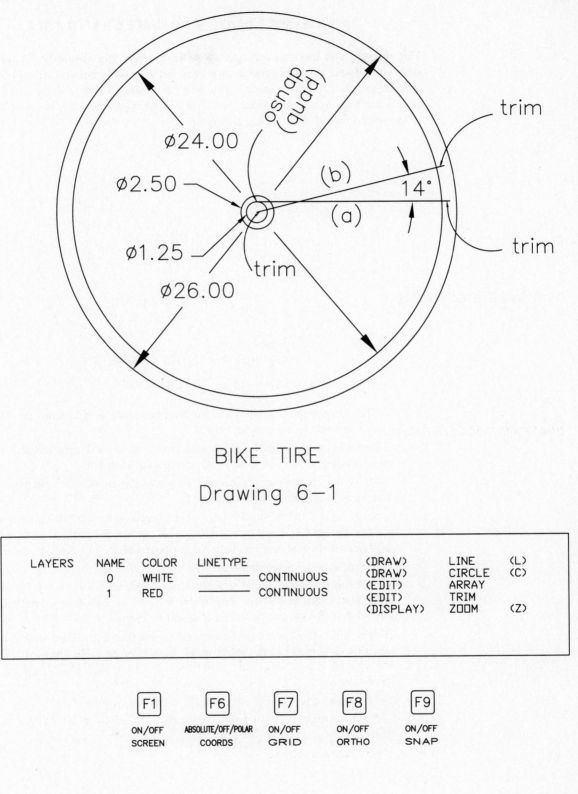

BIKE TIRE

Drawing 6–1

LAYERS	NAME	COLOR	LINETYPE				
	0	WHITE	———— CONTINUOUS	(DRAW)	LINE	(L)	
	1	RED	———— CONTINUOUS	(DRAW)	CIRCLE	(C)	
				(EDIT)	ARRAY		
				(EDIT)	TRIM		
				(DISPLAY)	ZOOM	(Z)	

F1	F6	F7	F8	F9
ON/OFF	ABSOLUTE/OFF/POLAR	ON/OFF	ON/OFF	ON/OFF
SCREEN	COORDS	GRID	ORTHO	SNAP

DRAWING 6-2: ARCHIMEDES SPIRAL

This drawing and the next go together as an exercise you should find interesting and enjoyable. These are not technical drawings, but they will give you valuable experience with important CAD commands. You will be creating a spiral using a radial grid of circles and lines as a guide. Once the spiral is done, you will use it to create the designs in the next drawing, 6-3, "Spiral Designs."

DRAWING SUGGESTIONS

GRID = .5   LIMITS = (0,0) (18,12)

SNAP = .25   LTSCALE = .5

> The alternating continuous and hidden lines work as a drawing aid. If you have color they will be even more helpful.

> Begin by drawing all the continuous circles on layer 0, centered near the middle of your display. Use the continuous circle radii as listed.

> Draw the continuous horizontal line across the middle of your six circles and then array it in a three item polar array.

> Set to layer 2 for the hidden lines. The procedure for the hidden lines and circles will be the same as for the continuous lines, except the radii are different and you will array a vertical line instead of a horizontal one.

> Set to layer 1 for the spiral itself.

> Turn on a running osnap to intersection mode and construct a series of three-point arcs. Start points and end points will be on continuous line intersections; second points will always fall on hidden line intersections.

> When the spiral is complete, turn off layers 0 and 2. There should be nothing left on your screen but the spiral itself. Save it or go on to Drawing 6-3.

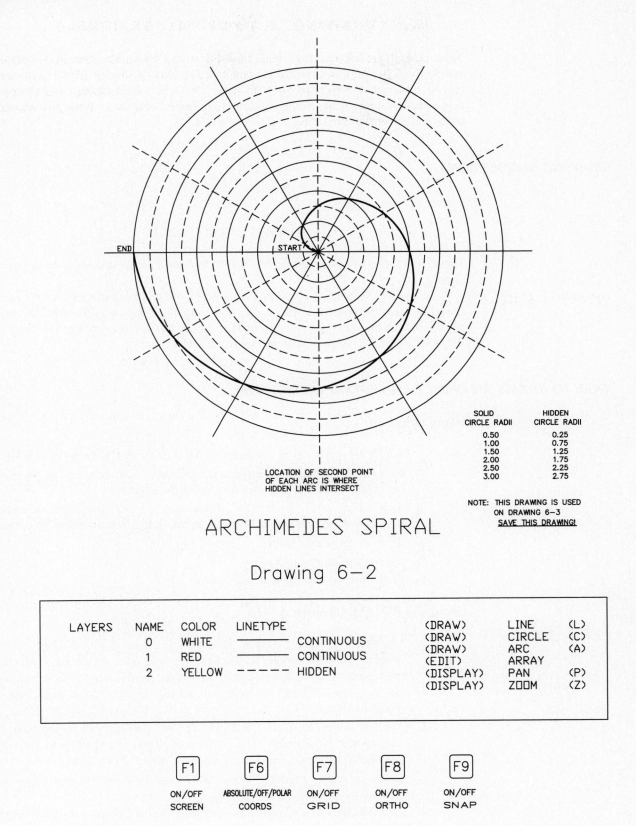

SOLID CIRCLE RADII	HIDDEN CIRCLE RADII
0.50	0.25
1.00	0.75
1.50	1.25
2.00	1.75
2.50	2.25
3.00	2.75

LOCATION OF SECOND POINT
OF EACH ARC IS WHERE
HIDDEN LINES INTERSECT

NOTE: THIS DRAWING IS USED
ON DRAWING 6–3
SAVE THIS DRAWING!

ARCHIMEDES SPIRAL

Drawing 6–2

LAYERS	NAME	COLOR	LINETYPE				
	0	WHITE	——————— CONTINUOUS	(DRAW)	LINE	(L)
	1	RED	——————— CONTINUOUS	(DRAW)	CIRCLE	(C)
	2	YELLOW	– – – – – HIDDEN	(DRAW)	ARC	(A)
				(EDIT)	ARRAY	
				(DISPLAY)	PAN	(P)
				(DISPLAY)	ZOOM	(Z)

F1	F6	F7	F8	F9
ON/OFF	ABSOLUTE/OFF/POLAR	ON/OFF	ON/OFF	ON/OFF
SCREEN	COORDS	GRID	ORTHO	SNAP

DRAWING 6-3: SPIRAL DESIGNS

These designs are different from other drawings in this book. There are no dimensions and you will use only edit commands now that the spiral is drawn. Below the designs is a list of the edit commands you will need. Don't be too concerned with precision. Some of your designs may come out slightly different from ours. When this happens, try to analyze the differences.

DRAWING SUGGESTIONS

$$LIMITS = (0,0) \; (34,24)$$

These large limits will be necessary if you wish to draw all of these designs on the screen at once.

In some of these designs and in Drawing 6-4 you will need to rotate a copy of the spiral and keep the original in place. You can accomplish this using the grip edit rotate procedure with the copy option, or by making a copy of the objects before you enter the ROTATE command. Both procedures are listed following.

HOW TO ROTATE AN OBJECT AND RETAIN THE ORIGINAL

Using Grip Edit

1. Select the objects to be rotated (i.e., the six arcs that make up the spiral).
2. Pick the grip around which you want to rotate, or any of the grips if you are not going to use the grip as a base point for rotation.
3. Type "b" or select "Base point", if necessary. In this exercise the base point you choose for rotation will depend on the design you are trying to create.
4. Type "c" or select "Copy".
5. Show the rotation angle.
6. Press enter to exit the grip edit system.

Using the ROTATE Command

1. Use COPY to make a copy of the objects you want to rotate directly on top of their originals. In other words, give the same point for the base point and the second point of displacement. When the copy is done your screen will not look any different, but there will actually be two spirals there, one on top of the other.
2. Type or select "ROTATE" and give "p" or "previous" in response to the "Select objects:" prompt. This will select all the original objects from the last COPY sequence, without selecting the newly drawn copies.
3. Rotate as usual, choosing a base point dependent on the design you are creating.
4. After the ROTATE sequence is complete, you will need to do a REDRAW before the objects copied in the original position will be visible.

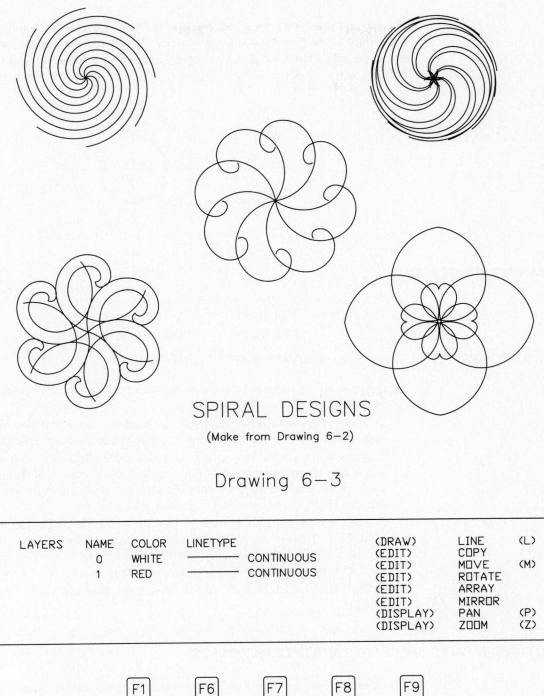

SPIRAL DESIGNS

(Make from Drawing 6-2)

Drawing 6-3

LAYERS	NAME	COLOR	LINETYPE		(DRAW)	LINE	(L)
	0	WHITE	———— CONTINUOUS		(EDIT)	COPY	
	1	RED	———— CONTINUOUS		(EDIT)	MOVE	(M)
					(EDIT)	ROTATE	
					(EDIT)	ARRAY	
					(EDIT)	MIRROR	
					(DISPLAY)	PAN	(P)
					(DISPLAY)	ZOOM	(Z)

F1	F6	F7	F8	F9
ON/OFF	ABSOLUTE/OFF/POLAR	ON/OFF	ON/OFF	ON/OFF
SCREEN	COORDS	GRID	ORTHO	SNAP

DRAWING 6-4: GROOVED HUB

This drawing includes a typical application of the rotation technique just discussed. The hidden lines in the front view must be rotated 120 degrees and a copy retained in the original position. There are also good opportunities to use MIRROR, object snap, and TRIM.

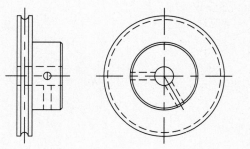

DRAWING SUGGESTIONS

GRID = .5   LIMITS = (0, 0) (18, 12)

SNAP = .0625   LTSCALE = 1

> Draw the circles in the front view and use these to line up the horizontal lines in the left side view.

> There are several different planes of symmetry in the left side view, which suggests the use of mirroring. We leave it up to you to choose an efficient sequence.

> A quick method for drawing the horizontal hidden lines in the left side view is to use a quadrant osnap to begin a line at the top and bottom of the .62 diameter circle in the front view. Draw this line across to the back of the left side view, and use TRIM to erase the excess on both sides.

> The same method can be used to draw the two horizontal hidden lines in the front view. Snap to the top and bottom quadrants of the .25 diameter circle in the left side view as a guide and draw lines through the front view. Then trim to the 2.25 diameter circle and the .62 diameter circle.

> Once these hidden lines are drawn, rotate them, retaining a copy in the original position.

PLOTTING IN PAPER SPACE WITH MULTIPLE VIEWPORTS

As you near the completion of Part I, now would be a good time to explore paper space and the use of multiple viewports to plot different views in a drawing. This drawing is used to illustrate multiple viewport plotting techniques in Chapter 15, Task 2. We recommend that you turn to that section when you have completed this drawing, or save it so that you can use it later.

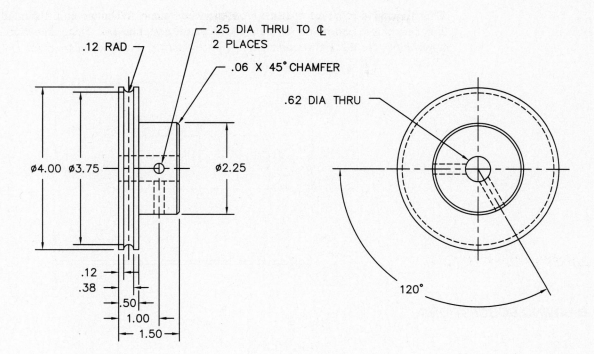

.12 RAD

.25 DIA THRU TO ℄
2 PLACES

.06 X 45° CHAMFER

Ø4.00　Ø3.75

Ø2.25

.62 DIA THRU

.12
.38
.50
1.00
1.50

120°

GROOVED HUB
Drawing 6–4

LAYERS	NAME	COLOR	LINETYPE		
	0	WHITE	————— CONTINUOUS		
	1	RED	————— CONTINUOUS		
	2	YELLOW	- - - - - HIDDEN		
	3	GREEN	— — — CENTER		

(DRAW) LINE (L)
(DRAW) CIRCLE (C)
(DRAW) ARC (A)
(EDIT) CHAMFER
(EDIT) COPY
(EDIT) BREAK
(EDIT) TRIM
(EDIT) MIRROR
(EDIT) ROTATE
(DISPLAY) ZOOM (Z)

F1	F6	F7	F8	F9
ON/OFF	ABSOLUTE/OFF/POLAR	ON/OFF	ON/OFF	ON/OFF
SCREEN	COORDS	GRID	ORTHO	SNAP

DRAWING 6–5: CAP IRON

This drawing is of a type of blade used in a wood plane. When wood is planed, the cap iron causes it to curl up out of the plane so that it does not jam. There are several good applications for the TRIM command.

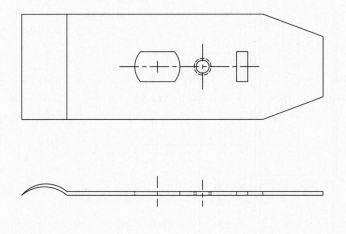

DRAWING SUGGESTIONS

GRID = 1.00   LIMITS = (0, 0) (48, 36)

SNAP = .25   LTSCALE = .25

> The circle with a hidden line outside a continuous line indicates a tapped hole. The dimension is given to the hidden line; the continuous inner line is drawn with a slightly smaller radius that is not specified.

> You may find it helpful to use the DIST command to position the smaller figures within the top view.

> The figure near the center of the top view that has two arcs with .38 radii can be drawn exactly the same way as the "band aid", *Figure 6-14* in Task 4 of this chapter. Draw a circle and two horizontal lines and then trim it all down.

> The .54 and .58 arcs in the front view can be drawn using Start, End, Radius.

> The small vertical hidden lines in the front view can be done using a system introduced in the previous drawing. Draw lines down from the figures in the top view and then trim them. For the tapped hole and the arced opening in the middle, you will have to use osnaps to right and left quadrant points to locate the start of these lines.

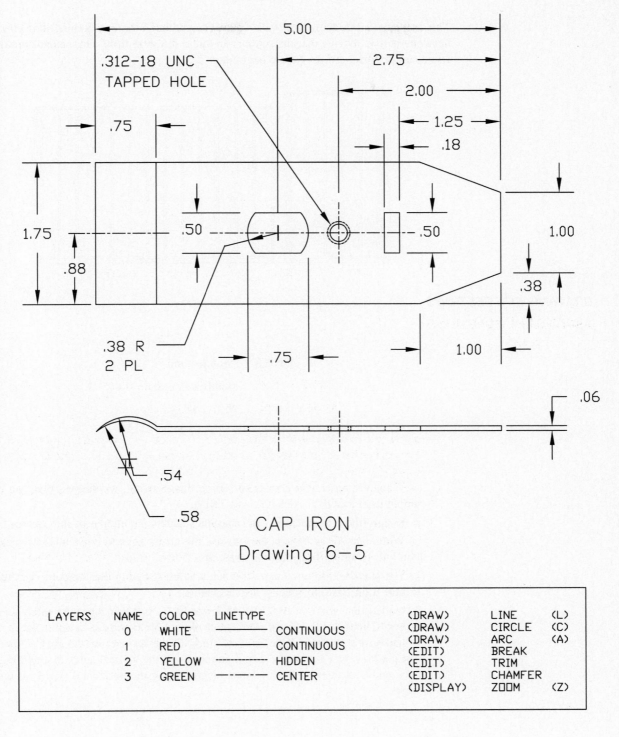

CAP IRON
Drawing 6-5

LAYERS	NAME	COLOR	LINETYPE				
	0	WHITE	———— CONTINUOUS		(DRAW)	LINE	(L)
	1	RED	———— CONTINUOUS		(DRAW)	CIRCLE	(C)
	2	YELLOW	------------ HIDDEN		(DRAW)	ARC	(A)
	3	GREEN	—·—·— CENTER		(EDIT)	BREAK	
					(EDIT)	TRIM	
					(EDIT)	CHAMFER	
					(DISPLAY)	ZOOM	(Z)

F1	F6	F7	F8	F9
ON/OFF	ABSOLUTE/OFF/POLAR	ON/OFF	ON/OFF	ON/OFF
SCREEN	COORDS	GRID	ORTHO	SNAP

DRAWING 6–6: DECK FRAMING

This architectural drawing may take some time, although there is nothing in it you have not done before. Notice that the settings are quite different from our standard prototype, so be sure to change them before beginning.

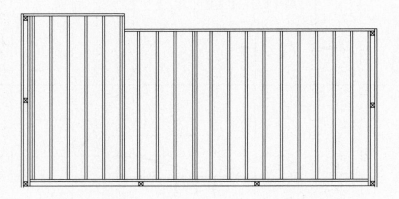

DRAWING SUGGESTIONS

UNITS = Architectural

smallest fraction = 1

LIMITS = (0, 0) (48′, 36′)

GRID = 1′

SNAP = 2″

> Whatever order you choose for doing this drawing, we suggest that you make ample use of COPY, ARRAY, and TRIM.

> Keep ortho on, except to draw the lines across the middle of the squares.

> With snap set at 2″ it is easy to use the arrow keys to copy lines 2″ apart, as you will be doing frequently to draw the 2″ x 8″ studs.

> You may need to turn snap off when you are selecting lines to copy, but be sure to turn it on again to specify displacements.

> Notice that you can use ARRAY effectively, but that there are three separate arrays. They are all 16″ on center, but the double boards in several places make it inadvisable to do a single array of studs all the way across the deck. What you can do, however, is to draw, copy, and array all the vertical studs first and then go back and trim them to their various lengths using the horizontal boards as cutting edges.

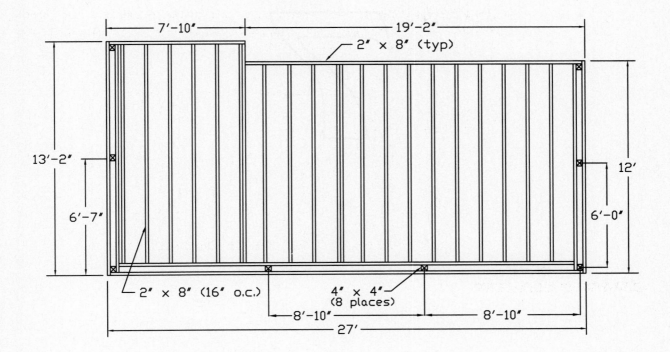

DECK FRAMING
Drawing 6–6

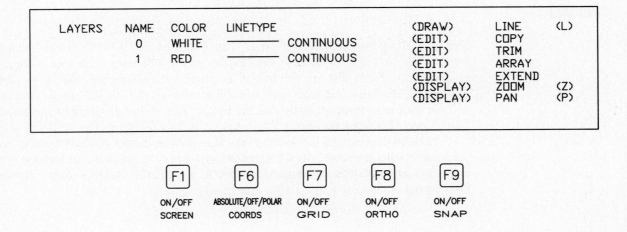

LAYERS	NAME	COLOR	LINETYPE				
	0	WHITE	———— CONTINUOUS		(DRAW)	LINE	(L)
	1	RED	———— CONTINUOUS		(EDIT)	COPY	
					(EDIT)	TRIM	
					(EDIT)	ARRAY	
					(EDIT)	EXTEND	
					(DISPLAY)	ZOOM	(Z)
					(DISPLAY)	PAN	(P)

F1	F6	F7	F8	F9
ON/OFF	ABSOLUTE/OFF/POLAR	ON/OFF	ON/OFF	ON/OFF
SCREEN	COORDS	GRID	ORTHO	SNAP

CHAPTER

COMMANDS

DRAW	EDIT
TEXT	CHANGE
DTEXT	SCALE
STYLE	DDEDIT

OVERVIEW

This chapter begins Part II of the book. Part I focused on basic 2D entities such as lines, circles, and arcs. In the next five chapters you will be learning to draw a number of AutoCAD entities that are constructed as groups of lines, circles, and arcs. Text, dimensions, polylines, and blocks are all entities made up of basic 2D entities, but you will not have to treat them line by line, arc by arc. Also in Part II, you will continue to learn AutoCAD editing features.

Now it's time to add text to your drawings. In this chapter you will learn to find your way around the AutoCAD TEXT commands and subcommands. In addition, you will learn two new editing commands, CHANGE and SCALE, that are often used with text but that are equally important for editing other objects.

TASKS

1. Enter standard text using seven placement options.
2. Enter multiline text.
3. Enter multiline text using the DTEXT command.
4. Change fonts and styles.
5. Use DDEDIT to edit previously drawn text.

6. Use CHANGE to edit previously drawn text.
7. Use CHANGE to edit other entities.
8. Change properties of objects other than text.
9. Use SCALE to change the size of objects on the screen.
10. Do Drawing 7-1 ("Title Block").
11. Do Drawing 7-2 ("Gauges").
12. Do Drawing 7-3 ("Stamping").
13. Do Drawing 7-4 ("Control Panel").

TASK 1: Entering Text in Standard Style

Procedure.

1. Type or select "TEXT".
2. Type or select an option.
3. Pick a location.
4. Answer prompts regarding height and rotation.
5. Type text.

Discussion. TEXT is one of the more complex of the AutoCAD commands. There are fourteen options for placing text and a variety of fonts to use and styles that can be created from them. In the first three tasks we will focus on placement and stick to the standard text style. In Task 4 we will explore other styles and fonts.

> To prepare for this exercise, draw a 4.00 horizontal line beginning at (1,1). Then create a 6 row by 1 column array with 2.00 between rows, as shown in *Figure 7-1*. These lines are for orientation in this exercise only, they are not essential for drawing text.

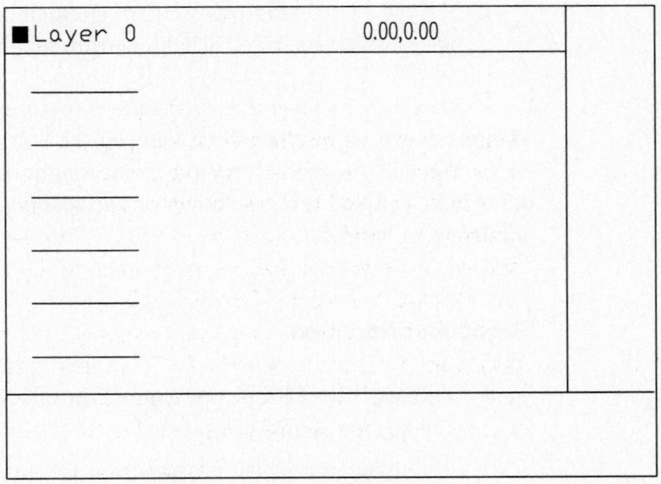

Figure 7-1

> Type or select "TEXT". You will see a prompt with three options:

Justify/Style/<Start point>:

"Style" will be explored in Task 4. In this task we will be looking at different options for placing text in a drawing. These are all considered text justification methods and will be listed if you choose the "Justify" option at this prompt. But first let's try the default method by picking a start point. This will give us standard, left-justified text.

> Pick a start point at the left end of the upper line.

Look at the prompt that follows and be sure that you do not attempt to enter text yet:

Height <0.20>:

This gives you the opportunity to set the text height. The number you type specifies the height of uppercase letters in the units you have specified for the current drawing. For now we will accept the default height.

> Press enter to accept the default height (0.20).

The prompt that follows allows you to place text in a rotated position.

Rotation angle <0>:

The default of 0 degrees orients text in the usual horizontal manner. Other angles can be specified by typing a degree number relative to the polar coordinate system, or by showing a point. If you show a point it will be taken as the second point of a baseline along which the text string will be placed. For now we will stick to horizontal text.

> Press enter to accept the default angle (0).

Now, at last, it is time to enter the text itself. AutoCAD prompts:

Text:

For our text we will type the word "Left" since this is an example of left-justified text.

> Type "Left" and press enter. (Remember that you cannot use the space bar in place of the enter key when entering text.)

Figure 7-2 shows the left-justified text you have just drawn along with the other options as we will demonstrate them in the rest of this exercise.

We will proceed to try out some of the other text placement options, beginning with right-justified text, as shown on the second line of *Figure 7-2*. We will also specify a change in height.

Right-justified Text

> Repeat the TEXT command. You will see the same prompt as before.

> Type "r" or select "right".

Now AutoCAD prompts you for an end point instead of a start point:

End point:

We will choose the end of the second line.

> Point to the right end of the second line.

This time we will change the height to .50. Notice that AutoCAD gives you a rubber band from the end point. It can be used to specify height and rotation angle by pointing, if you like.

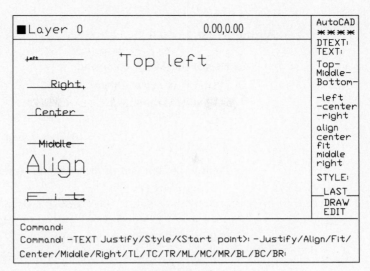

Figure 7-2

> Type ".5" and press enter or show a height of .50 by pointing.

> Press enter to retain 0 degrees of rotation. You are now prompted to enter text.

> Type "Right" and press enter. Your screen should now include the second line of text.

Centered Text

> Repeat the TEXT command.

> Type "c" or select "center".

AutoCAD prompts:

Center point:

> Point to the midpoint of the third line.

> Press enter to retain the current height, which is now set to .50.

> Press enter to retain 0 degrees of rotation.

> Type "Center" and press enter.

Middle Text

> Repeat the TEXT command.

> Type "m" or select "middle".

AutoCAD prompts:

Middle point:

> Point to the midpoint of the fourth line.

> Press enter to retain the current height of .50.

> Press enter to retain 0 degrees of rotation.

> Type "middle" and press enter.

Notice the difference between center and middle. Center refers to the midpoint of the baseline below the text. Middle refers to the middle of the text itself, so that the line now runs through the text.

Aligned Text

> Repeat the TEXT command.
> Type "a" or select "align".
AutoCAD prompts:

First text line point:

> Point to the left end of the fifth line. AutoCAD prompts for another point:

Second text line point:

> Point to the right end of the fifth line.

Notice that there is no prompt for height. AutoCAD will calculate a height based on the space between the points you chose. There is also no prompt for an angle, because the angle between your two points (in this case 0) will be used. You could put text at an angle using this option.

> Type "Align" and press enter.

Text Drawn To Fit Between Two Points

> Repeat the TEXT command.
> Type "f" or select "fit".
You will be prompted for two points as in the "align" option.
> Point to the left end of the sixth line.
> Point to the right end of the sixth line.
> Press enter to retain the current height.
As in the align option, there will be no prompt for an angle of rotation.
> Type "Fit" and press enter.

Even though the text is considerably stretched to make it fit between the given points, the height is .50, as specified. This is the difference between fit and align. In the align option, text height is determined by the width you show. With fit, the specified height is retained and the text is stretched or compressed to fill the given space. This option also can be used to place text at an angle.

Other Justification Options

Before proceeding to the next task, take a moment to look at the list of justification options.

> Select "Justify" from the screen menu. You could type "J", but using the screen menu will allow you to see both the command area prompt and the screen menu list.

AutoCAD will show you a prompt listing fourteen options.

Align/Fit/Center/Middle/Right/TL/TC/TR/ML/MC/MR/BL/BC/BR:

These are spelled out on the screen menu, as shown in *Figure 7-2*. We already have explored the first five plus the default option. For the others, study *Figure 7-3*. As shown on the chart and the screen menu, T is for top, M is for middle, and B is for bottom. L, C, and R stand for left, center, and right. So we have "Top Left", "Top Center", "Top Right", "Middle Center", etc. All of these options work the same way. Notice that it is not necessary to see the list to enter the option. Just enter the TEXT command and then the one or two letters of the option. Let's try one.

> Type "TL" or select "Top-" and then "-Left" from the screen menu.

AutoCAD will ask for a "Top/Left point". As shown in *Figure 7-3*, top left refers to the highest potential text point at the left of the word. If you begin with a lowercase letter, the point will be above the text.

> Pick a top/left point as shown in *Figure 7-2*.

> Press enter twice to accept the height and rotation angle settings and arrive at the "Text:" prompt.

> Type "top left".

Your screen should resemble *Figure 7-2*.

TEXT JUSTIFICATION	
<START POINT> TYPE ABBREVIATION	TEXT POSITION + INDICATES START POINT or PICK POINT
A	ALIGN
F	FIT
C	CENTER
M	MIDDLE
R	RIGHT
TL	TOP LEFT
TC	TOP CENTER
TR	TOP RIGHT
ML	MIDDLE LEFT
MC	MIDDLE CENTER
MR	MIDDLE RIGHT
BL	BOTTOM LEFT
BC	BOTTOM CENTER
BR	BOTTOM RIGHT

Figure 7-3

TASK 2: Entering Multiline Text

Procedure.

1. Enter a line of text using any of the placement options.
2. Press enter to repeat the TEXT command.
3. Press enter at the "Justify/Style/<Start point>:" prompt.
4. Type text and press enter.

Discussion. If you have several lines of text to enter in one place on your drawing, you will want to avoid having to position each line separately. To do this, enter the first line of text in the usual manner, with any of the placement options discussed previously. Then press enter twice to repeat the TEXT command and bring back the "Text:" prompt. New text will be positioned directly beneath the previous line with the same height and rotation angle. Line spacing will be determined by AutoCAD based on text height.

In this exercise we will create three lines of left-justified text, one below the other, all rotated 45 degrees.

> Repeat the TEXT command.

You will see the familiar prompt:

Justify/Style/<Start point>:

> Pick a starting point near (9.50,7.50), as shown by the blip next to the word "These" in *Figure 7-4*.

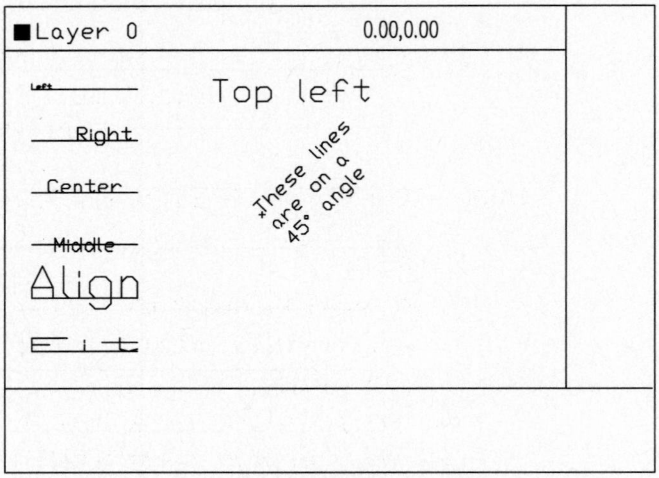

Figure 7-4

> Press enter to retain the current height.
> Type "45" or show an angle of 45 degrees.
> Type "These lines" and press enter.

The text will be drawn on the screen at a 45 degree angle and you will be returned to the "Command:" prompt. The steps that follow are the new ones for drawing multiline text.

> Press enter to repeat the TEXT command.
> Press enter again.

This tells AutoCAD that you want to continue entering text below the previous line. Other prompts will be skipped and you will be prompted for text.

> Type "are on a" and press enter.

> Press enter again to repeat the TEXT command.

> Press enter once more to indicate that you want to add another line of multiline text.

Other prompts will be skipped and you will be prompted for text.

The Degree Symbol and Other Special Characters

The next line contains a degree symbol. Since you do not have this character on your keyboard, AutoCAD provides a special method for drawing it. Type the text with the %% signs just as shown following and then study *Figure 7-5*, which lists other special characters that can be drawn this way.

> Type "45%%d angle" and press enter.

Your screen should now resemble *Figure 7-4*.

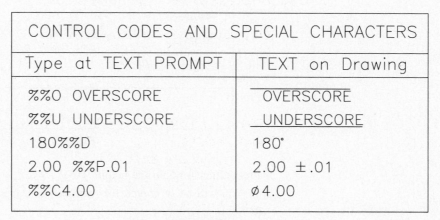

CONTROL CODES AND SPECIAL CHARACTERS	
Type at TEXT PROMPT	TEXT on Drawing
%%O OVERSCORE	O̅V̅E̅R̅S̅C̅O̅R̅E̅
%%U UNDERSCORE	U̲N̲D̲E̲R̲S̲C̲O̲R̲E̲
180%%D	180°
2.00 %%P.01	2.00 ±.01
%%C4.00	⌀4.00

Figure 7-5

TASK 3: Writing Text Directly to the Screen with DTEXT

Procedure.

1. Type or select "DTEXT".
2. Type or select an option.
3. Pick a location.
4. Answer prompts regarding height and rotation.
5. Type a line of text and press enter.
6. Type another line of text and press enter.
7. Type another line of text and press enter...
8. Press enter to exit the command.

Discussion. The DTEXT command ("dynamic text") is a variation of the TEXT command, which allows you to see how your text will appear on the screen as you enter it. It also creates multiline text automatically, without having to repeat the command, and allows you to edit by backspacing through these multiple lines.

> Type or select "DTEXT". (Under "Draw" on either menu, Pick "Text" and then "Dynamic" on the pull down.)

You will be prompted as if you were in the TEXT command:

Justify/Style/<Start point>:

Notice that the command sequence is identical for TEXT and DTEXT. Any of the options could be selected, but left-justified text works best. With other options you will not see the text correctly positioned until after you have completed the command sequence.

> Pick a start point near (9.50,5.00), as shown by the blip next to the word "Dynamic" in *Figure 7-6*.

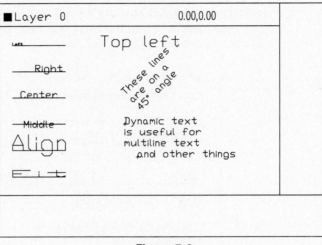

Figure 7-6

> Press enter to retain the height (0.5).

You will be prompted for rotation angle next. Notice that the current angle is now 45°:

Rotation angle <45>:

> Type "0" to return to horizontal orientation.

You should see the prompt for text. You will also see that a text location box has been placed next to your start point. This box is the height and width of your text. As you type, watch the screen to see how DTEXT works.

> Type "Dynamic text" and press enter.

Instead of exiting the command after drawing the text, DTEXT returns you to the text prompt for another line of text.

> Type "is useful for" and press enter.

> Type "multiline text" and press enter.

You should be at the "Text:" prompt again to try out one more convenient feature of the DTEXT command. Move your cursor and notice that you still have control of the cross hairs. If you select a new start point now, your next line of text will be placed there. Try it.

> At the "Text:" prompt, pick a new start point near (10.50, 2.00), as shown by the blip near the word "and" in *Figure 7-6*.

> Type "and other things".

DTEXT will continue to return the "Text:" prompt until you press enter in response.

> Press enter to exit DTEXT.

TASK 4: Changing Fonts and Styles

Procedure.

1. Type or select "STYLE".
2. Type a new style name.
3. Type a font file name.
4. Answer prompts for height, width, angle, and orientation.

Or, from the pull down menu bar:

1. Select "Draw".
2. Select "Text".
3. Select "Set Style".
3. Select a font from the icon menu.
4. Answer prompts for height, width, angle, and orientation.

Discussion. By default, the current text style in any AutoCAD drawing is one called "STANDARD." It is a specific form of a font called "txt" that comes with the software. All the text you have entered so far has been drawn with the standard style of the "txt" font.

Changing fonts is a simple matter. However, there is a lot of room for confusion in the use of the words "style" and "font." You can avoid this confusion if you remember that fonts are the basic patterns of character and symbol shapes that can be used with the TEXT and DTEXT commands, while styles are variations in the size, orientation, and spacing of the characters in those fonts. It is possible to create your own fonts, but for most of us this is an esoteric activity. In contrast, creating your own styles is easy and practical.

We will begin by creating a variation of the STANDARD style you have been using. There is a convenient dialogue box with an icon menu that we will get to shortly. However, the whole system will make more sense if you do not use the pull down menu yet.

> Type or select "STYLE".

You will be prompted as follows:

Text style name (or ?) <STANDARD>:

By now you should be familiar with the elements of this prompt. We will use the "?" first to see a list of available styles.

> Type "?".

AutoCAD will offer you the opportunity to limit the list of styles by using wild card characters.

Text style(s) to list <*>:

> Press enter to list all available styles.

AutoCAD will switch over to the text screen and give you the following information:

Text styles:

Style name: STANDARD Font files: txt
Height: 0.00 Width factor: 1.00 Obliquing angle: 0 Generation: Normal

Current text style: STANDARD

If anyone has used text commands in your prototype drawing it is possible that there will be other styles listed. However, STANDARD is the only one that is certain to be there, because it is created automatically. We will create our own variation of the STANDARD style and call it "VERTICAL". It will use the same "txt" character font, but will be drawn down the display instead of across.

> Press enter to repeat the STYLE command. You will see this prompt again:

Text style name (or ?) <STANDARD>:

> Type "vertical".

AutoCAD will respond by displaying the Select Font File dialogue box shown in *Figure 7-7*.

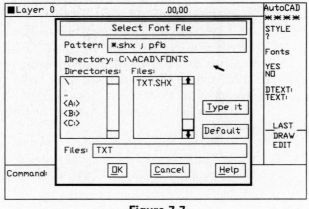

Figure 7-7

> Press enter to retain the current txt font.

AutoCAD closes the font dialogue box and prompts:

Height <0.00>:

It is important to understand what 0 height means in the STYLE command. It does not mean that your characters will be drawn 0.00 units high. It means that there will be no fixed height, so you will be able to specify a height whenever you use this style. Notice that STANDARD currently has no fixed height. That is why you are prompted for a height whenever you use it. In general, it is best to leave height variable unless you know that you will be drawing a large amount of text with one height. For practice, try giving our new "VERTICAL" style a fixed height.

> Type ".5".

AutoCAD prompts:

Width factor <1.00>:

This prompt allows you to stretch or shrink characters in the font based on a factor of one. Let's double the width to see how it looks.
> Type "2".
AutoCAD prompts:

Obliquing angle:

This allows you to put any font on a slant, right or left, creating an italic effect. We will leave this one alone for the moment; italics look better in horizontal text.
> Press enter to retain 0 degrees of slant.
AutoCAD follows with a series of three prompts regarding the orientation of characters. The first one is:

Backwards? <N>:

Obviously this is for special effects. You can try this one in a moment.
> Press enter to retain "frontwards" text.
The second orientation prompt is even more peculiar:

Upside down? <N>:

> Press enter if you want your text to be drawn right side up.
Finally, the one we've been waiting for:

Vertical? <N>:

This is what allows us to create a vertical style text.
> Type "y".
Before returning the "Command:" prompt AutoCAD will tell you that your new style is now current:

VERTICAL is now the current text style.

To see your new style in action you will need to enter some text.
> Type or select "TEXT".
> Pick a start point, as shown by the blip near the letter "V" in *Figure 7-8*.
Notice that you are not prompted for a height because the current style has height fixed at .50.
> Press enter to retain 270 degrees of rotation.
> Type "Vertical".
Your screen should resemble *Figure 7-8*.

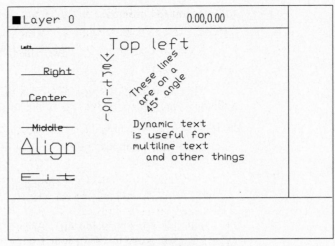

Figure 7-8

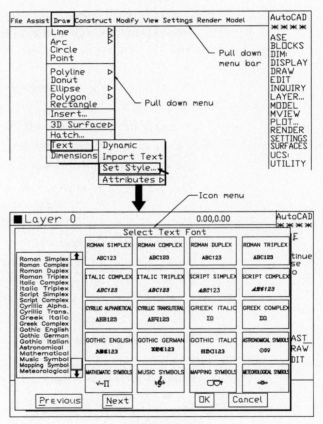

Figure 7-9

The Text Font Icon Menu

Now that you are familiar with the STYLE command, try creating a new style from the pull down icon menu.

> Select "Draw" from the pull down menu bar.

> Select "Text" from the menu.

> Select "Set Style..." from the submenu.

You will see the Select Text Font dialogue box illustrated in *Figure 7-9*. This box has a standard list box with a scroll bar on the left and an icon menu showing the fonts on the right. There are 38 fonts to choose from.

> Click on the "Roman Duplex" image box.

"Roman Duplex" will be highlighted on the list as well.

> Click on "OK".

The icon menu will disappear, leaving you in the middle of the STYLE command sequence as follows:

Text style name (or ?) <VERTICAL>: romand

New style. Font file <txt>: romand Height <0.0000>:

Reading this series of prompts and responses will show what the dialogue box has done for you. It has entered the STYLE command and initiated a new style called "romand" (Roman Duplex). The font file to be used in the creation of this style has the same name as the style itself, "romand." Now AutoCAD is asking you to complete the style definition, beginning with a height.

> Press enter to retain variable height (0.00).

The rest of the command sequence will be familiar from the STYLE command. We will retain all the defaults except for the obliquing angle.

> Press enter to retain a width factor of 1.

> Type "−45" and press enter.

This will cause your text to be slanted 45 degrees to the left. For a right slant, of course, you would type a positive number.

> Press enter three more times to retain the defaults for backward, upside-down, and vertical.

Now AutoCAD will tell you:

ROMAND is now the current text style.

Now enter some text to see how this slanted Roman Duplex style looks.

> Type or select "TEXT" or "DTEXT" and answer the prompts to draw the words "Roman Duplex" with a .50 height, as shown in *Figure 7-10*.

After you have completed the Roman Duplex text, use the icon menu to create two more lines of text, as shown in *Figure 7-10*. The bottom line is in mathematical symbols, the characters that are called out by typing "abcdefghijklm" when the "symath" font file has been chosen and styled with all the defaults and a .50 height.

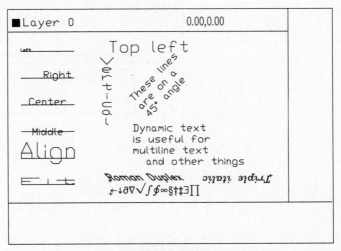

Figure 7-10

For a complete chart of alphabet-to-symbol correspondence in all the symbolic fonts, see the *AutoCAD Reference Manual*.

NOTE: Once you have a number of styles defined in a drawing, you can switch from one to another with the Style option of the TEXT and DTEXT commands. This option is only for switching previously defined styles; it will not allow you to define new ones.

TASK 5: Editing Previously Drawn Text with DDEDIT

Procedure.

1. Type or select "DDEDIT" (under "EDIT" on the screen menu).
2. Select a line of text. (Steps 1 and 2 may be reversed.)
3. Edit text as shown in the dialogue box.
4. Click "OK" to exit.

Discussion.   DDEDIT provides a quick and easy way to change the wording or spelling of previously drawn text. It only works on one text entity at a time and does not allow for other types of changes (style, height, layer, rotation, etc.). For these you will need to use the CHANGE command or the DDMODIFY dialogue, introduced in Task 6. Try this.

> Type "ddedit" or select DDEDIT from the screen menu under "EDIT".

AutoCAD prompts you to select text:

<Select a TEXT or ATTDEF object>/Undo:

ATTDEF is the attribute definition command. "Attributes" are a special kind of text item attached to "blocks." Blocks and attributes are discussed in Chapter 10.
> Pick the line of text that says "Dynamic text".

AutoCAD immediately produces a simple dialogue box, as illustrated in *Figure 7-11*. The main feature of this dialogue is an edit box containing the text you want to change. You can edit in this box as in any edit box.

The text will be highlighted, indicating that if you type now, the entire text will be replaced.

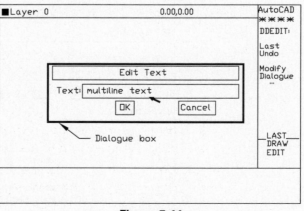

Figure 7-11

> Type "DDEDIT".
> Click on "OK".

The dialogue box will close and your changes will be reflected immediately on your screen.

AutoCAD will stay in the DDEDIT command sequence and ask for another text object to edit, or you can undo your last edit by typing "u" or selecting "Undo" from the screen menu.

> Pick the line of text that says "multiline text."

The dialogue box will appear again with this new selection in the edit box.

> Place the arrow at the beginning of the word "multiline," press the pick button, and drag across the word. Do not include the word "text."

The word "multiline" now should be highlighted.

> Type "editing".

> Click on "OK".

Your screen should resemble *Figure 7-12*.

Notice that DDEDIT, as convenient as it is, will not allow you to select more than one text object at a time. For situations where you want to change many lines, or where you want to change more than the wording, you will need to use CHANGE or DDMODIFY, as follows.

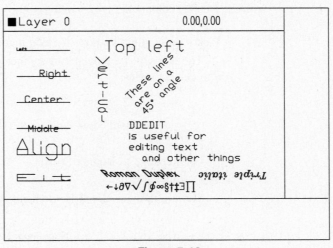

Figure 7-12

TASK 6: Changing Previously Drawn Text with CHANGE

Procedure.

1. Type or select "CHANGE".
2. Select objects (text). (Steps 1 and 2 can be reversed if noun/verb selection is enabled.)
3. Pick a new location or press enter for no change.
4. Type or select a new text style or press enter for no change.
5. Type or show a new height or press enter for no change.
6. Type or show a new rotation angle or press enter for no change.
7. Type new text or press enter for no change.

Discussion. The CHANGE command is a very useful tool that allows you to change a number of different entities, text being only one of them. The qualities of previously drawn text that can be changed are location, style, height, rotation angle, and the text itself. You can change all the properties at once if need be, but more often you will be changing only one or two. Properties you do not wish to change are retained by pressing enter. In this exercise we will use the CHANGE command twice to edit some of the text you have already drawn.

> Type or select "CHANGE". (CHANGE is under "Edit" on the screen menu. On the pull down, select "Modify" and then "Points" on the "Change" submenu.)

You will be prompted to select objects.

> Point to the word "Left", the first line of text you entered in Task 1.

> Press enter to end selection.

AutoCAD will issue the first of a series of prompts that ask you to specify what you would like to change:

Properties/<Change point>:

"Properties" refers to a list of options, including color, layer, and linetype, which we will discuss in Task 8. "Change point" has different meanings with different types of entities. In the case of text, it allows you to relocate the text (this can also be done with the MOVE command or by moving a grip point).

> Pick a point slightly above the line that the text is written on.

The text will be moved and another prompt issued. This prompt will allow you to change styles:

Text style:
Standard New style or RETURN for no change:

Let's change to Roman Duplex.

> Type "romand".

You are now prompted for a change in height:

New height <0.20>:

We will change to .50 so that this line of text matches the ones below it.

> Type ".5".

The next prompt is for a change in rotation angle:

New rotation angle <0>:

We will retain this angle.

> Press enter to retain horizontal orientation.

Finally, AutoCAD prompts for a change in the characters themselves:

New Text <Left>:

Two common applications for this option are rewording and respelling. A less obvious but very useful application is shown in Drawing 7-2, "Gauges." We will change the wording to "Left justified."

> Type "Left justified".

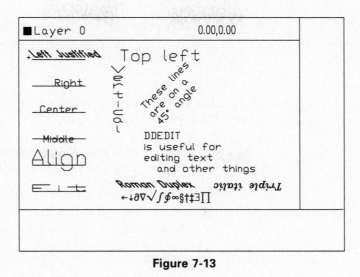

Figure 7-13

Your screen now should resemble *Figure 7-13*.

NOTE: Grips can be used to edit text in the usual grip edit modes of moving, copying, rotating, mirroring, and scaling. The stretch mode works the same as moving. Grips on text are located at the left-justified start point and at the original point actually used to position the text. Grips cannot be used to reword, respell, or change text properties.

Changing Text with DDMODIFY

The DDMODIFY dialogue offers the same types of changes that can be made using the CHANGE command, but like DDEDIT, it only allows you to select one object at a time, whereas CHANGE allows you to select many objects and cycle through the command sequence for one after another of the selected items. Try this.

> Type "ddmodify" or type "ddedit" and then select "Modify Dialogue" from the screen menu.

AutoCAD will ask you to select an object to modify.

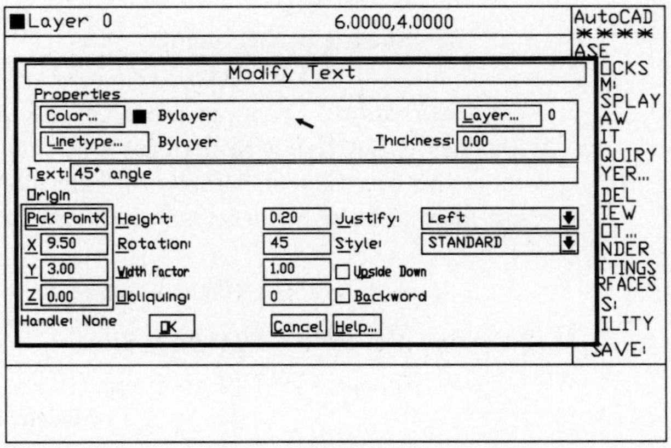

Figure 7-14

> Select the text "45° angle".

You will see a dialogue box similar to the one illustrated in *Figure 7-14*. Take a moment to look at all the properties of this one piece of text you can modify. They should all be familiar to you at this point.

> Double click in the edit box to the right of "Rotation:".

This box should show the highlighted number 45.

> Type "0".

> Click on "OK".

The line you just modified should now be horizontal and your screen should resemble *Figure 7-15*.

Now that you have seen what is available in this dialogue box, we are sure that you will have no trouble using it to change any of the other properties.

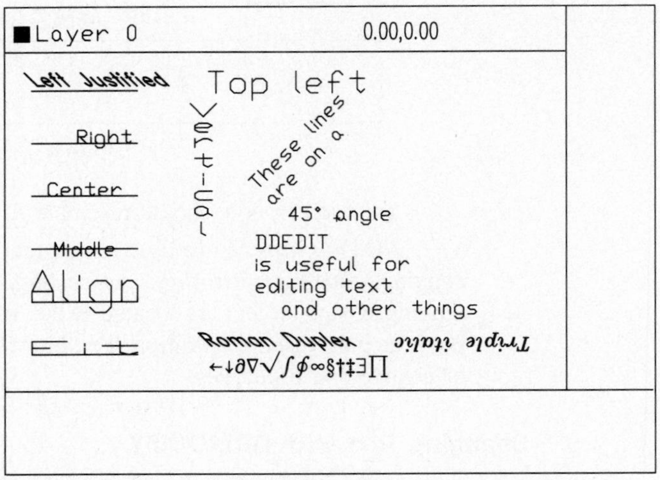

Figure 7-15

TASK 7: Using Change Points with Other Entities

Procedure.

1. Type or select "CHANGE".
2. Define a selection set. (Steps 1 and 2 can be reversed if noun/verb selection is enabled.)
3. Show a change point.

Discussion. You can use a change point to alter the size of lines and circles. With lines, CHANGE will perform a function similar to the EXTEND command, but without the necessity of defining an extension boundary. With circles, CHANGE will cause them to be redrawn so that they pass through the change point.

> Repeat the CHANGE command.

You will be prompted to:

Select objects:

> Select the first two lines, under the words "Left justified" and "Right".

> Press enter to end selection.

AutoCAD prompts:

Properties/<Change point>:

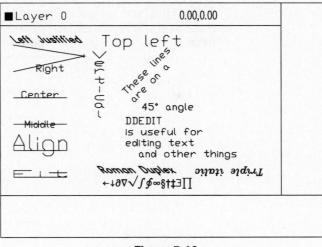

Figure 7-16

We will use a change point first to alter the selected lines, as shown in *Figure 7-16*.

> If ortho is on turn it off (F8).

> Pick a point between the two lines and to the right, in the neighborhood of (6.50,10.00).

The lines will be redrawn so that the change point becomes the new end point of both lines.

To maintain horizontal or vertical orientation of lines while using the change point option of the CHANGE command, turn ortho on. Try it.

> Turn ortho on.

> Repeat the CHANGE command.

> Select the third, fourth, fifth, and sixth lines where the words "center", "middle", "align", and "fit" are drawn.

> Press enter to end selection.

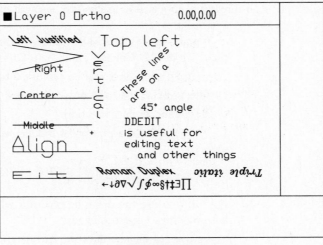

Figure 7-17

> Pick a change point to the right of the lines, as shown by the blip in *Figure 7-17*.

Be careful not to pick this point too low or too high. This could cause AutoCAD to redraw one or more of the lines vertically. All four lines will be extended horizontally, as in *Figure 7-17*.

NOTE: If you use the change point option to edit a circle, the circle will be redrawn so that it passes through the change point. See *Figure 7-18*.

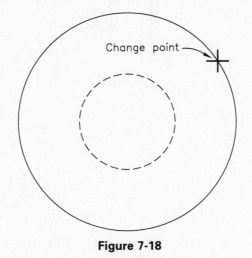

Figure 7-18

TASK 8: Changing Properties of Objects Other Than Text

Procedure.

1. Type or select "CHPROP".
2. Select objects. (Steps 1 and 2 may be reversed if noun/verb selection is enabled.)
3. Type or select a property to change.
4. Enter a new value for the property.

Discussion.   You can change the properties, including layer, color, linetype, and thickness (3D), of any entity using CHANGE, CHPROP, or the DDCHPROP dialogue. The three are similar, but CHPROP and DDCHPROP skip the change point option and go directly to properties. In this task we will move an object to a different layer.

> Type or select "CHPROP" (under "Edit" on the screen menu; on the pull down, pick "Modify", "Change", and then "Properties").

In all cases you will be prompted to select objects.

> Select any of the lines on your screen.
> Press enter to end selection.

You will see a prompt or a dialogue box with a list of options:

Change what property (Color/LAyer/LType/Thickness)?

If you use the dialogue box you will see that there are subdialogues for all the properties except thickness.

You can change the color or linetype of an individual entity, but in this book we are adhering to a system of associating colors and linetypes with layers. This "BYLAYER" system is common practice and is usually best for keeping drawings well organized.

The only property change option we will make use of at this time is the layer option. This is an important editing capability for correcting the common mistake of drawing an object on the wrong layer and for those instances where it is convenient to draw objects on one layer and then move them to other layers after they are drawn.

> Type "la" or select "Layer".

Notice that you must type two letters to avoid confusion between "layer" and "ltype".

AutoCAD will prompt for a new layer or display a subdialogue with a list of layers to choose from. We will move this line to layer 2, so that it will appear as a yellow, hidden line.

> Type "2" and press enter, or pick layer 2 in the dialogue box and then click on "OK" twice.

The line will be redrawn on the new layer.

Changing Properties with DDMODIFY

You can also change properties of objects using the DDMODIFY dialogue box, introduced in the last task. Lines, for example, can be selected to change their color, linetype, layer, thickness, and even their end points. We have not included a specific exercise, but encourage you to explore this feature.

TASK 9: SCALEing Previously Drawn Entities

Procedure.

1. Type or select "SCALE".
2. Select objects. (Steps 1 and 2 can be reversed if noun/verb selection is enabled.)
3. Pick a base point.
4. Enter a scale factor.

Discussion. Any object or group of objects can be scaled up or down using the SCALE command or the grip edit scale mode. In this exercise we will practice scaling some of the text and lines that you have drawn on your screen. Remember, however, that there is no special relationship between SCALE and TEXT and that other types of entities can be scaled just as easily.

> Type or select "SCALE" (under "Modify" on the pull down and under "Edit" on the screen menu).

AutoCAD will prompt you to select objects.

> Use a crossing box (right to left) to select the set of six lines and text drawn in Task 1.

> Press enter to end selection.

You will be prompted to pick a base point:

Base point:

Imagine for a moment that you are looking at a square and you want to shrink it using a scale-down procedure. All the sides will, of course, be shrunk the same amount, but how do you want this to happen? Should the lower left corner stay in place and the whole square shrink toward it? Or should everything shrink toward the center? Or toward some other point on or off the square (see *Figure 7-19*)?

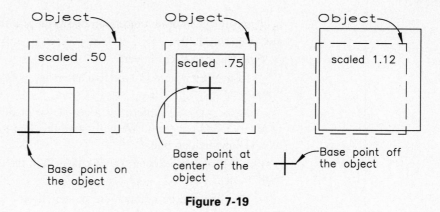

Figure 7-19

This is what you will tell AutoCAD when you pick a base point. In most applications you will choose a point somewhere on the object.

> Pick a base point at the left end of the bottom line of the selected set (the blip in *Figure 7-20*).

AutoCAD now needs to know how much to shrink or enlarge the objects you have selected:

<Scale factor>/Reference:

We will get to the reference method in a moment. When you enter a scale factor, all lengths, heights, and diameters in your set will be multiplied by that factor and redrawn accordingly. Scale factors are based on a unit of 1. If you enter .5, objects will be reduced to half their original size. If you enter 2, objects will become twice as large.

> Type ".5" and press enter.

Your screen should now resemble *Figure 7-20*.

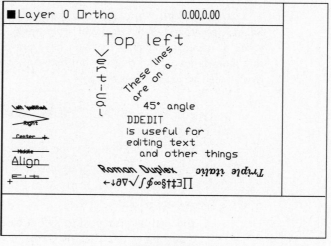

Figure 7-20

SCALEing by Reference

This option can save you from doing the arithmetic to figure out scale factors. It is useful when you have a given length and you know how large you want that length to become after the scaling is done. For example, we know that the lines we just scaled are now 2.00 long. Let's say that we want to scale them again to become 2.33 long (a scale factor of 1.165, but who wants to stop and figure that out?). This could be done using the following procedure:

1. Type or select "SCALE".

2. Select the "previous" set.

3. Pick a base point.

4. Type "r" or select "reference".

5. Type "2" for the reference length.

6. Type "2.33" for the new length.

NOTE: You can also perform reference scaling by pointing. In the procedure above, you could point to the ends of the 2.00 line for the reference length and then show a 2.33 line for the new length.

Scaling with Grips

Scaling with grips is very similar to scaling with the SCALE command. To illustrate this, try using grips to return the text you just scaled back to its original size.

> Use a window or crossing box to select the six lines and the text drawn in Task 1.

There will be a large number of grips on the screen, three on each line and two on most of the text entities. Some of these will overlap or duplicate each other.

> Pick the grip at the lower left corner of the word "Fit," the same point used as a base point in the last scaling procedure.

> Select "SCale" from the screen menu, or press enter three times to bypass stretch, move, and rotate.

> Move the cursor slowly and observe the dragged image.

AutoCAD will use the selected grip point as the base point for scaling unless you specify that you want to pick a different base point.

Notice that you also have a reference option as in the SCALE command. Unlike the SCALE command you also have an option to make copies of your objects at different scales.

As in SCALE, the default method is to specify a scale factor by pointing or typing.

> Type "2" or show a length of 2.00.

Your text will return to its original size and your screen will resemble *Figure 7-17* again.

TASKS 10, 11, 12, and 13

The drawings that follow contain typical applications of TEXT, DTEXT, STYLE, CHANGE, and SCALE. Pay particular attention to the suggestions on the use of DTEXT in the first drawing, and CHANGE in the second, third, and fourth drawings. These will save you time and help you to become a more efficient CAD operator.

DRAWING 7-1: TITLE BLOCK

This title block will give you practice in using a variety of text styles and sizes. You may want to save it and use it as a title block for future drawings. In Chapter 10 we will show you how to insert one drawing into another, so you will be able to incorporate this title block into any drawing.

QTY REQ'D
DESCRIPTION
PART NO.
ITEM NO.
BILL OF MATERIAL
UNLESS OTHERWISE SPECIFIED DIMENSIONS ARE IN INCHES
DRAWN BY:
B. A. Cad Designer
DATE
YOUR CAD CO.
REMOVE ALL BURRS & BREAK SHARP EDGES
APPROVED BY:
TOLERANCES
FRACTIONS ± 1/64
ANGLES ± 0°-15'
DECIMALS
XX ± .01
XXX ± .005
ISSUED:
DRAWING TITLE:
MATERIAL:
FINISH:
SIZE
C
CODE IDENT NO.
38178
DRAWING NO.
REV.
SCALE:
DATE:
SHEET
OF

DRAWING SUGGESTIONS

GRID = 1

SNAP = .0625

> Make ample use of DIST and TRIM as you draw the line patterns of the title block. Take your time and make sure that at least the major divisions are in place before you start entering text into the boxes.

> Set to the "text" layer before entering text.

> Use DTEXT with all the STANDARD, .09, left-justified text. This will allow you to do all of these in one command sequence, moving the cursor from one box to the next and entering the text as you go.

> Remember that once you have defined a style you can make it current using the TEXT or DTEXT commands. This will save you from having to restyle more than necessary.

> Use "%%D" for the degree symbol and "%%P" for the plus or minus symbol.

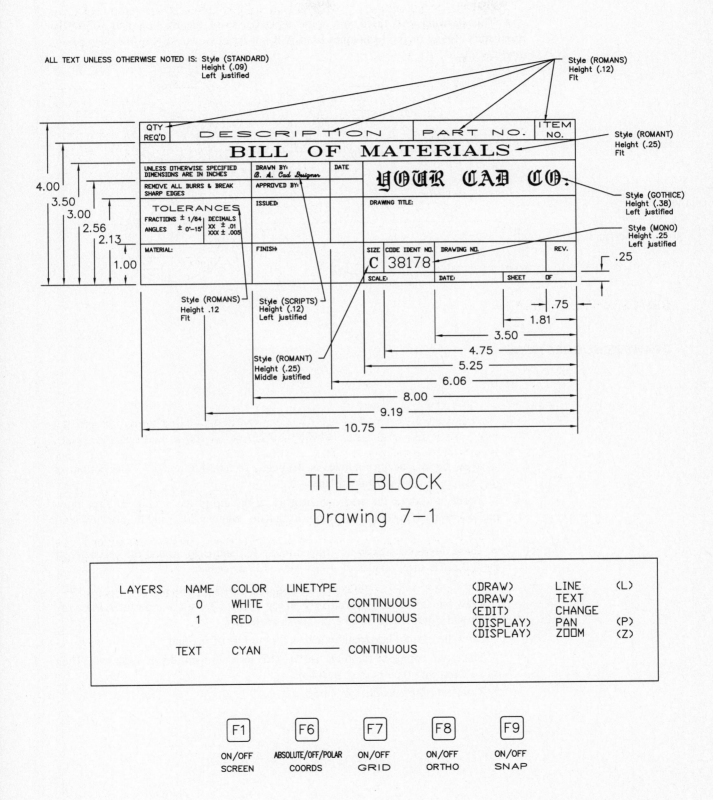

ALL TEXT UNLESS OTHERWISE NOTED IS: Style (STANDARD)
Height (.09)
Left justified

Style (ROMANS)
Height (.12)
Fit

Style (ROMANT)
Height (.25)
Fit

Style (GOTHICE)
Height (.38)
Left justified

Style (MONO)
Height .25
Left justified

TITLE BLOCK

Drawing 7-1

LAYERS	NAME	COLOR	LINETYPE			
	0	WHITE	CONTINUOUS	(DRAW)	LINE	(L)
	1	RED	CONTINUOUS	(DRAW)	TEXT	
				(EDIT)	CHANGE	
	TEXT	CYAN	CONTINUOUS	(DISPLAY)	PAN	(P)
				(DISPLAY)	ZOOM	(Z)

F1	F6	F7	F8	F9
ON/OFF	ABSOLUTE/OFF/POLAR	ON/OFF	ON/OFF	ON/OFF
SCREEN	COORDS	GRID	ORTHO	SNAP

DRAWING 7-2: GAUGES

This drawing will teach you some typical uses of the SCALE and CHANGE commands. Some of the techniques used will not be obvious, so read the suggestions carefully.

DRAWING SUGGESTIONS

GRID = .5

SNAP = .125

> Draw three concentric circles at diameters of 5.0, 4.5, and 3.0. The bottom of the 3.0 circle can be trimmed later.

> Zoom in to draw the arrow-shaped tick at the top of the 3.0 circle. Then draw the .50 vertical line directly below it and the number "0" (middle-justified text) above it.

> These three objects can be arrayed to the left and right around the perimeter of the 3.0 circle using angles of +135 and −135 as shown.

> Use the CHANGE command to change the arrayed zeros into 10, 20, 30, etc.

> Draw the .25 vertical tick directly on top of the .50 mark at top center and array it left and right. There will be 20 marks each way.

> Draw the needle horizontally across the middle of the dial.

> Make two copies of the dial; use SCALE to scale them down as shown. Then move them into their correct positions.

> Rotate all three needles as shown.

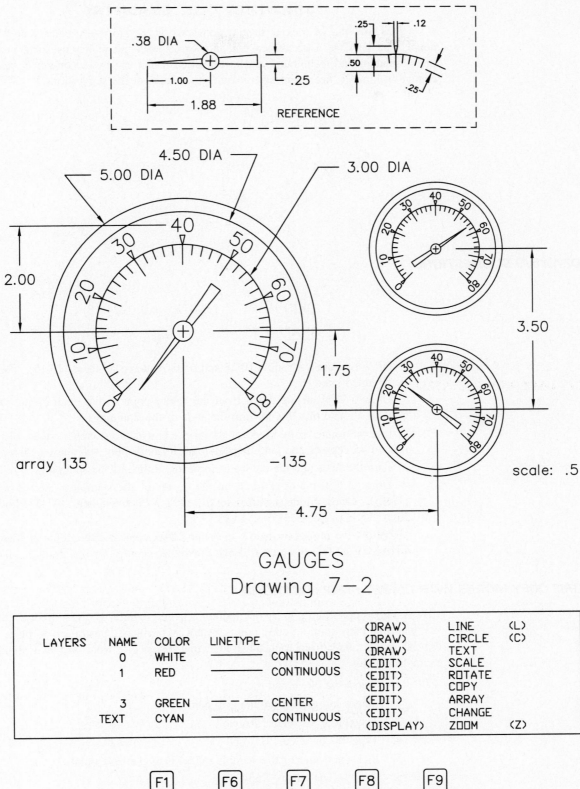

.38 DIA

1.00

1.88

.25

.25 .12

.50

.25

REFERENCE

5.00 DIA

4.50 DIA

3.00 DIA

2.00

40

50

30

20

60

10

70

0

80

array 135

-135

1.75

3.50

scale: .5

4.75

GAUGES
Drawing 7-2

LAYERS	NAME	COLOR	LINETYPE		(DRAW)	LINE	(L)
					(DRAW)	CIRCLE	(C)
	0	WHITE	————	CONTINUOUS	(DRAW)	TEXT	
	1	RED	————	CONTINUOUS	(EDIT)	SCALE	
					(EDIT)	ROTATE	
					(EDIT)	COPY	
	3	GREEN	– – – –	CENTER	(EDIT)	ARRAY	
	TEXT	CYAN	————	CONTINUOUS	(EDIT)	CHANGE	
					(DISPLAY)	ZOOM	(Z)

F1	F6	F7	F8	F9
ON/OFF	ABSOLUTE/OFF/POLAR	ON/OFF	ON/OFF	ON/OFF
SCREEN	COORDS	GRID	ORTHO	SNAP

DRAWING 7–3: STAMPING

This drawing is trickier than it appears. There are many ways that it can be done. The way we have chosen not only works well but makes use of a number of the commands and techniques you have learned in the last two chapters. Notice that a change in limits is needed to take advantage of some of the suggestions.

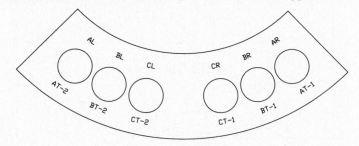

DRAWING SUGGESTIONS

$$\text{GRID} = .50 \qquad \text{LIMITS} = (0,0)(24,18)$$
$$\text{SNAP} = .25$$

> Draw two circles, radius 10.25 and 6.50, centered at about (13,15). These will be trimmed later.

> Draw a vertical line down from the center point to the outer circle. We will copy and rotate this line to form the ends of the stamping.

> Use the rotate, copy mode of the grip edit system to create copies of the line rotated 45 degrees and −45 degrees (coordinate display will show 315 degrees).

> Trim the lines and the circles to form the outline of the stamping.

> Draw a 1.50 diameter circle in the center of the stamping, 8.50 down from (13,15). Draw middle-justified text, "AR", 7.25 down, and "AT-1" down 9.75 from (13,15).

> Follow the procedure below to create offset copies of the circle and text, then CHANGE all text to agree with the drawing.

GRIP COPY MODES WITH OFFSET SNAP LOCATIONS

Here is a good opportunity to try out another grip edit feature. If you hold down the shift key while picking multiple copy points, AutoCAD will be constrained to place copies only at points offset from each other the same distance as your first two points. For example, try this:

1. Select the circle and the text.
2. Select any grip to initiate grip editing.
3. Type "RO" or select "Rotate".
4. Type "b" or select "Base pt".
5. Pick the center of the stamping (13,15) as the base point.
6. Type "c" or select "Copy".
7. Hold down shift and move the cursor to rotate a copy 11 degrees from the original.
8. *Keep holding down the shift key* as you move the cursor to create other copies. All copies will be offset 11 degrees.

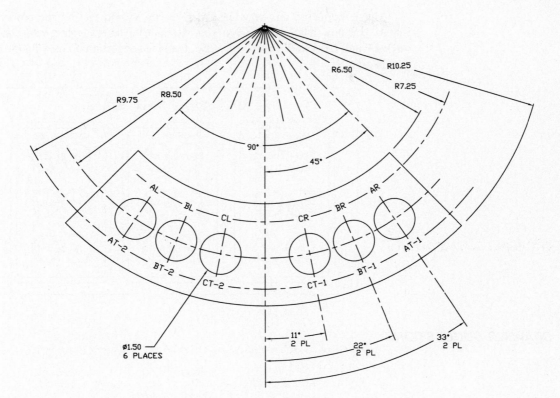

STAMPING
Drawing 7–3

LAYERS	NAME	COLOR	LINETYPE		
	0	WHITE	———— CONTINUOUS		
	1	RED	———— CONTINUOUS		
	3	GREEN	– – – CENTER		
	TEXT	CYAN	———— CONTINUOUS		

(DRAW)	LINE	(L)
(DRAW)	CIRCLE	(C)
(DRAW)	TEXT	
(EDIT)	COPY	
(EDIT)	TRIM	
(EDIT)	ROTATE	
(EDIT)	BREAK	
(EDIT)	CHANGE	
(DISPLAY)	ZOOM	(Z)

F1 — ON/OFF SCREEN
F6 — ABSOLUTE/OFF/POLAR COORDS
F7 — ON/OFF GRID
F8 — ON/OFF ORTHO
F9 — ON/OFF SNAP

DRAWING 7-4: CONTROL PANEL

Done correctly, this drawing will give you a good feel for the power of the commands you now have available to you. Be sure to take advantage of combinations of ARRAY and CHANGE described. Also, read the suggestion on moving the origin before you begin.

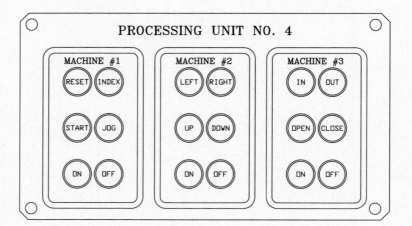

DRAWING SUGGESTIONS

GRID = .50

SNAP = .0625

> After drawing the outer rectangles, draw the double outline of the left button box, and fillet the corners. Notice the different fillet radii.

> Draw the "on" button with its text at the bottom left of the box. Then array it 2 × 3 for the other buttons in the box.

> CHANGE the lower right button text to "off" and draw the MACHINE # text at the top of the box.

> ARRAY the box 1 × 3 to create the other boxes.

> CHANGE text for buttons and machine numbers as shown.

> Complete the drawing.

MOVING THE ORIGIN WITH THE UCS COMMAND

The dimensions of this drawing are shown in ordinate form, measured from a single point of origin in the lower left-hand corner. In effect this establishes a new coordinate origin. If we move our origin to match this point, then we will be able to read dimension values directly from the coordinate display. This may be done by setting the lower left-hand limits to (-1,-1). But it also may be done using the UCS command to establish a User Coordinate System with the origin at a point you specify. User Coordinate Systems are discussed in depth in Chapter 12. For now, here is a simple procedure:

> Type "ucs".

> Type "o" for the "Origin" option.

> Point to the new origin.

That's all there is to it. Move your cursor to the new origin and watch the coordinate display. It should show "0.00,0.00", and all values will be measured from there.

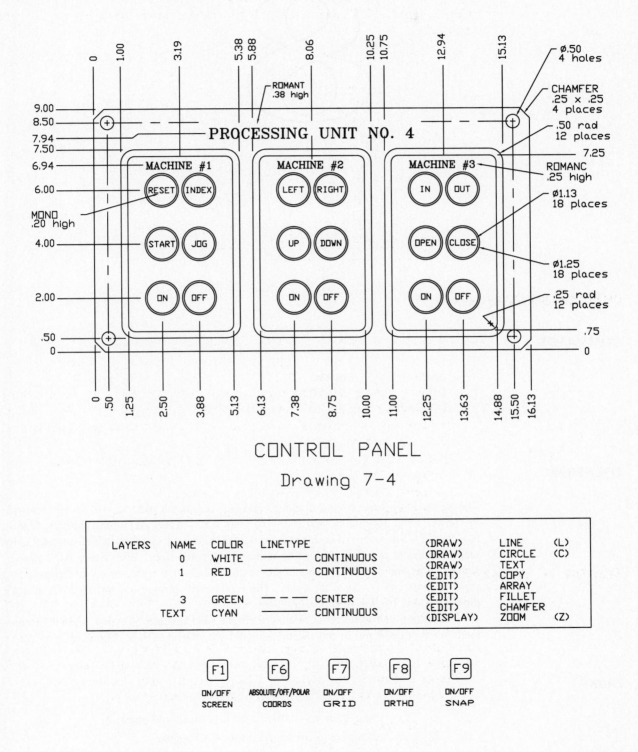

PROCESSING UNIT NO. 4

MACHINE #1 MACHINE #2 MACHINE #3

RESET INDEX   LEFT RIGHT   IN OUT

START JOG   UP DOWN   OPEN CLOSE

ON OFF   ON OFF   ON OFF

ROMANT
.38 high

Ø.50
4 holes

CHAMFER
.25 x .25
4 places

.50 rad
12 places

7.25

ROMANC
.25 high

Ø1.13
18 places

Ø1.25
18 places

.25 rad
12 places

.75

MONO
.20 high

CONTROL PANEL
Drawing 7–4

LAYERS	NAME	COLOR	LINETYPE				
	0	WHITE	——— CONTINUOUS		(DRAW)	LINE	(L)
	1	RED	——— CONTINUOUS		(DRAW)	CIRCLE	(C)
					(DRAW)	TEXT	
					(EDIT)	COPY	
					(EDIT)	ARRAY	
	3	GREEN	– – – CENTER		(EDIT)	FILLET	
	TEXT	CYAN	——— CONTINUOUS		(EDIT)	CHAMFER	
					(DISPLAY)	ZOOM	(Z)

F1 F6 F7 F8 F9

ON/OFF   ABSOLUTE/OFF/POLAR   ON/OFF   ON/OFF   ON/OFF
SCREEN   COORDS   GRID   ORTHO   SNAP

CHAPTER

DIM:	DRAW
DIM	BHATCH
DIM1	BPOLY
	HATCH

OVERVIEW

The ability to dimension your drawings and add crosshatch patterns will greatly enhance the professional appearance and utility of your work. AutoCAD's dimensioning feature is a complex subsystem of commands, subcommands, and variables which automatically measure objects and draw dimension text and extension lines. With AutoCAD's dimensioning tools and variables, you can create dimensions in a wide variety of formats, and these formats can be saved as styles. The time saved through not having to draw each dimension line by line is very significant.

Hatching in AutoCAD is relatively simple, and Release 12's new BHATCH command overcomes many of the shortcomings of the older HATCH command.

TASKS

1. Draw linear dimensions (horizontal, vertical, and aligned).
2. Draw baseline and continued linear dimensions.
3. Draw angular dimensions.
4. Draw center marks and diameter and radius dimensions.
5. Draw leaders to dimension objects.
6. Draw ordinate dimensions.

7. Change dimension variable settings and save dimension styles.
8. Add cross-hatching to previously drawn objects.
9. Do Drawing 8-1 ("Tool Block").
10. Do Drawing 8-2 ("Flanged Wheel").
11. Do Drawing 8-3 ("Shower Head").
12. Do Drawing 8-4 ("Nose Adaptor").
13. Do Drawing 8-5 ("Plot Plan").
14. Do Drawing 8-6 ("Panel").

TASK 1: Drawing Linear Dimensions

Procedure.

1. Type or select "DIM" or "DIM1".
2. Type or select an orientation (horizontal, vertical, etc.).
3. Select an object or show two extension line origins.
4. Type text or press enter to accept AutoCAD's measurement.

Discussion. The DIM command has more options than any other AutoCAD command. In addition to the options, there are numerous system variables that determine how dimensions will appear in your drawing. These exercises will not teach you everything there is to know about dimensioning in AutoCAD, but they will get you off to a good start.

The DIM command is really a complex subsystem of commands. It differs from most other commands in that you stay within it until you cancel. This is built into the command so that it will repeat until you decide to exit. This is a convenience, because you will be doing most of your dimensioning at one time. Typically you will finish the objects in a drawing and then go on to dimension them. This holds true if you execute DIM from either the "command" prompt or the screen menu. In Release 12, however, the pull down menu executes DIM1 instead of DIM. DIM1 is exactly like DIM except that it does not repeat. That said, we will use DIM throughout this discussion.

> To prepare for this exercise, draw a triangle (ours is 3.00, 4.00, 5.00) and a line (6.00) above the middle of the display, as shown in *Figure 8-1*. Exact sizes and locations are not critical.

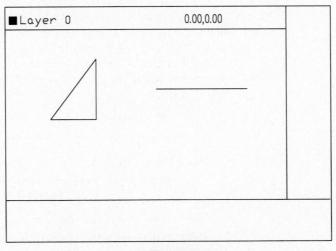

Figure 8-1

We will begin by adding dimensions to the triangle.

> Type "dim" or select "DIM".

AutoCAD simply acknowledges that you are now in the DIM command system and waits for your choice of an option.

Dim:

The options available for linear dimensions are horizontal, vertical, aligned, rotated, baseline, and continue. We will use the first three to dimension the three sides of the triangle, beginning with the base.

> Type "hor" or select "Horizontal".

You will be prompted to show what you want to dimension and where you want the dimension to go:

First extension line origin or RETURN to select:

There are two ways to proceed at this point. One is to show where the extension lines should begin, and the other is to select the base of the triangle itself and let AutoCAD position the extension lines. In most simple applications the latter is faster.

> Press enter (RETURN) to indicate that you will select an object.

AutoCAD will replace the cross hairs with a pickbox and prompt for your selection:

Select line, arc, or circle:

> Select the horizontal line at the bottom of the triangle, as shown by point 1 in *Figure 8-2*.

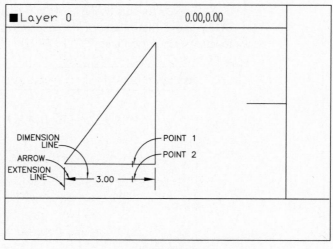

Figure 8-2

AutoCAD immediately creates a dimension, including extension lines, dimension line, and text, that you can drag out away from the selected line. AutoCAD will place the dimension line and text where you indicate, but will keep the text centered between the extension lines. The prompt is as follows:

Dimension line location (Text/Angle):

In the default sequence, you will show the location of the dimension, followed by the text. The other options allow you to specify the text first and to place the text at an angle other than 0 (horizontal text).

NOTE: If the dimension variable "dimsho" is set to 0 (off), you will not be given an image of the dimension to drag into place. The default setting is 1 (on), so this should not be a problem. If, however, it has been changed in your drawing, type "dimsho" and then "1" to turn it on again.

> Pick a location about .50 below the triangle, as shown by point 2 in *Figure 8-2*.

Notice that this figure and others in this chapter are shown zoomed in on the relevant object for the sake of clarity. You may zoom or not as you like.

Now AutoCAD shows you the dimension text from its own measurement and gives you the opportunity to change it if you like. In our drawing the line is 3.00 long, as you can see:

Dimension text <3.00>:

> Press enter to accept the dimension text.

Bravo! You have completed your first dimension.

At this point, take a good look at the dimension you have just drawn to see what it consists of.

As in *Figure 8-2*, you should see the following components: two extension lines, two "arrows," a dimension line on each side of the text, and the text itself.

Notice also that AutoCAD has automatically placed the extension line origins a short distance away from the triangle base (you may need to zoom in to see this). This distance is controlled by a dimension variable called "dimexo". It is one of many variables that control the look of AutoCAD dimensions. Another example of a dimension variable is "dimasz", which controls the size of the arrows at the end of the extension lines. Variables are discussed in Task 6.

> You should be at the "Dim:" prompt before continuing.

> Type "ver" or select "Vertical".

You will be prompted for extension line origins as before:

First extension line origin or RETURN to select:

This time we will show the extension line origins manually.

> Pick the right angle corner at the lower right of the triangle, point 1 in *Figure 8-3*. AutoCAD will prompt for a second point:

Second extension line origin:

Even though you are manually specifying extension line origins, it is not necessary to show the exact point where you want the line to start. AutoCAD will automatically set the dimension lines slightly away from the line as before.

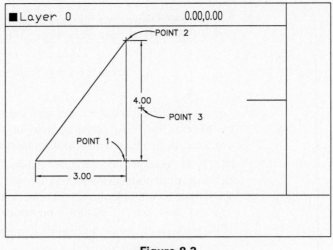

Figure 8-3

> Pick the top intersection of the triangle, point 2 in the figure.

From here on, the procedure will be the same as before. You should have a dimension to drag into place, and the following prompt:

Dimension line location (Text/Angle):

> Pick a point about .50 to the right of the triangle.

AutoCAD prompts:

Dimension text <4.00>:

> Press enter.

Your screen should now include the vertical dimension, as shown in *Figure 8-3*.

NOTE: You can use "U" within the DIM command just as in the LINE command. If you type "U" at the "Dim:" prompt, your last dimension will be undone. If you have drawn a series of dimensions without leaving DIM, you can "walk backward" through them, undoing them one by one. But be careful, there is no REDO within the DIM subsystem.

Now let's place a dimension on the diagonal side of the triangle. For this we will need the "align" option. You should be at the "Dim:" prompt before continuing.

> Type "ali" or select "Aligned".
> Press enter (RETURN), indicating that you will select an object.

AutoCAD will give you the pickbox and prompt you to select a line, arc, or circle.

> Select the hypotenuse of the triangle.
> Pick a point approximately .50 above and to the left of the line.
> Press enter to accept the dimension text.

Your screen should resemble *Figure 8-4*.

NOTE: The last option for an individual linear dimension is "rotated". Try it if you like. It works much like "aligned", except that you will be prompted for a rotation angle first and the dimension line will be oriented according to this angle. The

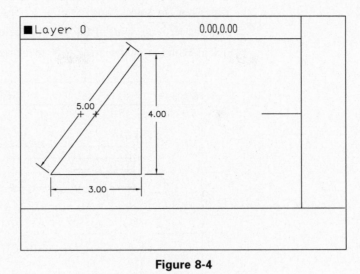

Figure 8-4

difficulty with "rotated" is that AutoCAD will measure the distance between its own extension lines instead of the length of the line you are dimensioning. Because of this we recommend that you use "aligned" unless your application requires a specific rotation that is different from the line itself. In these cases you may need to use a rotated dimension, but do not depend on AutoCAD's measurement.

TASK 2: Drawing Multiple Linear Dimensions—Baseline and Continued

Procedure.

1. Draw an initial linear dimension.
2. Type "bas" or "con" or select "Baseline" or "Continue".
3. Pick a second extension line origin.
4. Press enter or type text.

Discussion. "Baseline" and "continue" allow you to draw multiple linear dimensions more efficiently. In baseline format you will have a series of dimensions all measured from the same initial origin. In continue there will be a string of dimensions in which the second extension line for one dimension becomes the first extension for the next.

> To prepare for this exercise, be sure that you have a 6.00 horizontal line as shown in *Figure 8-1* at the beginning of Task 1. Although the figures in this exercise will show only the line, leave the triangle in your drawing, because we will come back to it in the next task.

In this exercise we will be placing a set of baseline dimensions on top of the line and a continued series on the bottom.

> To begin, you should be at the "Dim:" prompt. (If necessary, type or select "DIM".)
    In order to use either baseline or continue, you must have one linear dimension already drawn on the line you wish to dimension. So we will begin with this.

> Type "hor" or select "horizontal".

> Pick the left end point of the line for the origin of the first extension line.

> Pick a second extension origin 2.00 to the right of the first, as shown in *Figure 8-5*.

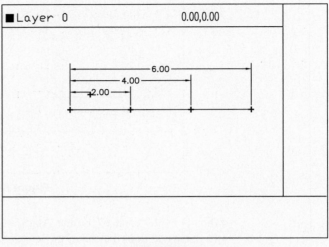

Figure 8-5

> Pick a point .50 above the line for dimension text.

> Press enter to accept AutoCAD's text.

    You should now have the initial 2.00 dimension shown in *Figure 8-5*. We will use baseline to add the other dimensions above it.

> At the "Dim:" prompt, type "bas" or select "baseline".

    AutoCAD uses the first extension line origin you picked again and prompts for a second:

        Second extension line origin or RETURN to select:

> Pick a point 4.00 to the right of the first extension line (in other words, 4.00 to the right of the original extension line at the left end of the 6.00 line).

    AutoCAD prompts for text and shows its own measure of the distance from the left end of the line to the point you selected. Ours looks like this:

        Dimension text <4.00>:

> Press enter to accept the dimension text.

    The second baseline dimension shown in *Figure 8-5* should be added to your drawing. We will add one more.

NOTE: Within the DIM command you can press enter or the space bar to repeat an option.

> Press enter to repeat the baseline option.

> Pick the right end point of the line.

> Press enter to accept AutoCAD's text.

    Your screen should resemble *Figure 8-5*.

Continued Dimensions

Now we will place three continued dimensions along the bottom of the line, as shown in *Figure 8-6*. You should need little help to do this at this point.

> Begin by placing an initial horizontal dimension .50 below the line, showing a length of 2.00 from the left end, as shown in *Figure 8-6*.

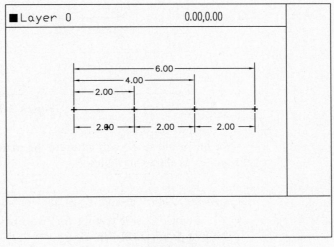

Figure 8-6

> Type "con" or select "continue".
> Pick a second extension line origin 2.00 to the right of the last extension line.

Be sure to pick this point on the 6.00 line, otherwise the extension line will be left hanging.
> Press enter to accept AutoCAD's dimension text.

You now should have a set of two continued dimensions below the line. We leave it to you to complete the exercise by drawing the third continued dimension shown in *Figure 8-6*.

TASK 3: Drawing Angular Dimensions

Procedure.

1. Type or select "DIM".
2. Type "ang" or select "angular".
3. Select two lines that form an angle.
4. Pick an arc location.
5. Type text or press enter.
6. Pick a text location or press enter.

Discussion. Angular dimensioning works much like linear dimensioning, except that you will be prompted for an arc location as well as a text location. AutoCAD will compute an angle based on the geometry that you select (two lines, an arc, part of a circle, or a vertex and two points) and construct extension lines, a dimension arc, and text specifying the angle.

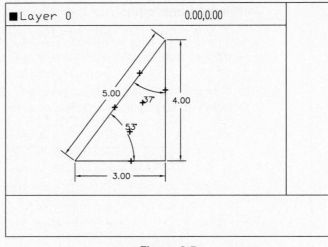

Figure 8-7

For this exercise we will return to the triangle and add angular dimensions to two of the angles as shown in *Figure 8-7*.

> At the "Dim:" prompt type "ang" or select "angular".

AutoCAD will prompt for two lines and will measure the angle between. The first prompt will be:

Select arc, circle, line, or RETURN:

The prompt shows that you can use angular dimensions to specify angles formed by arcs and portions of circles as well as angles formed by lines. If you press enter (RETURN) you can specify an angle manually by picking its vertex and a point on each side of the angle. We will begin by picking lines, the most common use of angular dimensions.

> Select the base of the triangle.

You will be prompted for another line:

Second line:

> Select the hypotenuse.

As in linear dimensioning, AutoCAD now shows you the dimension lines and lets you drag them into place (assuming dimsho is on). The prompt asks for an arc location and also allows you the option of changing the text or the text angle.

Dimension arc line location (Text/Angle):

> Pick a point between the two selected lines, as shown by the blip in *Figure 8-7*.

The dragged dimension will disappear temporarily, and AutoCAD will prompt you for text, giving its own measure of the angle as the default:

Dimension text <53>:

> Press enter to accept the given angle measure.

Now you will be prompted for a text location:

Enter text location (or RETURN):

This seems redundant, but if you move the cursor you will see that now the dimension arc stays in place and only the text itself moves. This will allow you to place the text anywhere, but most often you will want it to stay near the middle of the arc.

> Press enter to place the text in the middle of the arc.

The lower left angle of your triangle should now be dimensioned, as in *Figure 8-7*. Notice that the degree symbol is automatic in angular dimension text.

We will dimension the upper angle by showing its vertex, using the RETURN option. This time we will place the text outside the arc, as shown in *Figure 8-7*.

> At the "Dim:" prompt, type "ang" or select "angular" (or press enter to repeat the option).
> Press enter.

AutoCAD prompts for an angle vertex.

> Select the vertex of the angle at the top of the triangle.

AutoCAD prompts:

First angle endpoint:

> Pick any point along the hypotenuse.

AutoCAD prompts:

Second angle endpoint:

> Pick any point along the vertical side of the triangle.
> Move the cursor slowly up and down within the triangle.

Notice how AutoCAD places the arrows outside the angle when you approach the vertex and things get crowded.

> Pick a location for the dimension arc as shown in *Figure 8-7*.
> Press enter to accept the default text.
> Place the text just outside the arc, as shown in the figure.

Angular Dimensions on Arcs and Circles

You also can place angular dimensions on arcs and circles. In both cases AutoCAD will construct extension lines and a dimension arc. When you dimension an arc with an angular dimension, the center of the arc becomes the vertex of the dimension angle, and the end points of the arc become the start points of the extension lines. In a circle the same format is used, but the dimension line origins are determined by the point used to select the circle and a second point, which AutoCAD prompts you to select. These options are illustrated in *Figure 8-8*.

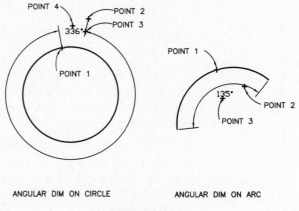

Figure 8-8

TASK 4: Dimensioning Arcs and Circles

Procedure.

1. Type or select "DIM".
2. Type "rad", "dia", or "cen", or select "radius", "diameter", or "center".
3. Pick the arc or circle at the point where you want the dimension line or leader to start.
4. Type text or press enter.
5. Pick a leader line end point location.

Discussion.   The basic process for dimensioning circles and arcs is simpler than those we have already covered. There are only three options, one for a diameter dimension, one for a radius, and one to draw a center mark. It can get tricky, however, when AutoCAD does not place the dimension where you want it. Text placement can be controlled by adjusting dimension variables and using the TEDIT subcommand.

> To prepare for this exercise, draw three circles across the bottom of your screen, as shown in *Figure 8-9*. The circles we have used have radii of 2.00, 1.50, and 1.00.

Although the remaining figures in this section will show the circles only, keep the triangle and the line in your drawing, because they will be used again in Task 6.

> Type or select "DIM".

Center marks resemble blips, but they are actual lines and will appear on a plotted drawing. They are the simplest of all dimension features to create and are created automatically as part of some radius and diameter dimensions.

> At the "Dim:" prompt, type "cen" or select "center".
AutoCAD prompts:

                        Select arc or circle:

> Select the middle circle.

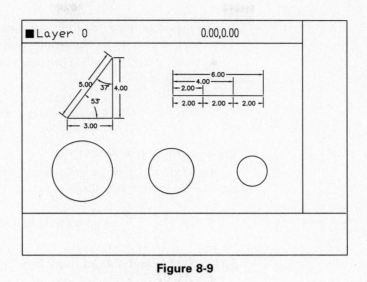

Figure 8-9

A center mark will be drawn, as shown in *Figure 8-10*. You may want to REDRAW your display to see the difference between blips and center marks.

NOTE: A different type of center mark can be produced by changing the dimension variable "dimcen" from .09 to −.09. The result is shown in the dimension variables chart, *Figure 8-20*, later in this chapter. You may recall that this technique was introduced previously in Drawing 4-4.

Now we will add the diameter dimension shown on the largest circle in *Figure 8-10*.

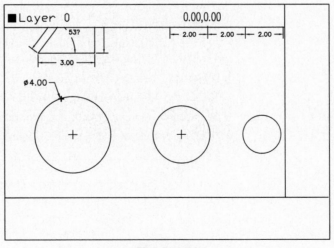

Figure 8-10

> At the "Dim:" prompt, type "dia" or select "diameter".

    AutoCAD will prompt:

                              Select arc or circle:

> Select the largest circle.

The important thing about this selection is that the point you choose will be taken as the end point of the dimension leader.

As usual, AutoCAD will show you its default text and give you the opportunity to change it:

Dimension text <4.00>:

> Press enter to accept the text.

AutoCAD will draw an angled leader line and a short extension with the text at the end and prompt as follows:

Enter leader length for text:

> Pick a point a short distance away from the circle as shown in *Figure 8-10*.

Notice that the diameter symbol is added automatically.

The placement of diameter dimensions is an important consideration. Diameter dimensions are often shown inside the circle, though this can be problematic if other dimensions, text, or objects are in the way. Release 12 offers substantial flexibility through the "dimtix" dimension variable and the TEDIT subcommand. Try this:

> At the "Dim:" prompt, type "dimtix".

AutoCAD responds:

Current value <Off> New value:

> Type "on" or "1".

You have changed the value of dimtix from off to on. Turning dimtix on forces AutoCAD to draw the dimension text inside the circle.

> Type "dia" or select "Diameter".

> Select the 4.00 diameter circle again.

> Press enter to accept the dimension text.

Your screen should resemble *Figure 8-11*.

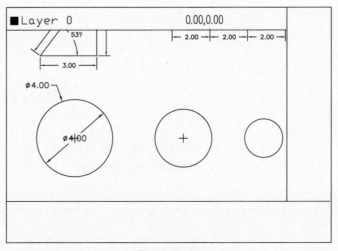

Figure 8-11

Moving Dimension Text with TEDIT

Now suppose you want to move the dimension text "4.00" away from the center of the circle, but keep it within the extension lines. This is easily done using the TEDIT command.

> At the "Dim:" prompt, type "tedit". (You can also reach TEDIT by selecting "Edit" from the DIM: screen menu, or from the pull down Modify menu under "Edit Dims").

AutoCAD will prompt you to select a dimension.

> Pick the diameter dimension just drawn. Dimensions are block entities and can be selected by picking any part of the block.

When you have picked the dimension you will see a rubber band stretching from the original text location to the current location of the cross hairs. AutoCAD will prompt:

Enter text location (Left/Right/Home/Angle):

The first two options will allow you to automatically move the text to the right or to the left along the diameter line. "Home" will bring text back to its default position, in this case the center of the circle. "Angle" will allow you to rotate the text.

You can also move the text by pointing, as we do here.

> Pick a point above and to the right of the center to produce the text placement shown in *Figure 8-12*. Ortho must be off to do this.

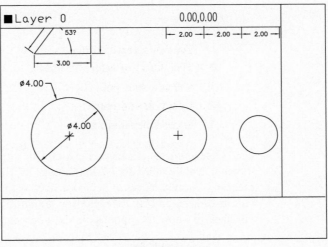

Figure 8-12

Before proceeding, turn dimtix off.

> At the "DIM:" prompt, type "dimtix".

> Type "0" or "off".

Radius Dimensions

The procedures for radius dimensioning are exactly the same as those for diameter dimensions.

> At the "Dim:" prompt, type "rad" or select "radius".

> Select the 1.50 (middle) circle.

> Press enter to accept the given text.

> Pick a point outside the circle, a short distance away, as shown in *Figure 8-13*.

The "R" for radius is added automatically.

NOTE: If dimtix is "on" the radius dimension will be placed inside the circle, halfway between the center and the point used to select the circle.

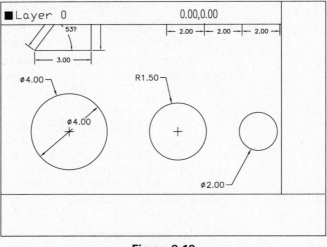

Figure 8-13

TASK 5: Dimensioning with Leaders

Procedure.

1. Type or select "DIM".
2. Type "lea" or select "leader".
3. Select a start point.
4. Select an end point.
5. Type dimension text.

Discussion. Leaders are useful in dimensioning objects in crowded areas of a drawing. Unlike other dimension formats in which you select an object or show a length, a leader is simply a line or series of lines with an arrow at the end to connect an object with its dimension text. Because you do not select an object when drawing a leader, you will need to know the dimension text you want to use *before* you begin. Let's try it.

> At the "Dim:" prompt type "lea" or select "leader".

AutoCAD will prompt you for a start point:

Leader start:

Usually you will want the leader arrow to start on the object, not offset like an extension line would be. This suggests that an object snap may be in order.

> Type "nea", or select "NEArest" from an OSNAP menu (under "Assist" on the AutoCAD pull down menu and under "* * * *" on the screen menu).

This specifies that you want to snap to the nearest point on the circle. You will see that the pickbox has been added to the cross hairs.

> Position the cross hairs so that the 1.00 radius circle crosses the aperture and press the pick button.

The leader will be snapped to the circle and a rubber band shown extending to the cross hairs. AutoCAD will prompt for a second point just as in the LINE command:

To point:

> Pick an end point for the leader, as shown in *Figure 8-13*.

AutoCAD will continue to prompt for points so that you can draw a broken leader. This is sometimes necessary in order to maneuver around other objects. More often, however, you will need only a single line.

> Press enter to end the leader at the second point.

AutoCAD will now give you the familiar text prompt:

Dimension text <1.50>:

Notice that the text is not taken from a measurement of the present circle. Instead it is "left over" from the last dimension you entered and is of no use at this point. You can get the AutoCAD measurement by first drawing a dummy dimension, then using a leader to create the actual dimension, and then erasing the dummy.

In our case we know the diameter, but we need to add the diameter symbol.

> Type "%%c2.00".

The leader and text are drawn, as in *Figure 8-13*.

TASK 6: Drawing Ordinate Dimensions

Procedure.

1. Define a coordinate system with origin at the corner of the object to be dimensioned.
2. Type or select "dim".
3. Type "ord" or select "Ordinate".
4. Select a location to be dimensioned.
5. Pick a leader end point.
6. Press enter or change dimension text.

Discussion. Ordinate, or datum line, dimensions are another way to specify linear dimensions. They are used to show multiple horizontal and vertical distances from a single point or the corner of an object. Since these fall readily into a coordinate system, it is efficient to show these dimensions as the x and y displacements from a single point of origin. AutoCAD will ordinarily specify points based on the point (0,0) on your screen, therefore it will be necessary to move the origin so that DIM will show the appropriate dimension text. Drawing 7-4 in the last chapter was dimensioned in this way.

> To prepare for this exercise, exit DIM and erase the baseline and continued dimensions created in Task 3. This is a good opportunity to apply the "remove" option in the ERASE command, as follows:

1. Enter the ERASE command.
2. Select all of the baseline and continued dimensions with a window or crossing box. This also will select the line.

3. Type "r" or select "Remove".

4. Select the line only.

5. Press enter to carry out the command.

The dimensions will be erased, but not the line, since it has been removed from the selection set.

> Now draw a 3.00 vertical line at the left end of the 6.00 horizontal line, as shown in *Figure 8-14*.

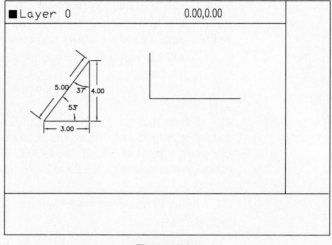

Figure 8-14

We will use ordinate dimensions to specify a series of horizontal and vertical distances from the intersection of the two lines. First, we need to define a temporary User Coordinate System with its origin at the intersection. User coordinate systems are extremely useful in 3D drawing and are explored in depth in Chapter 12.

> Type or select "UCS" (On the main screen menu or under "Settings" on the pull down menu).

> Type "o" or select "origin".

Specifying a new coordinate system by moving the point of origin is the simplest of many options in the UCS command. AutoCAD prompts:

Origin point <0,0,0>:

> Pick the intersection of the two lines.

If you move your cursor to the intersection and watch the coordinate display, you will see that this point is now read as (0.00,0.00).

> Type or select "Dim".

> Type "or" or select "Ordinate".

AutoCAD prompts:

Select Feature:

In actuality, all you will do is show AutoCAD a point and then an end point for a leader. Depending on where the end point is located relative to the first point, AutoCAD will show dimension text for either an x or a y displacement from the origin of the current coordinate system.

> Pick a point along the 6.00 line, one unit to the right of the intersection, as shown in *Figure 8-15*.

AutoCAD prompts:

Leader endpoint (Xdatum/Ydatum

You can manually indicate whether you want the x or y coordinate by typing "x" or "y". However, if you choose the end point correctly, AutoCAD will pick the right coordinate automatically.

> Pick an endpoint .5 below the line, as shown in *Figure 8-15*.

AutoCAD shows you its dimension text and gives you the opportunity to change it:

Dimension text <1.00>:

> Press enter to accept the text.

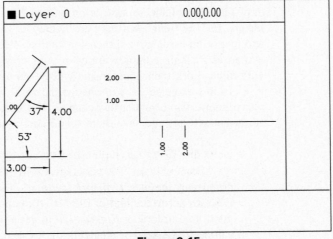

Figure 8-15

Your screen should now include the 1.00 ordinate dimension shown in the figure. To complete this exercise, repeat the ordinate option three times and add the other ordinate dimensions shown. When you are done, you should return to the "world" coordinate system. This is the default coordinate system and the one we have been using all along.

> Type "e" to exit the DIM command.

> Type or select "UCS".

> Press enter to return to the world coordinate system.

This will return the origin to its original position at the lower left of your screen.

TASK 7: Using Styles and Dimension Variables

Procedure.

1. Type or select "DIM".
2. Type a variable name.
3. Type a new value.
4. To save a dimension style, type or select "save" and then give a new name.

5. To restore a style, type or select "restore" and then give the name of a previously saved style.

Discussion. Setting dimension variables is easy, but the sheer number of them can be overwhelming. The chart included in this chapter (*Figure 8-20*) will show you some of the most commonly used variables. By studying it carefully you will gain a good sense of the possibilities. For more information, see the *AutoCAD Reference Manual*.

Because of the large range of possibilities available through changing dimension variables, AutoCAD also allows you to save sets of variable settings as styles, which can be restored whenever you wish.

In the following discussion and exercises we will create a style using the current settings, change a variable called "dimscale", and later restore the value to its current setting. Along the way we will demonstrate some other commands and features having to do with dimension variables and associative dimensions.

Associative Dimensioning

This exercise assumes that no one has changed the dimaso variable in your prototype drawing. By default, dimaso is on and all dimensions you draw are associative. This means, for one thing, that they are treated as single entities. All the lines, arrowheads, and text of an associative dimension can be selected for editing with one pick. They are treated as a single complex entity in your drawing database. If dimensions are drawn with dimaso off, their components will be stored and treated separately.

In this exercise we will change the value of dimscale and then UPDATE some of your dimensions to reflect this change. But before changing anything, let's take a look at current settings and save them so we can return to them easily.

> At the "Dim:" prompt, type "sta" or select "status".

You will see 42 variables listed with their current settings and a phrase describing the effect of each setting. You will have to press enter (RETURN) twice to get to the end of the list. As you glance over this list, it also would be a good time to look at *Figure 8-20* to get a sense of what a few dimension variables can do in the way of changing the look of dimensions.

> At the "Dim:" prompt, type "save".

AutoCAD prompts:

> ?/Name for a new dimension style:

> Type "standard" or any other suitable name.

Now the 42 settings just listed are saved under this dimension style name and can be recalled at any time.

Next, we will change the variable dimscale so that the size of dimension features will be doubled.

> At the "Dim:" prompt, type "dimscale". (From the DIM: screen menu you will have to first select "Dim Vars".)

AutoCAD will show you the current value of the variable so that you can either retain it or type a new value:

> Current value <1.0000> New value:

> Type "2".

You will be returned to the "Dim:" prompt.

Nothing has changed on your screen, but you would find that, if you drew new dimensions now, the size of the text and the arrows would be doubled. Instead of drawing new dimensions, we will use UPDATE to change some of your previously drawn dimensions according to the new scale.

UPDATEing Dimensions

The UPDATE subcommand can be used with previously drawn dimensions to reflect changes in dimension variables that have been made since the dimensions were drawn. Otherwise you would have to erase dimensions and recreate them with the new settings.

> Type "up" or select "Update". (From the DIM: screen menu first select "Edit".)

You are prompted to select objects.

> Select the triangle and all of its dimensions using a window or crossing.

> Press enter to end selection.

Your dimensions will be redrawn as shown in *Figure 8-16*. (If nothing has changed, check to be sure that the variable dimaso is on. If it is off, you will have to turn it on and draw some new dimensions to achieve the results shown in this exercise.)

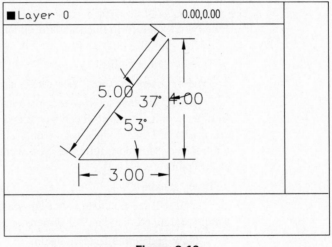

Figure 8-16

For contrast, and to demonstrate the power of associative dimensions, let's see what happens when you use SCALE to scale up the object itself along with its associated dimensions.

> Cancel or exit the DIM command.

> Enter the SCALE command.

> Select the triangle and all its dimensions using a window or crossing.

> Pick a base point near the center of the triangle.

> Type a scale factor of "1.25".

Your screen should resemble *Figure 8-17*.

As the triangle is scaled up, AutoCAD changes the associated dimension text to reflect the new measurements and repositions all of the dimension entities. This can cause problems, such as dimensions placed on top of each other or crossing objects. Usually you can solve such problems using TEDIT to move some of the dimension text.

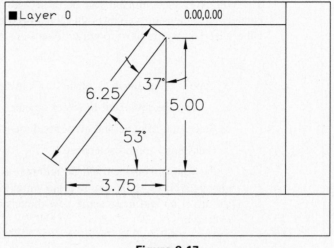

Figure 8-17

Finally, let's return to our standard dimension style and update the triangle again.

> Type or select "DIM".

> Type or select "restore". (Restore is under "Dim Styl" on the screen menu.)

AutoCAD first tells us that the current dimension style is "*UNNAMED". In other words, it has not been saved and will not be available to restore later. In our case that's okay, since we've only changed one variable. If you had changed a number of variables, however, you would want to consider creating a new style at this point.

> Type "standard".

You will see no change, but dimscale will be changed back to 1.00, as it was when we defined the standard dimension style.

Now update the triangle again.

> Type "up" or select "Update".

> Select the triangle and its dimensions, using a crossing or window.

Dimension text and arrows will be restored to their former size, as shown in *Figure 8-18*. Note that the changes in the scale of the triangle are still reflected in the dimension text.

Changing Dimension Text with NEWTEXT

Before leaving the DIM command, here is another useful DIM subcommand: NEW-TEXT.

> At the "Dim:" prompt, type "new" or select "Newtext" from the screen menu.

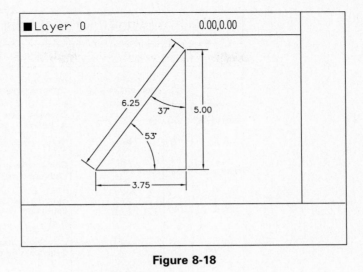

Figure 8-18

> Enter a new value, such as "5.0000" or "5.00 mm".

> Select the vertical text ("5.00") on the right of the triangle.

The text will be redrawn, as shown in *Figure 8-19*. This command is very convenient when all you want to do is change the text of a dimension.

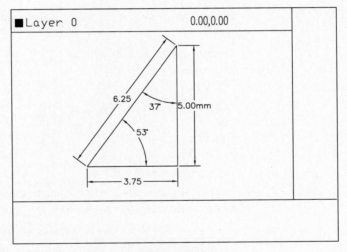

Figure 8-19

The DDIM Dialogue Box

Release 12 also includes a dialogue box for setting variables and defining dimension styles. The dialogue is opened by typing "DDIM" or selecting "Dimension Style..." under "Settings" on the pull down menu. In the DDIM dialogue box you will find seven subdialogues for specifying many aspects of the appearance of dimensions. These dialogue boxes are another way to change the settings of the 42 dimension variables.

You are now on your own with AutoCAD's dimensioning commands. Once again, we highly recommend that you take a good look at *Figure 8-20* before moving on to the BHATCH command.

COMMONLY USED DIMENSION VARIABLES

VARIABLE	DEFAULT VALUE	APPEARANCE	DESCRIPTION	NEW VALUE	APPEARANCE
dimaso	on	All parts of dim are one entity	Associative dimensioning	off	All parts of dim are separate entities
dimscale	1.00	⊢—2.00—⊣	Changes size of text & arrows, not value	2.00	⊢—2.00—⊣
dimasz	.18	▶	Sets arrow size	.38	▶
dimcen	.09	(+)	Center mark size and appearance	−.09	⊕
dimdli	.38		Spacing between continued dimension lines	.50	
dimexe	.18		Extension above dimension line	.25	
dimexo	0.06		Extension line origin offset	.12	
dimtp	0.00	1.50	Sets plus tolerance	.01	$1.50^{+0.01}_{-0.00}$
dimtm	0.00	1.50	Sets minus tolerance	.02	$1.50^{+0.00}_{-0.02}$
dimtol	off	1.50	Generate dimension tolerances (dimtp & dimtm must be set) (dimtol & dimlim cannot both be on)	on	$1.50^{+0.01}_{-0.02}$
dimlim	off	1.50	Generate dimension limits (dimtp & dimtm must be set) (dimtol & dimlim cannot both be on)	on	1.51 1.48
dimtad	off	⊢—1.50—⊣	Places text above the dimension line	on	⊢—1.50—⊣
dimtxt	.18	1.50	Sets height of text	.38	1.50
dimtsz	.18	⊢—1.50—⊣	Sets tick marks & tick height	.25	⊬—1.50—⊬
dimtih	on	1.50	Sets angle of text When off rotates text to the angle of the dimension	off	1.50
dimtix	off	∅0.71 (+)	Forces the text to inside of circles and arcs. Linear and angular dimensions are placed inside if there is sufficient room.	on	∅0.71

Figure 8-20

TASK 8: Using the BHATCH Command

Procedure.

1. Type or select "bhatch".
2. Select a pattern.
3. Define style parameters.
4. Define boundaries of object to be hatched.

Discussion. Automated hatching always has been an immense timesaver. However, the HATCH command is also one of the most cumbersome of the AutoCAD commands and is likely to perform in undesirable ways. Fortunately, Release 12 includes a new method of hatching, using the BHATCH command. BHATCH differs from HATCH in that it automatically defines the nearest boundary surrounding a point you have specified. The HATCH command requires you to manually specify each segment of the boundary. In other words, with BHATCH you can point to the area you want to hatch and AutoCAD will go looking for its boundaries, while with HATCH you select the boundaries and AutoCAD hatches what's inside.

> To prepare for this exercise, clear your screen of all previously drawn objects and then draw three rectangles, one inside the other, with the word "TEXT" at the center, as shown in *Figure 8-21*.

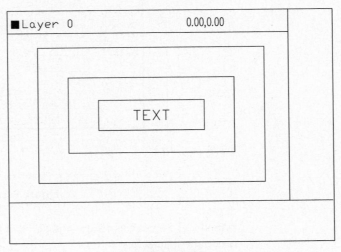

Figure 8-21

> Type "bhatch" or select "Bhatch..." from the screen menu under "Draw".

    Whether typed or entered from a menu, BHATCH always calls the Boundary Hatch dialogue box shown in *Figure 8-22*. At the top of the box you will see the phrase "No hatch pattern selected." Before we can hatch anything we need to specify a pattern, using the Hatch Options dialogue box.

> Click on "Hatch Options...".

    This brings up the second dialogue box shown in the figure. Look at the two options shown under "Pattern Type". The radio buttons allow us to choose from among Release 12's fifty-three stored hatch patterns, or to define a simple user-defined pattern of lines drawn at a specified angle. We will demonstrate both in this exercise, beginning with a user-defined pattern.

> Click on "User-Defined Pattern (U)".

    When you create a user pattern you will need to specify an angle and a spacing. There is also an option to create double hatching, with hatch lines running perpendicular to each other according to the specified angle.

> Double click in the Angle edit box, and then type "45".

> Double click in the Spacing edit box, and then type ".5".

> Click on "OK" to exit "Hatch Options".

    At the top of the Boundary Hatch dialogue box you will now see "U,N" as the current hatch pattern. "U" is the name given to user-defined patterns. "N" refers to the "normal" style of hatching. We will discuss hatching styles in a moment.

    Looking down the dialogue box, the next item is "Define Hatch Area", with the options "Pick Points" and "Select Objects". Using the first option, you can have AutoCAD locate a boundary when you point to the area inside it. The second

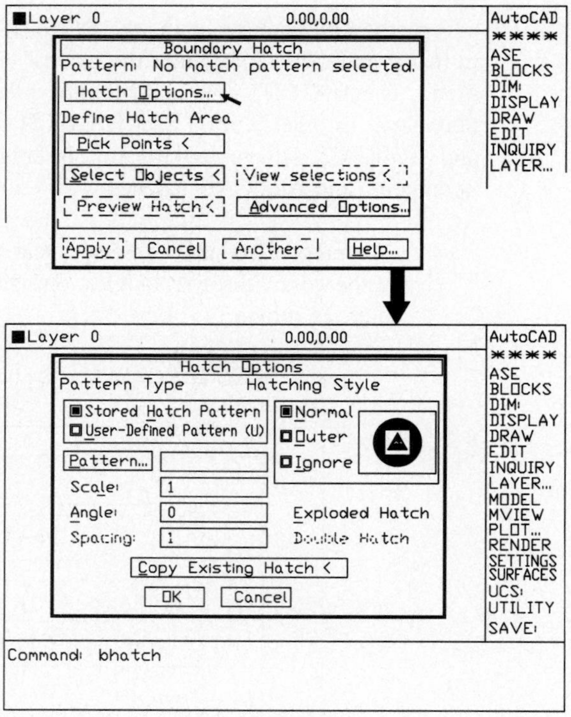

Figure 8-22

option can be used to create boundaries the old way, by selecting entities that lie along the boundaries.

> Click on "Pick Points <".

The dialogue box will disappear temporarily and you will be prompted as follows:

Select internal point.

> Pick any point inside the smallest, inner rectangle.

AutoCAD displays the message:

Analyzing the selected data . . .

In a large drawing this process can be time consuming, as the program searches all visible entities to locate the appropriate boundary. When the process is complete the inner rectangle will be highlighted. It will happen very quickly in this case.

AutoCAD continues to prompt for internal points so that you can define multiple boundaries, as we will do momentarily. For now, let's return to the dialogue box and see what we've done so far.

> Press enter to end internal point selection.

The dialogue box will reappear. You may not have noticed, but several of the options that were "grayed out" before are now accessible. We will make use of the "Preview Hatch" option. This allows us to preview what has been specified without leaving the command, so that we can continue to adjust the hatching until we are satisfied.

> Click on "Preview Hatch <".

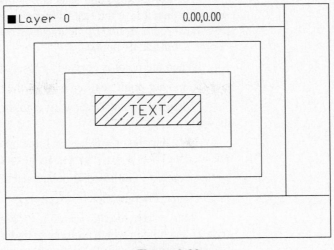

Figure 8-23

Your screen should resemble *Figure 8-23*, except that your hatching will run through the text. We can correct this flaw by using "Select Objects" to hatch around the text.

> Press enter (RETURN) to return to the dialogue box.

> Click on "Select Objects <".

> Select the word "TEXT".

> Press enter to return to the dialogue box.

> Click on "Preview Hatch <".

Your screen should now resemble *Figure 8-23*.

> Press enter to return to the dialogue box.

Next, we will pick two more points to define the boundaries of the outer rectangles.

> Click on "Pick Points <".

The inner square will be highlighted. This is the only boundary defined so far.

> Pick a point near any side of the second rectangle, as shown in *Figure 8-24*.

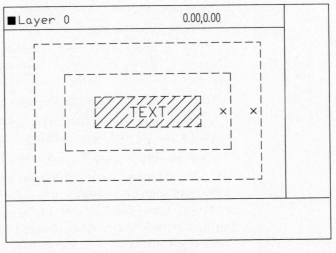

Figure 8-24

The key to this point selection is that the point must be closer to the second rectangle than it is to the first. Otherwise, AutoCAD will look at the inner rectangle and show you a Boundary definition error dialogue box with a message that says "Point is outside of boundary".

When the point is correctly chosen, the second rectangle will be highlighted.

> Pick another point near any side of the third rectangle, as shown in *Figure 8-24*.

When this point is correctly chosen, the third rectangle will be highlighted as well.

Now that AutoCAD has multiple boundaries to deal with, how will the hatching be done? Let's use preview again to see.

> Press enter to end internal point selection.

> Click on "Preview Hatch <".

Your screen should resemble *Figure 8-25*. This demonstrates the "normal" style of hatching in which multiple boundaries are hatched or left clear in alternating fashion, beginning with the outermost boundary and working inward. You can see the effect of the other styles by looking at the Hatch Options dialogue box.

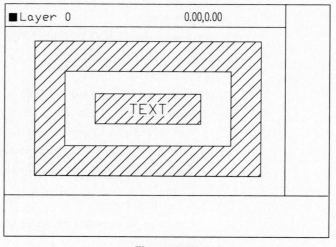

Figure 8-25

> Press enter to return to the Boundary Hatch dialogue box.

> Click on "Hatch Options...".

At the upper right under "Hatching Style" you will see the three options "Normal", "Outer", and "Ignore" with radio buttons. There is also an image box that shows an example of the current style, as shown previously in *Figure 8-22*.

> Click on "Outer" and watch the black image box.

It now shows the "Outer" style in which only the area between the outermost boundary and the first inner boundary is hatched.

> Click on "Ignore" and watch the image box.

In the "Ignore" style, all interior boundaries are ignored and the entire area including the text is hatched.

You can see the same effects in your own drawing, if you like, by clicking on "Preview Hatch" after changing from the "Normal" style to either of the other styles. Of course, the three styles are indistinguishable if you do not have boundaries within boundaries to hatch.

> When you are done experimenting, you should select "Normal" style hatching again.

Now let's take a look at some of the fancier stored hatch patterns that AutoCAD provides.

> Click on the Stored Hatch Pattern radio button at the top left of the Hatch Options dialogue box.

When you switch on this radio button, the "Pattern..." edit box becomes accessible and the name "U" is highlighted. If you know the name of the pattern you want, you can type it here. Or, you can access a dialogue box with icons showing examples of all fifty-three patterns.

> Click on "Pattern...".

You will see the Choose Hatch Pattern dialogue box shown in *Figure 8-26*. This menu of hatch patterns, shown in alphabetical order has five "pages" with twelve patterns on each of the first four pages and five on the last. Our illustration shows the third page. Move forward or backward through the pages by clicking on "Next" or "Previous".

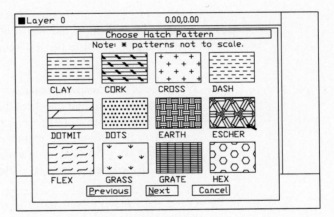

Figure 8-26

To produce the hatched image in *Figure 8-27*, choose the Escher pattern on the third page.

> Click on "Next" twice and then pick the Escher pattern.

The icons will disappear and "ESCHER" will be written in the edit box on the Hatch Options dialogue box. We have also used a larger scale in this hatching.

> Double click in the "Scale:" edit box and type "1.5".

> Click on "OK" to return to the Boundary Hatch dialogue box.

> Click on "Preview Hatch <".

Your screen should resemble *Figure 8-27*.

When you are through adjusting hatching, you have the choice of canceling the BHATCH command, so that no hatching is added to your drawing, or completing the process by clicking on "Apply". Apply will confirm the most recent choices of boundaries, patterns, and scales, making them part of your drawing.

> Click on "Apply" to exit BHATCH and confirm the hatching.

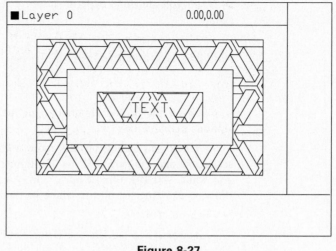

Figure 8-27

"Advanced Options" and the BPOLY Command

There are a number of worthwhile options and techniques that we have not explored in this exercise. Some of these options are available from the Advanced Options subdialogue box. For your information we offer the following notes:

1. When AutoCAD locates a boundary, it temporarily creates a polyline entity that completely outlines the boundaried area. A polyline (Chapter 9) is a single entity, which may be comprised of many straight and curved line segments. By default, the temporary polyline borders used by BHATCH are deleted after hatching is drawn. They may be retained for other uses, however, by checking the Retain Boundaries box in the Advanced Options dialogue box.

2. Using the BPOLY command, the same procedures that are used to create polyline hatch boundaries can be used to create polyline outlines independent of any hatching operation. BPOLY calls a dialogue box similar to the Advanced Options dialogue, but with no intervening steps through the BHATCH dialogues.

3. In very complex drawings it may be efficient to limit the number of entities AutoCAD needs to consider when looking for boundaries. This can be done by zooming in on the area to be hatched, or by defining a boundary set for AutoCAD to consider in its calculations. The boundary set does not need to be precise. By including all the entities in one portion of a drawing, for example, you would still substantially reduce the magnitude of AutoCAD's task. To specify a boundary set, click on "Make New Boundary Set" in the Advanced Options dialogue box.

4. "Ray casting" is the method AutoCAD uses to search out boundaries. The default option for ray casting is called "nearest." In this method AutoCAD begins by looking at the nearest entity that could be part of a border. Other options force the program to look in a specified direction relative to the coordinate system. You will see these options listed as +X, -X, +Y, and -Y on a pop up list under "Ray Casting:" in "Advanced Options". For most purposes the default method is all you will need. The other methods can speed up the boundary making process in tight, complex situations. See the *AutoCAD Reference Manual* for further information.

TASKS 9, 10, 11, 12, 13, and 14

DIM and BHATCH are two of AutoCAD's most powerful commands. They will do vast amounts of work for you and perform very well if used correctly. In general, you should complete other drawing procedures first and save hatching and dimensioning until the end. Dimensions and hatch patterns should also be allotted separate layers of their own so that they can be turned on and off at will.

Both dimensioning and hatching can be time consuming and require careful attention. But remember, in most applications your drawings will be of little use until the dimensions and appropriate hatching are clearly and correctly placed.

DRAWING 8–1: TOOL BLOCK

In this drawing the dimensions should work well without editing. The hatch is a simple user-defined pattern used to indicate that the front and right views are sectioned views.

DRAWING SUGGESTIONS

GRID = 1.0

SNAP = .125

HATCH line spacing = .125

> As a general rule, complete the drawing first, including all cross-hatching, then add dimensions and text at the end.

> Place all hatching on the hatch layer. When hatching is complete, set to the dim layer and turn the hatch layer off so that hatch lines will not interfere when you select lines for dimensioning.

> Zooming in on the area being hatched is advisable to see that the whole boundary is defined clearly. Remember that inner boundaries, such as the circle in the bottom view, must be defined as well as outer boundaries or BHATCH will hatch through them.

> The section lines in this drawing can be easily drawn as leaders in the DIM command. Set the "dimasz" variable to .38 first. Check to see that ortho is on, then begin the leader at the tip of the arrow, and make a right angle as shown. After picking the other end point of the leader, press the space bar to bring up the "Dimension text" prompt. Then press the space bar again so that you will have no text, and finally, press enter to complete the sequence.

> You will need to set the dimtix variable to "on" in order to place the 3.25 diameter dimension at the center of the circle in the top view, and "off" to create the leader style diameter dimension in the front section.

> Extra lines of text in a dimension must be drawn using the TEXT or DTEXT commands (stay on dim layer). Text height should match dimension text height (.18), and the style should be the same.

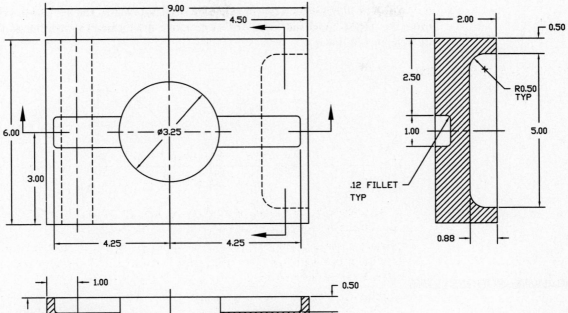

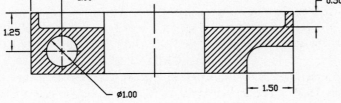

TOOL BLOCK
Drawing 8–1

LAYERS	NAME	COLOR	LINETYPE			
	0	WHITE	———— CONTINUOUS	(DRAW)	LINE	(L)
	1	RED	———— CONTINUOUS	(DRAW)	CIRCLE	(C)
	2	YELLOW	- - - - - HIDDEN	(DRAW)	HATCH	
	3	GREEN	— - — CENTER	(EDIT)	BREAK	
	TEXT	CYAN	———— CONTINUOUS	(EDIT)	FILLET	
	HATCH	BLUE	———— CONTINUOUS	(DISPLAY)	ZOOM	(Z)
	DIM	MAGENTA	———— CONTINUOUS			

F1	F6	F7	F8	F9
ON/OFF	ABSOLUTE/OFF/POLAR	ON/OFF	ON/OFF	ON/OFF
SCREEN	COORDS	GRID	ORTHO	SNAP

DRAWING 8-2: FLANGED WHEEL

Most of the objects in this drawing are straightforward. The keyway is easily done using the TRIM command. Use TEDIT to move the diameter dimension as shown in the reference following.

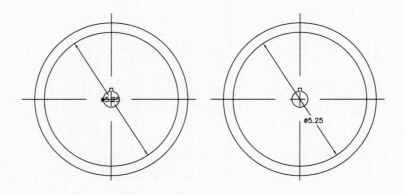

DRAWING SUGGESTIONS

$$GRID \ = .25$$

$$SNAP = .0625$$

$$HATCH \ line \ spacing \ = .50$$

> You will need a .0625 snap to draw the keyway. Draw a .125 x .125 square at the top of the .63 diameter circle. Drop the vertical lines down into the circle so they may be used to TRIM the circle. TRIM the circle and the vertical lines, using a window to select both as cutting edges.

> Remember to set to layer "hatch" before hatching, layer "text" before adding text, and layer "dim" before dimensioning.

MOVING DIAMETER DIMENSIONS

To create the diameter dimensions with text moved from the center as shown in the front view, follow this procedure (*Reference 8-2*):

    1.   Set dimtix to "on."

    2.   Draw the dimension, letting AutoCAD place the text in the center.

    2.   Type or select "tedit" (still in the DIM command).

    3.   MOVE the text to its final position as shown.

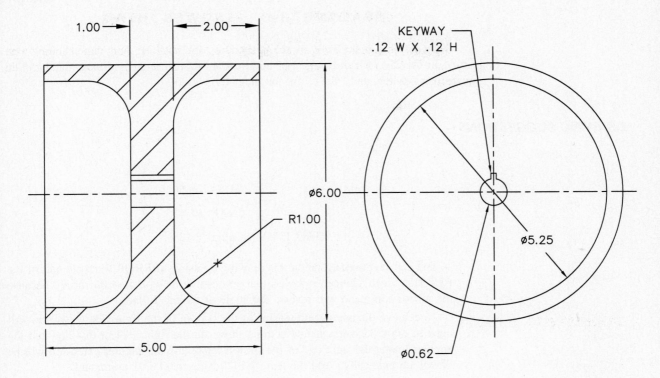

FLANGED WHEEL

Drawing 8–2

LAYERS	NAME	COLOR	LINETYPE				
	0	WHITE	——————— CONTINUOUS		(DRAW)	LINE	(L)
	1	RED	——————— CONTINUOUS		(DRAW)	CIRCLE	(C)
					(EDIT)	MOVE	(M)
					(EDIT)	BREAK	
	3	GREEN	— — — — CENTER		(EDIT)	HATCH	
	TEXT	CYAN	——————— CONTINUOUS		(EDIT)	FILLET	
	HATCH	BLUE	——————— CONTINUOUS		(EDIT)	EXPLODE	
	DIM	MAGENTA	——————— CONTINUOUS		(DISPLAY)	ZOOM	(Z)

F1	F6	F7	F8	F9
ON/OFF	ABSOLUTE/OFF/POLAR	ON/OFF	ON/OFF	ON/OFF
SCREEN	COORDS	GRID	ORTHO	SNAP

DRAWING 8–3:   SHOWER HEAD

This drawing makes use of the procedures for hatching and dimensioning you learned in the last two drawings. In addition, it uses an angular dimension, baseline dimensions, leaders, and "%%c" for the diameter symbol.

DRAWING SUGGESTIONS

GRID = .50

SNAP = .125

HATCH line spacing = .25

> You can save some time on this drawing by using MIRROR to create half of the right side view. Notice, however, that you cannot hatch before mirroring, because the mirror command will reverse the angle of the hatch lines.

> To achieve the angular dimension at the bottom of the right side view, you will need to draw the vertical line coming down on the right. Select this line and the angular line at the right end of the shower head, and the angular extension will be drawn automatically. Add the text "2 PL" using the TEXT command.

> Notice that the diameter symbols in the vertical dimensions at each end of the right side view are not automatic. Use %%c to add the diameter symbol to the text.

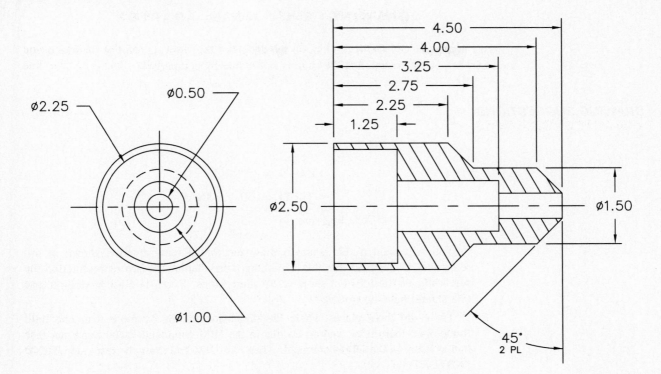

SHOWER HEAD

Drawing 8–3

LAYERS	NAME	COLOR	LINETYPE				
	0	WHITE	————— CONTINUOUS		(DRAW)	LINE	(L)
	1	RED	————— CONTINUOUS		(DRAW)	CIRCLE	(C)
	2	YELLOW	– – – – HIDDEN		(EDIT)	BREAK	
	3	GREEN	— – — CENTER		(EDIT)	MIRROR	
	TEXT	CYAN	————— CONTINUOUS		(EDIT)	HATCH	
	HATCH	BLUE	————— CONTINUOUS		(EDIT)	EXPLODE	
	DIM	MAGENTA	————— CONTINUOUS		(EDIT)	MOVE	(M)
					(DISPLAY)	ZOOM	(Z)

F1	F6	F7	F8	F9
ON/OFF	ABSOLUTE/OFF/POLAR	ON/OFF	ON/OFF	ON/OFF
SCREEN	COORDS	GRID	ORTHO	SNAP

DRAWING 8-4: NOSE ADAPTOR

Make ample use of ZOOM to work on the details of this drawing. Notice that the limits are set larger than usual, and the snap is rather fine by comparison.

DRAWING SUGGESTIONS

$$\text{LIMITS} = (0,0)\ (36,24)$$

$$\text{GRID} = .50 \qquad \text{SNAP} = .125$$

$$\text{HATCH line spacing} = .25$$

> You will need a .125 snap to draw the thread representation shown in the reference. Understand that this is nothing more than a standard representation for screw threads; it does not show actual dimensions. Zoom in close to draw it and you should have no trouble.

> There are three places where the dimension text is on more than one line. Remember, there is no way to do this in the DIM command itself. Draw the first line as usual in the DIM command. Then exit DIM and draw the rest using TEXT or DTEXT.

> This drawing includes two examples of "simplified drafting" practice. The thread representation is one, and the other is the way in which the counter bores are drawn in the front view. A precise rendering of these holes would show an ellipse, since the slant of the object dictates that they break through on an angle. However, to show these ellipses in the front view would make the drawing more confusing and less useful. Simplified representation is preferable in such cases.

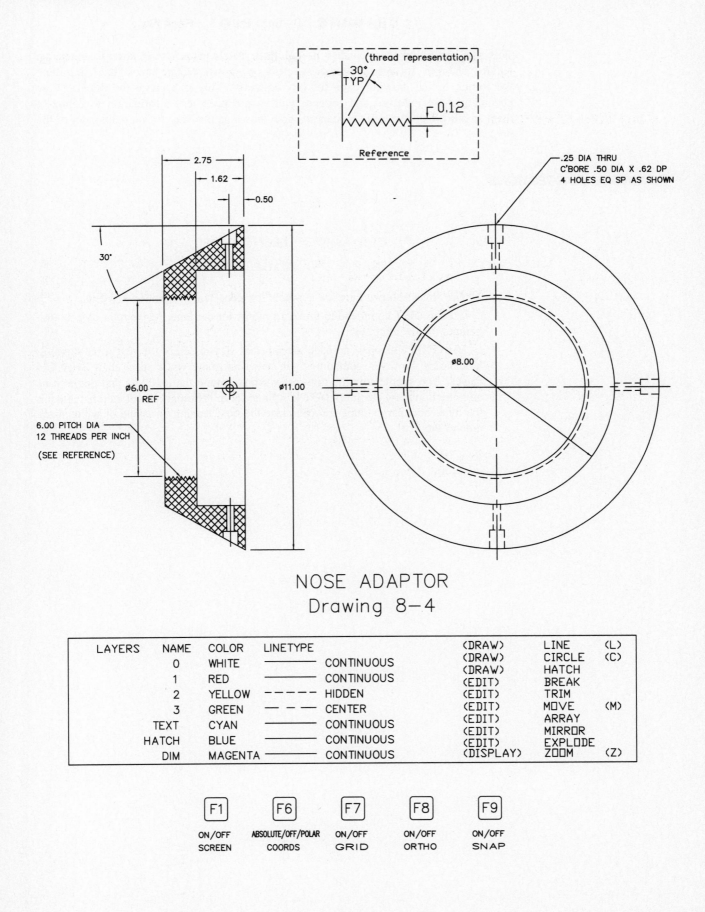

(thread representation)

30°
TYP

0.12

Reference

2.75

1.62

0.50

30°

Ø6.00
REF

Ø11.00

.25 DIA THRU
C'BORE .50 DIA X .62 DP
4 HOLES EQ SP AS SHOWN

Ø8.00

6.00 PITCH DIA
12 THREADS PER INCH

(SEE REFERENCE)

NOSE ADAPTOR
Drawing 8-4

LAYERS	NAME	COLOR	LINETYPE		(DRAW)	LINE	(L)
	0	WHITE	——————	CONTINUOUS	(DRAW)	CIRCLE	(C)
	1	RED	——————	CONTINUOUS	(DRAW)	HATCH	
	2	YELLOW	– – – –	HIDDEN	(EDIT)	BREAK	
	3	GREEN	— – — –	CENTER	(EDIT)	TRIM	
	TEXT	CYAN	——————	CONTINUOUS	(EDIT)	MOVE	(M)
	HATCH	BLUE	——————	CONTINUOUS	(EDIT)	ARRAY	
	DIM	MAGENTA	——————	CONTINUOUS	(EDIT)	MIRROR	
					(EDIT)	EXPLODE	
					(DISPLAY)	ZOOM	(Z)

F1
ON/OFF
SCREEN

F6
ABSOLUTE/OFF/POLAR
COORDS

F7
ON/OFF
GRID

F8
ON/OFF
ORTHO

F9
ON/OFF
SNAP

DRAWING 8-5: PLOT PLAN

This architectural drawing makes use of three hatch patterns and several dimension variable changes. Be sure to make these settings as shown. Notice that we have simplified the format of the drawing page for this drawing. This is because the drawings are becoming more involved and because you should need less information to complete them at this point. We will continue to show drawings this way for the remainder of the book.

DRAWING SUGGESTIONS

$$\text{GRID} = 10' \qquad \text{LIMITS} = 180', 120'$$

$$\text{SNAP} = 1' \qquad \text{LTSCALE} = 2'$$

> The "trees" shown here are symbols for oaks, willows, and evergreens.

> Use the DIST command to find start points for the inner rectangular objects (the garage, the dwelling, etc.).

> BHATCH will open a space around text if you select the text after defining boundaries; however, sometimes you will want more white space than BHATCH leaves. The simple solution is to draw a box around the text area and define it as an inner boundary. If the BHATCH style is set to "Normal" it will stop hatching at the inner boundary. Later you can erase the box, leaving an island of white space around the text.

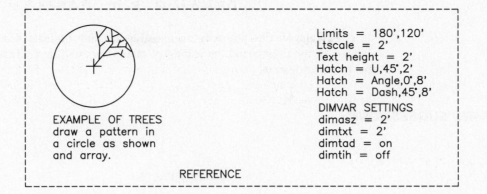

EXAMPLE OF TREES
draw a pattern in
a circle as shown
and array.

Limits = 180',120'
Ltscale = 2'
Text height = 2'
Hatch = U,45°,2'
Hatch = Angle,0°,8'
Hatch = Dash,45°,8'
DIMVAR SETTINGS
dimasz = 2'
dimtxt = 2'
dimtad = on
dimtih = off

REFERENCE

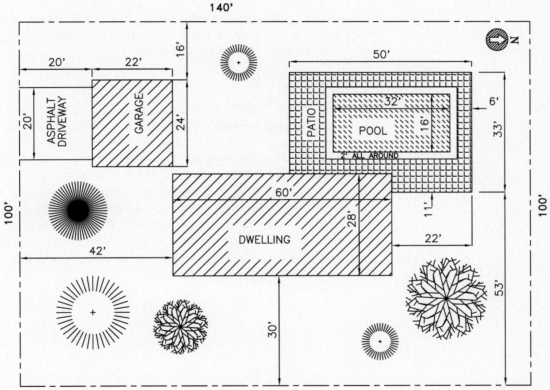

PLOT PLAN
Drawing 8–5

DRAWING 8-6: PANEL

This drawing is primarily an exercise in using ordinate dimensions. Both the drawing of the objects and the adding of dimensions will be facilitated dramatically by this powerful feature.

DRAWING SUGGESTIONS

GRID = .50

SNAP = .125

UNITS = 3-place decimal

> After setting grid, snap, and units, create a new user coordinate system with the origin moved in and up about 1 unit each way. This technique was introduced in Task 6. For reference, here is the procedure:

1. Type or select "UCS".
2. Type "o" for "Origin".
3. Pick a new origin point.

> From here on all of the objects in the drawing can be easily placed using the x and y displacements exactly as they are shown in the drawing.

> When objects have been placed switch to the dim layer and begin dimensioning using the ordinate dimension feature. You should be able to move along quickly, but be careful to keep dimensions on each side of the panel lined up. That is, the leader end points should end along the same vertical or horizontal line.

> Notice that several of the dimensions were drawn using a broken leader, rather than a simple ordinate dimension leader.

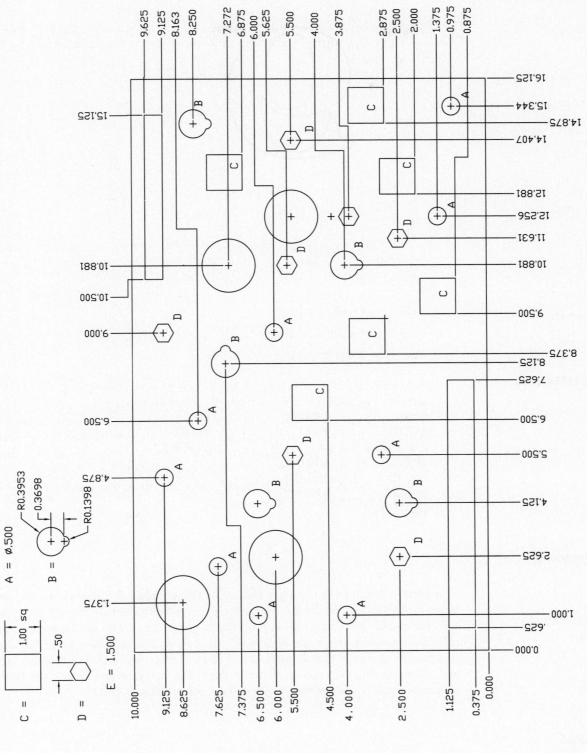

PANEL
DRAWING 8–6

CHAPTER

COMMANDS

DRAW	**DISPLAY**	**EDIT**
POINT	FILL	PEDIT
POLYGON		OFFSET
DONUT	**UTILITY**	
SOLID	VSLIDE	
PLINE	MSLIDE	
SKETCH		

OVERVIEW

This chapter should be fun. As you can see by the preceding list, you will be learning a large number of new commands. You will see new things happening on your screen with each command. The commands in this chapter are used to create special entities, some of which cannot be drawn any other way. All of them, like text, dimensions, and hatch patterns, are complex objects made up of lines, circles, and arcs, but they are stored and treated as singular entities. Some of them, like polygons and donuts, are familiar geometric figures, while others, like polylines, are peculiar to CAD.

TASKS

1. Draw POLYGONs.
2. Draw DONUTs.
3. Use the FILL command.
4. Draw straight polyline segments.
5. Draw polyline arc segments.

6. Edit polylines with PEDIT.
7. Use the OFFSET command to create parallel objects.
8. Draw SOLIDs.
9. Make and view slides.
10. Draw POINTs in various styles (optional).
11. Draw freehand lines using SKETCH (optional).
12. Do Drawing 9-1 ("Backgammon Board").
13. Do Drawing 9-2 ("Dart Board").
14. Do Drawing 9-3 ("Printed Circuit Board").
15. Do Drawing 9-4 ("Carbide Tip Saw Blade").
16. Do Drawing 9-5 ("Gazebo").

TASK 1: Drawing POLYGONS

Procedure.

1. Type or select "POLYGON".
2. Type number of sides.
3. Pick center point.
4. Indicate "Inscribed" or "Circumscribed".
5. Show radius of circle.

Discussion. Among the most interesting and flexible of the entities you can create in AutoCAD is the polyline. In this chapter we will begin with two regularly shaped polyline entities, polygons and donuts. These entities have their own special commands, separate from the general PLINE command (Tasks 4 and 5), but are created as polylines and can be edited just as any other polyline would be.

Polygons with any number of sides can be drawn using the POLYGON command. In the default sequence, AutoCAD will construct a polygon based on the number of sides, the center point, and a radius. Optionally, the "edge" method allows you to specify the number of sides and the length and position of one side (see *Figure 9-1*).

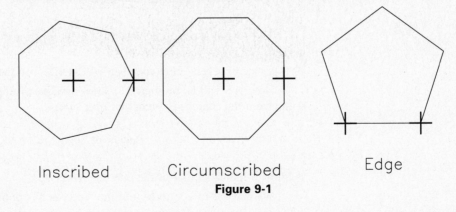

Inscribed   Circumscribed   Edge

Figure 9-1

> Type or select "polygon" (under "Draw" on the pull down and screen menus, but we suggest you do not use the pull down yet).

AutoCAD's first prompt will be for the number of sides:

Number of sides <4>:

> Type "8".

Now you are prompted to show either a center point or the first point of one edge:

Edge/<Center of polygon>:

> Pick a center point as shown by the blip on the left in *Figure 9-2*.

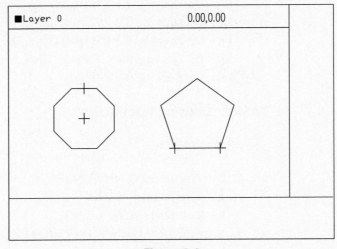

■Layer 0   0.00,0.00

Figure 9-2

From here the size of the polygon can be specified in one of two ways, as shown in *Figure 9-1*. The radius of a circle will be given and the polygon drawn either inside or outside the imaginary circle. Notice that in the case of the "inscribed" polygon, the radius is measured from the center to a vertex, while in the "circumscribed" polygon it is measured from the center to the midpoint of a side. You can tell AutoCAD which you want by typing "i" or "c" or selecting from the screen.

Inscribed in circle/Circumscribed about circle (I/C) <I>:

The default is currently "inscribed". We will use the "circumscribed" method instead.

> Type "c" or select "circumscribed" ("C-scribe" on the screen menu).

Now you will be prompted to show a radius of this imaginary circle (that is, a line from the center to a midpoint of a side).

Radius of circle:

> Show a radius similar to the one in *Figure 9-2*.

We leave it to you to try out the "inscribed" option.

We will draw one more polygon, using the "edge" method.

> Press enter to repeat the POLYGON command.

> Type "5" for the number of sides.

> Type "e" or select "Edge".

AutoCAD will issue a different series of prompts:

First endpoint of edge:

> Pick a point as shown on the right in *Figure 9-2*.

AutoCAD prompts:

Second endpoint of edge:

> Pick a second point as shown.

Your screen should resemble *Figure 9-2*.

The options on the pull down menu are exactly the same, but you must choose either "Edge", "Inscribed", or "Circumscribed" when you initiate the POLYGON command. Now that you know what all the options do, this slight difference will cause no difficulty.

TASK 2: Drawing "DONUTs"

Procedure.

1. Type or select "donut".
2. Type or show an inside diameter.
3. Type or show an outside diameter.
4. Pick a center point.
5. Pick another center point.
6. Press enter to exit the command.

Discussion.   The DONUT command is logical and easy to use. You show inside and outside diameters and then draw as many donut-shaped objects of the specified size as you like.

> Clear your display of polygons before continuing.

> Type or select "donut".

AutoCAD prompts:

Inside diameter <0.50>:

We will change the inside diameter to 1.00.

> Type "1".

AutoCAD prompts:

Outside diameter <1.00>:

We will change the outside diameter to 2.00.

> Type "2".

AutoCAD prompts:

Center of doughnut:

> Pick any point.

A donut will be drawn around the point you chose, as shown by the "fat" donuts in *Figure 9-3*. (If your donut is not filled, see Task 3.)

AutoCAD stays in the DONUT command, allowing you to continue drawing donuts.

> Pick a second center point.

> Pick a third center point.

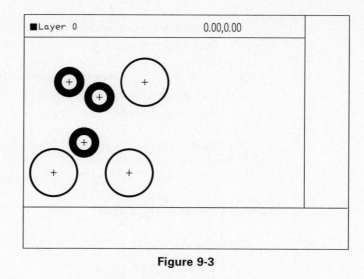

Figure 9-3

You should now have three donuts on your screen as shown.

> Press enter to exit the DONUT command.

Now reenter the donut command, change the inside diameter to 3.00 and the outer diameter to 3.25, and draw three "thin" donuts as shown in *Figure 9-3*. When you are done, leave the donuts on the screen so that you can see how they are affected by the FILL command.

TASK 3: Using the FILL Command

Procedure.

1. Type or select "FILL".
2. Type "on" or "off".
3. Type or select "regen".

Discussion. Donuts, polylines (Tasks 4 and 5), and solids (Task 8) are all affected by FILL. With FILL on, these entities are displayed and plotted as solid filled objects. With FILL off, only the outer boundaries are displayed (donuts are shown with radial lines between the inner and outer circles). Since filled objects are slower to regenerate than outlined ones, you may want to set FILL off as you are working on a drawing and turn it on when you are ready to print or plot.

> For this exercise you should have at least one donut on your screen from Task 2.

> Type "fill" or open the Drawing Aids (DDRMODES) dialogue box (under "Settings" on the pull down menu).

If you are typing, AutoCAD prompts:

ON/OFF <ON>:

If you are at the dialogue box, "Solid Fill" will be the second check box under "Modes" on the left.

> Type "off" or click in the Solid Fill check box, and then click on "OK" to exit the box.

You will not see any immediate change in your display when you do this. In order to see the effect, you will have to regenerate your drawing.

> Type or select "regen".

Your screen will be regenerated with FILL off and will resemble *Figure 9-4*. Many of the special entities that we will be discussing in the remainder of this chapter can be filled, so we encourage you to continue to experiment with FILL as you go along.

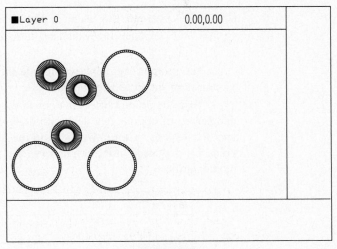

Figure 9-4

TASK 4: Drawing Straight "Polyline" Segments

Procedure.
1. Type or select "PLINE".
2. Pick a start point.
3. Type or select width, halfwidth, or other options.
4. Pick other points.

Discussion. In AutoCAD there are several ways in which collections of entities can be treated as one unit. In the last two chapters you saw how text, dimensions, and hatch patterns are all created as complex entities that can be selected and treated as single objects. In the next chapter you will see how to create blocks from groups of separate entities. Here you will see another kind of conglomerate entity, the polyline. You have already drawn several polylines without going through the PLINE command. Donuts and polygons both are drawn as polylines and therefore can be edited using the same edit commands that work on other polylines. You can, for instance, fillet all the corners of a polygon at once. Using the PLINE command itself, you can draw anything from a simple line to a series of lines and arcs with varying widths. Most important, polylines can be edited using many of the ordinary edit commands as well as a whole set of specialized editing procedures found in the PEDIT command.

We will begin by creating a simple polyline rectangle. The process will be much like drawing a rectangular outline with the LINE command, but the result will be a single object, rather than four distinct line segments.

> Type "pl" or select "Polyline" under "Draw" on the pull down, or "PLINE" under "Draw" on the screen menu. If you use the pull down menu, you will also need to select "2D".

AutoCAD begins with a prompt for a starting point:

> From point:

> Pick a start point, like P1 in *Figure 9-5*.

From here the PLINE prompt sequence becomes more complicated:

> Current line width is 0.00
> Arc/Close/Halfwidth/Length/Undo/Width/<Endpoint of line>:

The prompt begins by giving you the current line width, left from any previous use of the PLINE command.

Then the prompt offers options in the usual format. "Arc" will lead you into another set of options that deal with drawing polyline arcs. We will save polyline arcs for Task 5. "Close" works as in the LINE command to connect the last end point in a sequence to the original starting point. We will get to the other options momentarily.

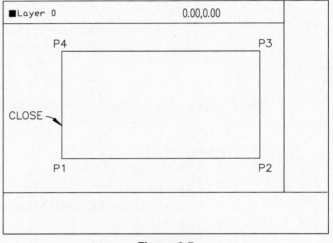

Figure 9-5

This time around we will draw a series of 0-width segments, just as we would in the LINE command.

> Pick an end point, like P2 in the figure.

AutoCAD will draw the segment and repeat the prompt.

> Pick another end point, like P3 in the figure.
> Pick another end point, like P4 in the figure.
> Type "c" or select "Close" to complete the rectangle, as shown in the figure.
> Now, select the rectangle by pointing to any of its sides.

You will see that the entire rectangle is selected, rather than just the side you point to. This means, for example, that you can FILLET or CHAMFER all four corners of the rectangle at once. Try it if you like, using the following procedure:

1. Type or select "Fillet".
2. Type "r" or select "Radius".
3. Specify a radius.
4. Repeat the FILLET command.

5. Type "p" or select "Polyline" to indicate that you want to fillet an entire polyline.

6. Select the rectangle.

NOTE: If a corner is left without a fillet, it is probably because you did not use the close option when you completed the rectangle.

Now let's create a rectangle with wider lines.

> Type "pl" or select the PLINE command.

> Pick a starting point as shown by P1 in *Figure 9-6*.

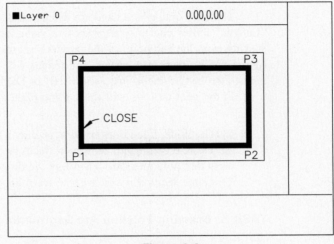

Figure 9-6

AutoCAD prompts:

Arc/Close/Halfwidth/Length/Undo/Width/<Endpoint of line>:

This time we need to make use of the "Width" option.

> Type "w" or select "width".

AutoCAD will respond with:

Starting width <0.00>:

You will be prompted for two widths, a starting width and an ending width. This makes it possible to draw tapered lines. For this exercise, our lines will have the same starting and ending width.

NOTE: The "halfwidth" option differs from "width" only in that the width of the line to be drawn is measured from the center out. With either option you can specify by showing rather than typing a value.

> Type ".25".

AutoCAD prompts:

Ending width <0.25>

Notice that the starting width has become the default for the ending width. To draw a polyline of uniform width, we accept this default.

> Press enter to keep starting width and ending width the same.

AutoCAD now returns to the previous prompt:

Arc/Close/Halfwidth/Length/Undo/Width/<Endpoint of line>:

> Pick an end point as shown by P2 in *Figure 9-6*.

> Continue picking points to draw a second rectangle as shown in the figure. Be sure to use the close option to draw the last side; otherwise the last two sides will overlap rather than join.

The only options we have not discussed in this exercise are "Length" and "Undo". "Length" allows you to type or show a value, and then draws a segment of that length starting from the end point of the previous segment and continuing in the same direction (if the last segment was an arc, the length will be drawn tangent to the arc). "Undo" undoes the last segment, just as in LINE or DIM.

In the next task we will draw some pline arc segments.

NOTE: Wide, filled lines of the type drawn in this exercise can also be drawn using the TRACE command. However, traces are less flexible and cannot be edited in the ways that polylines can. Therefore we do not recommend them. See the *AutoCAD Reference Manual* if you wish to learn about TRACE.

TASK 5: Drawing Polyline Arc Segments

Procedure.

1. Type or select "PLINE".
2. Pick a start point.
3. Specify a width.
4. Type "a" or select "arc".
5. Type or select options or pick an end point.

Discussion. A word of caution: Because of the flexibility and power of the PLINE command, it is tempting to think of polylines as always having weird shapes, tapered lines, and strange sequences of lines and arcs. Most books, including the *Auto-CAD Reference Manual*, perpetuate this by consistently giving peculiar examples to show the range of what is possible with polylines. This is useful but misleading. Remember, polylines are practical entities even for relatively simple applications like the rectangles drawn in Task 4.

Having said that, we will proceed to add our own bit of strangeness to the lore of the polyline. We will draw a polyline with three arc segments and one tapered straight line segment, as shown in *Figure 9-7*. We call this thing a "goosenecked funnel." You may have seen something like it at your local garage.

> Type or select "PLINE".

> Pick a new start point as shown by P1 in *Figure 9-7*.

> Type "w" or select "width" to set new widths.

> Type "0" for the starting width.

> Type ".50" for the ending width.

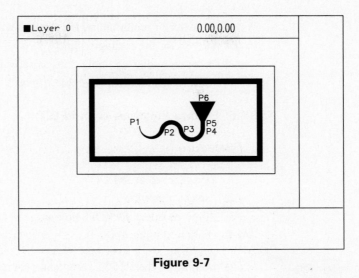

Figure 9-7

> Type "a" or select "arc". This will bring up the arc prompt, which looks like this:

Angle/CEnter/CLose/Direction/Halfwidth/Line/Radius/Second pt/Undo/Width/
<Endpoint of arc>:

Let's look at this prompt for a moment. To begin with there are four options that are familiar from the previous prompt. "CLose", "Halfwidth", "Undo", and "Width" all function exactly as they would in drawing straight polyline segments. The "Line" option returns you to the previous prompt so that you can continue drawing straight line segments after drawing arc segments.

The other options, "Angle", "CEnter", "Direction", "Radius", "Second pt", and "Endpoint of arc", allow you to specify arcs in ways similar to the ARC command. One difference is that AutoCAD assumes that the arc you want will be tangent to the last polyline segment entered. This is often not the case. The "center" and "direction"options let you override this assumption where necessary, or you can begin with a short line segment to establish direction before entering the arc prompt.

> Pick an end point to the right, as shown by P2 in the figure, to complete the first arc segment.

NOTE: If you did not follow the order shown in the figures and drew your previous rectangle clockwise, or if you have drawn other polylines in the meantime, you will find that the arc does not curve downward as shown in *Figure 9-7*. You can fix this by using the Direction option. Type "d" and then point straight down. Now you can pick an end point to the right as shown.

AutoCAD prompts again:

Angle/CEnter/CLose/Direction/Halfwidth/Line/Radius/Second pt/Undo/Width/
<Endpoint of arc>:

For the remaining two arc segments, retain a uniform width of .50.

> Enter points P3 and P4 to draw the remaining two arc segments as shown.

Now we will draw two straight line segments to complete the polyline.

> Type "L" or select "line" (this takes you back to the original prompt).

> Pick P5 straight up about 1.00 as shown.

> Type "w" or select "width".

> Press enter to retain .50 as the starting width.

> Type "3" for the ending width.

> Pick an end point up about 2.00 as shown.

Your screen should resemble *Figure 9-7*.

TASK 6: Editing Polylines with PEDIT

Procedure.

1. Type or select "PEDIT".
2. Select a polyline.
3. Type or select a PEDIT option.
4. Follow the prompts.

Discussion.   The PEDIT command provides a whole subsystem of special editing capabilities that work only on polylines. We will not attempt to have you use all of them; some you may never need. Most important is that you be aware of the possibilities so that when you find yourself in a situation calling for a PEDIT procedure you will know what is possible. After executing the following task, study *Figure 9-10*, the PEDIT chart. For further information see the *AutoCAD Reference Manual*.

We will perform two edits on the polylines already drawn.

> Type or select "PEDIT".

You will be prompted to select a polyline:

Select polyline:

> Select the outer 0-width polyline rectangle drawn in Task 4.

Notice that PEDIT works on only one object at a time and that selected polylines *do not* become dotted. You are prompted as follows:

Open/Join/Width/Edit vertex/Fit/Spline/Decurve/Ltype gen/Undo/eXit/ <X>:

"Open" will be replaced by "Close" if your polyline has not been closed. "Undo" and "eXit" are self-explanatory. Other options are illustrated in *Figure 9-10*. "Edit vertex" brings up the subset of options shown on the right side of the chart. When you do vertex editing, AutoCAD will mark one vertex at a time with an "x". You can move the x to other vertices by pressing enter, typing "n", or selecting "Next".

Now we will edit the selected polyline by changing its width.

> Type "w" or select "width".

This option allows you to set a new uniform width for an entire polyline. All tapering and variation is removed when this edit is performed.

AutoCAD prompts:

Enter new width for all segments:

> Type ".25".

Your screen will be redrawn to resemble *Figure 9-8*.

You should be at the "Close/Join/Width/Edit vertex . . ." prompt before continuing. The last polyline is still selected so that you can continue shaping it with other PEDIT options.

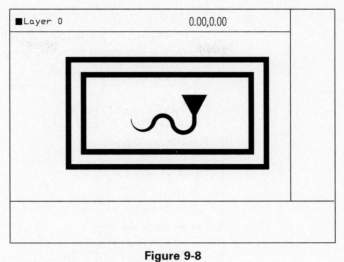

Figure 9-8

> Press enter to exit PEDIT.
> Press enter to repeat PEDIT.
> Select the "gooseneck funnel" polyline.

This time we'll try out the "Decurve" option. Decurve straightens all curves within the selected polyline.

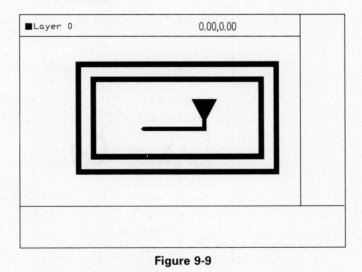

Figure 9-9

> Type "d" or select "Decurve".

Your screen will resemble *Figure 9-9*.

To complete this exercise, we suggest that you try out some of the other editing options. In particular, you will get interesting results from "Fit" and "Spline". Be sure to study the PEDIT chart *Figure 9-10* before going on to the next task.

TASK 7: Creating Parallel Objects with OFFSET

Procedure.

1. Type or select "OFFSET".
2. Type or show an offset distance.

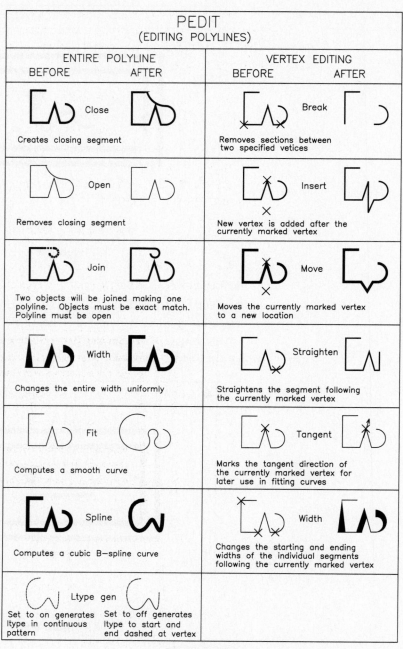

Figure 9-10

3. Select object to offset.
4. Show which side to offset.

Discussion.   Offset creates parallel copies of lines, circles, arcs, or polylines. You will find a number of typical applications in the drawings at the end of this chapter. In this brief exercise we will perform an offset operation to add a third border, as shown in *Figure 9-11*.

> Type or select "offset".
    AutoCAD prompts:

        Offset distance or Through <Through>:

There are two methods. You can type or show a distance or you can show a point that you want the new copy to run through. We will use the distance method. Then if you like you can undo the command and try it again using the "through point" system.

> Type ".75".

AutoCAD prompts for an object:

Select object to offset:

> Point to the outer rectangle.

AutoCAD now needs to know whether to create the offset image to the inside or outside of the rectangle:

Side to offset:

> Pick a point anywhere outside the rectangle.

Your screen should now resemble *Figure 9-11*.

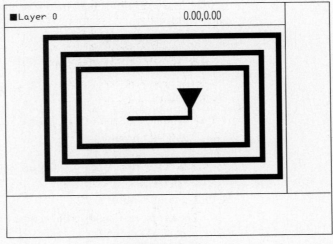

Figure 9-11

To create the same border using the through point method, follow this procedure:

1. Type or select "offset".
2. Type "t" or select "through".
3. Select the rectangle.
4. Pick a "through point" 0.75 out from any of the sides of the rectangle.

TASK 8: Drawing "SOLIDs"

Procedure.

1. Type or select "solid".
2. Pick a first point.
3. Pick a second point.
4. Pick a third point.
5. Pick a fourth point or press enter to draw a triangular section.
6. Pick another third point or press enter to exit the command.

Discussion. SOLID allows you to draw rectangular and triangular solid-filled shapes by specifying points that become corners or vertices. There is a trick to using SOLID for rectangular sections involving the order in which you enter points. If you enter them in the wrong order you will get the bow tie effect shown in *Figure 9-12*. It is natural to enter points in a rectangle by moving around the perimeter. However, AutoCAD solids are drawn with edges between point 1 and point 3, and between point 2 and point 4, so you need to be careful about the order in which you pick points.

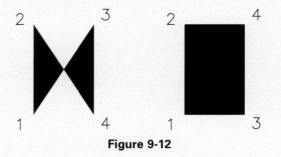

Figure 9-12

> To begin this task, clear the screen of polylines left over from Task 7.
> FILL and ORTHO should be on for this exercise. We will begin with a rectangular solid.
> Type or select "solid".

AutoCAD will prompt for a series of points, beginning with:

First point:

> Pick a point similar to P1 in *Figure 9-13*.

AutoCAD prompts:

Second point:

> Pick a point similar to P2.

These first two points will become the end points of one side of a rectangular solid. AutoCAD prompts:

Third point:

> Pick a point similar to P3.

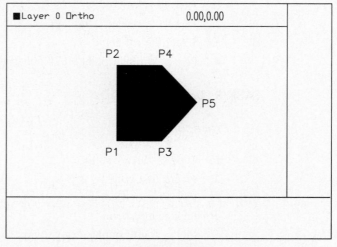

Figure 9-13

Remember that a side will be drawn between point 1 and point 3. AutoCAD prompts:

Fourth point:

> Pick a point similar to P4 in *Figure 9-13*.

When the fourth point is entered, AutoCAD will draw a solid rectangle and continue to prompt for points.

Third point:

If you continue entering points, the previous points 3 and 4 will become points 1 and 2 of the new section. You can draw a triangular section by picking a third point and then pressing enter in response to the prompt for a fourth point. This also means that you will need to press enter twice when you want to exit SOLID. We will draw a triangular solid before exiting.

> Turn ortho off and pick a point similar to P5 in *Figure 9-13*.

> Press enter in response to the "Fourth point:" prompt.

Your screen should resemble *Figure 9-13*.

> Press enter again to exit the command.

TASK 9: Making and Viewing Slides

Procedure.

1. Type or select "Mslide" or "Vslide".
2. Type or select the name of a .sld file.

Discussion.   Slides are simply "snapshots" of AutoCAD drawings that are saved in a reduced format so they can be loaded very quickly. They cannot be plotted or edited, but often are used in developing business presentations that can be shown on a computer screen.

Slides are very easily created using MSLIDE. Once created they can be displayed using the VSLIDE command. Since slides resemble drawings, it is important that you understand the primary difference: Slides cannot be edited, added to, or changed in any way. To change a slide you must overwrite the slide file with a new one of the same name.

To create a slide of your present display, follow this procedure:

> Type or select "MSLIDE".

MSLIDE stands for "make slide." It creates a slide from your current screen display. When the command is entered in Release 12, you will see a Create Slide File dialogue box. This is a standard file list box, listing files that have a .sld extension. When the box opens, the cursor will be blinking in the File: edit box so that you can type in a name for the slide you want to create.

> Type a name for the file, like "9-1" or "solid."

> Click on "OK".

It's that simple. Your display will be saved as a file with a .sld extension. To see that it is really there, you must first alter your screen in some way and then load the file using VSLIDE.

> Erase the solid from your screen.

>Type or select "vslide".

You will see another standard file list dialogue box. This one will be titled "Select Slide File".

> Type or select the file you just created with MSLIDE.

Your slide will appear.

> Try to select the solid or any other objects that appear in your slide.

You will find that you cannot. It is possible to draw new objects while a slide is showing on your screen. These are not part of the slide, but are part of your current drawing. If you REDRAW the screen, the newly drawn objects will remain and the slide will disappear.

> To clear the slide from your screen, type "r" or select "Redraw".

Most slide applications use a series of slides, exactly as you would in a photographic slide show. This process can be automated and timed using a special kind of file called a script file. There are a number of special commands used in the making of a script file, including SCRIPT, DELAY, RESUME, and RSCRIPT, in addition to MSLIDE and VSLIDE. See the *AutoCAD Reference Manual* for further information if your goals include the use of slide presentations.

TASK 10: Drawing "POINTs" (Optional)

Procedure.

1. Type or select "POINT".
2. Specify a point type and size.
3. Pick a point.

Discussion. On the surface this is the simplest DRAW command in AutoCAD. However, if you look at *Figure 9-14*, you will see figures that were drawn with the POINT command that do not look like ordinary points. This capability adds a bit of power and complexity to this otherwise simple command.

> Turn off the grid (F7).

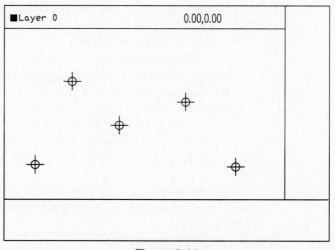

Figure 9-14

> Type or select "POINT".

> Pick a point anywhere on the screen.

AutoCAD will place a blip at the point and return you to the "Command:" prompt.

In order to see what has really happened, you will need to perform a RE-DRAW to clear away the blip.

> Type "r" or select "Redraw".

Look closely and you will see the point you have drawn. Beside those odd instances in which you may need to draw tiny dots like this, points can also serve as object snap "nodes." See the OSNAP chart, *Figure 6-8*, in Chapter 6.

But what about those circles and crosses in *Figure 9-14*? AutoCAD has 18 other simple forms that can be drawn as points. Before we change the point form, we need to see our options.

> Type "ddptype" or select "Type and Size . . ." under "POINT" on the "DRAW" screen menu.

AutoCAD displays a dialogue box with an icon menu, as shown in *Figure 9-15*. It shows you graphic images of your choices. You can pick any of the point styles shown by pointing. You can also change the size of points using the Point Size edit box.

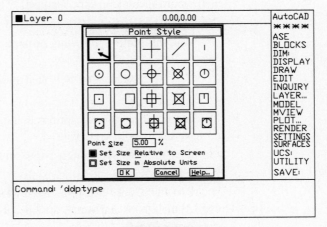

Figure 9-15

> Pick the style in the middle of the bottom row.

> Click on "OK" to exit the dialogue box.

> Type or select "Point".

> Pick a point anywhere on your screen.

AutoCAD will draw a point in the chosen style, as shown in the figure.

> Repeat POINT and pick another point.

Draw a few more points, or return to the dialogue box to try another style if you wish.

TASK 11: Using the SKETCH Command (Optional)

Procedure.

1. Type or select "SKETCH".
2. Type an increment.
3. Pick a start point (pen down).

4. Move cursor to sketch lines.

5. Pick an end point (pen up).

6. Record, exit, quit, or erase.

Discussion. The SKETCH command allows you to draw freehand lines. We include it here as an optional task so that you will know that it is available. It is not used in any of the drawings that follow.

The key to SKETCH is becoming familiar with its pen up, pen down action. Also, get used to the idea that SKETCHed lines are not part of your drawing until you "record" them or exit the SKETCH command.

> Type or select "sketch".

AutoCAD prompts:

SKETCH record increment <0.10>:

This will allow you to decide how fine or coarse you want your lines to be. Remember also that AutoCAD will continue to observe your snap. If you want a small record increment, turn snap off.

> Press enter to accept .10 as the record increment, or change it if you like.

You will see the following prompt:

Sketch. Pen eXit Quit Record Erase Connect.

We will discuss these options in a moment. They will make more sense after you have done some sketching.

> In order to begin sketching, choose any point on your screen and press the pick button once.

This puts your imaginary sketching pen down.

> Move the cursor and watch the lines that appear on the screen.

> Press the pick button again.

This picks your imaginary pen up again, resulting in an end point. If you move the cursor again, new lines will be drawn.

> Press the pick button once again and move the cursor.

The pen is down and you can continue sketching from a new start point.

Now look at the other options:

Sketch. Pen eXit Quit Record Erase Connect .

"P" picks the imaginary pen up and down, but the pick button is more convenient. "X" records the lines you have drawn and exits the command. "Q" exits without recording. "R" records without exiting. "E" allows you to erase some of the lines you have sketched in the last sequence. The action of this erase option is interesting and you should try it out. "C" connects you to the point where you last picked up your pen. "." draws a straight line from the point where you left off to the current position of the cross hairs.

NOTE: Since SKETCHed objects are made up of large numbers of very small lines, they take up a great deal of memory.

TASKS 12, 13, 14, 15, and 16

You now know how to draw nearly all of AutoCAD's two-dimensional entities. In the next chapter we will explore ways to create and manipulate blocks made up of multiple entities, all of which will be drawn and edited using the commands you already know. The drawings you are about to do are intended to be fun and interesting as well as to give you experience with the new entities you have learned in this chapter.

DRAWING 9-1: BACKGAMMON BOARD

This drawing should go very quickly. It is a good warm-up and will give you practice with SOLID and PLINE. Remember that the dimensions are always part of your drawing now, unless otherwise indicated.

DRAWING SUGGESTIONS

GRID = 1.00

SNAP = .125

> First draw a 0-width 15.50 × 13.50 polyline rectangle and then OFFSET it .125 to the inside. The inner polyline is actually .25 wide; but it is drawn on center, so the offset must be half the width.

> Enter the PEDIT command and change the width of the inner polyline to .25. This will give you your wide border.

> Draw the four triangles at the left of the board and then array them across. The filled triangles are drawn with the SOLID command; the others are just outlines drawn with LINE. (Notice that you cannot draw some solids filled and others not filled.)

> The dimensions in this drawing are quite straightforward and should give you no trouble. Remember to set to layer "dim" before dimensioning.

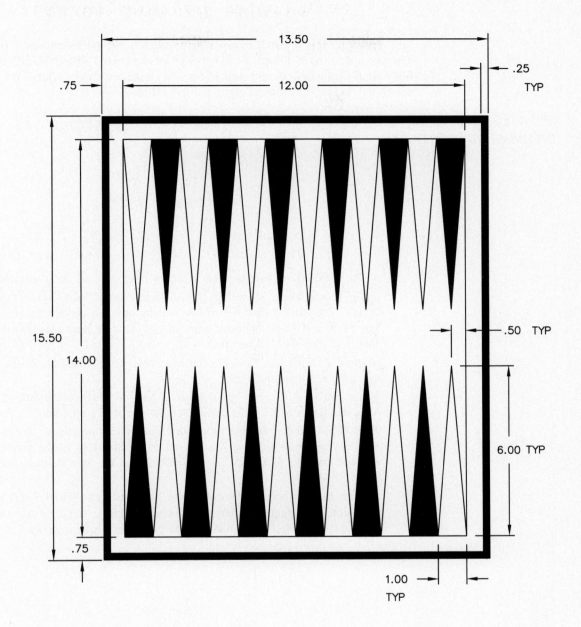

BACKGAMMON BOARD
Drawing 9-1

DRAWING 9-2: DART BOARD

Although this drawing may seem to resemble the previous one, it is quite a bit more complex and is drawn in an entirely different way. Using SOLID to create the filled areas here would be impractical because of the arc-shaped edges. We suggest you use DONUTs and TRIM them along the radial lines.

DRAWING SUGGESTIONS

LIMITS = (0, 0) (24, 18)

GRID = 1.00

SNAP = .125

> The filled inner circle is a donut with 0 inner and .62 outer diameters.

> The second circle is a simple 1.50 diameter circle. From here, draw a series of donuts. The outside diameter of one will become the inside diameter of the next. The 13.00 and 17.00 diameter outer circles must be drawn as circles rather than donuts so they will not be filled.

> Draw a radius line from the center to one of the quadrants of the outer circle and array it around the circle.

> You may find it easier and quicker to turn fill off before trimming the donuts. Also, use layers to keep the donuts separated visually by color.

> To TRIM the donuts, select the radial lines as cutting edges. This is easily done using a very small crossing box around the center point of the board. Otherwise you will have to pick each line individually in the area between the 13.00 and 17.00 circle.

> Draw the number 5 at the top of the board using a "middle" text position and a rotation of 2 degrees. Array it around the circle and then use the DDEDIT command to change the copied fives to the other numbers shown.

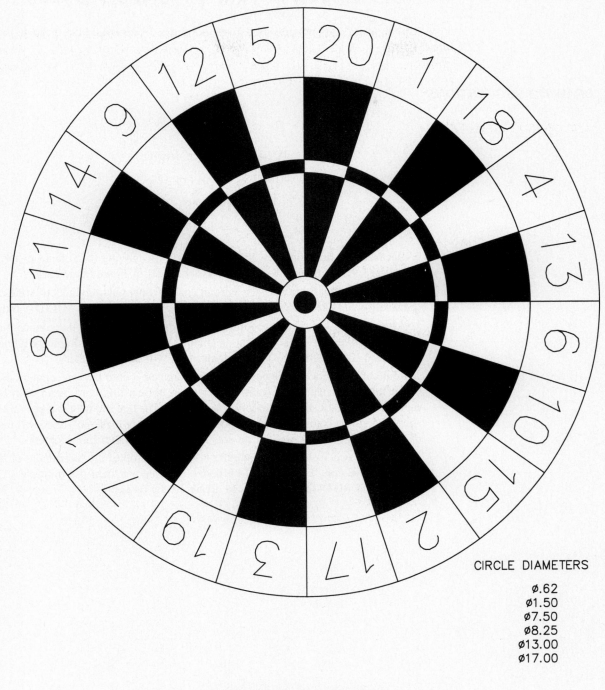

CIRCLE DIAMETERS

ø.62
ø1.50
ø7.50
ø8.25
ø13.00
ø17.00

DART BOARD

Drawing 9-2

DRAWING 9-3: PRINTED CIRCUIT BOARD

This drawing uses donuts, solids, and polylines. Also notice the ordinate dimensions.

DRAWING SUGGESTIONS

UNITS = 4-place decimal

LIMITS = (0,0) (18, 12)

GRID = 0.5000

SNAP = 0.1250

> Because this drawing uses ordinate dimensions, moving the 0 point of the grid using the UCS command will make the placement of figures very easy.

> The 26 rectangular tabs at the bottom can be drawn as polylines or solids. We drew solids and used DIST to lay out corners before entering the SOLID command.

> After placing the donuts according to the dimensions, draw the connections to them using polyline arcs and line segments. These will be simple polylines of uniform .03125 halfwidth. The triangular tabs will be added later.

> Remember, AutoCAD begins all polyline arcs tangent to the last segment drawn. Often this is not what you want. One way to correct this is to begin with a line segment that establishes the direction for the arc. The line segment can be extremely short and still accomplish your purpose. Thus many of these polylines will consist of a line segment, followed by an arc, followed by another line segment.

> There are two sizes of the triangular tabs, one on top of the rectangular tabs and one at each donut. Draw one of each size in place and then use multiple COPY, MOVE, and ROTATE commands to create all the others.

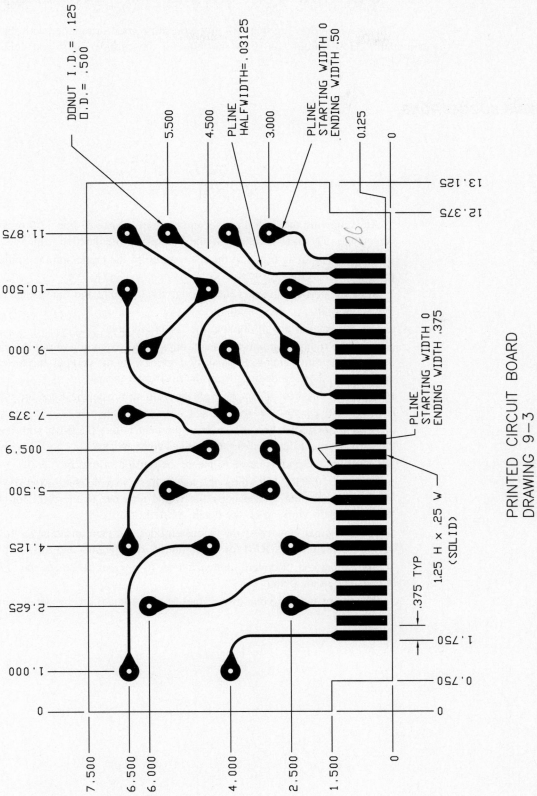

PRINTED CIRCUIT BOARD
DRAWING 9-3

DONUT I.D.= .125
O.D.= .500

5.500

4.500

PLINE
HALFWIDTH=.03125

3.000

PLINE
STARTING WIDTH 0
ENDING WIDTH .50

0.125

0

13.125

12.375

PLINE
STARTING WIDTH 0
ENDING WIDTH .375

1.25 H × .25 W
(SOLID)

.375 TYP

1.750

11.875

10.500

9.000

7.375

6.500

5.500

4.125

2.625

1.000

0

7.500

6.500

6.000

4.000

2.500

1.500

0

0.750

0

263

DRAWING 9-4: CARBIDE TIP SAW BLADE

This is a nice drawing that will give you some good experience with the OFFSET command. How would you draw the sides of the carbide tip if you could not use OFFSET?

DRAWING SUGGESTIONS

GRID = 1.00

SNAP = 0.125

> After drawing the 7.25 diameter circle, draw a vertical line 1.50 over from the center line. This line will become the left side of the detailed "cut."

> Use DIST with an osnap to the intersection of the circle and the vertical line to locate the .58 vertical distance.

> Draw the horizontal center line through the .58 point and the vertical center line .16 to the right.

> Use the center lines in drawing the .16 radius arc.

> From the right end point of the arc, draw a line extending out of the circle at 80 degrees. The dimension is given as 10 degrees from the vertical, but the coordinate display will show 80 degrees from the horizontal instead.

> OFFSET this line .06 to the right and left to create the lines for the left and right sides of the carbide tip.

> Draw a horizontal line .12 up from the center line. TRIM it with the sides of the carbide tip and create .06 radius fillets right and left.

> Draw the 3.68 radius circle to locate the outside of the tip.

> BREAK and TRIM the three 80 degree lines, leaving three extension lines for use in dimensioning. Then copy the whole area out to the right for the detail. When you start working on the detail, SCALE it up 2.00.

> In the original view erase the extension lines and then array the cut and carbide tip around the circle. TRIM the circle out of the new cuts and tips.

> You can use a "Rotated" dimension at 10 degrees to create the .12 and .06 dimensions in the detail.

> Be sure to type in your own values as you dimension the detail, since it has been scaled.

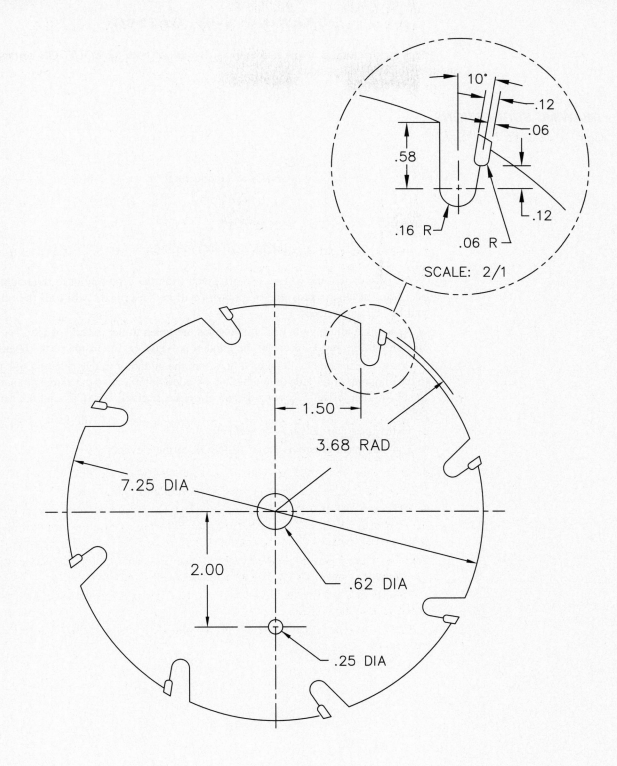

10°
.12
.06
.58
.12
.16 R
.06 R

SCALE: 2/1

1.50

3.68 RAD

7.25 DIA

.62 DIA

2.00

.25 DIA

CARBIDE TIP SAW BLADE

Drawing 9–4

DRAWING 9-5: GAZEBO

This architectural drawing makes extensive use of both the POLYGON command and the OFFSET command.

DRAWING SUGGESTIONS

UNITS = Architectural

GRID = 1$'$

SNAP = 2$''$

LIMITS = $(0', 0')$ $(48', 36')$

> All radii except the 6$''$ polygon are given from the center point to the midpoint of a side. In other words, the 6$''$ polygon will be "inscribed," while all the others will be "circumscribed."

> Notice that all polygon radii dimensions are given to the outside of the 2$'' \times 4''$. OFFSET to the inside to create the parallel polygon for the inside of the board.

> Create radial studs by drawing a line from the midpoint of one side of a polygon to the midpoint of the side of another, or the midpoint of one to the vertex of another as shown, then offset 1$''$ each side and erase the original. Array around the center point.

> TRIM lines and polygons at vertices.

> You can make effective use of MIRROR in the elevation.

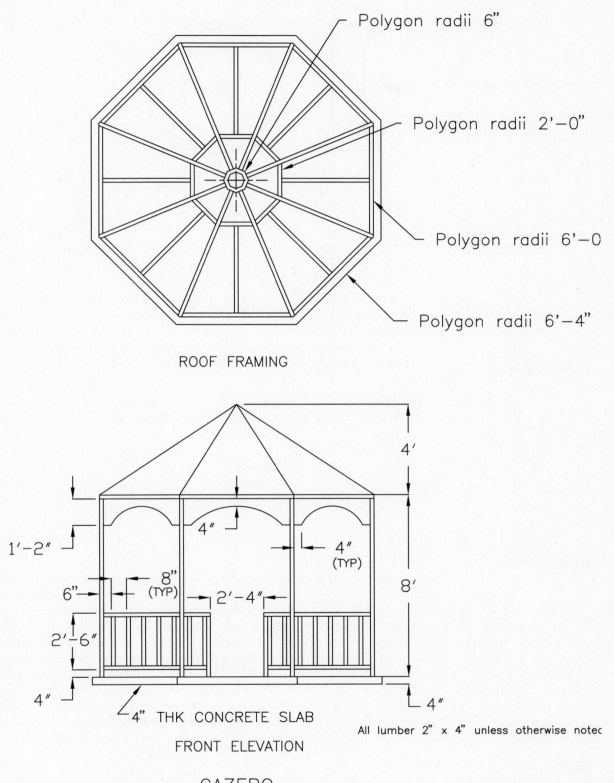

Polygon radii 6"

Polygon radii 2'–0"

Polygon radii 6'–0

Polygon radii 6'–4"

ROOF FRAMING

4'

1'–2"

4"

4"
(TYP)

8"
(TYP)

6"

8'

2'–4"

2'–6"

4"

4"

4" THK CONCRETE SLAB

All lumber 2" x 4" unless otherwise notec

FRONT ELEVATION

GAZEBO
Drawing 9–5

CHAPTER

10

COMMANDS

BLOCKS	EDIT	UTILITY
ATTDEF	ATTEDIT	ATTEXT
BLOCK	DDATTE	
DDATTDEF		
INSERT	**DISPLAY**	
XBIND	ATTDISP	
XREF		
WBLOCK		

OVERVIEW

You have seen several ways in which AutoCAD can treat a complex object as a single entity. In this chapter you will learn to create "blocks." A block is a group of entities defined as a single object. Blocks can be inserted repeatedly in many drawings and also can be given attributes. An attribute is an item of information about a block, such as a part number or price, that is stored along with the block definition. All the information stored in attributes can be extracted from a drawing and used to produce itemized reports. This is a powerful feature of CAD which has no direct counterpart in manual drafting.

Blocks may be stored within individual drawings or saved as complete drawings in themselves. In the latter case they can then be inserted into other drawings as blocks or linked to other drawings as "external references," using the XREF command. These features allow you to create symbol libraries made up of commonly used objects.

TASKS

1. Create blocks using BLOCK.
2. INSERT and assemble blocks.
3. Create attributes using DDATTDEF.

4. Edit attributes using DDATTE and ATTEDIT.

5. EXPLODE blocks.

6. Do Drawing 10-1 ("CAD Room").

7. Do Drawing 10-2 ("Base Assembly").

8. Do Drawing 10-3 ("Double Bearing Assembly").

9. Do Drawing 10-4 ("Scooter Assembly").

TASK 1: Creating BLOCKs

Procedure.

1. Type or select "BLOCK".

2. Type a name.

3. Pick an insertion point.

4. Select objects to be included in the block definition.

Discussion. Blocks can be stored as part of an individual drawing or as separate drawings. In general, the most useful blocks are those that will be used repeatedly and therefore can become part of a library of predrawn objects used by you and others in your work group. In mechanical drawing, for instance, you may want a set of screws drawn to standard sizes that you can call out any time you wish. Or, if you are doing architectural drawing, you might find a library of doors and windows useful.

In this chapter we will create a set of simple symbols for some of the tools we know you will be using no matter what kind of CAD you are doing—namely, computers, monitors, keyboards, digitizers, plotters, and printers. We will draw them, define them as blocks, and then assemble them into a workstation. Later we will insert workstations into an architectural drawing called "CAD ROOM."

> Begin by making the following changes in the drawing setup:

1. Set to layer 0 (see following note).

2. Change to architectural units, with smallest fraction = 1.

3. Set GRID = $1'$.

4. Set SNAP = $1''$.

5. Set LIMITS = $(0',0')$ $(48',36')$.

NOTE: There is a special relationship between blocks and layer 0. If you create a block on layer 0 you can insert it later on any other layer and it will take on the linetype and color of that layer. If you create a block on a layer other than 0 it will be fixed in that layer.

> Zoom into an area approximately $12' \times 9'$.

> Draw the four objects in *Figure 10-1*.

The text and dimensions in the figure are for your reference only; do not draw them on your screen.

We will define each of these symbols as a block, beginning with the "computer."

> Type or select "block".

The first thing AutoCAD wants is a name for the block:

Block name (or ?):

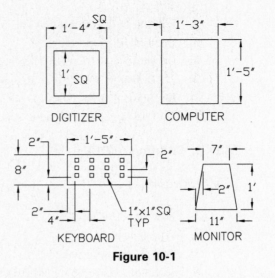

Figure 10-1

A "?" will get you a list of blocks defined within the current drawing. Right now there are none.

> Type "computer".

AutoCAD prompts:

Insertion base point:

Insertion points and insertion base points are critical in the whole matter of using blocks. The insertion base point is the point on the block which will be at the intersection of the cross hairs when you insert the block. Therefore, when defining a block, try to anticipate the point on the block you would most likely use to position the block on the screen.

> Use a midpoint osnap to pick the middle of the bottom line of the computer as the insertion point, as shown in *Figure 10-2*.

Finally, AutoCAD needs to know what to include in the block.

Select objects:

> Use a window to select the whole computer box.

When a block is defined, the first thing that happens is that it is erased from the display. The block definition is now part of the drawing database, and you can insert the block anywhere in the drawing, but the original is gone. This facilitates the practice of creating a number of blocks, one after the other, and then assembling them at the end. If the originals did not disappear you would have the added step of erasing them or panning to another part of the display to find room for the next block.

NOTE: If for any reason you want the original back right away, the OOPS command will bring it back, just as it does in the ERASE command. Do not use U, because this would undo the block definition.

You have created a "computer" block definition. Now repeat the process to make a "monitor" block.

> Type or select "block".

> Type "monitor".

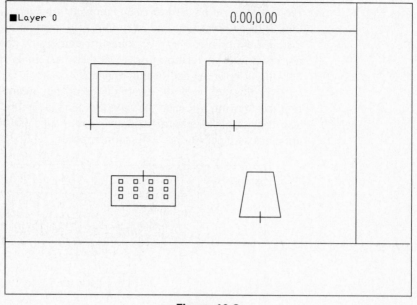

Figure 10-2

> Pick the midpoint of the bottom line of the monitor as the insertion base point.
> Select the monitor with a window.

Repeat the blocking process two more times to create "keyboard" and "digitizer" blocks, with insertion base points as shown in *Figure 10-2*. When you are done, your screen should be blank. Look at this description of the WBLOCK command before proceeding to Task 2.

WBLOCK

The WBLOCK command is very similar to BLOCK, except that it writes a block out to a separate file so that it may be inserted in other drawings. You can WBLOCK a previously defined block or create a new block definition as you write the block out. You can also WBLOCK an entire drawing. This can be quite useful, since a WBLOCKed drawing takes up less memory than a SAVEd one. We will be using WBLOCK as well as BLOCK extensively in the drawings at the end of this chapter.

TASK 2: INSERTing Previously Defined Blocks

Procedure.

1. Type or select "INSERT".
2. Type a block name.
3. Pick an insertion point.
4. Answer prompts for horizontal and vertical scale and rotation angle.

Discussion. The INSERT command is used to call out blocks. The four block definitions you created in Task 1 are now part of the drawing database and can be inserted in this drawing anywhere you like. INSERT or DDINSERT, the dialogue box version, also can be used to insert complete drawings into other drawings. Among other things, these procedures are very useful in creating assembly drawings. You will find that assembling blocks can be done efficiently using appropriate OSNAP modes to place objects in precise relation to one another. Assembly drawing will be the focus of the drawing tasks at the end of this chapter.

In this task we will insert the computer, monitor, keyboard, and digitizer back into the drawing to create the "workstation" assembly shown in *Figure 10-3*. We will also discuss other options for drawing file management including the use of complete drawings as blocks or as "external references."

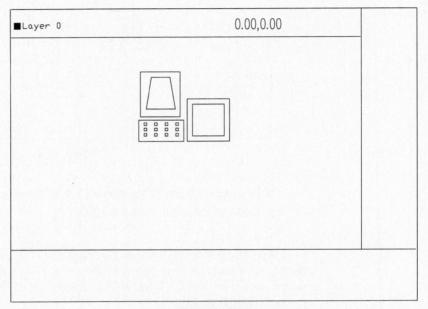

Figure 10-3

> Type or select "insert".

AutoCAD needs to know which block to insert:

Block name (or ?):

Now is a good time to see that your block definitions are still in your database, even though there is nothing on the screen.

> Type "?" to see a list of blocks.

You should see a list like this:

Defined blocks.

COMPUTER
MONITOR
KEYBOARD
DIGITIZER

User	**Unnamed**
Blocks	
4	0

> Repeat the INSERT command.
> At the "Block name (or ?):" prompt, type "computer". AutoCAD now needs to know where to insert the computer:

Insertion point:

Notice that AutoCAD gives you a block to drag into place and that it is positioned with the block's insertion base point at the intersection of the cross hairs.
> Pick a point near the middle of the screen, as shown in *Figure 10-3*.

What comes next is a set of prompts that allow you to scale and rotate the block as you insert it. This vastly increases the flexibility and power of the blocking system, although in many instances, including this one, you will accept all the defaults.

The first prompt asks for a scale factor:

X scale factor <1> / Corner / XYZ:

Unlike the SCALE command, which automatically scales both horizontally and vertically, blocks can be stretched or shrunk in either direction independently as you insert them. You can type an X scale factor or specify both an X and a Y factor at once by showing two corners of a window using the Corner option. The third option, XYZ, is reserved for 3D applications. Pressing enter will retain the block's present length.
> Press enter to retain an X scale factor of 1.

AutoCAD follows with a prompt for vertical scale:

Y scale factor (default = X):

> Press enter to retain a Y factor of 1.

You now have the opportunity to rotate the object:

Rotation angle <0>:

> Press enter to retain 0 degrees of rotation.

Now let's add a monitor.
> Repeat the INSERT command.

Notice that the last block inserted becomes the default block name. This facilitates procedures in which you insert the same block in several different places in a drawing.
> Type "monitor".
> Pick an insertion point two or three inches above the insertion point of the computer, as shown.
> Press enter three additional times to retain X and Y scale factors of 1, and a rotation of 0.

You should have the monitor sitting on top of the computer, and be back at the "command" prompt. We will insert the keyboard, as shown in *Figure 10-3*.

> Repeat the INSERT command.
> Type "keyboard".

> Pick an insertion point one or two inches below the computer, as shown.

> Press enter three additional times to retain X and Y scale factors of 1, and a rotation of 0.

You should now have the keyboard in place.

> Repeat the INSERT command once more and place the digitizer block to the right of the other blocks as shown.

Congratulations, you have completed your first assembly. Now that you are familiar with BLOCK, WBLOCK, and INSERT, you have the primary tools needed to create and utilize a symbol library. The tasks that follow introduce you to attributes. First we will create attributes to hold information about CAD workstations and include them in the definition of a new "ws" block. Then we will insert several workstations into our drawing and edit some of the attribute information. But before going on, let's look at "external references," another way to bring information from one drawing into another.

External References

An external reference is a drawing that is "attached" to another drawing through the use of the XREF command. External references are similar to blocks and can be used for many of the same purposes. They are particularly important in network environments.

In the previous exercise we inserted blocks that were defined within our current drawing. We can use exactly the same procedure with the INSERT command to insert a complete drawing file into our current drawing. The inserted drawing would then become a block within the current drawing, although its original drawing file would still exist separately. The XREF command is an alternative to INSERTing complete drawings. The principal difference between inserted drawings and externally referenced drawings is that inserted drawings are actually merged with the current drawing database, whereas externally referenced drawings are only linked. You cannot edit an external reference from within the current drawing. However, if the XREFed drawing is changed, the changes will be reflected in the current drawing the next time it is loaded, or when the Reload option of the XREF command is executed.

Since XREF only loads enough information to "point to" the externally referenced drawing, it does not increase the size of the current drawing file as significantly as INSERT does. The options of the XREF command are as follows:

?	Produces a list of external references attached to the current drawing.
Bind	Merges an external reference completely into the current drawing. The end result is the same as INSERTing a drawing, but binding does not have to occur until the final version of the drawing is complete. There is also an XBIND command which allows you to exclude certain types of information when you bind an external reference. The dimensions, for example, can be left out if they are drawn on a separate layer.
Detach	Removes the link between the current drawing and specified external references.
Path	Tells AutoCAD where to locate an external reference. This option is used to update a link when file structure is changed, or the externally referenced drawing is moved. Otherwise, the link cannot be maintained.
Reload	Reloads an external reference without leaving the current drawing. This is most useful in networked environments in which one person may be working on a drawing that is referenced in another person's drawing. Using this option, the most recent changes can be brought into the current drawing.
Attach	Creates a link between the current drawing and another drawing.

Management of Named Objects

What happens when an externally referenced or inserted drawing has layers, linetypes, text styles, dimension styles, blocks, or views with names that conflict with those in the current drawing? Good question. In the case of INSERTed drawings, name definitions in the current drawing override those in the inserted block. In the case of XREFed drawings, named objects are given special designations that eliminate the confusion. For example, if drawing A is attached to drawing B and both have a layer called FLOOR, a new layer is created in B called A—FLOOR.

TASK 3: Defining Attributes with DDATTDEF

Procedure.

1. Type or select ATTDEF or DDATTDEF.
2. Specify attribute modes.
3. Type an attribute tag.
4. Type an attribute prompt.
5. If desired, type a default attribute value.
6. Include the attribute in a block definition.

Discussion.   Attributes can be confusing and you should not spend too much time worrying over their details unless you are currently involved in an application that requires their use. On the other hand, they are a powerful tool, and if you have a basic understanding of what they can do, you could be the one in your work setting to recognize when to use them.

One of the difficulties of learning about attributes is that you have to define them before you see them in action. It is therefore a little hard to comprehend what your definitions mean the first time around. Bear with us and follow instructions closely; it will be worth your effort.

In this task we will define attributes that will hold information about CAD workstations. The attributes will be defined in a flexible manner so that the workstation block can represent any number of hardware configurations.

When we have defined our attributes, we will create a block called "ws" that includes the whole assembly and its attributes.

> To begin this task, you should have the assembled workstation from Task 2 on your screen.

First we will define an attribute that will allow us to specify the type of computer in any individual occurrence of the "ws" block. As is often the case in Release 12, you have a choice between a command sequence and a dialogue box. We will show you the DDATTDEF dialogue box. The older ATTDEF command covers exactly the same specifications, but works in a step-by-step sequence of commands.

> Type "ddattdef" or select "BLOCKS", "ATTDEF", and then "AttDef Dialogue..." from the screen menu.

This will open the Attribute Definition dialogue box shown in *Figure 10-4*.

Look first at the check boxes at the left under "Mode". We will be using all the default modes in this first attribute definition. This means that when our workstation block is inserted, the computer attribute value will be visible in the drawing (because "Invisible" is not checked), variable with each insertion of the block (because "Constant" is not checked), verified only once ("Verify" is not checked), and not preset to a value ("Preset" is not checked).

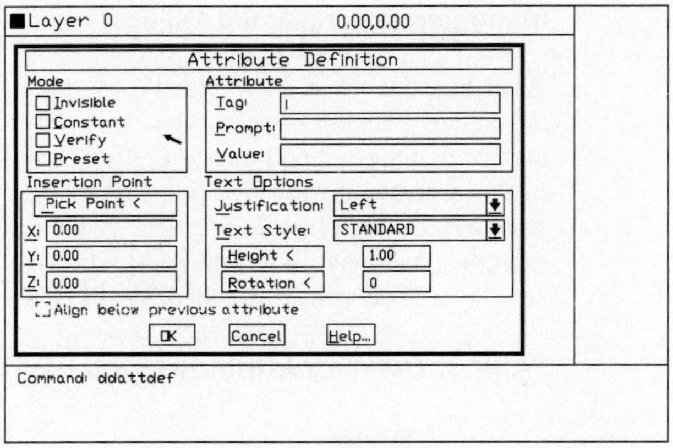

Figure 10-4

Next look at the box under "Attribute". The cursor should be blinking in the Tag edit box. Like a field name in a database file, a tag identifies the kind of information this particular attribute is meant to hold. The tag appears in the block definition as a field name. In occurrences of the block, the tag is replaced by a specific value. "Computer," for example, could be replaced by "IBM."

> Type "Computer" in the Tag edit box.

> Move the cursor to the "Prompt" edit box.

As with the tag, the key to understanding the attribute prompt is to be clear about the difference between block definitions and actual occurrences of blocks in a drawing. Right now we are defining an attribute. The attribute definition will become part of the definition of the ws block and will be used whenever ws is inserted. Attribute definitions function as containers for information. Each time we insert ws we can specify some or all of the information that its attributes hold. This is what will allow us to use our ws block to represent different hardware configurations. With the definition we are creating, there will be a prompt whenever we insert ws that asks us to enter information about the computer in a given configuration.

> Type "Enter computer type:".

We also have the opportunity to specify a default attribute value, if we wish, by typing in the Value edit box. This time, we will use no default in our attribute definition.

The box labelled "Text Options" allows you to specify text parameters as you would in TEXT or in DTEXT. Visible attributes appear as text on the screen. Therefore, the appearance of the text needs to be specified. The only change we will make is to specify a height.

> Click in the edit box to the right of "Height <" and then type "4".

Finally, AutoCAD needs to know where to place the visible attribute information in the drawing. You can type in x, y, and z coordinate values, but you are much more likely to show a point.

> Click on "Pick Point <".

The dialogue box will disappear temporarily to allow access to the screen. You will also see a "Start point:" prompt in the command area.

We will place our attributes 8 inches below the keyboard, as shown in *Figure 10-5*.

> Pick a start point 8 inches below the left side of the keyboard, as shown.

The dialogue box will reappear.

> Click on "OK" to complete the dialogue.

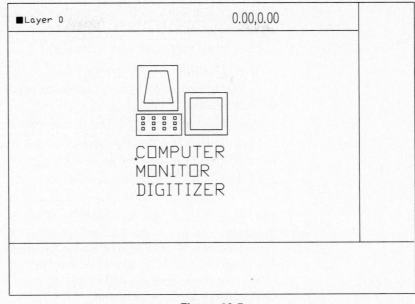

Figure 10-5

The dialogue box will disappear and the attribute tag "Computer" will be drawn as shown. Remember, this is an attribute definition, not an occurrence of the attribute. "Computer" is our attribute tag. After we define the workstation as a block and the block is inserted, you will answer the "Enter computer type:" prompt with the name of a computer, and the name itself will be in the drawing rather than this tag.

Now we will proceed to define three more attributes, using some different options.

> Repeat DDATTDEF.

We will use all the default modes again, but we will provide a default monitor value in this attribute definition.

> Type "Monitor" for the attribute tag.

> Type "Enter monitor type:" for the attribute prompt.

> Type "NEC Multisync" for the default attribute value. Now when AutoCAD shows the prompt for a monitor type, it will also show NEC Multisync as the default.

You can align a series of attributes by checking the Align below previous attribute box.

> Click in the check box labeled "Align below previous attribute".

> Click on "OK" to complete the dialogue.

The attribute tag "Monitor" should be added to the workstation below the "Computer" tag.

Next, we will add an "invisible, preset" attribute for the digitizer. Invisible means that the attribute text will not be visible when the block is inserted, although the information will be in the database and can be extracted. Preset means that the attribute has a default value and does not issue a prompt to change it. However, unlike "constant" attributes, you can change preset attributes using the ATTEDIT command, which we will explore in Task 5.

> Repeat DDATTDEF.

> Click in the check box next to "Invisible".

NOTE: If you use the ATTDEF command instead of the dialogue box, you must change modes by typing the first letter of the mode. To change a mode from N (no) to Y (yes), you will type the first letter of the mode, as shown in the parentheses in the prompt (ICVP).

> Click in the check box next to "Preset".

> Type "Digitizer" for the attribute tag.

You will not need a prompt, since the preset attribute is automatically set to the default value.

> Type "SummaSketch II" for the default attribute value.

> Click in the Align below previous attribute check box to position the attribute below "Monitor" in the drawing.

> Click on "OK" to complete the dialogue.

The "Digitizer" attribute tag should be added to your screen, as shown. Once again, remember that this is the attribute definition. When ws is inserted the attribute value "SummaSketch II" will be written into the database, but nothing will appear on the screen since the attribute is defined as invisible.

Finally, the most important step of all: We must define the workstation as a block that includes all our attribute definitions.

> Type or select "block".

> Type "ws" for the block name.

> Pick an insertion point at the midpoint of the bottom of the keyboard.

> Window the workstation assembly and all three attribute tags.

> Press enter to end object selection.

As usual, the newly defined block will disappear from the screen. In the next task we will insert several workstations back into your drawing and use DDATTE to change an attribute value.

TASK 4: Editing Attributes with DDATTE and ATTEDIT

Procedure.   (for ATTEDIT)

1. Type or select "ATTEDIT".
2. Specify one-by-one or global editing.
3. Specify blocks and attributes to include in the editing process.
4. In one-by-one editing, specify property to be edited and edit it.
5. In global editing, specify string to change and new string.

Discussion.   The DDATTE and ATTEDIT commands provide the capacity to change values and text properties of attributes in blocks that have been inserted. They do *not* allow you to edit attribute definitions. *Block definitions and attribute definitions can be changed only by recreating them.*

There are two ways to use ATTEDIT. One-by-one editing allows you to change individual attribute values, text position, height, angle, style, layer, and color. Global editing allows you to change values only. DDATTE can only be used to change individual attribute values and cannot be used to change any text specifications.

> To begin this task, you should have a clear screen, but the ws block with its attributes as defined in the previous task must be stored in your current drawing.

> Insert three workstations, using the following procedure (note the attribute prompts):

1. Type or select "INSERT".

2. Type "ws" for the block name.

3. Pick an insertion point.

4. Press enter for X and Y scale factors and rotation angle.

5. Answer the attribute prompts for monitors and computers.

We specified two Zenith computers and one IBM computer for this exercise and retained all the monitor defaults (NEC Multisync). Your hardware information may be entirely different, but this exercise will be simpler if you use ours. Notice that you are not prompted for digitizers because that attribute is preset.

When you are done, your screen should resemble *Figure 10-6*.

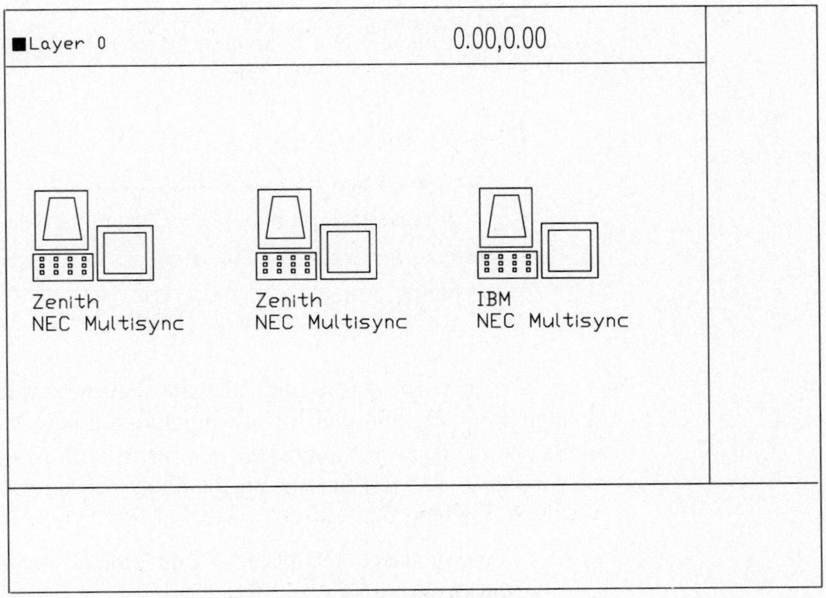

Figure 10-6

NOTE: The INSERT command can be used with a dialogue box. The box displays attribute prompts and defaults in a table of edit boxes. The dialogue box will be displayed in place of the command line prompts if the system variable "ATTDIA" is set to 1. By default it is set to 0.

The first thing we will do with the inserted blocks is use ATTDISP ("attribute display") to turn invisible attributes on.

Displaying Invisible Attributes

The ATTDISP command allows control of the visibility of all attribute values, regardless of their defined visibility mode.

> Type or select "ATTDISP" (under "DISPLAY" on the screen menu).

The prompt shows you three options:

Normal/On/Off <Normal>:

"Normal" means that visible attributes are visible and invisible attributes are invisible. "On" turns all attributes on. "Off" turns all attributes off.

> Type "on".

Your screen will be regenerated with invisible attributes on, as shown in *Figure 10-7*.

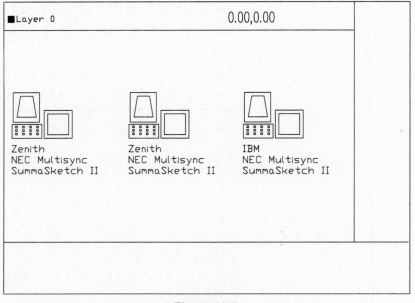

Figure 10-7

Now we will do an edit. Imagine that these three workstations represent part of a small work site and that we just purchased a new Multisync 4FG monitor. We could erase one of the workstations and reinsert it with new attribute information, but it will be simpler to edit just the one attribute that needs to change.

> Type or select "DDATTE" ("Edit", then "Attedit", then "Dialogue" on the screen menu).

This type of editing, in which we only want to change the values of attributes in a single block, is most efficiently handled with the DDATTE dialogue box.

When the command is entered, AutoCAD will prompt you to select a block.

> Select the middle workstation.

You will see the Edit Attributes dialogue box shown in *Figure 10-8*. Notice that all defined attributes are available, including the preset digitizer attribute.

> Click in the Monitor edit box and add "4FG".

> Click on "OK" to end the dialogue.

The attribute text will be changed as shown in *Figure 10-9*.

Now let's use ATTEDIT to perform a global edit.

> Type or select "ATTEDIT".

The first prompt allows you to choose between global and individual editing:

```
Edit attributes one at a time?  <Y>:
```

> Type "n" for global editing.

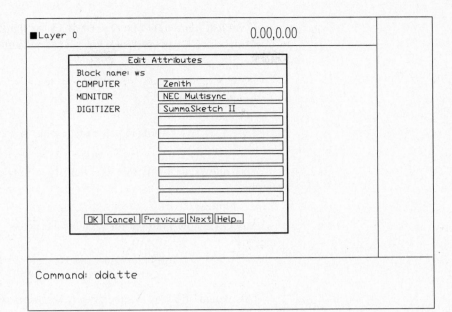

Figure 10-8

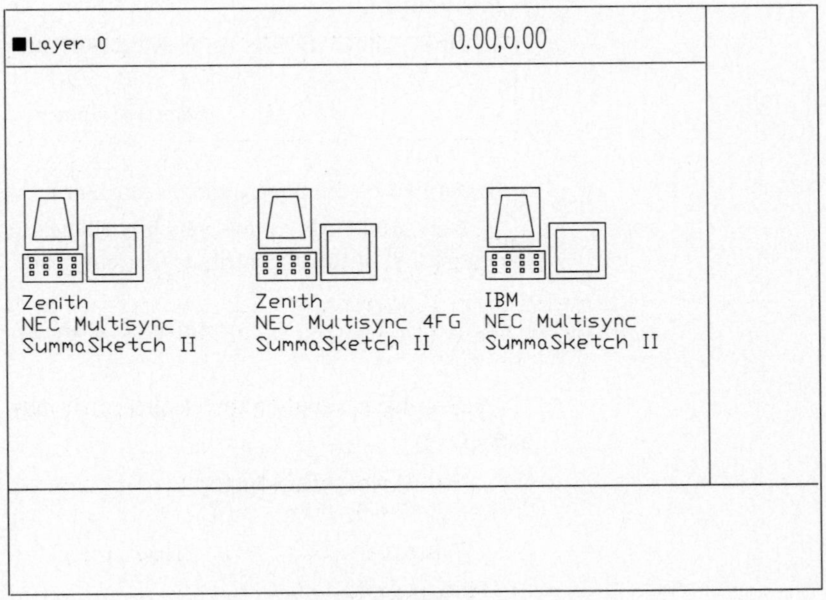

Figure 10-9

AutoCAD prompts:

Edit only attributes visible on the screen? <Y>

Since we set ATTDISP to "on" and because we have not zoomed away from any of our inserted blocks, all of our attributes are visible.

> Press enter to edit only visible attributes.

AutoCAD issues a series of three prompts that allow you to narrow down the field of attributes to be edited.

Block specification <*>:

If we had more than one type of block on the screen, we could limit editing to occurrences of whatever block we wished to name. But we have only the ws block.

> Press enter.

AutoCAD prompts:

Attribute tag specification <*>:

This allows us to narrow the field to a single tag—all the digitizers, for example.

> Type "digitizer".

AutoCAD now prompts for an attribute value:

Attribute value specification <*>:

This would allow us to specify only digitizers with the value "SummaSketch II", for example. Since all of our workstations have the same value at this point, this would be useless.

> Press enter.

Now AutoCAD asks us to select attributes by pointing or windowing:

Select Attributes:

> Select two of the three digitizer attributes.

Now AutoCAD knows which attributes to edit. It will allow you to change the entire text of the two attributes, or only part. It does this by requesting a string:

String to change:

A string is simply a text sequence. It may be part or all of the text.

> Type "II".

Now AutoCAD prompts:

New string:

> Type "III".

The two selected attributes will be changed, as shown in *Figure 10-10*.

The ATTEDIT command gives you a lot of power, but it can be tricky. See the *AutoCAD Reference Manual* if you need additional information.

Extracting Attribute Information from Drawings

Although there are many good reasons to use attributes, the most impressive is the ability to create extract files (the ATTEXT and DDATTEXT commands), which can be processed by other programs to generate reports, bills of materials, inventories, parts lists, and quotations. This means, for example, that with a well-managed CAD system you can do a drawing of a construction project and get a complete price breakdown and supply list directly from the drawing database, all processed by computer. In order to

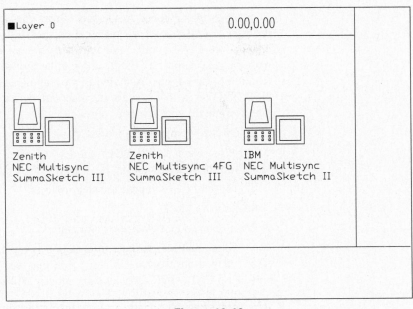

Figure 10-10

accomplish this, you need a complete library of parts with carefully defined attributes and a program like dBASE III or LOTUS 1-2-3 that is capable of receiving the extract information and formatting it into a useful report.

Unfortunately, since we have no way of knowing what programs are available to you and since we want to keep the focus of this book on drawing rather than programming, it is beyond our scope to create the files and formats necessary for extracting attributes. With a little imagination, however, you should be able to see the possibilities. With dBASE III, for example, we could match the computer, monitor, and digitizer names in our block references to a price list contained in a database file, calculate totals and subtotals, and format an elaborate report. This is a matter worthy of a whole book of its own, and we have only scratched the surface here. If you want additional information, see the *AutoCAD Reference Manual*.

TASK 5: EXPLODEing Blocks

Procedure.

1. Type or select "EXPLODE".
2. Select objects.
3. Press enter to carry out the command.

Discussion. The EXPLODE command undoes the work of the BLOCK command. It takes a group of objects that have been defined as a block and recreates them as independent entities. EXPLODE works on dimensions and hatch patterns as well as on blocks created in the BLOCK command. It does not work on XREF drawings until they have been attached permanently through the bind option.

> To begin this task, you should have at least one ws block on your screen.

> To see why you need this command, select a ws block by pointing.

You will see grips at the insertion point of the block and at the start point of the three attributes.

> Try selecting the monitor independently.

You will be unable to do this. Since the monitor, computer, keyboard, and digitizer are all part of a single entity, the ws block, they cannot be selected or edited except as a unit. The attributes are an exception. They can be edited with DDATTE and ATTEDIT, and can be moved independently using the stretch feature of grip editing. Actually, in most applications you will not want to explode block references that contain attribute information, because EXPLODE replaces the information with attribute tags.

Let's try exploding a workstation.

> Type or select "EXPLODE" (under "Modify" on the pull down menu, under "Edit" on the screen menu).

You will be prompted to select objects.

> Select a ws block.

> Press enter to carry out the command.

Notice that the attribute information is replaced by tags, as shown in *Figure 10-11*. If you are working in color, you may see a change in color as well. This is because EXPLODE automatically moves exploded objects to layer 0.

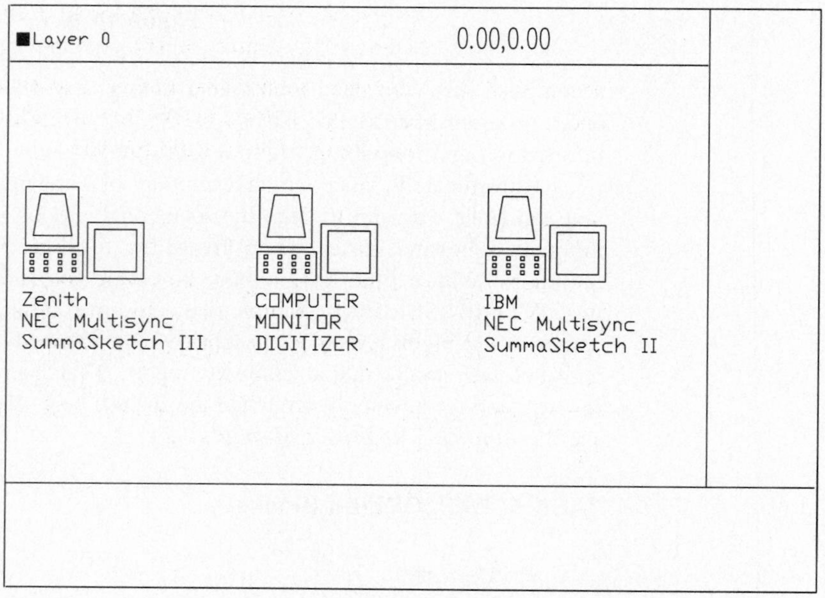

Figure 10-11

> Now try selecting the monitor again.

> Try selecting other parts of the workstation.

All of the component parts of the previously blocked workstation can now be edited separately. However, notice that there are still blocks within this configuration. Try selecting one of the buttons on the keyboard, for example. You will see that the keyboard is still considered a single entity. This is an example of a nested block. The keyboard block is one component of the former workstation block. Since EXPLODE moves through levels of nesting one at a time, blocks that were included in the definition of the ws block are still blocks when it is exploded.

Before going on, take a look at the following chart, Other Commands to Use with Blocks. It is a list and description of other commands that are frequently used in conjunction with blocks.

OTHER COMMANDS TO USE WITH BLOCKS

COMMAND	USAGE
BASE	Allows you to specify a base insertion point for an entire drawing. The base point will be used when the drawing is inserted in other drawings.
DBLIST	Displays information for all entities in the current drawing database. Information includes type of entity and layer. Additional information depends on the type of entity. For blocks it includes insertion point, X scale, Y scale, rotation, and attribute values. Due to length, a database list usually must be printed using printer echo (Ctrl-Q) or viewed with scroll pause (Ctrl-S to pause, any key to resume scrolling). See "LIST", following.
LIST	Lists information about a single block or entity. Information listed is the same as that in DBLIST, but for the selected entity only.
MINSERT	Multiple Insert. Allows you to insert arrays of blocks. MINSERT arrays take up less memory than ARRAYs of INSERTed blocks.
PURGE	Deletes unused blocks, layers, linetypes, shapes, or text styles from a drawing. PURGE must be the first command executed when you enter the drawing editor; otherwise it will not work.
WBLOCK	Saves a block to a separate file so that it can be inserted in other drawings. Does not save unused blocks or layers, and therefore can be used to reduce drawing file size.

TASKS 6, 7, 8, and 9

The first drawing exercise focuses on the use of attributes, while the other three are purely assembly drawings. We will be making some suggestions on how to manage drawing files and blocks in assembly drawings. Such techniques will be useful and necessary in any industrial application, but they may not be required to complete the drawings as classroom exercises. Remember to create objects to be BLOCKed on layer 0, unless you have a specific reason for doing otherwise.

DRAWING 10-1: CAD ROOM

This architectural drawing is primarily an exercise in using blocks and attributes. Use your ws block and its attributes to fill in the workstations and text after you draw the walls and countertop. New blocks should be created for the plotters and printers, as described following. The drawing setup is the same as that used in the chapter.

DRAWING SUGGESTIONS

UNITS = Architectural, smallest fraction = 1

GRID = $1'$

SNAP = $1''$

LIMITS = $(0', 0')(48', 36')$

> The "plotter" block is a 1×3 rectangle, with two visible, variable attributes (all the default attribute modes). The first attribute is for a manufacturer and the second for a model. The "printers" are 2×2.5 with the same type of attributes. Draw the rectangles, define their attributes 8 inches below them, create the BLOCK definitions, and then INSERT plotters and printers as shown.

NOTE: Do not include the labels "plotter" or "laser printer" in the block, because text in a block will be rotated with the block. This would give you inverted text on the front countertop. Insert the blocks and add the text afterward. The attribute text can be handled differently, as described following.

> The "8 pen plotter" was inserted with a Y scale factor of 1.25.

THE MIRRTEXT SYSTEM VARIABLE

The two workstations on the front counter could be inserted with a rotation angle of 180 degrees, but then the attribute text would be inverted also and would have to be turned around using ATTEDIT. Instead, we have reset the "mirrtext" system variable so that we could mirror blocks without attribute text being inverted:

1. Type "mirrtext".
2. Type "0".

Now you can mirror objects on the back counter to create those on the front. With the "mirrtext" system variable set to "0", text included in a MIRROR procedure is not inverted as it would be with mirrtext set to "1" (the default). This applies to attribute text as well as ordinary text. However, it does not apply to ordinary text included in a block definition.

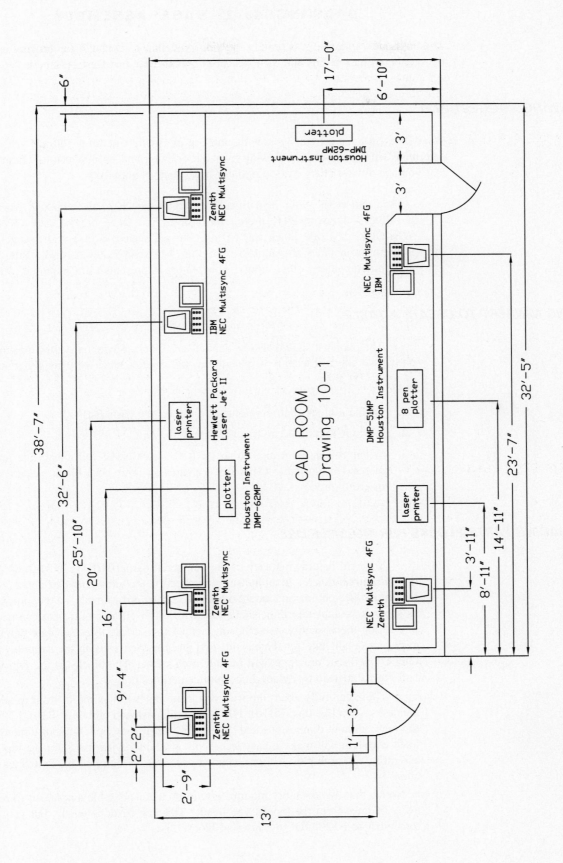

CAD ROOM
Drawing 10-1

DRAWING 10-2: BASE ASSEMBLY

This is a good exercise in assembly drawing procedures. You will be drawing each of the numbered part details and then assembling them into the "Base Assembly."

DRAWING SUGGESTIONS

We will no longer provide you with units, grid, snap, and limit settings. You can determine what you need by looking over the drawing and its dimensions. Remember that you can always change a setting later if it becomes necessary.

> You can create your own title block from scratch or develop one from "Title Block," Drawing 7-1, if you have saved it. Once created and SAVEd or WBLOCKed, a title block can be inserted and scaled to fit any drawing. Also, Release 12 includes an AutoLISP program, MVSETUP, which draws title blocks and borders, among other things. This feature is presented in Chapter 15, Task 5.

USING MINSERT TO CREATE A TABLE

The parts list should also be defined as a block. Since many drawings include parts lists, you will want to be able to quickly create a table with any given number of rows. Try this:

1. Define a block that represents one row of the parts list.
2. WBLOCK it so it can be used in any drawing.
3. When you insert it, use either ARRAY or MINSERT to create the number of rows in the table (MINSERT creates an array of a block as part of the insertion process).

MANAGING PARTS BLOCKS FOR MULTIPLE USE

You will be drawing each of the numbered parts (B101-1, B101-2, etc.) and then assembling them. In an industrial application the individual part details would be sent to different manufacturers or manufacturing departments, so they must exist as separate, completely dimensioned drawings as well as blocks that can be used in creating the assembly. An efficient method is to create three separate blocks for each part detail: one for dimensions and one for each view in the assembly. The dimensioned part drawings will include both views. The blocks of the two views will have dimensions, hidden lines, and centerlines erased.

Think carefully about the way you name blocks. You might want to adopt a naming system like this: "B101-1D" for the dimensioned drawing "B101-1T" for a top view without dimensions and "B101-1F" for a front view without dimensions. Such a system will make it easy to call out all the top view parts for the top view assembly, for example. A more detailed procedure is outlined for Drawings 10-3 and 10-4.

> Notice that the assembly requires you to do a considerable amount of trimming away of lines from the blocks you insert. This can be done easily, but you must remember to EXPLODE the inserted blocks first.

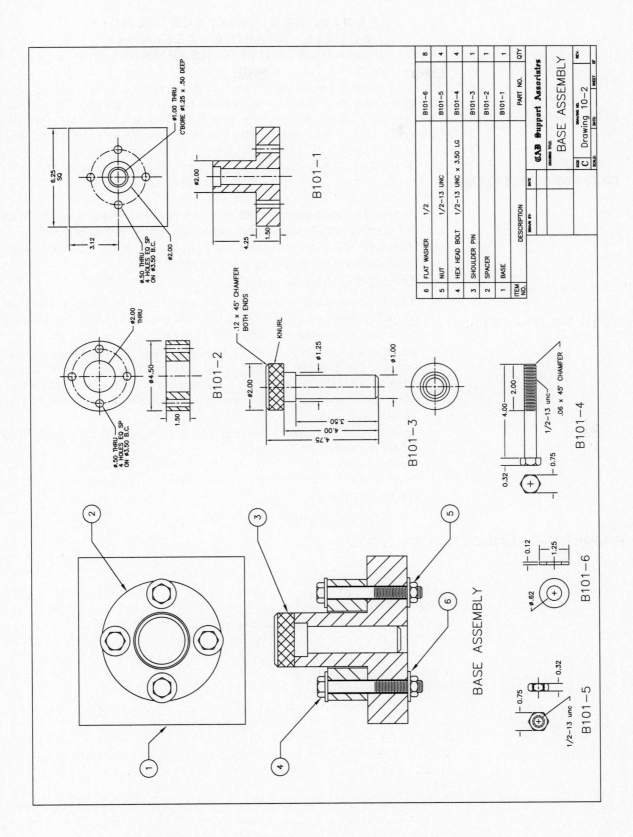

BASE ASSEMBLY

B101-1

B101-2

B101-3

B101-4

B101-5

B101-6

.12 x 45° CHAMFER
BOTH ENDS

KNURL

∅2.00 THRU

∅.50 THRU
4 HOLES EQ SP
ON ∅3.50 B.C.

∅4.50

1.50

∅1.25

∅1.00

4.75
4.00
3.50

.06 x 45° CHAMFER

1/2-13 unc

4.00
2.00
0.75
0.32

1/2-13 unc

0.75
0.32

0.12
1.25

∅.62

∅1.00 THRU
C'BORE ∅1.25 x .50 DEEP

6.25
SQ

3.12

∅2.00

∅.50 THRU
4 HOLES EQ SP
ON ∅3.50 B.C.

∅2.00

4.25

1.50

ITEM NO.	DESCRIPTION		PART NO.	QTY
6	FLAT WASHER	1/2	B101-6	8
5	NUT	1/2-13 UNC	B101-5	4
4	HEX HEAD BOLT	1/2-13 UNC x 3.50 LG	B101-4	4
3	SHOULDER PIN		B101-3	1
2	SPACER		B101-2	1
1	BASE		B101-1	1

CAD Support Associates

DRAWING TITLE: BASE ASSEMBLY

DRAWING NO. Drawing 10-2

SIZE C

SCALE | DATE | SHEET | OF | REV.

DRAWN BY: | DATE

DRAWINGS 10–3 AND 10–4:
DOUBLE BEARING ASSEMBLY
AND SCOOTER ASSEMBLY

All of the specific drawing techniques required to do the individual part details in these two drawings are ones that you have encountered in previous chapters. What is new is the blocking and assembly process. The procedure outlined below is a step-by-step elaboration of the kind of block management system we introduced in the last drawing.

DRAWING SUGGESTIONS

1. Draw each part detail in whatever two-or three-view form is given. Make the drawing complete with hidden lines, centerlines, and dimensions.

2. WBLOCK the part, giving it a file name that identifies it as a complete, dimensioned drawing. For example: "CAPD".

3. Use OOPS to return the part to the display.

4. ERASE dimensions, hidden lines, and centerlines. If you have kept your layers separated, you can turn off layer 0 and then erase everything left using a window or crossing box. Then turn 0 on again.

5. BLOCK the views separately, giving each a name that will identify it with its view. For example: "CAPT" for the top view of the cap, "CAPF" for cap front, and "CAPR" for cap right. It is essential that your naming system keep these BLOCKed views distinct from the WBLOCKed dimensioned drawing of step 2.

6. Insert blocks from step 5 to create the assembly. EXPLODE and TRIM where necessary.

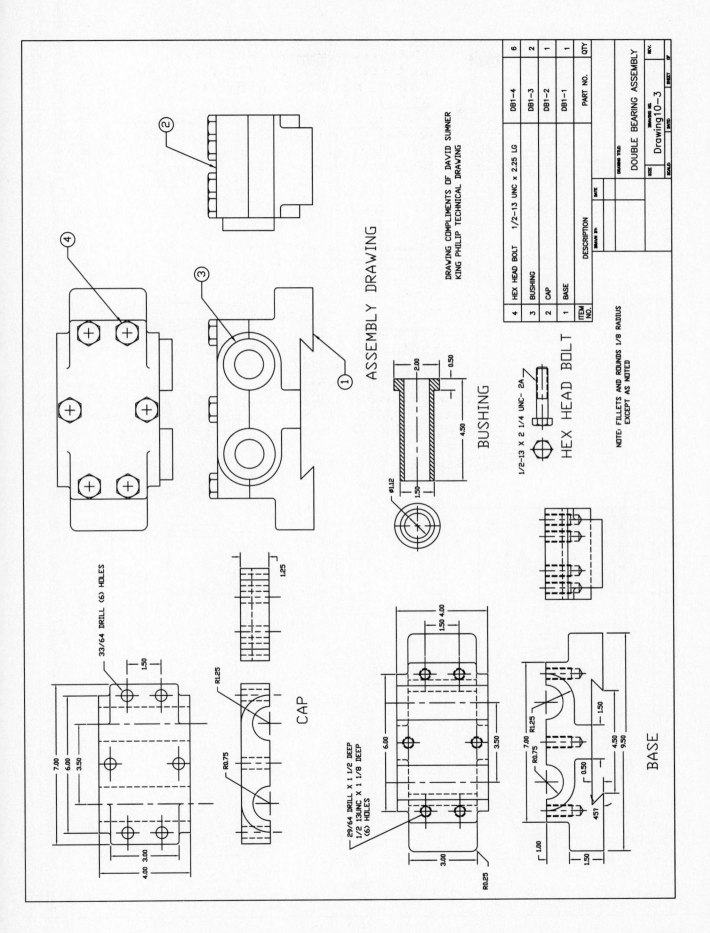

ASSEMBLY DRAWING

DRAWING COMPLIMENTS OF DAVID SUMNER
KING PHILIP TECHNICAL DRAWING

ITEM NO.		DESCRIPTION		PART NO.	QTY
4	HEX HEAD BOLT	1/2-13 UNC x 2.25 LG		DB1-4	6
3	BUSHING			DB1-3	2
2	CAP			DB1-2	1
1	BASE			DB1-1	1

DRAWN BY:		DATE

DRAWING TITLE:	
DOUBLE BEARING ASSEMBLY	

SIZE	DRAWING NO. Drawing10-3	REV.
SCALE	DATED:	SHEET	OF

NOTE: FILLETS AND ROUNDS 1/8 RADIUS
EXCEPT AS NOTED

BUSHING

HEX HEAD BOLT

1/2-13 X 2 1/4 UNC- 2A

CAP

33/64 DRILL (6) HOLES

R1.25

R0.75

29/64 DRILL x 1 1/2 DEEP
1/2 13UNC x 1 1/8 DEEP
(6) HOLES

BASE

R0.25

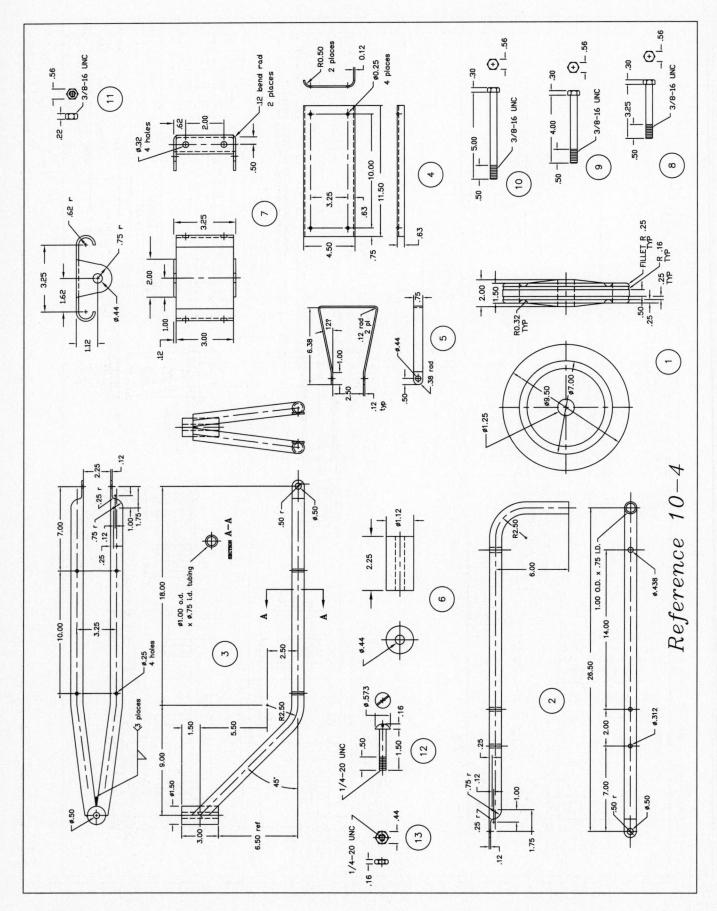

Reference 10-4

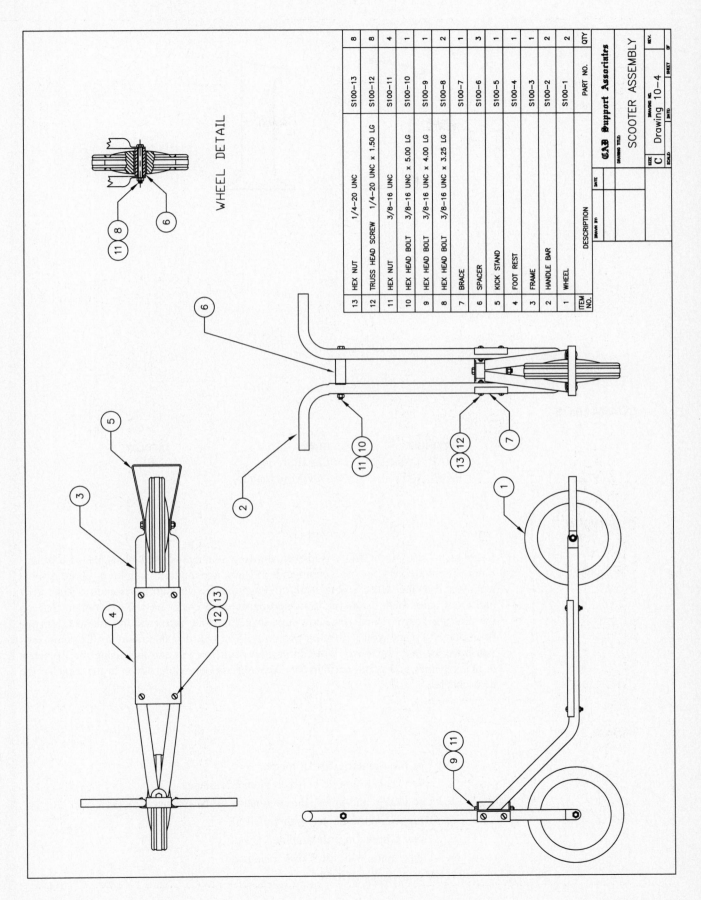

WHEEL DETAIL

ITEM NO.	DESCRIPTION		PART NO.	QTY
13	HEX NUT	1/4–20 UNC	S100-13	8
12	TRUSS HEAD SCREW	1/4–20 UNC x 1.50 LG	S100-12	8
11	HEX NUT	3/8–16 UNC	S100-11	4
10	HEX HEAD BOLT	3/8–16 UNC x 5.00 LG	S100-10	1
9	HEX HEAD BOLT	3/8–16 UNC x 4.00 LG	S100-9	1
8	HEX HEAD BOLT	3/8–16 UNC x 3.25 LG	S100-8	2
7	BRACE		S100-7	1
6	SPACER		S100-6	3
5	KICK STAND		S100-5	1
4	FOOT REST		S100-4	1
3	FRAME		S100-3	1
2	HANDLE BAR		S100-2	2
1	WHEEL		S100-1	2

CAB Support Associates

DRAWING TITLE:
SCOOTER ASSEMBLY

DRAWING NO.
Drawing 10-4

SIZE: C   REV.

DRAWN BY: DATE:

SCALE: DATE: SHEET: OF:

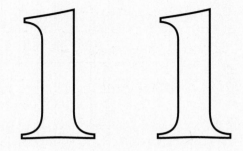

COMMANDS

SETTINGS	DRAW	DISPLAY
SNAP (isometric)	ELLIPSE	VIEW
ISOPLANE	ZOOM (dynamic)	

OVERVIEW

Learning to use AutoCAD's isometric drawing features should be a pleasure at this point. There are very few new commands to learn, and anything you know about manual isometric drawing will translate easily to the computer. In fact, the isometric snap, grid, and cross hairs make isometric drawing considerably easier on a CAD system than on the drafting board. Once you know how to get into the isometric mode and to change from plane to plane, you will be on your way. You will find that many of the commands you have learned previously will continue to work for you and that using the isometric drawing planes is a good warmup for 3D wireframe drawing, which is the topic of the next chapter.

TASKS

1. Use the isometric SNAP mode.
2. Use Ctrl-E to toggle between isometric planes.
3. Use COPY and other edit commands in the isometric mode.
4. Draw isometric circles with ELLIPSE.
5. Draw ellipses in orthographic views.
6. Save zooms with the VIEW command.
7. Use dynamic ZOOM.

8. Do Drawing 11-1 ("Mounting Bracket").
9. Do Drawing 11-2 ("Radio").
10. Do Drawing 11-3 ("Fixture Assembly").
11. Do Drawing 11-4 ("Flanged Coupling").
12. Do Drawing 11-5 ("Garage Framing").

TASK 1: Using Isometric SNAP

Procedure.

1. Type or select SNAP.
2. Type "s" or select "style".
3. Type "i" or select "isometric".

Discussion. To begin drawing isometrically you need to switch to the isometric snap style. When you do, you will find the grid and cross hairs behaving in ways that may seem odd at first, but you will quickly get used to them.

> Type or select "snap".

You will see a familiar prompt:

Snap spacing or ON/OFF/Aspect/Rotate/Style <0.25>:

> Type "s" or select "style".

AutoCAD will prompt for a snap style:

Standard/Isometric <S>:

Standard refers to the orthographic grid and snap you have been using since Chapter 1.

> Type "i" or select "isometric".

At this point your grid and cross hairs will be reoriented so that they resemble *Figure 11-1*.

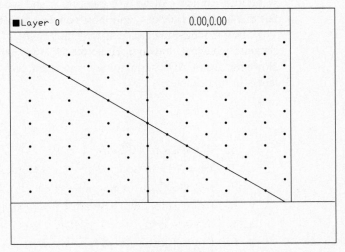

Figure 11-1

NOTE: You can also enter the isometric snap style by clicking in the On check box under "Isometric Snap/Grid" in the Drawing Aids dialogue box.

This is the isometric grid. Grid points are placed at 30, 90, and 150 degree angles from the horizontal. The cross hairs are initially turned to define the left isometric plane. The three isoplanes will be discussed in Task 2.

> To get a feeling for how this snap style works, enter the LINE command and draw some boxes, as shown in *Figure 11-2*. Make sure that ortho is off and snap is on, or you will be unable to draw the lines shown.

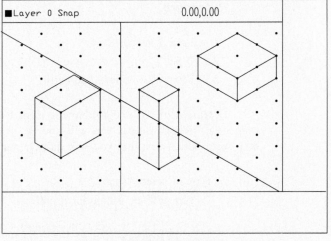

Figure 11-2

TASK 2: Switching Isometric Planes

Procedure.

1. Press Ctrl-E once to switch to the "top" plane.
2. Press Ctrl-E again to switch to the "right" plane.
3. Press Ctrl-E again to return to the "left" plane.

Discussion. If you tried to draw the boxes in Task 1 with ortho on, you have discovered that it is impossible. Without changing the orientation of the cross hairs you can draw in only one of the three isometric planes. We need to be able to switch planes so that we can leave ortho on for accuracy and speed. There are several ways to do this, but the simplest, quickest, and most convenient is to use Ctrl-E.

Before beginning, take a look at *Figure 11-3*. It shows the three planes of a standard isometric drawing. These planes are usually referred to as top, front, and right. However, AutoCAD's terminology is top, left, and right. We will stick with AutoCAD's labels in this chapter.

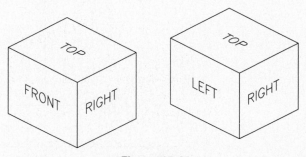

Figure 11-3

Now look at *Figure 11-4* and you will see how the isometric cross hairs are oriented to draw in each of the planes.

> Hold down Ctrl and press E to switch from "left" to "top."

Learn to use Ctrl-E with one hand, probably your left, so that you can keep the other hand on the cursor.

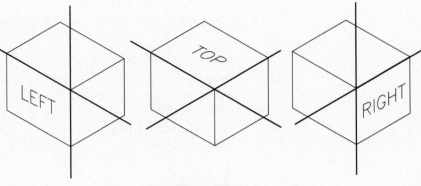

Figure 11-4

> Press Ctrl-E again to switch from "top" to "right."
> Press Ctrl-E once more to switch back to "left."

If you like, try switching planes using the radio buttons in the Drawing Aids dialogue box or by entering the ISOPLANE command and typing "L", "T", or "R". The problem with the pull down method is that it requires four picks, and the menu obstructs your view of the drawing. The problem with ISOPLANE is that you must type it or locate it on the screen menu, and it interrupts the command in progress.

> Now turn ortho on and draw a box outline like the one in *Figure 11-5*.

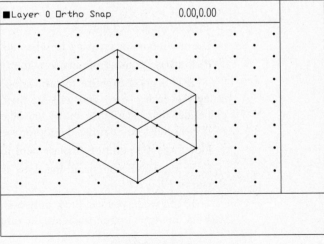

Figure 11-5

You will need to switch planes several times to accomplish this. Notice that you can switch planes using Ctrl-E without interrupting the LINE command. If you find that you are in the wrong plane to construct a line, switch planes. Since every plane allows movement in two of the three directions, you will always be able to move in the direction you want with one switch. However, you may not be able to hit the snap point you want. If you cannot, switch planes again.

TASK 3: Using COPY and Other Edit Commands

Discussion. Most commands work in the isometric planes just as they do in standard orthographic views. In this exercise we will construct an isometric view of a bracket using the LINE, COPY, and ERASE commands. Then we will draw angled corners using CHAMFER. In the next task we will draw a hole in the bracket with ELLIPSE, COPY, and TRIM.

> To begin this exercise, clear your screen of boxes and check to see that ortho is on.

> Draw the L-shaped surface shown in *Figure 11-6*.

Notice that this is drawn in the left isoplane and that it is 1.00 unit wide.

Next, we will copy this object 4.00 units back to the right to create the back surface of the bracket.

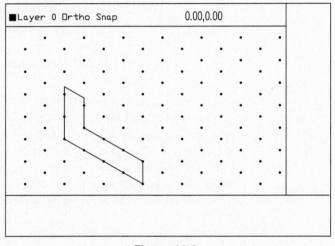

Figure 11-6

> Type or select "COPY".

> Use a window or crossing to select all the lines in the L.

> Pick a base point at the inside corner of the L.

It is a good exercise to turn ortho on, switch planes, and move the object around in each plane. You will see that you can move in two directions in each plane and that in order to move the object back to the right as shown in *Figure 11-7*, you must be in either the top or the right plane.

> Pick a second point of displacement four units back to the right, as shown.

> Enter the LINE command and draw the connecting lines in the right plane, as shown in *Figure 11-8*.

If you wish, you can draw only one of the lines and use the COPY command with the multiple option to create the others.

Creating Chamfers in an Isometric View

Keep in mind that angular lines in an isometric view do not show true lengths. Angular lines must be drawn between end points located along paths that are vertical or horizontal in one of the three drawing planes. In our exercise we will create angled lines by using the CHAMFER command to cut the corners of the bracket. This will be no different from using CHAMFER in orthographic views.

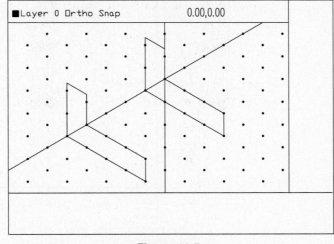

Figure 11-7

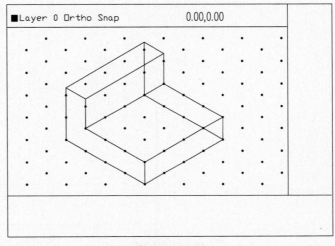

Figure 11-8

> Type or select "chamfer".

> Type "D" or select "distance".

AutoCAD will prompt for a first chamfer distance.

> Type "1".

> Press enter to accept 1.00 as the second chamfer distance.

> Repeat the CHAMFER command.

> Pick two edges of the bracket to create a chamfer, as shown in *Figure 11-9*.

> Repeat CHAMFER.

Chamfer the other three corners so that your drawing resembles *Figure 11-9*.

> ERASE the two small lines left hanging at the previous corners.

> To complete the bracket, enter the LINE command and draw lines between the new chamfer end points.

> Finally, ERASE the two unseen lines on the back surface to produce *Figure 11-10*.

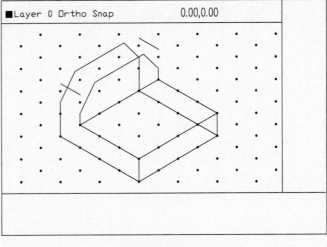

Figure 11-9

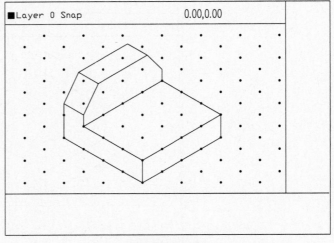

Figure 11-10

TASK 4: Drawing Isometric Circles with ELLIPSE

Procedure.

1. Locate the center point.
2. Type or select "ELLIPSE".
3. Type "I" or select "isocircle".
4. Pick the center point.
5. Type or show the radius or diameter.

Discussion.   The ELLIPSE command can be used to draw true ellipses in orthographic views or circles which appear as ellipses in isometric views (called "isocircles" in AutoCAD). In this task we will use the latter capability to construct a hole in the bracket.

> To begin this task you should have the bracket shown in *Figure 11-10* on your display.

The first thing you will need in order to draw an isocircle is a center point. Often it will be necessary to locate this point carefully using DIST, temporary lines, or point filters (Chapter 12). So you must be sure that you can locate the center point *before* entering the ELLIPSE command.

In our case it will be easy since the center point will be on a snap point.
> Type or select "ELLIPSE".

AutoCAD will prompt:

<Axis endpoint 1>/Center/Isocircle:

Notice that the default option is first on the list this time. The option we want is "Isocircle". We will ignore the others for the time being.
> Type "I" or select "Isocircle".

AutoCAD prompts:

Center of circle:

If you could not locate the center point you would have to exit the command now and start over.
> Switch into the top isoplane, if you are not already there, and use the snap and grid to pick the center of the surface, as shown in *Figure 11-11*.

AutoCAD gives you an isocircle to drag, as in the CIRCLE command, and prompts:

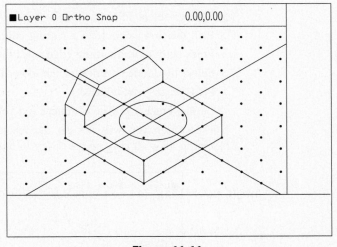

Figure 11-11

<Circle radius>/Diameter:

A radius specification is the default here, as it is in the CIRCLE command.
> Type a value or pick a point so that your isocircle resembles the one in *Figure 11-11*.

Next, we use the COPY and TRIM commands to create the bottom of the hole.
> Enter the COPY command.
> Select the isocircle by pointing, or type "last".
> Pick the center of the isocircle as the base point.

Actually any point could be used as the base point. Another good choice would be the top of the front corner. Then choosing the bottom of the front corner as a second point would give you the exact thickness of the bracket.
> Switch to either the top or left isoplane if you have not already done so.

> Pick a second point 1.00 unit below the base point.

Your screen should now resemble *Figure 11-12*.

The last thing we must do is TRIM the hidden portion of the bottom of the hole.

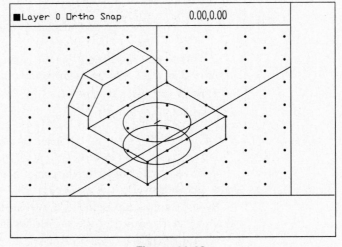

Figure 11-12

> Type or select TRIM.
> Pick the first isocircle as a cutting edge.
> Press enter to end cutting edge selection.
> Select the hidden section of the lower isocircle.
> Press enter to exit TRIM.

The bracket is now complete and your screen should resemble *Figure 11-13*.

NOTE: Often you will not get the results you expect when using TRIM in an isometric view. It may be necessary to use BREAK and ERASE as an alternative.

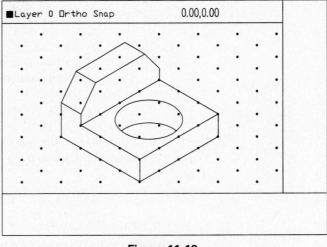

Figure 11-13

This completes the present discussion of isometric drawing. You will find more in the drawing suggestions at the end of this chapter.

Now we will go on to explore the nonisometric use of the ELLIPSE command and then to show you two new tricks for controlling your display.

TASK 5: Drawing Ellipses in Orthographic Views

Procedure.

1. Type or select "ellipse".
2. Pick one end point of an axis.
3. Pick the second end point.
4. Pick a third point showing the length of the other axis.

Discussion. The ELLIPSE command is important for drawing isocircles, but also for drawing true ellipses in orthographic views.

An ellipse is determined by a center point and two mutually perpendicular axes. In AutoCAD, these specifications can be shown in two nearly identical ways, each requiring you to show three points (see *Figure 11-14*). In the default method you will show two end points of an axis and then show half the length of the other axis, from the midpoint of the first axis out (the midpoint of an axis is also the center of the ellipse). The other method allows you to pick the center point of the ellipse first, then the end point of one axis, followed by half the length of the other axis.

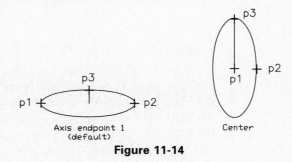

Figure 11-14

> In preparation for this exercise, return to the standard snap mode using the following procedure:

1. Type or select "snap".
2. Type "s" or select "style".
3. Type "s" or select "standard".

You will see that your grid is returned to the standard pattern and the cross hairs are horizontal and vertical again. Notice that this does not affect the isometric bracket you have just drawn.

We will briefly explore the ELLIPSE command and draw some standard ellipses.

> Type or select "ellipse" (under "Draw" on the pull down and screen menus).

AutoCAD prompts:

    <Axis endpoint 1>/Center:

If you select "Ellipse" from the Draw pull down menu, you will also have to choose between "Axis, Eccentricity" and "Center, Axis, Axis". These choices name the same two options as the command prompt in different language. We will use the first option first.

> Pick an axis end point as shown by point 1 on the ellipse at the lower left of the display in *Figure 11-15*.

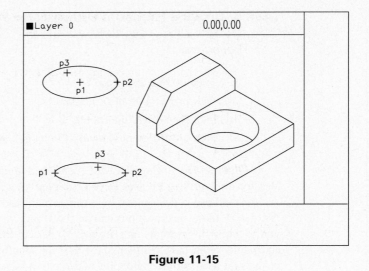

Figure 11-15

AutoCAD prompts for the other end point:

Axis endpoint 2:

> Pick a second end point as shown by point 2.

AutoCAD gives you an ellipse to drag and a rubber band so that you can show the length of the other axis. Only the length of the rubber band is significant; the angle is already determined to be perpendicular to the first axis. This is why the third point will only fall on the ellipse if the rubber band is perpendicular to the first axis.

The prompt that follows allows you to show the second axis distance as before, or a rotation around the first axis:

<Other axis distance>/Rotation:

We will not explore the rotation option here; see the *AutoCAD Reference Manual* for more information.

> Pick a point 3 as shown.

This point will show half the length of the other axis.

The first ellipse should now be complete.

Now we will draw one showing the center point first.

> Repeat the ELLIPSE command.

> At the "<Axis endpoint 1>/Center:" prompt, type "c" or select "center". (This step will be automated if you select "Center, Axis, Axis" from the pull down).

AutoCAD will give you a prompt for a center point:

Center of Ellipse:

> Pick a center point (point 1), as shown at the upper left of *Figure 11-15*.

Now you will have a rubber band stretching from the center to the end of an axis and the following prompt:

Axis endpoint:

> Pick an end point as shown in the figure (point 2).

The prompt that follows allows you to show the second axis distance as before, or a rotation around the first axis:

<Other axis distance>/Rotation:

> Pick an axis distance as shown by point 3.

Here again the rubber band is significant for distance only. The point you pick will fall on the ellipse only if the rubber band is stretched perpendicular to the first axis.

Your screen should now resemble *Figure 11-15*.

TASK 6: Saving and Restoring Displays with VIEW

Procedure.

1. Type or select "VIEW".
2. Type "s" to save or "r" to restore a view.
3. Type a view name.

Discussion. The word "view" in connection with the VIEW command has a special significance in AutoCAD. It refers to any set of display boundaries that have been named and "saved" using the VIEW command. Views that have been saved can be restored rapidly and by direct reference rather than by redefining the location and size of the area to be displayed. This feature can be useful when you know that you will be returning frequently to a certain area of a large drawing. It saves having to zoom out to look at the complete drawing and then zoom back in again on the area you want. Imagine that we have to do some extensive detail work on the area around the hole in the bracket and also on the top corner. We can define each of these as a view and jump back and forth at will.

> To begin this exercise, you should have the bracket on your screen as shown in *Figure 11-16*.

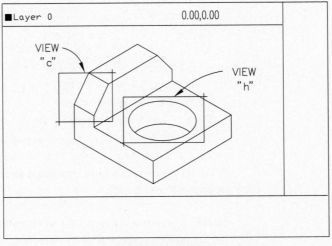

Figure 11-16

> Type or select "view".

　AutoCAD responds:

?/Delete/Restore/Save/Window:

　Notice that there is no default in this prompt. You must specify an option. In this exercise we will use "window" and "restore". The "?" is well known by now, it will get you a list of previously saved views. "Delete" erases previously saved views from the drawing database. "Restore" calls out a defined view. "Save" uses the current display window as the view definition. And "window" allows you to define a new view without actually displaying it.

> Type "w" or select "window".

　AutoCAD prompts for a view name:

View name to save:

> Type "h" for "hole".

　Views are designed for speed, so it makes sense to assign them short names. AutoCAD now prompts for corners as usual in a window selection process.

> Pick first and second corners to define a window around the hole in the bracket, as shown in *Figure 11-16*.

　When this is done, the command sequence is complete. The window you selected is now defined as a view that can be "restored," or called up, using the view name "h". But first, let's repeat the process once more to define a second view called "c" for corner.

> Repeat the VIEW command.

> Type "w" or select "window".

> Type "c" for the view name.

> Define a window, as shown in *Figure 11-16*.

　You have now defined two views. To see the command in action we must restore them.

> Repeat the VIEW command.

> Type "r" or select "restore".

　AutoCAD prompts:

View name to restore:

> Type "h" to switch to the view of the hole.

　Your screen should resemble *Figure 11-17*.

　Now switch to the corner view.

> Repeat the VIEW command.

> Type "r" or select "restore".

> Type "c". Your screen should resemble *Figure 11-18*.

It would be worthwhile at this point to switch back and forth a few more times. How rapidly can you do it?

NOTE: There is a dialogue box version of the VIEW command accessible through the DDVIEW command or by selecting "Set View" and then "Named view..." on the pull down menu, or "View Dialogue" on the screen menu.

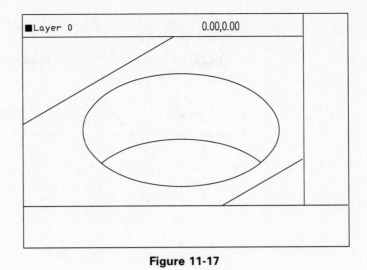

Figure 11-17

Figure 11-18

The dialogue includes the same choices plus an option that offers information about the defining features of each saved view. This information is most useful in 3D drawings.

TASK 7: Using Dynamic ZOOM

Procedure.

1. Type "z" or select "ZOOM".
2. Type "d" or select "dynamic".
3. Show a pan.
4. Show a zoom.
5. Press enter or the enter button.

Discussion. Dynamic ZOOM allows you to choose your display area while looking at the complete drawing area, without having to wait for the drawing to regenerate. Particularly in large, slow-to-regenerate drawings, this can be an efficient time-saver.

> To begin this exercise, your screen should be showing one of the views defined in Task 6. Either will do.

> Type "z" or select "Zoom" to enter the ZOOM command.

> Type "d" or select "dynamic".

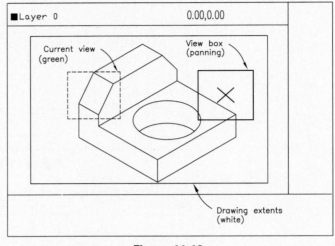

Figure 11-19

AutoCAD immediately will switch to a screen that resembles *Figure 11-19*, without the text. In order to see the white view box shown, you will need to move the cursor.

This screen display can be bewildering. Take a minute to look at the text in the figure to see what each of the boxes is used for. There are three boxes. The most significant is the white view box with the x inside. This is the only box you can move and the one you will use to define the area you want to display.

The dotted box (green if you have a color monitor) frames the current view, that is, the area you were looking at before entering dynamic zoom.

The solid white box represents the drawing extents. Extents refer to the actual drawing area currently in use.

In larger drawings you may also see four corner brackets (red on a color monitor). These show the boundaries of the area that is currently generated. If you zoom within these boundaries, AutoCAD will merely REDRAW the screen. If you zoom out of bounds, a regeneration will be required, causing some delay in a large drawing. AutoCAD will warn you of this by displaying an hourglass—as shown in *Figure 11-20*.

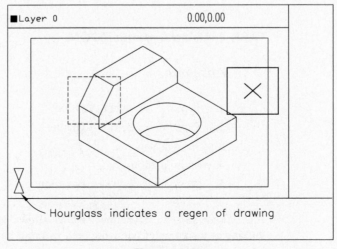

Figure 11-20

To use dynamic zoom, you must become accustomed to the two ways in which you can move the view box. When the x is showing, you can move the view box anywhere on the screen to frame a new area to display. Let's try it.

> Move the view box around the screen.

Notice that the box remains the same size as you move.

> Press the *pick* button (not the enter button).

You should see an arrow at the right of the view box, instead of the x in the center, as shown in *Figure 11-21*. The pick button switches between panning and zooming. In other words, with the x showing you can reposition the box, whereas with the arrow you can change its size.

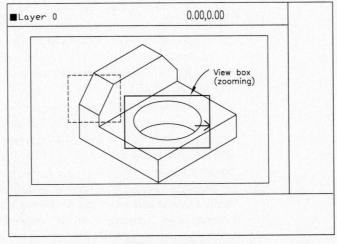

Figure 11-21

> Move the cursor to the right and left.

Notice how the box stretches and shrinks in both the horizontal and vertical directions. Unlike the usual ZOOM window, this box is always proportioned to show the area that will actually be displayed.

> Press the pick button again.

This brings back the x so that you can move the box again.

> Press enter, the space bar, or the enter button on your cursor.

This completes the dynamic ZOOM procedure and displays the area you defined with the view box.

Now that you know how to control the size and position of the box, try using dynamic ZOOM to display the area around the hole in the bracket, similar to the area you defined previously as the "h" view. Then use dynamic ZOOM to display the front corner, as in the "c" view.

TASKS 8, 9, 10, 11, and 12

The five drawings that follow will give you a range of experience in isometric drawing. The bracket drawing is an extension of the previous tasks, the radio drawing uses the "box method" and text on isometric angles, both the fixture and the flanged coupling drawings require you to work off an isometric centerline, and the garage drawing is an architectural drawing that introduces methods for multiple copying or using the ARRAY command in the isometric planes.

DRAWING 11–1: MOUNTING BRACKET

This drawing is a direct extension of the exercise in the chapter. It will give you practice in basic AutoCAD isometrics and in transferring dimensions from orthographic to isometric views.

DRAWING SUGGESTIONS

> When the center point of an isocircle is not on snap, as in this drawing, you will need to create a specifiable point and snap onto it. Draw intersecting lines from the midpoints of the sides so that you can snap to that intersection, or use DIST and draw a point there. Then use a "node" snap.

> Often when you try to select a group of objects to copy, there will be many crossing lines that you do not want to include in the copy. This is an ideal time to use the "remove" option in object selection. First window the objects you want along with those nearby that are unavoidable, and then remove the unwanted objects one by one.

> Frequently you will get unexpected results when you try to TRIM an object in an isometric view. AutoCAD will divide an ellipse into a series of arcs, for example, and only trim a portion. If you do not get the results you want, use the BREAK command to control how the object is broken, and then erase what you do not want.

> There are no isometric options in the ARC command, so semicircles like those at the top and bottom of the slots must be constructed by first drawing isocircles (ellipses) and trimming or erasing unwanted portions.

> Use COPY frequently to avoid duplicating your work. Since it may take a considerable amount of editing to create holes and fillets, do not COPY until edits have been done on the original.

> The row of small arcs that show the curve in the middle of the bracket are multiple copies of the fillet at the corner.

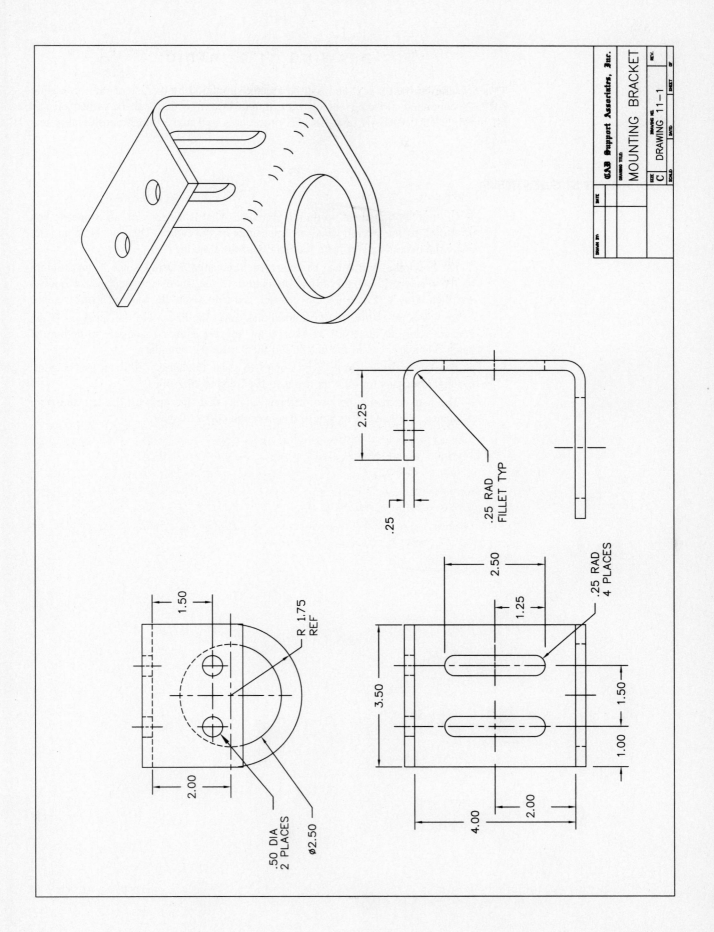

MOUNTING BRACKET

DRAWING 11-1

CAD Support Associates, Inc.

2.25

.25

.25 RAD
FILLET TYP

2.50

1.25

.25 RAD
4 PLACES

3.50

1.50

1.00

4.00

2.00

1.50

2.00

R 1.75
REF

.50 DIA
2 PLACES

Ø2.50

DRAWING 11–2: RADIO

This drawing introduces text and will be greatly simplified by the use of the rectangular ARRAY command. Placing objects on different layers so they can be turned on and off during TRIM, BREAK, and ERASE procedures will make things considerably less messy.

DRAWING SUGGESTIONS

> Use the "box method" to do this drawing. That is, begin with an isometric box according to the overall outside dimensions of the radio. Then go back and cut away the excess as you form the details of the drawing.

> The horizontal "grill" can be done with a rectangular array, since it runs straight on the vertical. Look carefully at the pattern to see where it repeats. Draw one set and then array it. Later you can go back and trim away the dial and speaker areas.

> Draw isocircles over the grill and break away the lines over the speaker. When you are ready to hatch the speaker, draw another trimmed isocircle to define the hatch boundary, create the hatch, and then erase the boundary.

> The knobs are isocircles with copies to show thickness. You can use tangent-to-tangent osnaps to draw the front-to-back connecting lines.

> The text is created on two different angles that line up with the left and right isoplanes. We leave it to you to discover the correct angles.

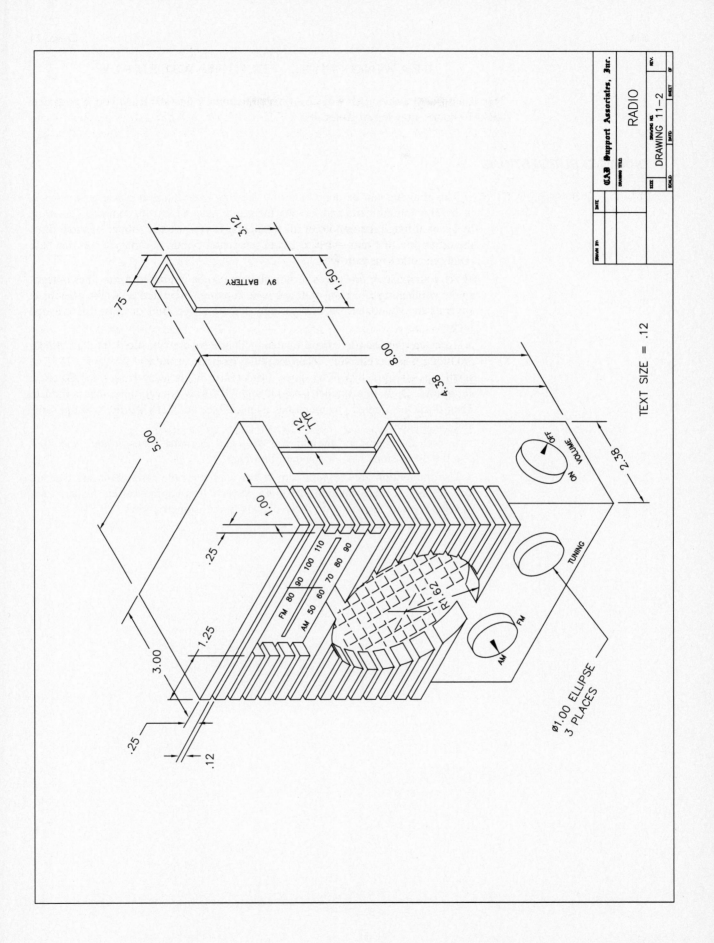

9V BATTERY

3.12

.75

1.50

8.00

5.00

4.38

2.38

.12 TYP

1.00

.25

FM 80 90 100 110
AM 50 60 70 80 90

R1.62

VOLUME
ON OFF

TUNING

AM FM

1.25

3.00

.25

.12

Ø1.00 ELLIPSE
3 PLACES

TEXT SIZE = .12

CAE Support Associates, Inc.

DRAWN BY:
DATE

DRAWING TITLE:
RADIO

DRAWING NO.
DRAWING 11-2
REV.

SIZE
SCALE
DATED
SHEET
OF

DRAWING 11-3: FIXTURE ASSEMBLY

This is a difficult drawing. It will take time and patience but will teach you a great deal about isometric drawing in AutoCAD.

DRAWING SUGGESTIONS

> This drawing can be done either by drawing everything in place as you see it, or by drawing the parts and moving them into place along the common centerline that runs through the middle of all the items. If you use the former method, draw the centerline first and use it to locate the center points of isocircles and as base points for other measures.

> As you go, look for pieces of objects that can be copied to form other objects. Avoid duplicating efforts by editing before copying. In particular, where one object covers part of another, be sure to copy it before you trim or erase the covered sections.

> To create the chamfered end of item 4, begin by drawing the 1.00 dia cylinder 3.00 long with no chamfer. Then copy the isocircle at the end forward .125. The smaller isocircle is .875 (7/8), since .0625 (1/16) is cut away from the 1.00 circle all around. Draw this smaller isocircle and TRIM away everything that is hidden. Then draw the slanted chamfer lines using LINE, not CHAMFER. Use the same method for item 5.

> In both the screw and the nut you will need to create hexes around isocircles. Use the dimensions from a standard bolt chart.

> Use three-point arcs to approximate the curves on the screw bolt and the nut. You are after a representation that looks correct. It is impractical and unnecessary to achieve exact measures on these objects in the isometric view.

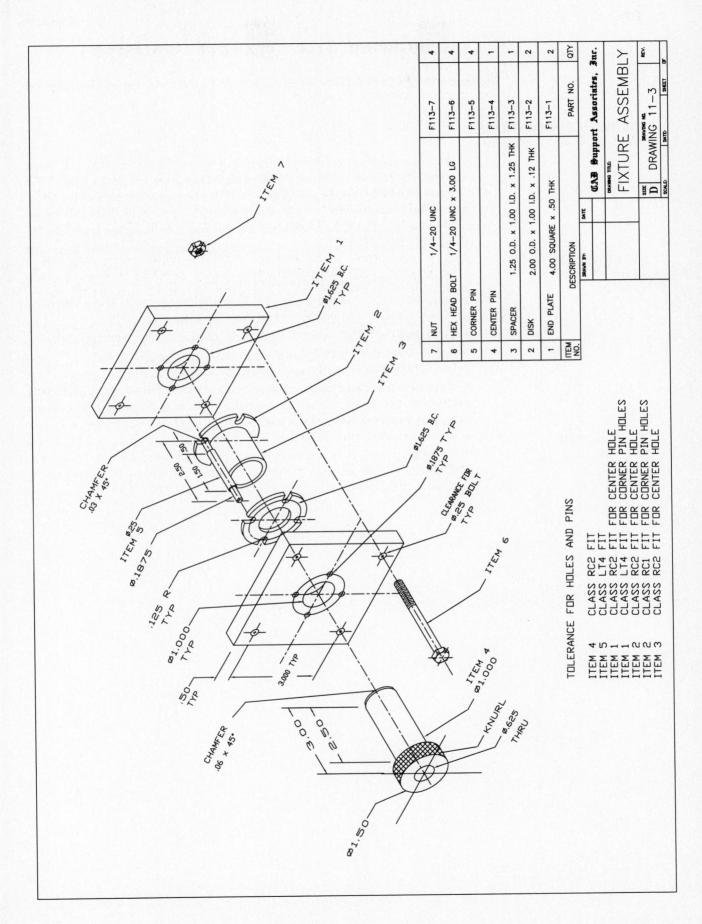

FIXTURE ASSEMBLY

ITEM NO.	DESCRIPTION		PART NO.	QTY
7	NUT	1/4-20 UNC	F113-7	4
6	HEX HEAD BOLT	1/4-20 UNC x 3.00 LG	F113-6	4
5	CORNER PIN		F113-5	4
4	CENTER PIN		F113-4	1
3	SPACER	1.25 O.D. x 1.00 I.D. x 1.25 THK	F113-3	1
2	DISK	2.00 O.D. x 1.00 I.D. x .12 THK	F113-2	2
1	END PLATE	4.00 SQUARE x .50 THK	F113-1	2

CAD Support Associates, Inc.

DRAWING TITLE: FIXTURE ASSEMBLY

DRAWING NO. DRAWING 11-3

SIZE **D**   REV.

SCALE: DATED: SHEET: OF

DRAWN BY: DATE:

TOLERANCE FOR HOLES AND PINS

ITEM 4   CLASS RC2 FIT
ITEM 5   CLASS LT4 FIT
ITEM 1   CLASS RC2 FIT FOR CENTER HOLE
ITEM 1   CLASS LT4 FIT FOR CORNER PIN HOLES
ITEM 2   CLASS RC1 FIT FOR CENTER HOLE
ITEM 2   CLASS RC2 FIT FOR CORNER PIN HOLES
ITEM 3   CLASS RC2 FIT FOR CENTER HOLE

ITEM 7

ITEM 1

Ø1.625 B.C.
TYP

ITEM 2

ITEM 3

CHAMFER
.03 x 45°

.50

.250

.50

.150

ITEM 5

Ø.25

Ø.1875

.125 R
TYP

Ø1.000
TYP

.50
TYP

3.000 TYP

Ø1.625 B.C.

Ø.1875 TYP
TYP

CLEARANCE FOR
Ø.25 BOLT
TYP

ITEM 6

ITEM 4
Ø1.000

CHAMFER
.06 x 45°

3.00

2.50

KNURL
Ø.625
THRU

Ø1.50

315

DRAWING 11-4: FLANGED COUPLING

The isometric view in this three-view drawing must be done working off the centerline.

DRAWING SUGGESTIONS

> Draw the major centerline first. Then draw vertical center lines at every point where an isocircle will be drawn. Make sure to draw these lines extra long so that they can be used to trim the isocircles in half. By starting at the back of the object and working forward, you can take dimensions directly from the right side view.

> Draw the isocircles at each centerline and then trim them to represent semicircles.

> Use end point, intersection, and tangent-to-tangent osnaps to draw horizontal lines.

> Trim away all obstructed lines and parts of isocircles.

> Draw the four slanted lines in the middle as vertical lines first. Then, with ortho off, CHANGE their end points, moving them in .125.

> Remember, MIRROR will not work in the isometric view, although it can be used effectively in the right side view.

> Use BHATCH to create the cross-hatching.

> If you have made a mistake in measuring along the major centerline, STRETCH can be used to correct it. Make sure that ortho is on and that you are in an isoplane that lets you move the way you want.

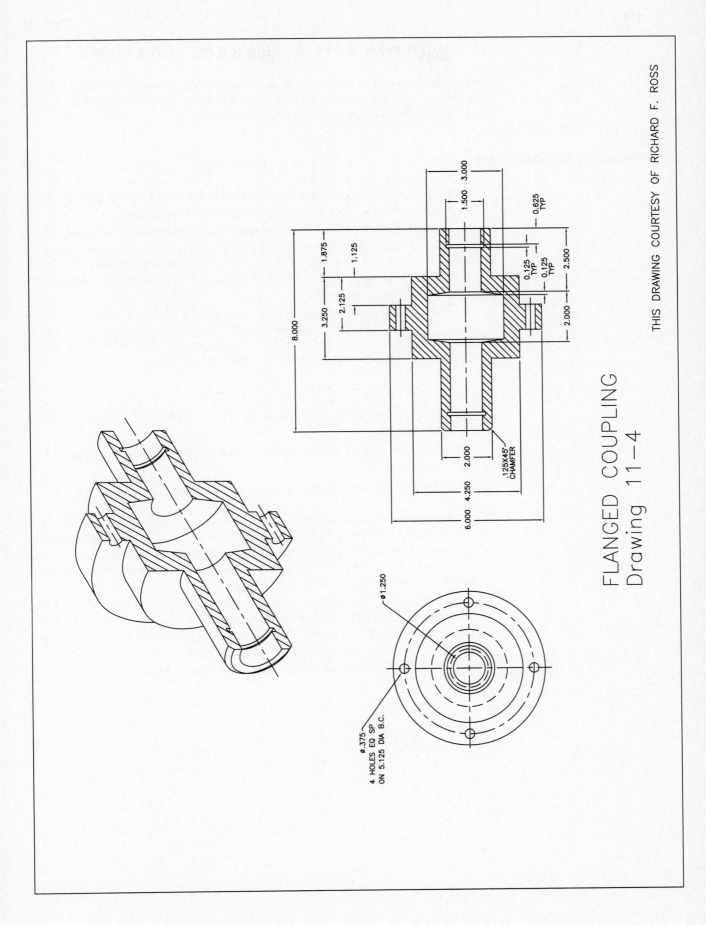

FLANGED COUPLING
Drawing 11-4

3.000

1.500

0.625
TYP

1.875

1.125

0.125
TYP

0.125
TYP

8.000

3.250

2.125

2.500

2.000

2.000

.125X45°
CHAMFER

4.250

6.000

Ø1.250

ø.375
4 HOLES EQ SP
ON 5.125 DIA B.C.

DRAWING 11-5: GARAGE FRAMING

This is a fairly complex drawing that will take lots of trimming and careful work. Changing the "snapang" (snap angle) variable so that you can draw slanted arrays is a method that can be used frequently in isometric drawing.

DRAWING SUGGESTIONS

> You will find yourself using COPY, ZOOM, and TRIM a great deal. OFFSET also will work well. This is a good place to use dynamic zoom.

> You may want to create some new layers of different colors if you have a color monitor. Keeping different parts of the construction walls, rafters, and joists on different layers will allow you to have more control over them and add a lot of clarity to what you see on the screen. Turning layers on and off can considerably simplify trimming operations.

> You can cut down on repetition in this drawing by using arrays on various angles. For example, if the snapang variable is set to 150 degrees, the 22″ wall in the left isoplane can be created as a rectangular array of studs with 1 row and 17 columns set 16 inches apart. To do so, follow this procedure:

1. Type "snapang".

2. Enter a new value so that rectangular arrays will be built on isometric angles (30 or 150).

3. Enter the ARRAY command and create the array. Use negative values where necessary.

4. Trim the opening for the window.

> One alternative to this array method is to set your snap to 16″ temporarily and use multiple COPY to create the columns of studs, rafters, and joists. Another alternative is to use the grip edit offset snap method beginning with an offset snap of 16″ (i.e., press shift when you show the first copy displacement and continue to hold down shift as you make other copies).

> The cutaway in the roof that shows the joists and the back door is drawn using the standard nonisometric ELLIPSE command. Then the rafters are trimmed to the ellipse and the ellipse is erased. Do this procedure before you draw the joists and the back wall. Otherwise you will be trimming these as well.

> Use CHAMFER to create the chamfered corners on the joists.

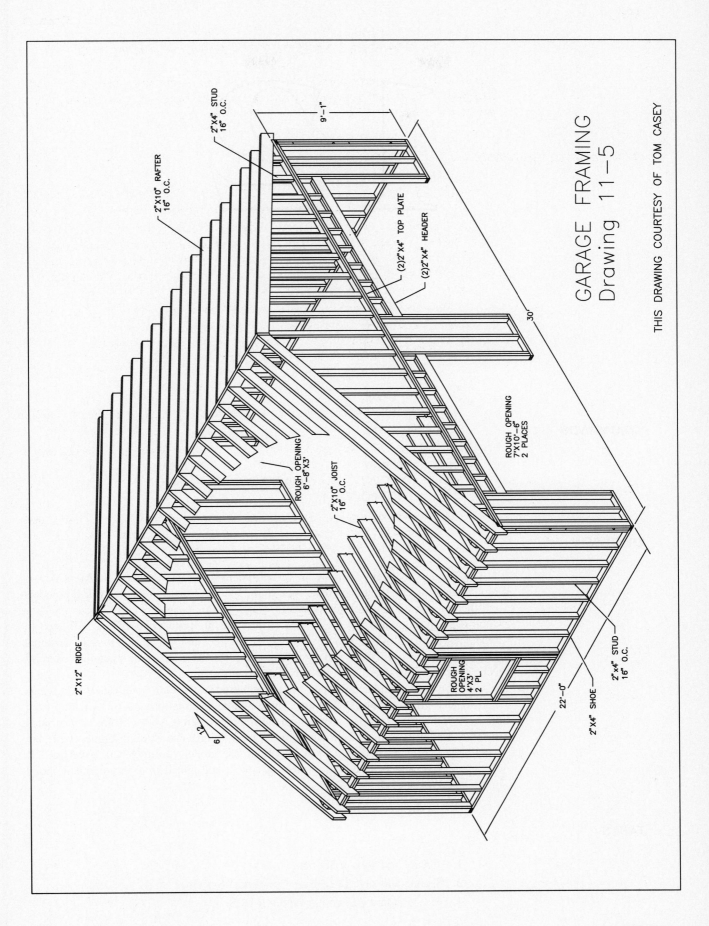

2"X10" RAFTER
16" O.C.

2"X4" STUD
16" O.C.

9'-1"

(2)2"X4" TOP PLATE

(2)2"X4" HEADER

30

ROUGH OPENING
7'X10'-6"
2 PLACES

ROUGH OPENING
6'-8"X3'

2"X10" JOIST
16" O.C.

2"X12" RIDGE

12
6

ROUGH
OPENING
4'X3'
2 PL.

22'-0"

2"X4" STUD
16" O.C.

2"X4" SHOE

GARAGE FRAMING
Drawing 11—5

THIS DRAWING COURTESY OF TOM CASEY

319

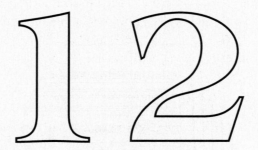

CHAPTER

COMMANDS

UCS	DISPLAY	3D	SETTINGS
UCS	VPOINT	RULESURF	UCSICON
	DDVPOINT		

OVERVIEW

It is now time to begin thinking in three dimensions. 3D drawing in AutoCAD is logical and efficient. You can create wire frame models, surface models, or solid models and display them from multiple points of view. In this chapter we will focus on User Coordinate Systems and 3D viewpoints. These are the primary tools you will need to understand how AutoCAD allows you to work in three dimensions on a two-dimensional screen. Tasks 1–5 will take you through a complete 3D wire frame modeling exercise using four different coordinate systems that we will define.

If you have completed Chapter 11, you will find that working on isometric drawings has prepared you well for 3D drawing. There will be a similar process of switching from plane to plane, but there are two primary differences. First, you will not be restricted to three isometric planes: You can define a User Coordinate System aligned with any specifiable plane. Second, and most important, the model you draw will have true 3D characteristics. You will be able to view it, edit it, and plot it from any definable point in space.

TASKS

1. Create and view a 3D box.
2. Define and save three User Coordinate Systems.
3. Use standard edit commands in a UCS.

4. Construct a slot through an angled surface in 3D.
5. Create a 3D fillet using FILLET and RULESURF.
6. Explore other methods of using the VPOINT command.
7. Do drawing 12-1 ("Clamp").
8. Do drawing 12-2 ("Guide Block").
9. Do drawing 12-3 ("Slide Mount").
10. Do drawing 12-4 ("Stair Layout").

TASK 1: Creating and Viewing a 3D Wireframe Box

Discussion.   In this task we will create a simple 3D box that we can edit in later tasks to form a more complex object. The 3D tasks you will be performing here are not possible with versions of AutoCAD before Release 10.

In Chapter 1 we showed how to turn the coordinate system icon (see *Figure 12-1*) off and on. For drawing in 3D you will definitely want it on. If your icon is not visible, follow this procedure to turn it on:

1. Type or select "ucsicon".
2. Type or select "on".

For now, simply observe the icon as you go through the process of creating the box, and be aware that you are currently working in the same coordinate system that you have always used in AutoCAD. It is called the World Coordinate System, to distinguish it from others you will create yourself beginning in Task 2.

Currently, the origin of the WCS is at the lower left of your screen. This is the point (0,0,0) when you are thinking 3D, or simply (0,0) when you are in 2D. *x* coordinates increase to the right horizontally across the screen, and *y* coordinates increase vertically up the screen as usual. The Z axis, which we have ignored up until now, currently extends out of the screen towards you and perpendicular to the X and Y axes. This orientation of the three planes is also called a plan view. Soon we will switch to a "front, right, top" view.

Let's begin.

> Draw a 2.00 by 4.00 rectangle near the middle of your screen, as shown in *Figure 12-1*.

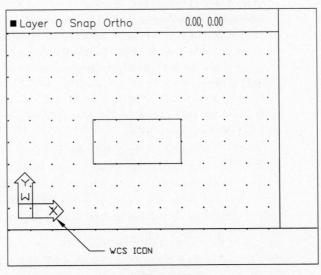

Figure 12-1

Changing Viewpoints

In order to move immediately into a 3D mode of drawing and thinking, our first step will be to change our viewpoint on this object. There are two commands that allow you to create 3D points of view, VPOINT and DVIEW. DVIEW, which is discussed at the end of Chapter 15, is complex and best suited for creating carefully adjusted presentation images, including perspective views. The VPOINT command is somewhat simpler and best used for setting up basic views during the drawing and editing process. A good understanding of all the VPOINT options will increase your understanding of AutoCAD's 3D space. For this reason we have included at the end of the chapter an optional discussion of the different methods available in the VPOINT command.

A simple and efficient method, however, is to use the preset Viewpoints dialogue box from the pull down menu. For our purposes, this is the only method you will need.

Preset views are accessed through the DDVPOINT dialogue box found on the "View" pull down menu. This Viewpoint Presets dialogue box is shown in *Figure 12-2*. We will use this menu to create a "front, right, top" view.

> Select "View" from the pull down menu bar.

A pull down menu will appear.

> Run down the menu until "Set View" is highlighted, then move the cursor to the right.

This will call up a cascading submenu beginning with "Dview", as shown in *Figure 12-2*.

> Run down the submenu to highlight "Viewpoint" and then move the cursor to the right.

This will call a second cascading submenu beginning with "Axes", as shown.

> Pick "Presets..." from the submenu.

This will call up the Viewpoint Presets dialogue box, as shown in *Figure 12-2*.

Using this method, AutoCAD needs two angles to create a new viewpoint. First is a viewing angle within the XY plane, described as an angle from the X axis. It takes the object's current orientation as 0 degrees from the X axis and rotates it around the Z axis. The second angle "elevates" our viewpoint on the object by moving us up or down out of the XY plane.

The angle from the X axis can be specified by selecting one of the squares with icons at the top of the box, or by typing a number in the edit box at the bottom. The angle from the XY plane can be typed or shown using the scroll bar at the right of the dialog box.

> Set the angle from the X axis by picking the bottom right box, "315" as shown in the figure.

Notice that selecting this box enters the value 315.0 in the From X Axis edit box and moves the white pointer to 315. The angle of 315 gives us our "right, front" viewpoint. It may be easier to visualize the rotation if you keep in mind that +315 is the equivalent of −45. When the rotation is complete, the front and back edges of the square will be at −45 degree angles from the horizontal, as shown in *Figure 12-3*.

The second angle specification (the angle from the XY plane) can be shown in a similar manner by picking a box from the semicircle at the right, or by typing a value

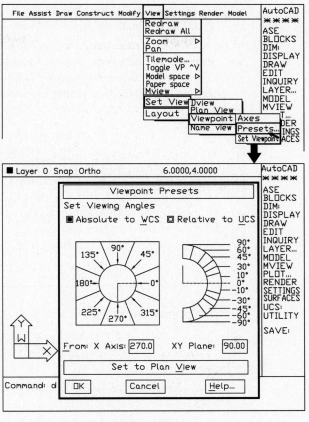

Figure 12-2

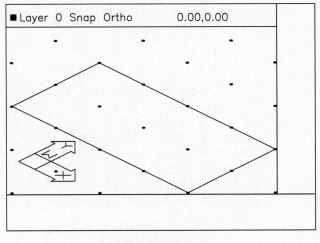

Figure 12-3

in the edit box at the bottom. The angle you specify will be a Z dimension viewing position. Think of this as a viewing height above or below the object, or at ground level, even with it. We will choose to look down at an angle of 30 degrees.

> Pick the box labelled +30.

This will move the white pointer and enter the value 30 in the XY Plane edit box.

> When your dialogue box shows 315.00 and 30.00 as the two viewing angles, pick OK to create the new viewpoint.

Your screen should be redrawn as shown in *Figure 12-3*. Notice how the grid and the coordinate system icon have altered to show our current orientation. These visual aids are extremely helpful in viewing 3D objects on the flat screen and imagining them as if they were positioned in space.

Using the two angles in the dialogue box to set rotation in the XY plane and the viewing height, you can create a large variety of points of view. We encourage you to experiment with these now. First see the note that follows. Then try changing the first angle to 225 to create a left, front, top view. What two angles will give you a front view at ground level? What will a view from below the object look like? As you experiment, pay attention to the UCS icon. Variations of the icon you may encounter here and later on are shown in *Figure 12-4*. With some views you will have to think carefully and watch the icon to understand which way the object is being presented.

ICON	DESCRIPTION
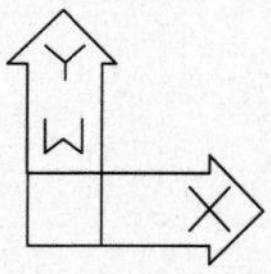	WCS (WORLD COORDINATE SYSTEM) "W" appears on "Y" arm
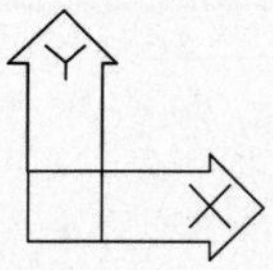	UCS (USER COORDINATE SYSTEM) NO "W" appears on "Y" arm
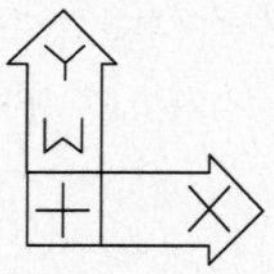	+ appears in box and "W" appears on "Y" arm if the current UCS is the same as the WCS
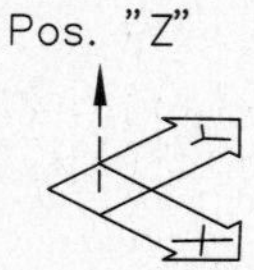 Pos. "Z"	Box appears at the base of ICON if viewing UCS from above its X—Y plane
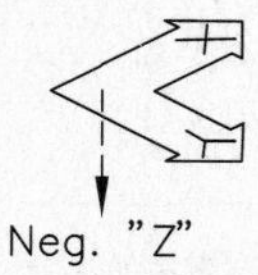 Neg. "Z"	Box is missing if viewing UCS from below its X—Y plane
	Broken pencil ICON appears if viewing direction is "EDGE ON" or near "EDGE ON" X—Y plane of current UCS

Figure 12-4

NOTE: Remember that AutoCAD saves your pull down menu selections. When you have opened the two cascading menus shown in *Figure 12-2*, they will appear automatically the next time you pick "View" from the menu bar. Now if "Presets..." is highlighted on the submenu you can reopen the dialog box by clicking on "View" in the menu bar again. This will save you time when you are using the same dialogue box repeatedly.

When you are done experimenting, be sure to return to our previous front, right, top view (angles 315 and 30, as in *Figure 12-3*). We will use this view frequently throughout this chapter and the next.

Whenever you change viewpoints, AutoCAD displays the drawing extents, so that the object fills the screen and is as large as possible. Often you will need to zoom out a bit to get some space to work in. This is easily done using the "Scale(X)" option of the ZOOM command.

> Type "z" or select "zoom".

Do not use the pull down menu, as this does not allow for the Scale(X) option.

AutoCAD prompts:

All/Center/Dynamic/Extents/Left/Previous/Vmax/Window/<Scale(X/XP)>:

> In response to the ZOOM prompt, type ".5x".

Don't forget the "x". This tells AutoCAD to adjust and redraw the display so that objects appear half as large as before.

Next, we will create a copy of the rectangle placed 1.25 above it. This brings up a basic 3D problem: AutoCAD interprets all point selections as being in the XY plane, so how does one indicate a point or a displacement in the Z direction? There are three possibilities: typed 3D coordinates, X/Y/Z point filters, and object snaps. Object snap requires an object already drawn above or below the XY plane, so it will be of no use right now. We will use typed coordinates first, then discuss how point filters could be used as an alternative. Later we will be using object snap as well.

Entering 3D Coordinates

3D coordinates can be entered from the keyboard in the same manner as 2D coordinates. Often this is an impractical way to enter individual points in a drawing. However, within COPY or MOVE it provides a simple method for specifying a displacement in the Z direction.

> Type or select "COPY".

AutoCAD will prompt for object selection.

> Select the square with a window.

> Press enter, the space bar, or the enter equivalent button on your pointing device to end object selection.

AutoCAD now prompts for the base point of a vector or a displacement value:

<Base point or displacement>/Multiple:

Typically, you would respond to this prompt and the next by showing the two end points of a vector. However, we cannot show a displacement in the Z direction this way. This is important for understanding AutoCAD coordinate systems. Unless an object snap is used, all points picked on the screen with the pointing device will be interpreted as being in the XY plane of the current UCS. Without an entity outside the XY plane to use in an object snap, there is no way to point to a displacement in the Z direction.

> Type "0,0,1.25".

AutoCAD now prompts:

Second point of displacement:

You can type the coordinates of another point, or press enter to tell AutoCAD to use the first entry as a displacement from (0,0,0). In this case, pressing enter will indicate a displacement of 1.25 in the Z direction, and no change in X or Y.

> Press enter.

AutoCAD will create a copy of the rectangle 1.25 directly above the original. Your screen should resemble *Figure 12-5*.

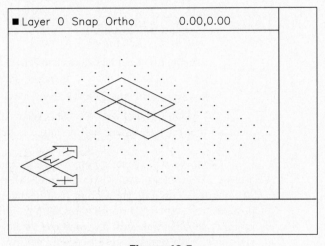

Figure 12-5

X/Y/Z Point Filters (Optional)

Point filters can be very useful in 3D, although they may seem odd until you get a feel for when to use them. Notice that in the displacement we just entered, the only thing that changes is the *z* value. Note also that we could specify the same displacement using any point in the xy plane as a base point. For example, (3,6,0) to (3,6,1.25) would have the same effect. In fact, we don't even need to know what *x* and *y* are as long as we know that they don't change.

That is how an ".XY" point filter works. We borrow, or "filter," the *x* and *y* values from a point, without pausing to find out what the values actually are, and then specify a new *z* value. Other types of filters are possible, of course, such as ".Z" or ".YZ".

You can use a point filter, like an object snap, any time AutoCAD asks for a point. After a point filter is specified, AutoCAD will always prompt with an "of". In our case you are being asked, "You want the *x* and *y* values of what point?" In response, you pick a point, then AutoCAD will ask you to fill in *z*. Notice that point filters can be "chained" so that, for example, you can filter the *X* value from one point and combine it with the filtered *Y* value from another point.

To use an .XY filter in the COPY command instead of typing coordinates, for example, you follow this procedure:

1. Enter the COPY command.
2. Select the rectangle.

3. For the displacement base point, pick any point in the XY plane.

4. At the prompt for a second point, type or select ".xy" (filters are on a submenu of the object snap menu, on the third button of your cursor, if you have four or more buttons).

5. At the "of" prompt, type "@" or pick the same point again.

6. At the "(need Z):" prompt, type "1.25". The result would be *Figure 12-5*, as before.

Using Object Snap

We now have two rectangles floating in space. Our next job is to connect the corners to form a wire frame box. This is done easily using "ENDpoint" object snaps. This is a good example of how object snaps allow us to construct entities not in the XY plane of the current coordinate system.

> Type or select "OSNAP" to turn on a running osnap mode.

AutoCAD prompts:

Object snap modes:

> Type "end" or select "ENDpoint".

The running ENDpoint object snap is now on and will affect all point selection. You will find that object snaps are very useful in 3D drawing and that ENDpoint mode can be used frequently.

Now we will draw some lines.

> Enter the LINE command and connect the upper and lower corners of the two rectangles, as shown in *Figure 12-6*. (We have removed the grid for clarity, but you will probably want to leave yours on.)

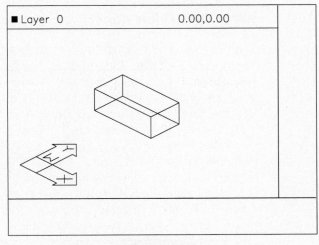

Figure 12-6

Before going on, pause a moment to be aware of what you have drawn. The box on your screen is a true wire frame model. Unlike an isometric drawing, it is a 3D model that can be turned, viewed, and plotted from any point in space. It is not, however, a solid model or a surface model. It is only a set of lines in 3D space. Removing hidden lines or shading would have no effect on this model.

In the next task you will begin to define your own coordinate systems that will allow you to perform drawing and editing functions in any plane you choose.

TASK 2: Defining and Saving User Coordinate Systems

Procedure.

1. Type "UCS".
2. Choose an option.
3. Specify a coordinate system.
4. Repeat the UCS command to name and save the new coordinate system.

Discussion. In this task you will begin to develop new vocabulary and techniques for working with objects in 3D space. The primary tool will be the UCS command. You will also learn to use the UCSICON command to control the placement of the coordinate system icon.

Until now we have had only one coordinate system to work with. All coordinates and displacements have been defined relative to a single point of origin. In Task 1 we changed our point of view, but the UCS icon changed along with it, so that the orientations of the X, Y, and Z axes relative to the object were retained. With the UCS command you can define new coordinate systems at any point and any angle in space. When you do, you can use the coordinate system icon and the grid to help you visualize the planes you are working in, and all commands and drawing aids will function relative to the new system.

The coordinate system we are currently using is unique. It is called the World Coordinate System and is the one we always begin with. The "w" at the base of the coordinate system icon indicates that we are working in the world system. A User Coordinate System is nothing more than a new point of origin and a new orientation for the X, Y, and Z axes.

We will begin by defining a User Coordinate System in the plane of the top of the box, as shown in *Figure 12-7*.

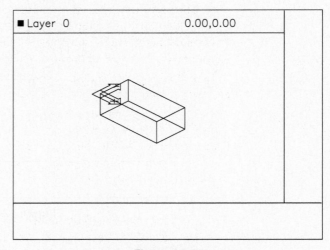

Figure 12-7

> Leave the ENDpoint osnap mode on for this exercise.

> Type or select "UCS".

The UCS command gives you the following prompt:

Origin/ZAxis/3point/Entity/View/X/Y/Z/Prev/Restore/Save/Del/?/<World>:

In this chapter we will explore all options except "ZAxis", "Entity", and "Del". For further information see the *AutoCAD Reference Manual* and the UCS icon chart, *Figure 12-4*.

First we will use "Origin" to create a UCS that is parallel to the WCS.

> Type "o" to specify the origin option.

AutoCAD will prompt for a new origin:

Origin point <0,0,0>:

This option does not change the orientation of the three axes. It simply shifts their intersection to a different point in space. We will use this simple procedure to define a UCS in the plane of the top of the box.

> Use the ENDpoint osnap to select the top left front corner of the box, as shown by the location of the icon in *Figure 12-7*.

You will notice that the "w" is gone from the icon. However, the icon has not moved. It is still at the lower left of the screen. It is visually helpful to place it at the origin of the new UCS, as in the figure. In order to do this we need the UCSICON command.

> Type or select "UCSICON". (There is an "Icon" selection under "Settings" and "UCS" on the pull down menu that is easy to use.)

If you are typing, AutoCAD prompts:

ON/OFF/All/Noorigin/ORigin <ON>:

The first two options allow you to turn the icon on and off. The "All" option affects icons used in multiple view ports, which we will discuss in Chapter 15. "Noorigin" and "ORigin" allow you to specify whether you want to keep the icon in the lower left corner of the screen or place it at the origin of the current UCS.

> Type "or" for the "ORigin" option. (Select "Origin" from the submenu if you are using the pull down.)

The icon will move to the origin of the new current UCS, as in *Figure 12-7*. With UCSICON set to origin, the icon will shift to the new origin whenever we define a new UCS. The only exception would be if the origin were not on the screen or too close to an edge for the icon to fit. In these cases the icon would be displayed in the lower left corner again.

The "top" UCS we have just defined will make it easy to draw and edit entities that are in the plane of the top of the box and also to perform editing in planes that are parallel to it, such as the bottom. In the next task we will begin drawing and editing using different coordinate systems, and you will see how this works. For now, we will spend a little more time on the UCS command itself. We will define two more User Coordinate Systems, but first, let's save this one so that we can recall it quickly when we need it later on.

> Type or select "UCS".

This time we will use the "Save" option.

> Type "s" or select "Save".

AutoCAD will ask you to name the current UCS so that it can be called out later:

?/Desired UCS name:

We will name our UCS "top." It will be the UCS we use to draw and edit in the top plane. This UCS would also make it easy for us to create an orthographic top view later on.

> Type "top".

The top UCS is now saved and can be recalled using the "Restore" option or by making it "current" using the UCS Control dialog box under "Settings".

NOTE: Strictly speaking, it is not necessary to save every UCS. However, it usually saves time, since it is unlikely that you will have all your work done in any given plane or UCS the first time around. More likely, you will want to move back and forth between major planes of the object as you draw. Be aware also that you can return to the last defined UCS with the "Previous" option.

Next we will define a "front" UCS using the "3point" option of the UCS command.

> Press enter or the space bar to repeat the UCS command.

> Type "3" to specify the "3point" option.

AutoCAD prompts:

Origin point <0,0,0>:

In this option you will show AutoCAD a new origin point, as before, and then a new orientation for the axes as well. Notice that the default origin is the current one. If we retained this origin, we could define a UCS with the same origin and a different axis orientation.

Instead, we will define a new origin at the lower left corner of the front of the box, as shown in *Figure 12-8*.

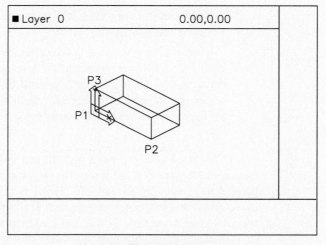

Figure 12-8

> With the ENDpoint osnap on, pick point 1, as shown in the figure.

AutoCAD now prompts you to indicate the orientation of the X axis:

Point on positive portion of the X axis <1.00,0.00,-1.25>:

> Pick the right front corner of the box, point 2, as shown.

The osnap ensures that the new X axis will now align with the front of the object. AutoCAD prompts for the Y axis orientation:

Point on positive-Y portion of the UCS XY plane <0.00,1.00,-1.25>:

By definition, the Y axis will be perpendicular to the X axis, therefore AutoCAD needs only a point that shows the plane of the Y axis and its positive direction. Because of this, any point on the positive side of the Y plane will specify the Y axis correctly. We have chosen a point that is on the Y axis itself.

> Pick point 3, as shown.

When this sequence is complete, you will notice that the coordinate system icon has rotated along with the grid and moved to the new origin as well. This UCS will be convenient for drawing and editing in the front plane of the box, or editing in any plane parallel to the front, such as the back.

Now save the "front" UCS.

> Press enter to repeat the UCS command.

> Type "s" to save.

> Type "front" to name the UCS.

Finally, we will use the "Origin" and "Y" axis rotation options together to create a right side UCS.

> Repeat the UCS command.

> Type "o" or select "Origin".

> Pick the lower front corner of the box for the origin, as shown in *Figure 12-9*.

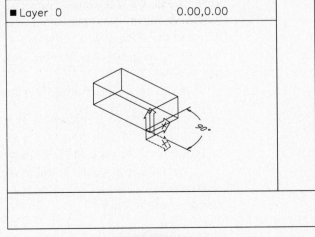

Figure 12-9

> Repeat the UCS command.

We will rotate the UCS icon around its Y axis to align it with the right side of the box.

In using any of the rotation options ("X", "Y", and "Z"), the first thing you have to decide is which axis is the axis of rotation. If you look at the current position of the icon and think about how it will look when it aligns with the right side of the box, you will see that the Y axis retains its position and orientation while the X axis turns through 90 degrees. In other words, since X rotates around Y, Y is the axis of rotation.

> Type "Y".

Now AutoCAD prompts for a rotation:

Rotation angle around Y axis <0.0>:

It takes some practice to differentiate positive and negative rotation in 3D. If you like, you can use AutoCAD's "right hand" rule, which can be stated as follows: If you are hitchhiking (pointing your thumb) in a positive direction along the axis of rotation, your fingers will curl in the direction of positive rotation for the other axis. In our case, align your right thumb with the positive Y axis, and you will see that your fingers curl in the direction we want the X axis to rotate. Therefore, the rotation of X around Y is positive.

> Type "90".

You should now have the UCS icon aligned with the right side of the box, as shown in *Figure 12-9*. Save this UCS before going on to Task 3.

> Repeat the UCS command.

> Type "s".

> Type "right".

TASK 3: Using Draw and Edit Commands in a UCS

Discussion. Now the fun begins. Using our three new coordinate systems and one more we will define later, we will give the box a more interesting "slotted wedge" shape. In this task we will cut away a slanted surface on the right side of the box. Since the planes we will be working in are parallel to the front of the box, we will begin by making the "front" UCS current. All our work in this task will be in this UCS.

> Repeat the UCS command, or select "Named UCS..." under "Settings" on the pull down menu. Now that we have three new coordinate systems defined, you may find the dialogue box a simple way to switch between them.

> Type "r" to specify the "Restore" option, or highlight "Front" in the dialog box and click on "Current".

If you are typing, AutoCAD will ask for the UCS to restore:

?/Name of UCS to restore:

> Type "front", or click on "OK" in the dialogue box.

The UCS icon should return to the front plane.

NOTE: In this case we also could have used the "Previous" option since "front" was the previous UCS.

Before going on, we need to turn off the running ENDpoint osnap.

> Type or select "osnap".

> Press enter or select "None" at the prompt for object snap modes.

Now there will be no running object snap modes in effect.

Look at *Figure 12-10*. We will draw a line down the middle of the front (line 1) and use it to trim another line coming in at an angle from the right (line 2).

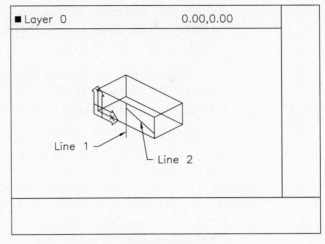

Figure 12-10

> Type "l" or select "Line".
> At the "From point:" prompt, type "mid" or select a "MIDpoint" osnap.
> Point to the top front edge of the box.

AutoCAD will snap to the midpoint of the line.

> Make sure that ortho is on (F8).

Notice how ortho works as usual, but relative to the current UCS.

> Pick a second point anywhere below the box.

This line will be trimmed later, so the exact length does not matter.

Next we will draw line 2 on an angle across the front. This line will become one edge of a slanted surface. Your snap setting will need to be at .25 or smaller, and ortho will need to be off. The grid, snap, and coordinate display all work relative to the current UCS, so it is a simple matter to draw in this plane.

> Check your snap setting and change it if necessary.
> Turn ortho off (F8).
> Repeat the LINE command.
> With snap on (F9), pick a point .25 down from the top edge of the box on line 1, as shown in *Figure 12-10*.
> Pick a second point .25 up along the right front edge of the box.

Now trim line 1.

> Type or select "trim".

You will see the following message in the command area:

View is not plan to UCS. Command results may not be obvious.

In the language of AutoCAD 3D, a view is plan to the current UCS if the XY plane is in the plane of the monitor display and its axes are parallel to the sides of the screen. This is the usual 2D view in which the Y axis aligns with the left side of the display and the X axis aligns with the bottom of the display. In previous chapters we always worked in plan view. In this chapter we have not been in plan view since the beginning of Task 1.

With this message, AutoCAD is warning us that boundaries, edges, and intersections may not be obvious as we look at a 3D view of an object. For example, lines that appear to cross may be in different planes.

Having read the warning, we continue.

> Select line 2 as a cutting edge.

> Press enter to end cutting edge selection.

> Point to the lower end of line 1.

> Press enter to exit TRIM.

Your screen should resemble *Figure 12-11*.

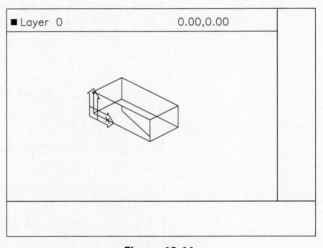

Figure 12-11

Now we will copy our two lines to the back of the box. Since we will be moving out of the front plane, we will require the use of ENDpoint object snaps to specify the displacement vector. We will also be using the ENDpoint osnap in the next sequence, so let's turn on the running mode again.

> Type or select "osnap".

> Type "end" or select "ENDpoint".

> Type or select "copy".

> Pick lines 1 and 2.

> Press enter to end object selection.

> Use the ENDpoint osnap to pick the lower front corner of the box, point 1 as shown in *Figure 12-12*.

> At the prompt for a second point of displacement, use the ENDpoint osnap to pick the lower right back corner of the box, point 2 as shown.

Your screen should now resemble *Figure 12-12*.

What remains is to connect the front and back of the surfaces we have just outlined and then trim away the top of the box. We will continue to work in the front UCS and to use ENDpoint osnaps.

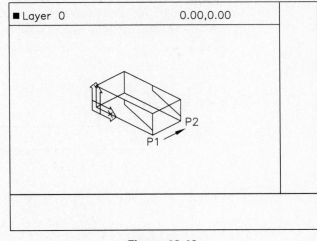

Figure 12-12

We will use a multiple COPY to copy one of the front-to-back edges in three places.

> Enter the COPY command.

> Temporarily override the end point osnap by typing "non" or selecting "None" from an object snap menu.

This is a single point override, which will leave the ENDpoint osnap in effect. It is convenient when you need to make a selection without an object snap but want to leave the running osnap on for points that follow.

> Pick any of the front-to-back edges for copying.

> Press enter to end object selection.

> Type "m" or select "multiple".

> Pick the front ENDpoint of the selected edge to serve as a base point of displacement.

> Pick the top end point of line 1 (point 1 in *Figure 12-13*).

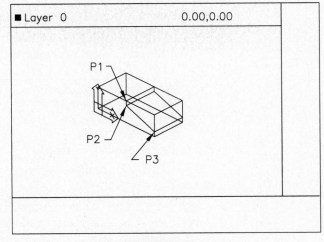

Figure 12-13

> Pick the lower end point of line 1 (point 2) as another second point.

> Pick the right end point of line 2 (point 3) as another second point.

> Press enter to exit the COPY command.

Finally, we need to do some trimming.

> Type or select "Osnap" and turn off the running "ENDpoint" mode by pressing enter or selecting "None" at the prompt.

> Type or select "trim".

> For cutting edges, select lines 1 and 2 and their copies in the back plane (lines 3 and 4 in *Figure 12-14*).

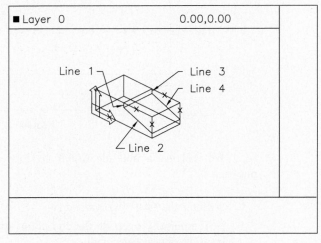

Figure 12-14

A quick alternative to selecting these four separate lines is to use a crossing box to select the whole area. As long as your selection includes the four lines, it will be effective.

NOTE: Trimming in 3D can be tricky. Remember where you are. Edges that do not run parallel to the current UCS may not be recognized at all.

> Press enter to end cutting edge selection.

> One by one, pick the top front and top back edges to the right of the cut, and the right front and right back edges above the cut, as shown by the Xs in *Figure 12-14*.

> Press enter to exit the TRIM command.

> Enter the ERASE command and erase the top edge that is left hanging in space.

Your screen should now resemble *Figure 12-15*.

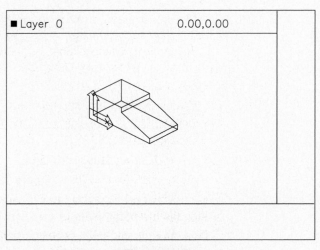

Figure 12-15

TASK 4: Working on an Angled Surface

Discussion. In this task we will take our 3D drawing a step further by constructing a slot through the new slanted surface and the bottom of the object. This will require the creation of a new UCS. In completing this task, you also will use the OFFSET command and continue to develop a feel for working with multiple coordinate systems.

> Type or select "UCS".

> Type "3" for the "3point" option.

> Using an ENDpoint osnap, pick point 1, as shown in *Figure 12-16*.

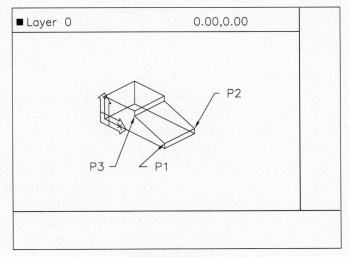

Figure 12-16

> Using an ENDpoint osnap, pick point 2, as shown.

> Using an ENDpoint osnap, pick point 3, as shown.

> Press enter to repeat the UCS command.

> Type "s" for the "Save" option.

> Type "angle" for the name of the UCS.

Now we are ready to work in the plane of the angled surface.

NOTE: From here on, we have moved our UCS icon back to the lower left of the screen for the sake of clarity in our illustrations. You may leave it at its origin on your screen, if you like, or move it by entering the UCSICON command again and typing "no" or selecting "NOorigin".

> If ortho is off, turn it on (F8).

We will create line 1 across the angled surface, as shown in *Figure 12-17*, by offsetting the right front edge of the wedge.

> Type or select "OFFSET".

> Type or show a distance of 1.50.

> Pick the right front edge.

> Point anywhere above and to the left of the edge.

> Exit the OFFSET command.

> Draw lines 2 and 3 perpendicular to the first, as shown. They will be over .50 and 1.50 from the current Y axis.

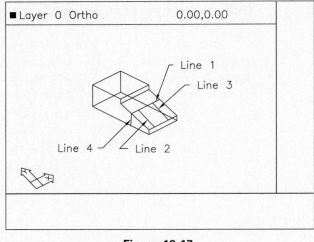

Figure 12-17

Watch the coordinate display and notice how the coordinates work in this UCS as in any other.

> Turn ortho off.

> Using snap for the top point and a "PERpendicular" osnap (single point override) for the lower point, drop line 4 down to the bottom front edge.

Notice again how osnap modes work for you, especially to locate points that would be difficult to define in the current UCS.

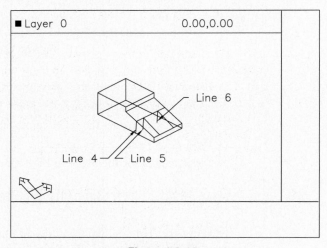

Figure 12-18

> Create lines 5 and 6, as shown in *Figure 12-18*, by making two copies of line 4, extending down from the ends of lines 2 and 3, as shown.

> ERASE line 4 from the front plane.

> Using ENDpoint osnaps, connect lines 5 and 6 to each other in the plane of the bottom of the object.

> Using ENDpoint and PERpendicular osnaps, connect lines 5 and 6 to the bottom edge of the right side.

> Using ENDpoint osnaps, draw two short vertical lines on the right side, connecting to lines 2 and 3.

> TRIM line 1 and the two lines on the right side across the opening of the slot.

When you are done, your screen should resemble *Figure 12-19*.

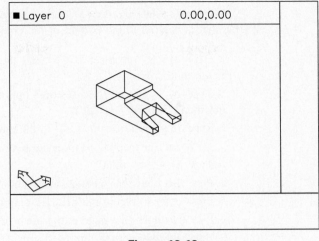

Figure 12-19

TASK 5: Using RULESURF to Create 3D Fillets

Procedure.

1. Create fillets in two planes.
2. Type or select RULESURF.
3. Pick a fillet.
4. Pick the corresponding side of the fillet in the other plane.

Discussion.   There are two parts to completing this task. First, we will fillet the top and bottom corners of the slot drawn in Task 4. Then we will use the RULESURF command to create filleted surfaces between the top and bottom of the slot.

The top and bottom fillets will be constructed in the usual manner, except that we will need to pay attention to our coordinate systems. We will use the "angle" UCS to fillet the top of the slot and the "top" UCS to fillet the bottom. The "top" UCS can be used this way because the top of the object is parallel to the bottom.

> To begin this task you should be in the angle UCS, as in Task 4, and your screen should resemble *Figure 12-19*.

> Type or select "Fillet".

AutoCAD will remind us that our view is not plan to our UCS and then prompt as usual:

```
View is not plan to UCS. Command results may not be obvious.
Polyline/Radius/<Select first object>:
```

> Type "r" to choose the "Radius" option.

> Type ".25" for the radius value.

> Press enter to repeat the FILLET command.

> Pick two lines that meet at one of the upper corners of the slot.

> Press enter to repeat the FILLET command.

> Pick two lines that meet at the other upper corner of the slot.

The upper fillets are done. Before we can do the lower ones, we must change to a UCS that is parallel to the bottom of the object.

> Type "UCS" or select "UCS" and then "Named UCS..." from the pull down menu under "Settings".
> Type "r" to choose the "Restore" option, or highlight "top" in the dialogue box and then click on "Current".
> Type "top" or click on "OK" in the dialogue box to restore the top UCS.
  We are now ready to fillet the bottom of the slot.
> Type or select "fillet".
> Pick two lines that meet at one of the lower corners of the slot.
> Press enter to repeat the FILLET command.
> Pick two lines that meet at the other lower corner of the slot.
> Erase the two vertical lines left outside the fillets.

Your screen should resemble *Figure 12-20*.

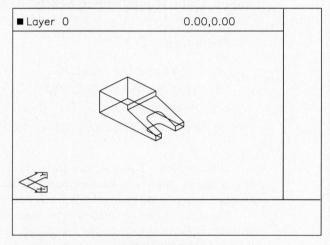

Figure 12-20

Now we will use a new command to connect the upper and lower fillets with 3D surfaces. RULESURF is one of several commands that create 3D surfaces. These commands create entities called "3D polygon meshes," which are discussed in detail in Chapter 13. This will serve as a quick introduction.

The RULESURF command allows you to create a 3D surface between two lines or curves in 3D space. Our two curves will be the upper and lower fillets at each of the two corners.

> Type or select "rulesurf".
  AutoCAD will prompt:

             Select first defining curve:

> Pick one of the top fillets, as shown in *Figure 12-21*.
  AutoCAD will prompt for a second curve:

             Select second defining curve:

> Pick the corresponding fillet in the bottom plane, with a pick point on the corresponding side, as shown.

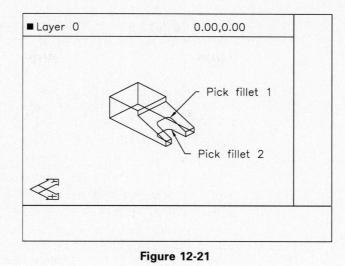

Figure 12-21

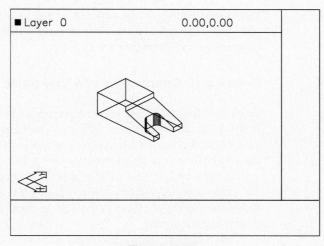

Figure 12-22

AutoCAD will draw a set of faces to represent the surface curving around the fillet radius, as shown in *Figure 12-22*.

The trick in using RULESURF is to be sure that you show a pick point toward one side of the curve, and that you pick the next curve with a point on the corresponding side. Otherwise you will get an hourglass effect, as shown in *Figure 12-23*.

We'll work more with 3D surfaces in the next chapter. To complete this task, repeat the RULESURF command and draw the fillet at the other corner of the groove. When you are done, your screen should resemble *Figure 12-22*.

TASK 6: Other Methods of Using the VPOINT Command (Optional)

Discussion. This discussion of other methods of using VPOINT is intended as a reference. The information presented here is not necessary to completing the drawings in this chapter, and no specific exercise is intended. However, if you are interested in gaining a complete understanding of the VPOINT command and its options, try creating

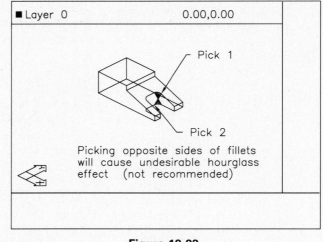

Figure 12-23

the views described and outlined in the charts and figures. In Chapter 15 you will also find a complete discussion of the DVIEW command for fine tuning and creating perspective and cutaway views.

Entering 3D Coordinates of a Viewpoint

From the "Rotate/<View point>" prompt of the VPOINT command, the default method is to type in 3D coordinates. When you first enter the VPOINT command from the WCS plan view, the default viewpoint is given as (0,0,1). This means that you are viewing the object from a point somewhere along the positive z axis. You are at 0 in the x and y directions and at +1 in the z direction. In other words, you are directly above the XY plane looking straight down, a plan view. Think of the x coordinate as controlling right-left orientation, the y coordinate as controlling back-front, and the z coordinate as controlling up-down.

By changing the x coordinate to 1 (right), leaving y at 0 (neither front nor back), and z at 1 (above), you can create a viewpoint above and to the right of the object (1,0,1). Similarly, (1,−1,1) would move you to the right (X = 1), back you up a bit (Y = −1) so that you are in front of the object, and raise your point of view (Z = 1) so that you are above the object looking down. This common (1,−1,1) viewpoint is the same as the right, front, top viewpoint used throughout this chapter, but previously we have defined it using the Viewport Preset dialogue box.

We will explore other methods of specifying viewpoints in a moment, but first look at the following chart. It summarizes the effects of the x, y, and z coordinates and gives you coordinates for some standard views. You should have a good understanding of why each view appears as it does.

X Right-Left	Y Back-Front	Z Up-Down	View Description
0	0	1	Plan
0	0	−1	"Worm's eye"
1	0	0	Right side
−1	0	0	Left side
0	1	0	Back
0	−1	0	Front
1	1	1	Right, Back, Top
1	−1	1	Right, Front, Top
	etc.	etc.	

We suggest that you try some of these viewpoints and experiment with others not listed. Your goal should be to get a feel for how different coordinate combinations move your point of view in relation to objects on the screen.

Rotation

The other option shown in the prompt is "Rotation". This is the option that is used by the Release 12 Viewport Preset dialogue box, used earlier in this chapter. Rotation can also be adjusted by typing "r" or selecting "Rotation" at the "Rotate/<View point>" prompt. Then AutoCAD will prompt for two angles. The first is an angle in the XY plane. It is measured from the X axis, with 0 being straight out to the right, as usual.

The second angle goes up or down from the XY plane, with 0 being ground level. Thus an angle of 90 degrees from the XY plane would define the plan view.

The following chart will give you the rotation versions of some of the same major views shown on the pull down menu and the previous chart.

From X	From XY	View Description
0	0	Right
0	90	Plan
90	0	Back
180	0	Left
270	0	Front
45	30	Back, Right, Top
−45 (or +315)	30	Front, Right, Top
45	−30	Back, Right, Bottom
etc.	etc.	

The Compass and Axes System

If you enter the VPOINT command and then press enter in response to the "Rotate/<View point>" prompt, you will see a display that resembles *Figure 12-24*.

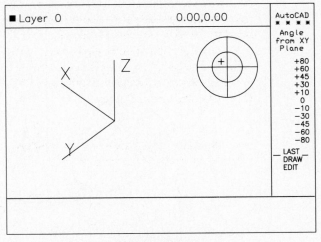

Figure 12-24

The triple axes represent the orientation of the object. When you move your cursor, you will see these rotating. Some users may find this visualization easier to comprehend because it represents the object itself rather than your point of view in relation to the object. However, this effect is much more clearly realized in the DVIEW command, discussed in Chapter 15.

The other part of the display is a rather unusual representation of a globe. The horizontal and vertical axes show the X and Y dimensions as you would expect, and the circles show the Z dimension. This actually shows a globe transformed into a cone and then flattened. The "north pole" of the globe has become a point at the center of the compass, while the "south pole" has been widened into a circle at the outside of the compass. In between is another circle representing the "equator," or ground 0 region.

This simply means that anywhere inside the first circle will give you a top-down view; outside the first circle will give you a bottom-up view. Anywhere on the middle circle will give you a ground-level view.

Notice the blip that moves as you move your cursor. This represents your point of view in the coordinate system.

Figure 12-25 gives you a good summary of the compass points and how they relate to standard views. Try them out if you like.

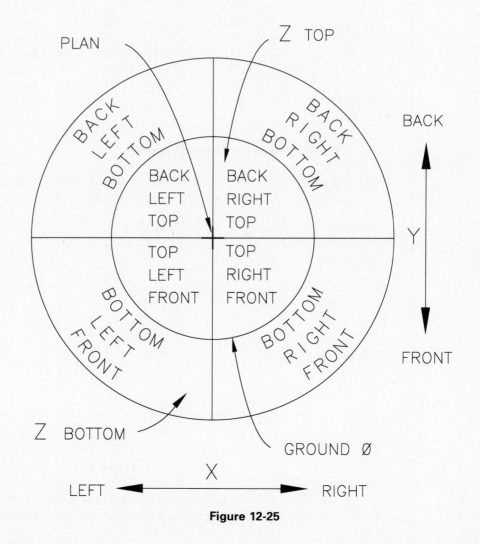

Figure 12-25

TASKS 7, 8, 9, and 10

The drawings that follow are all 3D wire frame models that use the techniques and procedures introduced in this chapter. Drawing 12-1 also introduces 3D dimensioning technique. Drawing 12-4 is a 3D architectural detail. Your primary objective in completing these drawings should be to gain facility with User Coordinate Systems and 3D space.

DRAWING 12–1: CLAMP

This drawing is similar to the one you did in the chapter. Two major differences are that it is drawn from a different viewpoint and that it includes dimensions in the 3D view. This will give you additional practice in defining and using User Coordinate Systems. Your drawing should include dimensions, border, and title.

DRAWING SUGGESTIONS

> We drew the outline of the clamp in a horizontal position and then worked from a front, left, top point of view.

> Begin in WCS plan view drawing the horseshoe shaped outline of the clamp. This will include fillets on the inside and outside of the clamp. The more you can do in plan view before copying to the top plane, the less duplicate editing you will need to do later.

> When the outline is drawn, switch to a front, left, top view.

> COPY the clamp outline up 1.50.

> Define User Coordinate Systems as needed, and save them whenever you are ready to switch to another UCS. You will need to use them in your dimensioning.

> The angled face, the slots, and the filleted surfaces can be drawn just as in the chapter.

Dimensioning in 3D

The trick to dimensioning a 3D object is that you will need to restore the appropriate UCS for each set of dimensions. Think about how you want the text to appear. If text is to be aligned with the top of the clamp (i.e., the 5.75 overall length), you will need to draw that dimension in a "top" UCS; if it is to align with the front of the object (the 17 degree angle and the 1.50 height), draw it in a "front" UCS, and so forth.

> Define a UCS with the "View" option in order to add the border and title. Type "UCS", then "v". This creates a UCS aligned with your current viewing angle.

Setting Surftab1

Notice that there are 8 lines defining the RULESURF fillets in this drawing, compared to six in the chapter. This is controlled by the setting of the variable Surftab1, which is discussed in Chapter 13. You can change it by typing "Surftab1" and entering "8" for the new value.

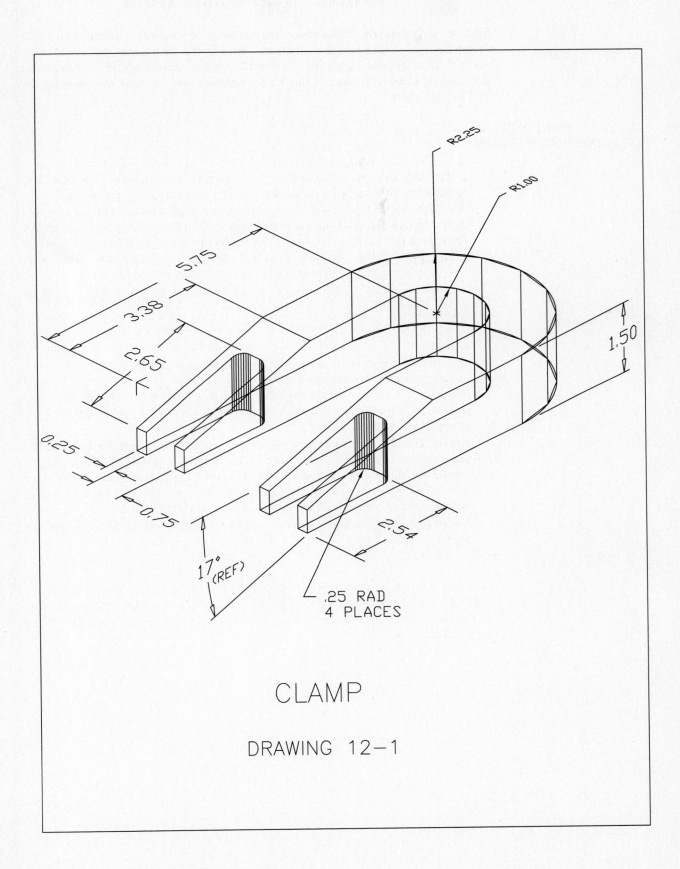

CLAMP

DRAWING 12–1

DRAWING 12-2: GUIDE BLOCK

In this drawing you will be working from dimensioned views to create a wire frame model. This brings up some new questions. Which view should you start with? How do you translate the views into the 3D image? A good general rule is this: Draw the top or bottom in the XY plane of the WCS, otherwise you will have trouble using the VPOINT command.

DRAWING SUGGESTIONS

> In this drawing it is tempting to draw the right side in WCS plan view first, because that is where most of the detail is. If you do this, however, you will have difficulty creating the view as shown. Instead, we suggest that you keep the bottom of the object in the WCS XY plane and work up from there, as has been the practice throughout this chapter. The reason for this is that the VPOINT command works relative to the WCS. Therefore, front-back, left-right, and top-bottom orientations will make sense only if the top and bottom are drawn plan to the WCS.

> Draw the 12.50 × 8.00 rectangle shown in the top view, and then copy it up 4.38 to form the top of the guide's base.

> Change over to the same front, right, left 3D viewpoint we used in the chapter.

> Connect the four corners to create a block outline of the base of the object.

> Now you can define a new UCS on the right side and do most of your work in that coordinate system, since that is where the detail is. Once you have defined the right side UCS, you may want to go into its plan view to draw the right side outline, including the arc and circle of the guide. Then come back to the 3D view to copy back to the left side.

NOTE: You can save some time switching viewpoints by using the save and restore options of the VIEW command. When a view is saved, it includes the 3D orientation along with the zoom factor that was current at the time of the save. Also, ZOOM previous can be used to restore a previous 3D point of view. It will not, however, restore a UCS.

> Use RULESURF with Surftab1 set to 16 to fill in surfaces between the arcs and circles.

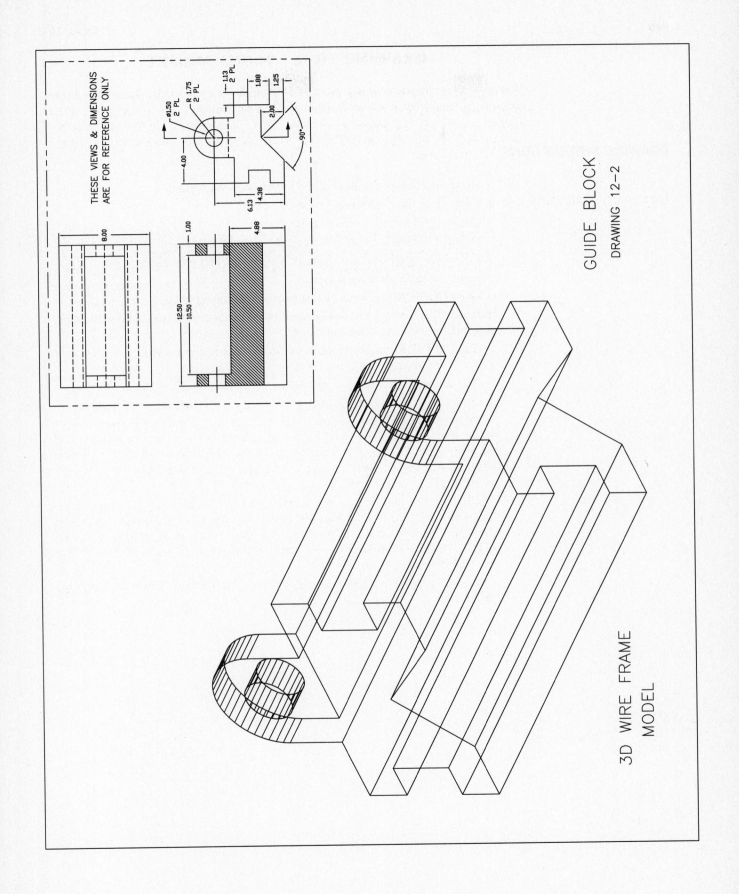

THESE VIEWS & DIMENSIONS ARE FOR REFERENCE ONLY

Ø1.50 2 PL
R 1.75 2 PL
1.13 2 PL
1.88
1.25
2.00
90°
4.00
6.13
4.38
8.00
1.00
4.88
12.50
10.50

3D WIRE FRAME MODEL

GUIDE BLOCK
DRAWING 12-2

349

DRAWING 12-3: SLIDE MOUNT

This drawing continues to use the same views, coordinate systems, and techniques as the previous drawings, but it has more detail and is a bit trickier.

DRAWING SUGGESTIONS

> Draw the H-shaped outline of the top view in WCS plan.

> Copy up in the Z direction.

> Connect the corners to create a 3D shape.

> Define a right side view, and create the slot and holes.

> Copy back to the left side, connect the corners, and trim inside the slot.

> Return to WCS (bottom plane).

> Use RULESURF between circles to create mounting holes.

> Draw filleted cutout and countersunk holes. Each countersunk hole will require three circles, two small and one larger.

> Use RULESURF to create inner surfaces of countersunk holes.

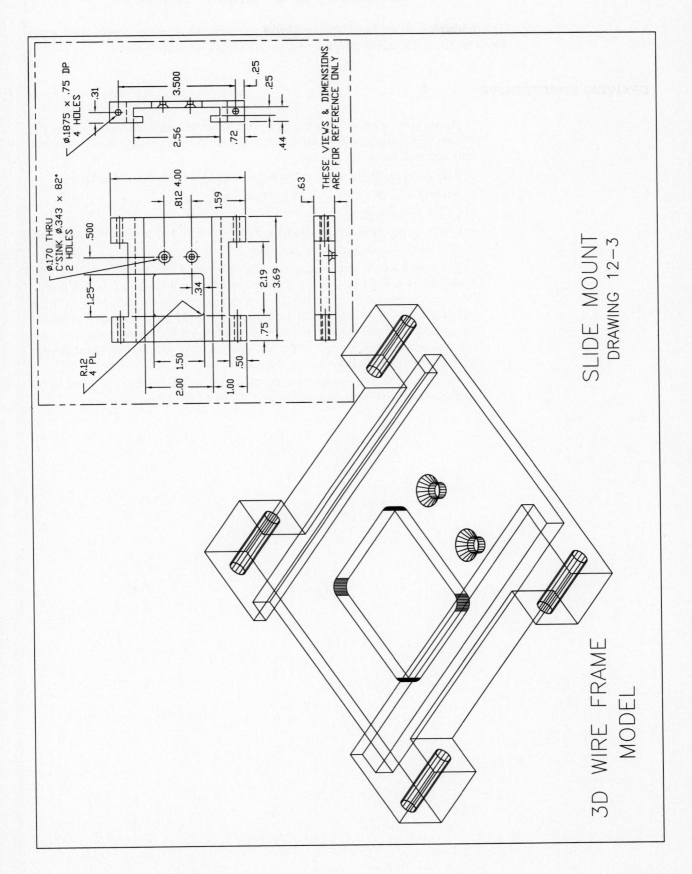

Ø.1875 × .75 DP
4 HOLES

.31
3.500
.25
.25

2.56
.72
.44

Ø.170 THRU
C'SINK Ø.343 × 82°
2 HOLES

4.00
.812
1.59

.500
.63

THESE VIEWS & DIMENSIONS
ARE FOR REFERENCE ONLY

1.25

.34
2.19
3.69

.75

R.12
4 PL

1.50
.50

2.00
1.00

SLIDE MOUNT
DRAWING 12-3

3D WIRE FRAME
MODEL

DRAWING 12–4: STAIR LAYOUT

This wire frame architectural detail will give you a chance to use architectural units and limits in 3D. It will require the use of a variety of edit commands.

DRAWING SUGGESTIONS

> In the WCS plan view, begin with a $2'' \times 12'$ rectangle that will become the bottom of a floor joist. This will keep the bottom floor in the plan view, consistent with our practice in this chapter.

> COPY the rectangle up $8''$ and connect lines to form the complete joist.

> ARRAY $16''$ on center to form the first floor.

> COPY all joists up $9'\text{-}6''$ to form the second floor.

> Create the stairwell opening in the second floor with double headers at each end.

> Add the $3/4''$ subfloor to the first floor.

> The outline of the stair stringers can be constructed in a number of ways. One possibility is as follows: Draw a guideline down from the front of the left double header and then another over $10'\text{-}10''$ to locate the end of the run; from the right end of the run, draw one $7\ 1/2''$ riser and one $9\ 1/2''$ tread, beginning from the top surface of the subflooring; use a multiple copy and ENDpoint osnaps to create the other steps; when you get to the top, you will find you need to TRIM the top tread slightly to bring it flush with the header.

> We leave it to you to construct the back line of the stringer. It needs to be parallel with the stringer line and down $1'$ from the top tread, as shown.

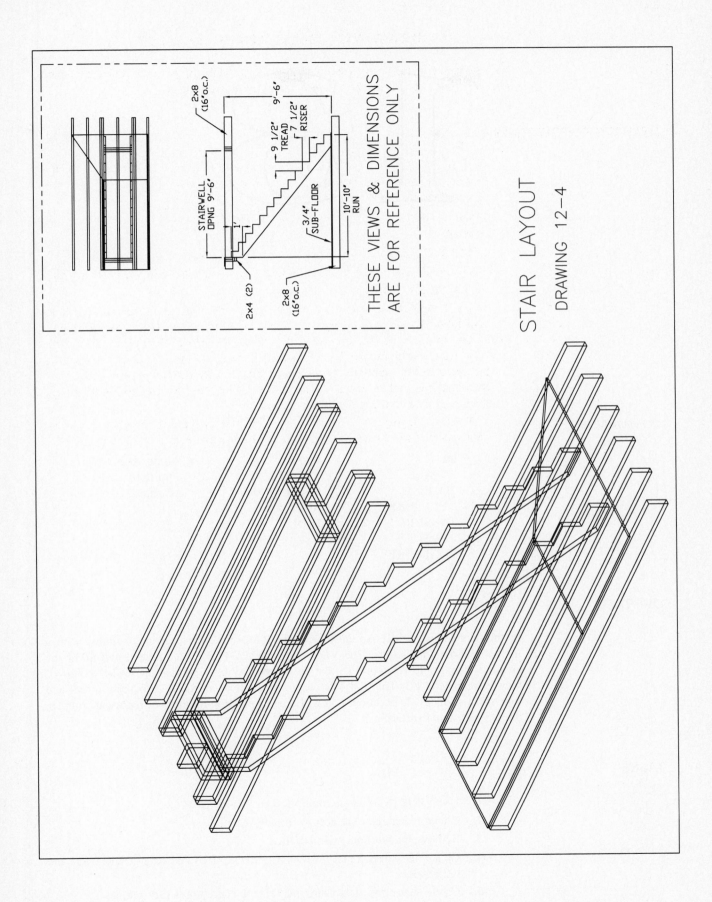

2x8
(16"o.c.)

STAIRWELL
OPNG 9'-6'

2x4 (2)

2x8
(16"o.c.)

9'-6'

9 1/2'
TREAD
7 1/2'
RISER

3/4'
SUB-FLOOR

10'-10'
RUN

THESE VIEWS & DIMENSIONS
ARE FOR REFERENCE ONLY

STAIR LAYOUT
DRAWING 12-4

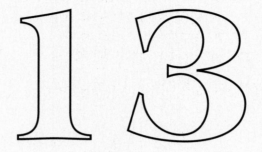

COMMANDS

3D	DISPLAY	VARIABLES
3DFACE	VPORTS	Surftab1
3DMESH	REDRAWALL	Surftab2
RULESURF	REGENALL	
TABSURF	HIDE	
REVSURF		
EDGESURF		

OVERVIEW

In this chapter we will continue to explore Release 12 3D drawing features, with a focus on surface modeling. The VPORTS (or VIEWPORTS) command will allow the creation of multiple viewports so that an object may be viewed from several points of view simultaneously. The 3DFACE command will be introduced to draw three- and four-sided surfaces. In addition, you will create "polygon meshes" to represent complex three-dimensional surfaces.

TASKS

1. Use VPORTS to create multiple tiled viewports.
2. Create rectangular surfaces with 3DFACE.
3. Remove hidden lines with HIDE.
4. Create 3D polygon meshes with TABSURF, RULESURF, EDGESURF, and REVSURF.
5. Create surface models using the "3D Objects" AutoLISP routines.

6. Create approximated surfaces using PEDIT (optional).
7. Do Drawing 13-1 ("REVSURF Designs").
8. Do Drawing 13-2 ("Picnic Table").
9. Do Drawing 13-3 ("Globe").
10. Do Drawing 13-4 ("Nozzle").

TASK 1: Using Multiple Tiled Viewports

Procedure.

1. Type or select "VPORTS".
2. Enter number of viewports desired.
3. Enter orientation of viewports.
4. Define views in each viewport.

Discussion. A major feature needed to draw effectively in 3D is the ability to view an object from several different points of view simultaneously as you work on it. The VPORTS, or VIEWPORTS, command is easy to use and can save you from having to jump back and forth between different views of an object. Viewports can be used in 2D to place several zoom magnifications on the screen at once, as shown in Chapter 3. More important, viewports can be used to place several 3D viewpoints on the screen at once. This can be a significant drawing aid. If you do not continually view an object from different points of view, it is easy to create entities that appear correct in the current view, but that are clearly incorrect from other points of view.

In this task we will divide your screen in half and define two views, so that you can visualize an object in plan view and a 3D view at the same time. As you work, remember that this is only a display command. The viewports we use in this chapter will be simple "tiled" viewports. Tiled viewports cover the complete drawing area, do not overlap, and cannot be plotted. Plotting multiple viewports can also be accomplished, but only in "paper space" with non-tiled viewports. We will explore these in Chapter 15.

> Type or select "VPORTS" (under "Settings" on the screen menu — or pick "View", "Layout", then "Tiled Viewports..." from the pull down).

AutoCAD will prompt:

Save/Restore/Delete/Join/SIngle/?/2/<3>/4:

The first three options allow you to save, restore, and delete viewport configurations. "Join" allows you to reduce the number of windows so that you move from, say, four windows to three. "SIngle" is the option that returns you to a single window. "?" will get you a list of previously saved viewport configurations. The numbers 2, 3, and 4 will establish the number of different viewports you want to put on the screen.

The pull down menu system has a dialogue box that will show you all the different ways in which the screen display may be split for multiple viewports. To use it, select "View", then "Layout", then "Tiled Viewports..." from the pull down. This will call out the dialogue box shown in *Figure 13-1*. Notice that the list on the left simply names the nine layout options on the right. Any of these can also be specified by typing and following the sequence of command prompts.

If you are typing, the default is three windows with a full pane on the right and a horizontal split on the left. This is called "Three: Right" in the pull down dialogue box.

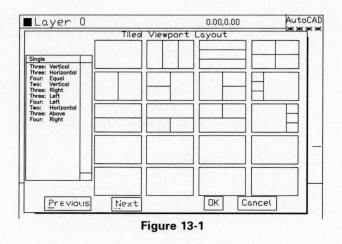

Figure 13-1

For our purposes we will create a simple two-way vertical split, the "Two: Vertical" option in the dialogue box.

> Type "2" or select the second box on the left of the icon menu.

If you type the number, AutoCAD will prompt for the direction of the split:

Horizontal/<Vertical>:

> Press enter to accept the default vertical split, or to complete the dialogue.

Your screen will be regenerated to resemble *Figure 13-2*.

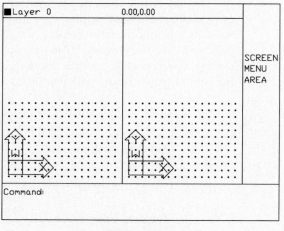

Figure 13-2

You will notice that the grid is rather small and confined to the lower part of each window. The shape of the viewports necessitates this reduction in drawing area. You can enlarge details as usual using the ZOOM command. Zooming and panning in one viewport will have no effect on other viewports. However, you can have only one UCS in effect at any time, so a change in the coordinate system in one viewport will be reflected in all viewports.

If you move your pointing device back and forth between the windows, you will see an arrow when you are on the left and the cross hairs when you are on the right. This indicates that the right window is currently active. Drawing and editing can be done only in the active window. To work in another window, you need to make it current by picking it with your pointing device. Often this can be done while a command is in progress.

> Move the cursor into the left window and press the pick button on your pointing device.

Now the cross hairs will appear in the left viewport, and you will see the arrow when you move into the right viewport.

> Move the cursor back to the right and press the pick button again.

This will make the right window active again.

There is no value in having two viewports if each is showing the same thing, so our next job will be to change the viewpoint in one of the windows. We will leave the window on the left in plan view and switch the right window to a 3D view. For consistency, we will use the familiar front, right, top view used in the last chapter.

> Select "View", "Set View", "Viewpoint", and then "Presets" from the pull down.

> Pick 315 degrees for the X axis rotation and 30 for the rotation in the XY plane.

> Click on "OK".

NOTE: As an alternative to using the dialogue box, you can type or select "vpoint" and then "1,-1,1". This will give you the same view.

Your screen should now be redrawn with a right, front, top view in the right viewport as shown in *Figure 13-3*.

Once you have defined viewports, any drawing or editing done in the active viewport will appear in all the viewports. As you draw, watch what happens in both viewports.

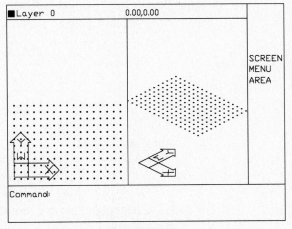

Figure 13-3

TASK 2: Creating Surfaces with 3DFACE

Procedure.

1. Type or select "3DFACE".
2. Pick three or four points going around the face.
3. Continue defining edges or press enter to exit the command.

Discussion. 3DFACE creates triangular and quadrilateral surfaces. 3D faces are built by entering points in groups of three or four to define the outlines of triangles or quadrilaterals, similar to objects formed by the SOLID command. The surface of a 3D face is not shown on the screen, but it is recognized by the HIDE command and by other rendering programs, such as RenderMan or 3D Studio.

Layering is critical in surface modeling. Surfaces quickly complicate a drawing so that object selection and object snap become difficult or impossible. Also, you may want to be able to turn layers off or freeze them to achieve the results you want from the HIDE command. You may eventually want a number of layers specifically defined for faces and surfaces, but this will not be necessary for the current exercise.

> Type or select "3DFace" (under "Draw" and then "3D Surfaces" on the pull down, under "DRAW" on the screen menu).

AutoCAD will prompt:

First point:

You can define points in either of the two viewports. In fact, you can even switch viewports in the middle of the command.

> Pick a point similar to point 1, as shown in *Figure 13-4*.

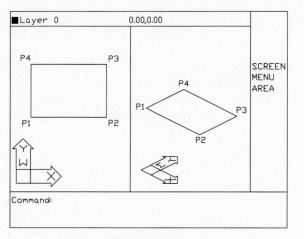

Figure 13-4

AutoCAD prompts:

Second point:

> Pick a second point, moving around the perimeter of the face, as shown.

Be aware that the correct order for defining 3D faces is different from the SOLID command (Chapter 9). It is important to pick points in order around the face, otherwise you will get a bow tie or hourglass effect.

AutoCAD prompts:

Third point:

> Pick a third point, as shown.

AutoCAD prompts:

Fourth point:

NOTE: If you pressed enter now, AutoCAD would draw the outline of a triangular face, using the three points already given.

> Pick the fourth point of the face.

AutoCAD draws the fourth edge of the face automatically when four points have been given.

AutoCAD will continue to prompt for third and fourth points so that you can draw a series of surfaces to cover an area with more than four sides. Keep in mind, however, that drawing faces in series is only a convenience. The result is a collection of independent three- and four-sided faces.

> Press enter to exit the 3DFACE command.

In the next task we will copy this face in order to demonstrate the HIDE command. But first, a word about invisible edges.

Invisible Edges in 3Dfaces

The edges of a 3Dface can be visible or invisible as desired. To define an invisible edge, type "i" before entering the first point of the edge. You can even define "phantom" 3D faces in which no edges are visible.

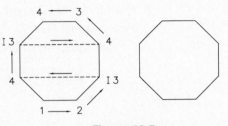

Figure 13-5

Take a look at *Figure 13-5*. This figure illustrates the need for invisible edges in 3Dfaces. Since 3DFACE only draws triangles or quadrilaterals, objects with more than four sides must be drawn as combinations of three- and four- sided objects. An octagon, for example, can be drawn as two trapezoids and a rectangle, as shown. However, you would not want the two horizontal edges across the middle showing, so the command allows you to make them invisible by typing "i" or selecting "Invisible" from the screen menu before picking the point that begins the invisible edge. This takes forethought and planning. You must remember that the end point of a visible edge also may be the starting point of the next invisible edge.

NOTE: Invisible edges will be hidden if the "Splframe" system variable is set to 0, the default setting. If the variable is set to 1, invisible edges will be displayed. This setting can be changed in the usual manner (Type "Splframe" and then "1") or by selecting "Showedge" from the screen menu.

TASK 3: Removing Hidden Lines with HIDE

Procedure.

1. Type or select HIDE.
2. Wait...

Discussion. The HIDE command is easy to execute. However, execution may be slow in large drawings, and a lot of careful work may be required to create a drawing that hides the way you want it to. This is a primary objective of surface modeling. When you've got everything right, HIDE will temporarily remove all lines and objects that would be obstructed in the current view, resulting in a more realistic representation of the object in space. Hiding has no effect on wireframe drawings, since there are no surfaces to obstruct lines behind them.

> To begin this exercise, you should have the 3Dface from the previous task on your screen.

> COPY the face up 2 units in the Z direction, using the following procedure.

1. Type or select "Copy".

2. Select the face.

3. Type "0,0,2".

4. Press enter.

You now have two 3Dfaces in your drawing. Since the second is directly over the first, you cannot see both in the plan view. From the viewpoint in the right viewport, however, the second face only partially covers the first. Since these are surfaces, rather than wire frames, the top face should hide part of the lower face.

> Make the right viewport active.

> Type or select "hide".

Your screen should be regenerated to resemble *Figure 13-6.*

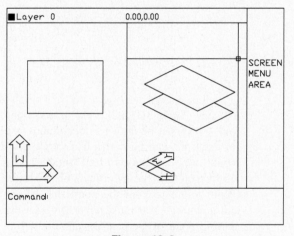

Figure 13-6

In the command line AutoCAD gives you a message that says:

Regenerating drawing.
Hidden lines: done 100%

In this case the hiding and regeneration will happen very quickly. In a larger drawing you will have to wait.

Following are some important points about hidden line removal which you should read before continuing:

1. Hidden line removal can be done at the time of a PLOT or PRPLOT. However, due to the time involved and the difficulty of getting a hidden view just right, it is usually better to experiment on the screen first, then plot with hidden lines removed when you know you will get the image you want.

2. Whenever the screen is regenerated, hidden lines are returned to the screen.

3. The image created through hidden line removal is *not* retained in BLOCKing, WBLOCKing, or saving VIEWs.

4. Hidden line removal can be captured in slides (the MSLIDE and VSLIDE commands, Chapter 9). But remember, slides cannot be plotted.

5. Layer control is important in hidden line removal. Layers that are frozen are ignored by the HIDE command, but layers that are off are treated like layers that are visible. This can, for example, create peculiar blank spaces in your display if you have left surfaces or solids on a layer that is off at the time of hidden line removal.

TASK 4: Using 3D Polygon Mesh Commands

Procedure

Figure 13-7

1. Create geometry to be used in defining the surface.
2. If necessary, set Surftab1 and Surftab2.
3. Enter a 3D polygon mesh command.
4. Use existing geometry to define the surface.

Discussion. 3DFACE can be used to create simple surfaces. However, most surface models require large numbers of faces to approximate the surfaces of real objects. Consider the number of faces in *Figure 13-7*, the globe you will be creating when you do Drawing 13-3. Obviously you would not want to draw such an image one face at a time.

AutoCAD includes a number of commands that make the creation of some types of surfaces very easy. These powerful commands create 3D polygon meshes. Polygon meshes are made up of 3D faces and are defined by a matrix of vertices. They can be treated as single entities and edited with the PEDIT command, or exploded into individual 3D faces.

> To begin this task, ERASE the two faces from the last task and draw an arc and a line below it as shown in *Figure 13-8*. Exact sizes and locations are not important.

The entities may be drawn in either viewport.

Now we will define some 3D surfaces using the arc and line you have just drawn.

TABSURF

The first surface we will draw is called a "tabulated surface." In order to use the TABSURF command, you need a line or curve to define the shape of the surface and a vector to show its size and direction. The result is a surface generated by repeating the shape of the original curve at every point along the path specified by the vector.

> Type or select "tabsurf" (or "Tabulated Surface" under "Draw" and "3D Surfaces" on the pull down menu).

AutoCAD will prompt:

Select path curve:

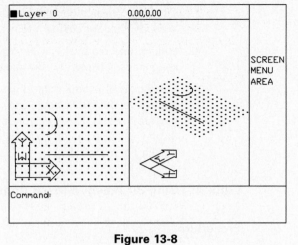

Figure 13-8

The path curve is the line or curve that will determine the shape of the surface. In our case it will be the arc.

> Pick the arc.

AutoCAD will prompt for a vector:

Select direction vector:

We will use the line. Notice that the vector does not need to be connected to the path curve. Its location is not significant, only its direction and length.

There is an oddity here to watch out for as you pick the vector. If you pick a point near the left end of the line, AutoCAD will interpret the vector as extending from left to right. Accordingly, the surface will be drawn to the right. By the same token, if your point is near the right end of the line, the surface will be drawn to the left. Most of the time you will avoid confusion by picking a point on the side of the vector nearest the curve itself.

> Pick a point on the left side of the line. Your screen will be redrawn to resemble *Figure 13-9*.

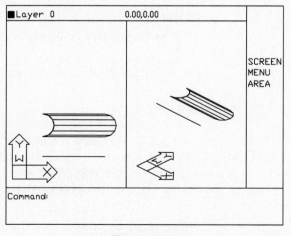

Figure 13-9

Notice that this is a flat surface even though it looks 3D. This may not be clear in the plan view, but is more apparent in the 3D view.

Tabulated surfaces can be fully 3D, depending on the path and vector chosen to define them. In this case we have an arc and a vector that are both entirely in the XY plane, so the resulting surface is also in that plane.

Surftab1

You will also notice that the surface is defined by long narrow faces that run parallel to the vector. If you zoom up on either end of the surface you will see that the arc is only approximated by the shorter edges of these six faces. Unlike the polygons or broken curves AutoCAD often uses to display arcs and circles in order to speed regeneration time, this mesh of faces is the actual current definition of this surface. In order to achieve a more accurate approximation, we need to increase the number of faces. This is done by changing the setting of a variable called "Surftab1" and drawing the object again. You will find Surftab1 and Surftab2 conveniently located in the middle of the 3D surfaces screen menu. We will discuss Surftab2 later.

Let's undo the tabulated surface so that we can draw it again with a new Surftab1 setting.

> Type "u" and then type "r" to execute a REDRAW.

Notice that only the current viewport is redrawn. In order to redraw all viewports simultaneously, you can enter a command called REDRAWALL. There is also a REGENALL command for regenerating all viewports.

> Type or select "Surftab1".

AutoCAD prompts:

```
New value for SURFTAB1 <6>:
```

The default value shows why we see six lines in the tabulated surface. When we change the setting, we will get a different number of lines and degree of accuracy.

> Type "12".

> Type or select "Tabsurf" (or "Tabulated Surface" on the pull down menu).

> Pick the arc for the path curve.

> Pick the line for the direction vector.

Your screen should now resemble *Figure 13-10*.

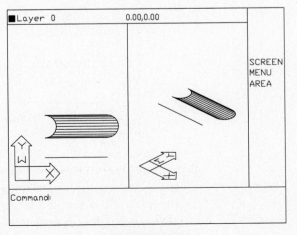

Figure 13-10

RULESURF

TABSURF is useful in defining surfaces that are the same on both ends, assuming you have one end and a vector. Often, however, you have no vector, or you need to draw a surface between two different paths. In these cases you will need the RULESURF command.

For example, what if we need to define a surface between the line and the arc? Let's try it.

> Type "u" to undo the last tabulated surface, then execute a REDRAW or RE-DRAWALL.

It is not absolutely necessary to do the REDRAW, but it makes it easier to pick the arc.

> Type or select "rulesurf" ("Ruled Surface" on the pull down, "RULSURF" on the screen menu).

You are familiar with this command sequence from Chapter 12. The first prompt is:

Select first defining curve:

> Pick the arc, using a point near the bottom.

Remember that you must pick points on corresponding sides of the two defining curves in order to avoid an hourglass effect.

AutoCAD prompts:

Select second defining curve:

> Pick the line, using a point near the left end.

Your screen should resemble *Figure 13-11*.

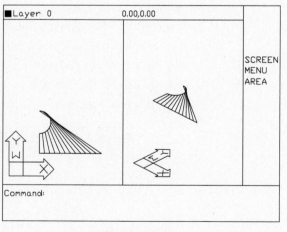

Figure 13-11

Again, notice that this surface is within the XY plane even though it looks 3D. Ruled surfaces may be drawn just as easily between curves that are not coplanar.

If you look closely, you will notice that this ruled surface is drawn with 12 lines, the result of our Surftab1 setting.

Some other typical examples of ruled surfaces are shown on the chart, *Figure 13-17*, at the end of this task.

EDGESURF

TABSURF creates surfaces that are the same at both ends and move along a straight line vector. RULESURF draws surfaces between any two boundaries. There is a third command, EDGESURF, which draws surfaces that are bounded by four curves. Edge-defined surfaces have a lot of geometric flexibility. The only restriction is that they must be bounded on all four sides. That is, they must have four edges that touch.

In order to create an EDGESURF, we need to undo our last ruled surface and add two more edges.

> Type "u" and execute a REDRAW or REDRAWALL.
> Add a line and an arc to your screen, as shown in *Figure 13-12*.

Remember, you can draw in either viewport.

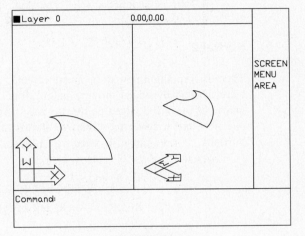

Figure 13-12

> Type or select "edgesurf", or select "Edge Defined Surface Patch" from the pull down menu.

AutoCAD will prompt for the four edges of the surface, one at a time:

Select edge 1:

> Pick the smaller arc.

AutoCAD prompts:

Select edge 2:

> Pick the larger arc.

AutoCAD prompts:

Select edge 3:

> Pick the longer line.

AutoCAD prompts:

Select edge 4:

> Pick the smaller line.

Your screen should now resemble *Figure 13-13*.

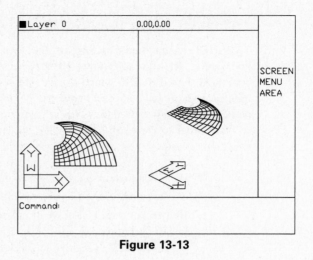

Figure 13-13

Surftab2

There is something new to be aware of here. With TABSURF and RULESURF, surfaces were defined by edges moving in only one direction. With EDGESURF, you have a matrix of faces and edges going two ways. You will notice that there are 12 edges going one way and 6 going the other, as shown in the figure. This brings us to the variable Surftab2. If we change its setting to 12 also, we will see 12 edges in each direction.

Try it.

> Type "u" to undo the EDGESURF command.
> Execute a REDRAW or REDRAWALL.
> Type or select "Surftab2".
> Type "12".
> Enter the EDGESURF command and select the four edges again.

The result should resemble *Figure 13-14*.

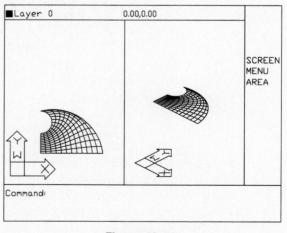

Figure 13-14

REVSURF

We have one more 3D polygon mesh command to explore, and this one is probably the most impressive of all. REVSURF creates surfaces by spinning a curve through a given angle around an axis of revolution. Just as tabulated surfaces are spread along a straight path, surfaces of revolution follow a circular or arc-shaped path. As a result, surfaces of revolution are always fully three-dimensional, even if their defining geometry is in a single plane, as it will be here.

> In preparation for this exercise undo the EDGESURF, and REDRAW (or RE-DRAWALL) your screen so that it resembles *Figure 13-12* again.

We will create two surfaces of revolution. The first will be a complete 360 degree surface using the smaller arc and the smaller line for definition. The second will be a 270 degree surface using the larger arc and the larger line.

> Type or select "revsurf", or select "Surface of Revolution" from the pull down menu.

AutoCAD needs a path curve and an axis of revolution to define the surface. The first prompt is:

Select path curve:

> Pick the smaller arc.
AutoCAD prompts:

Select axis of revolution:

> Pick the smaller line.

AutoCAD now needs to know whether you want the surface to begin at the curve itself or somewhere else around the circle of revolution:

Start angle <0>:

The default is to start at the curve.
> Press enter to begin the surface at the curve itself.
AutoCAD prompts:

Included angle (+=ccw, -=cw) <Full circle>:

Entering a positive or negative degree measure will cause the surface to be drawn around an arc rather than a full circle. The default will give us a complete circle.
> Press enter.
Your screen should be drawn to resemble *Figure 13-15*.

If you look closely, you will see that this globe has 12 lines in each direction. REVSURF, like EDGESURF, uses both Surftab1 and Surftab2. Also notice that this command gives us a way to create spheres. If the path curve is a true semicircle and the axis is along the diameter of the semicircle, then the result will be a sphere. There is another way to create a sphere, which we will discuss in Task 5.

Now we will create a larger surface that does not start at 0 degrees and does not include a full circle.

> Press enter to repeat the REVSURF command.
> Pick the larger arc for the curve path.
> Pick the left end of the longer line for the axis of revolution.

If you pick the right end, the positive and negative angles will be reversed in the two steps following.

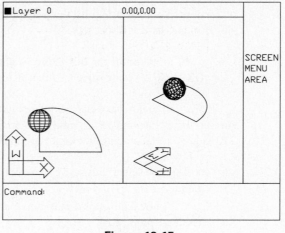

Figure 13-15

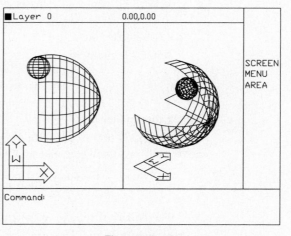

Figure 13-16

> Type "90" for the start angle.

This will cause the surface to begin 90 degrees up from the XY plane.

> Type "−270" for the included angle.

This will cause the surface to revolve 270 degrees clockwise around the axis. The result should resemble *Figure 13-16*. You may have to use PAN in one or both viewports to position the objects on the screen as we have shown them.

Next, we will demonstrate the use of the 3D Objects dialogue box, which contains AutoLISP routines to create nine more basic surface models. Take a look at the polygon mesh examples in *Figure 13-17* before proceeding.

TASK 5: Creating Surface Models Using the "3D Objects" AutoLISP Routines

Procedure.

1. Select an object from the icon menu.
2. Follow the prompts.

Discussion. The 3D Objects dialogue box shows nine objects that can be easily created as surface models. They are drawn using AutoLISP routines, which act just like commands. Like the 3D meshes explored in Task 4, 3D objects can be treated as single

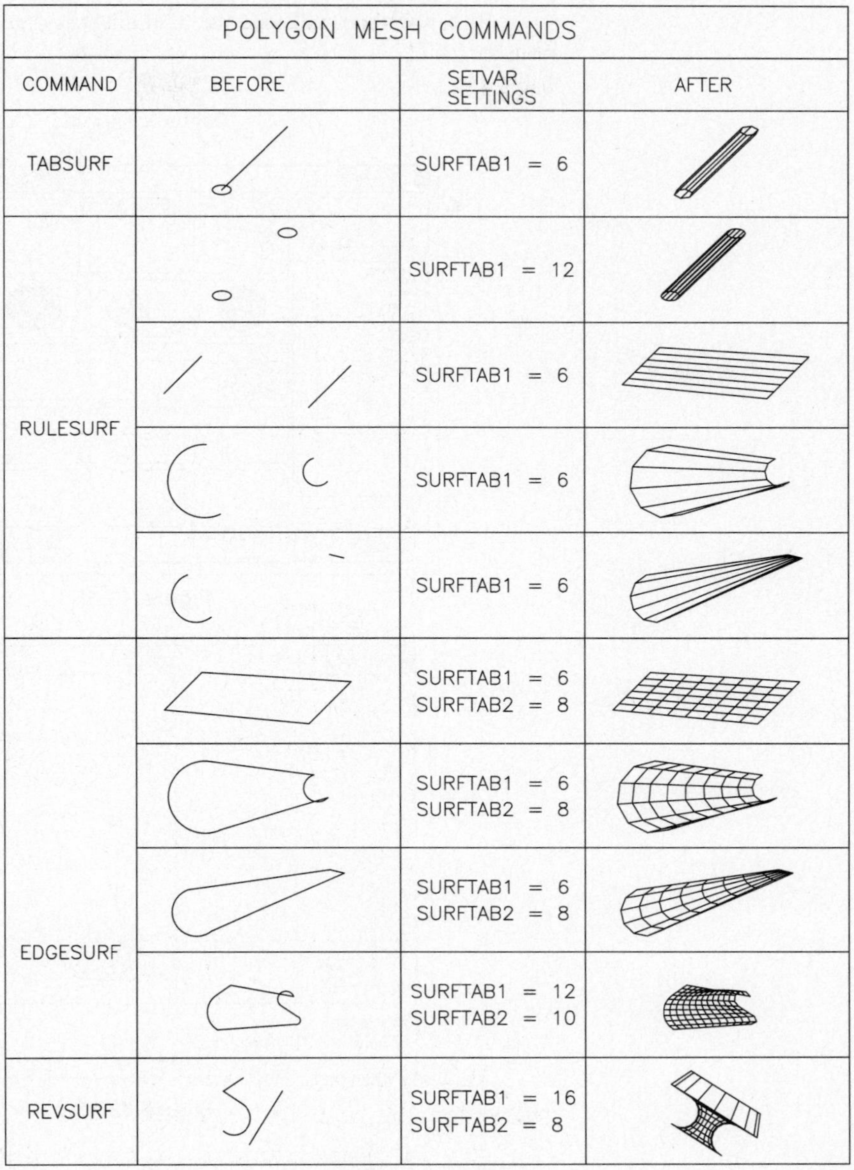

POLYGON MESH COMMANDS			
COMMAND	BEFORE	SETVAR SETTINGS	AFTER
TABSURF		SURFTAB1 = 6	
RULESURF		SURFTAB1 = 12	
		SURFTAB1 = 6	
		SURFTAB1 = 6	
		SURFTAB1 = 6	
EDGESURF		SURFTAB1 = 6 SURFTAB2 = 8	
		SURFTAB1 = 6 SURFTAB2 = 8	
		SURFTAB1 = 6 SURFTAB2 = 8	
		SURFTAB1 = 12 SURFTAB2 = 10	
REVSURF		SURFTAB1 = 16 SURFTAB2 = 8	

Figure 13-17

entities or EXPLODEd and edited as collections of 3D faces. Each of the objects has its own set of prompts, depending on its geometry. We will demonstrate one object in this task and leave the rest for you to explore on your own.

> To begin this task, clear your screen of objects left from Task 3.

> Pick "Draw", then "3D Surfaces", then "3D Objects..." from the pull down.

This will call up the 3D Objects dialogue box as shown in *Figure 13-18*.

NOTE: While "sphere", "cone", "torus", etc. appear to work just like commands, they are actually AutoLISP functions. Therefore, they will not work if AutoLISP is not loaded with appropriate memory allocation. If you have a problem, see the *AutoCAD Interface, Installation, and Performance Guide*.

> Pick the torus icon or the word "torus" on the list at the left and then click on "OK".

Either method will load the 3D Objects programs and then call the following prompt:

Center of torus:

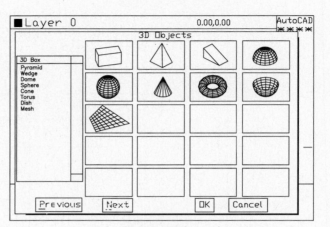

Figure 13-18

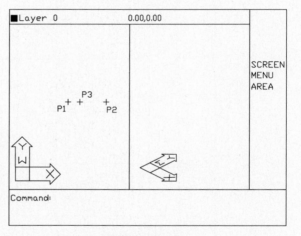

Figure 13-19

> Pick a center point as shown by P1 in *Figure 13-19*.

AutoCAD prompts:

Diameter/<radius> of torus:

The next point we pick will show the overall radius of the torus.

> Show a radius distance of about 6.00 units, as shown by P2 in the figure.

AutoCAD prompts:

Diameter/<radius> of tube:

This will be the diameter or radius of the torus tube. If you specify the tube size by pointing, remember that the distance is being shown from the center point of the torus, at P1, to P3, though the tube actually will be constructed from its own centerline at P2.

> Show a radius of about 2.00 units, as shown by P3 in the figure.

AutoCAD prompts:

Segments around tube circumference <16>:

You will be prompted for segment numbers around the tube and around the torus. These specify mesh density just like Surftab1 and Surftab2.

> Press enter to accept the default of 16 segments.

AutoCAD prompts:

Segments around torus circumference <16>:

> Press enter to accept the default of 16 segments.

Your screen should resemble *Figure 13-20*. As in the case of the 3D polygon mesh commands, notice how much surface modeling this AutoLisp routine accomplishes through a few simple prompts.

To appreciate the nature of surface models once again, we recommend that you make the right viewport active at this point and execute the HIDE command. You will see an image of the torus with hidden lines removed.

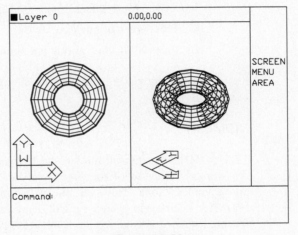

Figure 13-20

TASK 6: Creating Approximated Surfaces Using PEDIT (Optional)

Procedure.

1. Draw a 3DMESH in three dimensions.
2. Type or select "PEDIT".
3. Select the mesh.
4. Specify a surface type.
5. Type "s" or select "smooth".
5. Exit PEDIT.

Discussion. Within the PEDIT command there are some very impressive design features, which we introduce in this task and the next as optional exercises. These techniques will not be needed in the drawings that follow, but your knowledge of AutoCAD and surface modeling will be incomplete without them.

The techniques of curve and surface approximation are most useful when you have a curved object in mind but have not yet derived exact specifications for it, or when an irregular curved object passes through many different planes and would be very hard to draw face by face. You may be able to draw an outline and specify some key points, but beyond that, what you conceive may be simply a smooth curve that follows the basic shape of your outline. AutoCAD provides mathematical algorithms that can translate outlines into smooth curves. This can be accomplished with 2D and 3D polylines and with 3D meshes.

3D meshes can be curved according to three different formulas, controlled by the variable "Surftype" (not to be confused with Surftab1 and Surftab2). Surftype can be set to 5 for a quadratic approximation, 6 for cubic approximation, and 8 for bezier.

In this exercise we will create a simple rectangular 3D mesh in one plane, move two of its vertices to make it three dimensional, and then use the Smooth option of the PEDIT command to create approximated surfaces.

> To begin this task, clear your screen of all objects left from the last task, and return to a single viewport using the following procedure:

1. Make the right viewport active.
2. Type or select "Vports" (under "View", "Layout", and then "Tiled Vports..." on the pull down, under "Settings" on the screen menu).
3. Type "si" or select "single" or the single window icon.
4. Press enter or click on "OK".
5. Press F7 if your grid is not showing.

The screen will be redrawn with a single viewport resembling the currently active viewport.

3DMESH

The 3DMESH command allows you to create 3D polygon meshes "manually," vertex by vertex. Because of the time involved, the complete command is best used as a programmer's tool. However, the pull down menu has a very simple version of the 3DMESH command, which we will demonstrate here. Those interested in the full command sequence should see the *AutoCAD Reference Manual*, and the *AutoCAD Release 12 Tutorial*.

The pull down version of the 3DMESH command is the angled mesh at the middle left of the 3D Objects dialogue box shown in *Figure 13-18*. It allows you to create simple rectangular 3D meshes in one plane. We will use this tool to create a 3.00 × 4.00 mesh in the current XY plane with five vertices in each direction.

> Zoom in so that the grid covers more of the screen.
> Select "Draw" and then "3D Objects" from the pull down menu.
> Pick the mesh icon from the third line of the icon menu or the word "Mesh" from the list on the left.
> Click on "OK".

AutoCAD prompts:

First corner:

We will be prompted for four corners to define the outer boundaries of the mesh, and then for two numbers to specify the number of vertices.

> Pick a corner, as shown by point 1 in *Figure 13-21*.

AutoCAD will prompt for another corner:

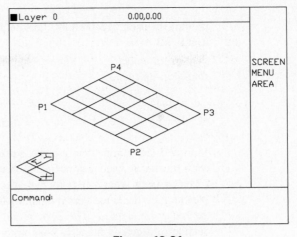

Figure 13-21

Second corner:

> Pick a second corner 4.00 to the right of point 1.

> Pick a third corner 3.00 in the Y direction from point 2.

> Pick point 4 as shown.

When you have picked four corners, your mesh should be outlined and one side highlighted. AutoCAD is asking for the number of vertices to be defined in the "M" direction:

Mesh M size:

The letters M and N are used to designate the two directions in which the mesh will be defined. The highlighted side shows the M direction. The M size is equivalent to the Surftab1 setting. The highlighted side will be divided equally by the number of vertices we specify.

> Type "5".

AutoCAD highlights a side perpendicular to the first, and prompts:

Mesh N size:

Like Surftab2, the "N" specification will determine the number of vertices in this direction.

> Type "5" again.

Your screen will be redrawn to resemble *Figure 13-21*.

The mesh will be drawn with five vertices in each direction. Later we will copy it twice so that we can produce three different types of smooth surfaces, but first we need to move some vertices up and down in the Z direction to give it three-dimensionality. This can be done using .XY filters and the grip edit stretch mode.

> First, zoom in so that the mesh covers more of the screen.

> Select the mesh.

The mesh will be highlighted and grips will appear at each vertex.

> Pick the grip at the back right corner of the mesh (point 3).

The stretch mode works the same as in previous chapters, except that now we will be moving vertices up and down out of the XY plane. If you have not previously used point filters, here is an opportunity to become familiar with this useful 3D tool.

> Type or select ".xy". (There is a Filters pop up box accessible from the Object snap pop up menu.)

AutoCAD prompts:

of

We are going to move the vertex straight up into the Z dimension, so we want the same x and y coordinates with a new z. The XY filter will take the x and y values from whatever point we specify and combine them with a new z value. We can pick the same vertex again to show x and y, or we can type "@", indicating the last point entered. The Z value will need to be typed since there are no objects outside of the X-Y plane to snap onto.

> Type "@" or pick the highlighted vertex grip again.

AutoCAD responds:

(need Z):

> Type "2".

This will move the corner vertex up 2.00, as shown in *Figure 13-22*.

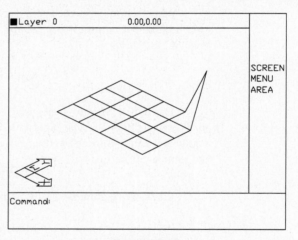

Figure 13-22

Now we will move the opposite corner down −3.00.

> Pick the grip at the front left corner, opposite the corner you just edited.

> Type or select ".xy".

> Type "@" or pick the same grip again.

> Type "−3".

We are now ready to create a quadratic-style smoothed surface from our 3D mesh.

> Type or select "PEDIT" or "PolyEdit".

AutoCAD will prompt for a polyline, but 3D polygon meshes may also be selected.

> Pick any point on the mesh.

> Press enter to end selection.

This will bring up a command prompt with the following options:

Edit Vertex/Smooth surface/Desmooth/Mclose/Nclose/Undo/eXit <X>:

The option we will be using is "Smooth surface".

> Type "s" or select "smooth".

Your screen will be redrawn to resemble *Figure 13-23*.

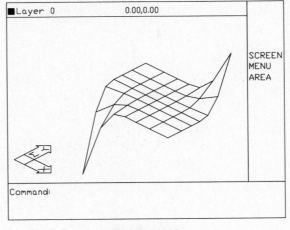

Figure 13-23

NOTE: If the variable "Splframe" is set to 1, your screen will show no change. Splframe shows the frame or outline used in defining an approximated curve. Because of the complexity of meshes, AutoCAD does not show a curved surface and its "frame" at the same time. With Splframe set to the default of 0, you will see the smoothed version with no frame. With a setting of 1 you see the original frame without the approximation.

Next we will make copies of the mesh and smooth the copies with the variable "surftype" set to create cubic and bezier surfaces.

> Press enter to exit the PEDIT command.

> Zoom all and make two copies of the mesh.

> Type "Surftype".

> Type "6".

> Type or select "PEDIT" or "PolyEdit" (under "Edit" on the screen menu, "Modify" on the pull down).

> Select the first copy of the mesh.

> Press enter to end selection.

> Type "s" or select "Smooth".

NOTE: The differences between cubic and quadratic surfaces in this object will be slight. In fact, you will have to look hard to see them. We have indicated them with arrows in *Figure 13-24* for your convenience. In order to show a more dramatic difference, you would need to create a more dramatic 3D figure by moving more vertices up or down. If you have the time, be our guest. Also consider changing the density of surface approximation through the variables "Surfu" and "Surfv". For more information see the *AutoCAD Reference Manual*, and the *AutoCAD Release 12 Tutorial*.

There is a dialogue box for changing curve and surface approximation styles. You can access this box by selecting "PolyVars" from the PEDIT screen menu. The dialogue can be used transparently, while you are in the PEDIT command. You might want to try this to smooth the last mesh.

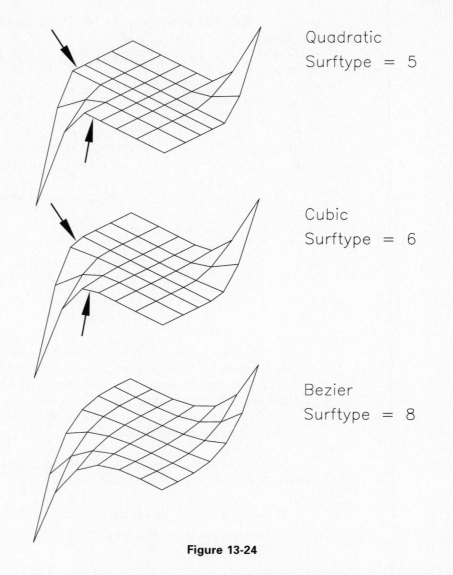

Quadratic
Surftype = 5

Cubic
Surftype = 6

Bezier
Surftype = 8

Figure 13-24

> Select "PEDIT" from the screen menu or "Polyedit" from the pull down menu.
> Select the remaining copy of the mesh.
> Press enter to end object selection.
> Select "PolyVars" from the screen menu.
    This will bring up a dialogue box with a list and an icon menu.
> Pick "Bezier" or the bezier icon.
> Click on "OK".
> Type "s" to smooth the mesh.
    Your meshes will resemble those in *Figure 13-24*.

Now that you know how to create smoothed surfaces, creating two-dimensional curve approximations should be easy. We include the following discussion as a reference.

Curve Approximation

Creating approximated curves in two dimensions is analogous to smoothing surfaces in three dimensions. The process is the same, with a few changes in variable names. Instead of beginning with a 3D mesh, you begin with a polyline. Polyline frames can be curved through the "Fit" or "Spline" options of the PEDIT command. Fit replaces all straight segments of a polyline with pairs of arc segments. The resulting curve passes through all existing vertices, and new vertices are created to join the arcs. Spline curves follow the shape of their frames, but they do not necessarily pass through all vertices. Instead they pass through the first and last points, and tend toward the ones between according to either the quadratic or cubic formula. (There is no Bezier option for spline curves.)

If the variable "Splframe" is set to 1 instead of the default 0, AutoCAD will display the defining frame along with the curve. Also, the degree of accuracy of curve approximation can be varied by changing the setting of the variable "Splinesegs". This variable controls the number of segments a polyline will be considered to have in the calculations of the spline formulae.

Examples of fit, cubic, and quadratic curves are shown in *Figure 13-25*.

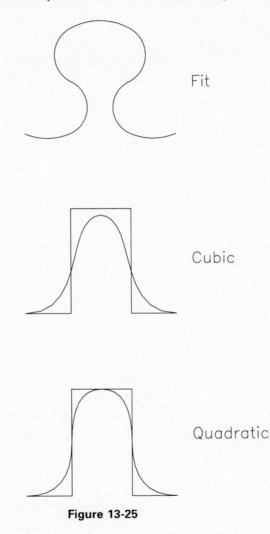

Fit

Cubic

Quadratic

Figure 13-25

TASKS 7, 8, 9, and 10

The drawings that follow will give you a wide range of experience with surface models. *Drawing 13-1* is an exercise in recognizing and creating a variety of surfaces using only the REVSURF command and some simple outlines. *Drawings 13-2* and *13-3* are more difficult and make use of 3D faces and polygon meshes. *Drawing 13-4* is a very challenging 3D drawing requiring careful use of the UCS command and several polygon mesh commands.

DRAWING 13-1: REVSURF DESIGNS

The REVSURF command is fascinating and powerful. As you get familiar with it, you may find yourself identifying objects in the world that can be conceived as surfaces of revolution. To encourage this process, we have provided this page of 12 REVSURF objects and designs.

To complete the exercise, you will need only the PLINE and REVSURF commands. In the first six designs we have shown the path curves and axes of rotation used to create the design. In the other six you will be on your own.

Exact shapes and dimensions are not important in this exercise. Imagination is. When you have completed our designs, we encourage you to invent a number of your own.

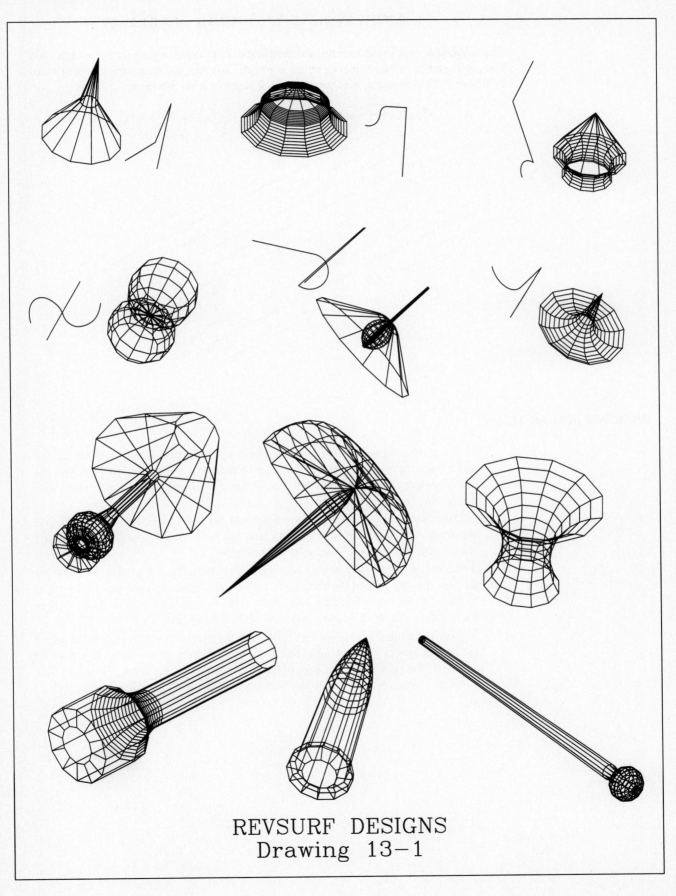

REVSURF DESIGNS
Drawing 13–1

DRAWING 13-2: PICNIC TABLE

This is a tricky drawing that must be done carefully. It requires efficient use of the UCS command along with a number of edit commands. In order to create an image that hides as shown in the reference, you must cover all surfaces with 3D faces.

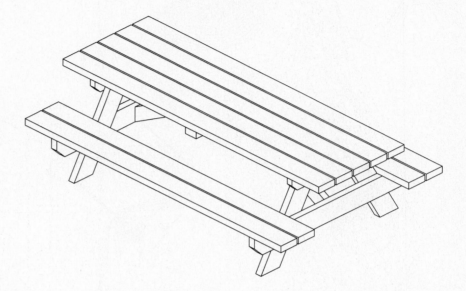

DRAWING SUGGESTIONS

> Use a three-viewport configuration, with top (plan) and front views on the left and a 3D view on the right. Be sure to keep an eye on all viewports as you go, since it is quite likely that you will create some lines that look correct in one view but not in others.

> Use a separate layer for 3D faces, and add the faces as you go. This will save you from retracing your steps. Notice that the faces on the chamfered braces are drawn with one invisible line across the middle.

> We recommend that you start with the top of the table and work down. Placing the legs directly behind the chamfered braces can be tricky. One way to do this is to draw the legs even with the side of the table first (in a UCS with its X-Y plane flush with a side of the table), and then MOVE them back 1'-2".

> Save the angled braces for last. Once the leg braces are drawn, you can locate the angled braces by drawing a line from the midpoint of the small brace in the middle of the table top to the midpoint of the bottom of a leg brace. Then OFFSET this line 1" each way to create the two lower edges of one angled brace.

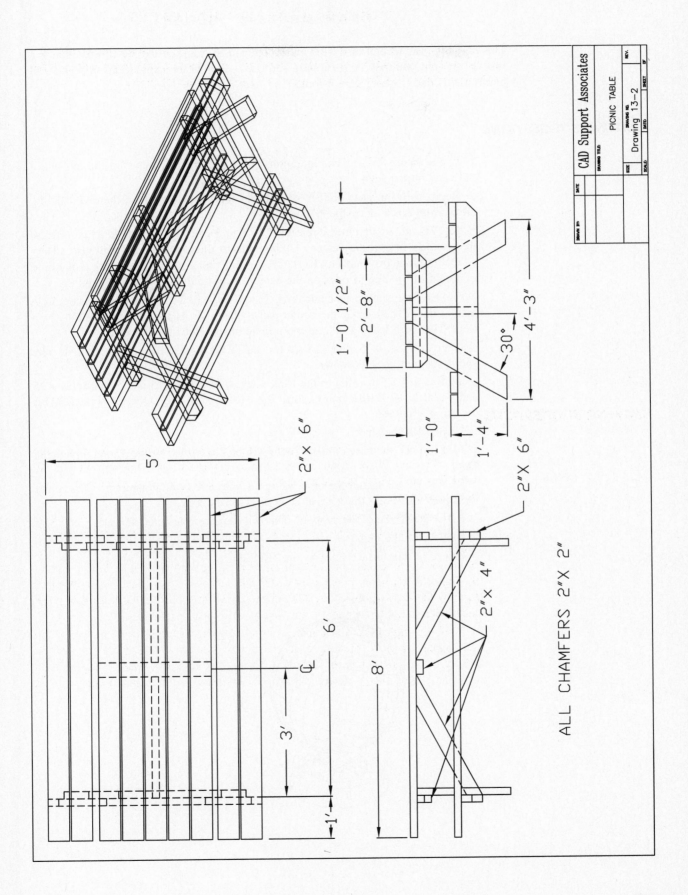

ALL CHAMFERS 2"X 2"

2"x 6"

5'

6'

3'

1'

2"X 6"

8'

2"x 4"

1'-0 1/2"

2'-8"

30°

4'-3"

1'-0"

1'-4"

CAD Support Associates

DRAWING TITLE:
PICNIC TABLE

DRAWING NO.
Drawing 13-2

REV.

DATE:

DRAWN BY:

SIZE

SCALE:

DATED

SHEET

OF

382

DRAWING 13-3: GLOBE

This drawing uses several of the 3D mesh commands. Some of the 3D construction is a little tricky, but you may be pleasantly surprised. Follow the suggestions and you will find that this one is easier than it looks.

DRAWING SUGGESTIONS

> Use a three-viewport configuration with top and front views on the left and a 3D view on the right.

> Begin with the base circles, drawing in the plan (top) view, then MOVE the circles into place along the Z axis.

> MOVE the small inner circle up 12.25 to locate the top of the shaft. Draw the centerline from the center of this circle to the top center of the base. Then COPY this line on itself and ROTATE the line and circle 23.5 degrees around the midpoint of the line to position the center of the shaft.

> OFFSET the shaft center line .125. Later, you will TRIM a 4.00 diameter circle to this line. Then using the centerline of the shaft as the axis of rotation for a REVSURF will leave a hole in the middle of the globe for the shaft.

> Draw the 4.00, 4.75, and 5.38 circles and TRIM them to the vertical, 23.5 degree, and 46 degree lines as shown.

> With your UCS parallel to the front view, COPY the 4.75 and 5.38 circles +.25 and −.25 in the Z direction to form the two sides of the globe support. ERASE the original circles.

> TABSURF the shaft.

> RULESURF the base circles. There will be three ruled surfaces to complete the base.

> REVSURF the top of the base, using a single line from a quadrant to the center for a path curve and the vertical centerline for the axis.

> RULESURF the globe support. This will require four ruled surfaces.

> REVSURF the globe.

> Freeze all nonsurface lines before HIDEing.

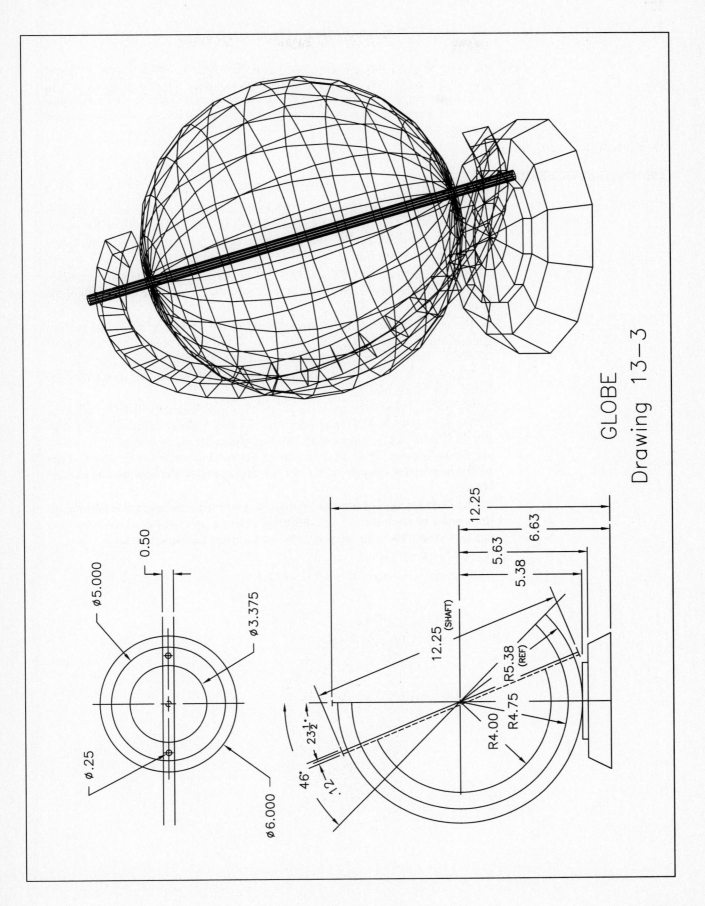

GLOBE
Drawing 13-3

Ø5.000
0.50
Ø3.375
Ø.25
Ø6.000

12.25
5.63
6.63
5.38
12.25 (SHAFT)
R5.38 (REF)
R4.75
R4.00
23½°
46°
1.2

383

DRAWING 13-4: NOZZLE

This is a tough drawing that will give you a real 3D workout. You will need to define numerous UCSs as you go. Your goal should be to create the two views A and B. Dimensioning is not part of the exercise. The dimensioned figure is not a complete wire frame, but a guide to show you the abstract relationships necessary to complete the surface model.

DRAWING SUGGESTIONS

We began in a front, right, top view. This puts the main centerline of the nozzle in the X-Y plane of the WCS, while the circles that show the outlines of the nozzle would be perpendicular to it. When we were done, we rotated the objects slightly to show them more clearly.

> Make ample use of COPY and OFFSET in drawing the circles and centerlines of the nozzle, the hexes and circles of the knob, and the polyline curve path of the nozzle.

> The circle and centerline at the right end of the 45 degree angle can be constructed using a COPY and ROTATE of the circle and centerline just in front of the angle. This must be done in a UCS parallel to the WCS.

> The curve in the nozzle is a -45 degree REVSURF around the centerline 1.00 to the right of the turn.

> The two darkened lines show the path curves used with REVSURF to draw the nozzle and the knob. Construct lines first and then go over them with PLINE or 3DPOLY. 3DPOLY is similar to PLINE, but it uses 3D points instead of 2D points and has no option to draw arcs. In general, 3D polylines are more flexible and can be drawn at times when the current UCS would not allow the construction of a 2D polyline.

> The centerline through the knob (along the arrow) runs perpendicular to the polyline outline of the nozzle. Use a PERpendicular osnap to construct the centerline and then define UCSs in relation to the centerline to construct the knob.

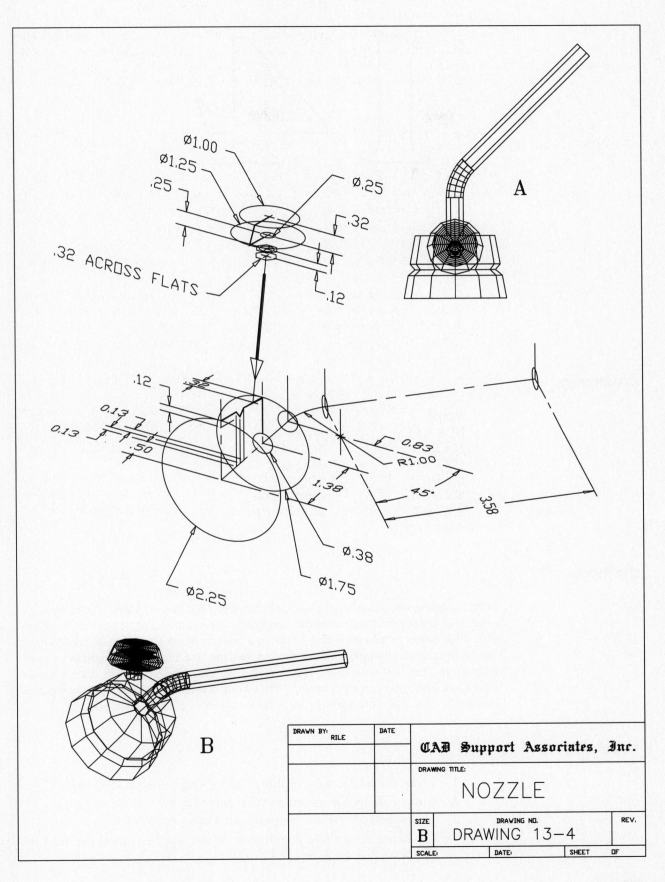

Ø1.00
Ø1.25
.25
Ø.25
.32
.32 ACROSS FLATS
.12

A

.12
.32
0.13
0.13
.50
0.83
R1.00
1.38
45°
3.58
Ø.38
Ø1.75
Ø2.25

B

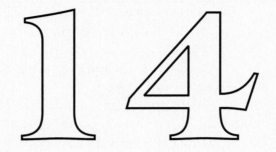

COMMANDS

MODEL

DDSOLPRM	SOLMASSP
SOLBOX	SOLMAT
SOLCHP	SOLSECT
SOLCUT	SOLSUB
SOLFEAT	SOLUNION
SOLLIST	SOLWEDGE
SOLMOVE	

OVERVIEW

Solid Modeling with AutoCAD's Advanced Modeling Extension (AME) is in many ways easier than either wire frame or surface modeling. In solid modeling you can draw a complete solid object by picking a few points, in a fraction of the time it would take to draw line by line, surface by surface. Furthermore, once the object is drawn it contains far more information than a wireframe or surface model. In this chapter you will draw a simple solid model using several solid drawing and editing commands. Note that the techniques introduced here will work only if your software includes the full AME package.

TASKS

1. Create a solid box using SOLBOX and a wedge using SOLWEDGE.
2. Create a composite solid from the union of the box and the wedge.
3. List information about a composite solid using SOLLIST.
4. Create box and cylinder primitives using the baseplane option and the AME Primitives dialogue box.

5. Create a composite solid by subtraction, using SOLSUB.
6. Edit primitives within composite solids, using SOLCHP.
7. Move solids with the SOLMOVE command.
8. Chamfer and fillet solid objects.
9. HIDE and SHADE solid models.
10. Create solids through extrusion using SOLEXT.
11. Create 2D region entities.
12. Create solids by revolving 2D entities using SOLREV.
13. Create solid cutaway views with SOLCUT.
14. Create sections with SOLSECT.
15. Copy edges and faces of solids with SOLFEAT.
16. Create profile images with SOLPROF.
17. Do Drawing 14-1 ("Bushing Mount").
18. Do Drawing 14-2 ("Link Mount").
19. Do Drawing 14-3 ("3D Assembly").
20. Do Drawing 14-4 ("Tapered Bushing").
21. Do Drawing 14-5 ("Pivot Mount").

TASK 1: Creating Solid Box and Wedge Primitives

Procedure.

1. Enter SOLBOX or SOLWEDGE.
2. Specify corner point and distances in the X-Y plane of the current UCS (or define a baseplane first and then specify points).
3. Specify a height.

Discussion. Solid modeling requires a somewhat different type of thinking than any of the drawings you have done so far. Instead of focusing on lines and arcs, edges and surfaces, you will need to imagine how 3D objects might be pieced together by combining or subtracting basic solid shapes, called "primitives." This building block process is called constructive solid geometry and includes joining, subtracting, and intersecting operations. A simple washer, for example, could be made by cutting a small cylinder out of the middle of a larger cylinder. In AutoCAD solid modeling you can begin with a flat outer cylinder, then draw an inner cylinder with a smaller radius centered at the same point, and then subtract the inner cylinder from the outer, as illustrated in *Figure 14-1*.

This "subtraction" is the equivalent of cutting a hole, and is one of three Boolean operations (after the mathematician George Booles) used to create composite solids. "Union" joins two solids to make a new solid, and "intersection" creates a composite solid in the space where two solids overlap (see *Figure 14-1*).

In this chapter you will create a composite solid from the union and subtraction of several solid primitives. Primitives are 3D solid building blocks—boxes, cones, cylinders, spheres, wedges, and torus. They all are regularly shaped and can be defined by specifying a few points and distances.

> To begin this task, go into a left front view (315 degrees from X, and 45 degrees from XY). Notice that this is a slightly higher viewing angle than we used in the previous two chapters.

> Type "box" or select "Solbox" (under "MODEL" and then "PRIMS." on the screen menu). Avoid the pull down for now.

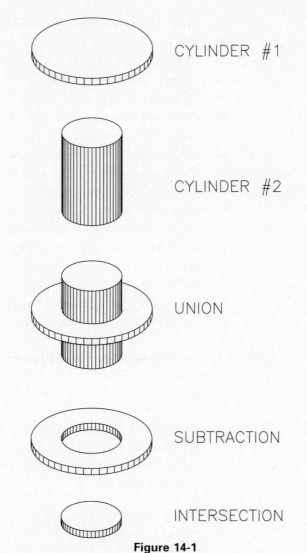

CYLINDER #1

CYLINDER #2

UNION

SUBTRACTION

INTERSECTION

Figure 14-1

AME is actually an add-on program, which must be loaded into basic Auto-CAD before any of the solid modeling commands will work. The first time you enter any of these commands during a drawing session, AutoCAD must pause to load the modeling package before proceeding. In the command area you will see the first two lines of the following prompt first and will have to wait for the third to appear:

Initializing...

Initializing Advanced Modeling Extension.

Baseplane/Center/<Corner of box> <0,0,0>:

The "Baseplane" option will allow you to specify a plane for the base of the box. Otherwise it will be drawn in the X-Y plane of the current UCS. "Center" allows you to begin defining a box by specifying its center point.

Here we will use the default "Corner of box" option to begin drawing a box in the baseplane of the current UCS. We will draw a box with a length of 4, width of 3, and height of 1.5.

> Pick a corner point similar to point 1 in *Figure 14-2*.

AutoCAD will prompt:

Cube/Length/<Other corner>:

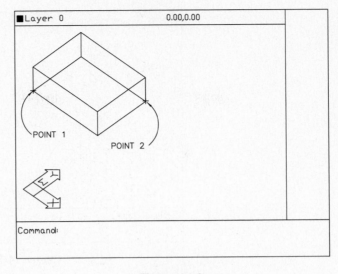

Figure 14-2

With the "Cube" option you can draw a box with equal length, width, and height simply by specifying one distance. The "Length" option will allow you to specify length, width, and height separately. If you have simple measurements that fall on snap points, as we do, you can show the length and width at the same time by picking the other corner of the base of the box (the default method).

> Move the cross hairs over 4 in the X direction and up 3 in the Y direction to point 2, as shown in the figure.

Notice that "length" is measured along the X axis, and "width" is measured along the Y axis.

> Pick point 2 as shown.

Now AutoCAD prompts for a height. "Height" is measured along the Z axis. As usual, you cannot pick points in the Z direction unless you have objects to snap to. Instead you can type a value or show a value by picking two points in the X-Y plane.

> Type "1.5" or pick two points 1.5 units apart.

AME performs some calculations and creates the mathematical data needed to store a solid model box. As it does it will show you the following in the command area:

> Phase I — Boundary evaluation begins.
>
> Phase II — Tessellation computation begins.
>
> Updating the Advanced Modeling Extension database.

When the process is complete, your screen should resemble *Figure 14-2*. Next we will create a solid wedge. The process will be exactly the same, but there will be no "Cube" option.

> Type "wed" or select "Solwedge".

AutoCAD prompts:

> Baseplane/<Corner of wedge> <0,0,0>:

> Pick a corner point as shown in *Figure 14-3*. Precise placement is not significant.

AutoCAD prompts for a length, or the other corner. This time let's use the length option.

> Type "L" or select "Length".

The rubber band will disappear and AutoCAD will prompt for a length, which you can define by typing a number or showing two points.

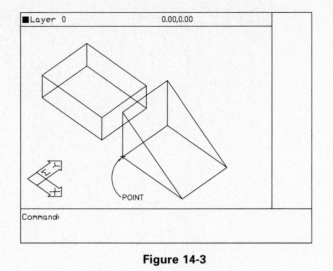

Figure 14-3

> Type "4" or show a length of 4 units.

As in SOLBOX, AutoCAD now prompts for a width. Remember, length is measured in the X direction, and width is measured in the Y direction.

> Type "3" or show a width of 3 units.

AutoCAD prompts for a height.

> Type "3" or show a distance of 3 units.

AutoCAD will go through the same computation phases and then draw the wedge you have specified. Notice that a wedge is simply half a box, cut along a diagonal plane.

Your screen should resemble *Figure 14-3*. Although the box and the wedge appear as wireframe objects, they are really quite different, as you will find. In Task 2 we will join the box and the wedge to form a new composite solid.

TASK 2: Creating a Composite with SOLUNION

Procedure.

1. Type or select "solunion".
2. Select solid objects to join. (Steps 1 and 2 may be reversed if noun/verb selection is enabled.)

Discussion.   Unions are simple to create and usually easy to visualize. The union of two objects is an object that includes all points that are on either of the objects. Unions can be performed just as easily on more than two objects. The union of objects can be created even if the objects have no points in common (i.e., they do not touch or overlap).

Here we will move the wedge adjacent to the box before entering the SOLUNION command. By the way, have you noticed that all solid modeling commands begin with "SOL", but that you can leave off the "sol" when you type the command?

> Select the wedge.

Notice that the wedge has only one grip. Solid primitives are actually blocks and are treated as such by many edit commands and functions. If "grips within blocks" are enabled you will see many grips. Otherwise you will see just one.

> Type "m" or select "move".

We will use midpoint object snaps to align the two adjacent faces of the box and the wedge.

> At the "Base point or displacement:" prompt type "mid" or open an object snap menu (pop up or screen) and select "Midpoint".

> Pick the lower left edge of the wedge.

> At the "Second point of displacement:" prompt, again type "mid" or open an object snap menu and select "Midpoint".

> Pick the lower right edge of the box.

AutoCAD will move the wedge against the box, matching midpoint to midpoint of the two lower edges. Your screen should resemble *Figure 14-4*.

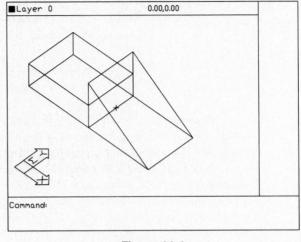

Figure 14-4

There are still two distinct solids on the screen; with SOLUNION we can join them.

> Type "union" or select "Solunion" (under "Model" on either menu, but the pull down will show simply "Union").

Now AutoCAD will prompt you to select objects.

> Point or use a crossing box to select both objects.

> Press enter to end object selection.

AutoCAD will go through a set of calculations, which will be reflected in the command area, ending with "2 solids unioned."

When the process is complete, your screen should resemble *Figure 14-5*.

NOTE: In practice it is efficient to reduce the number of union, subtraction, and intersection procedures used in creating solids. This can save time and make your solid model more memory-efficient. In this exercise, however, we are building our model in a step-by-step fashion because it makes a better learning sequence. More efficient sequencing will be suggested for the drawings at the end of the chapter.

TASK 3: Listing Information about Solids with SOLLIST

Procedure.

1. Type or select "SOLLIST".
2. Press enter to list object, type "t" or select "Tree" to list CSG tree.
3. Select objects to list.
4. Press enter to end object selection.

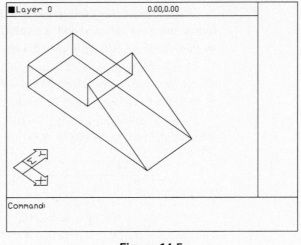

Figure 14-5

Discussion.   Using the regular LIST command to get information about an AME solid, you will find only that the solid is a block and, like other blocks, it has an insertion point and a "handle." Handles are ID numbers arbitrarily assigned to all AutoCAD entities. You can get more significant information about solids with the SOLLIST command. Among the types of information included are the handles of component primitives, the area of the object, its material, and how it is being represented on the screen. Further information and calculations of the type used by engineers performing finite element analysis (FEA) is available through the SOLMASSP command.

Let's see what SOLLIST has to tell about our composite model.

> Type or select "SOLLIST" (under "Model" and then "Inquiry" on the screen menu, under "Model", "Inquiry", and then "List Object" on the pull down menu).

AutoCAD will prompt:

Edge/Face/Tree/<Object>:

"Edge" and "Face" give coordinates, length, and orientation details about the edges and faces of a solid. We will concern ourselves with "Tree" and "Object". Object, the default option, will list information about a solid composite only, without listing the primitives from which it is constructed. Tree will list information about the composite and the components and procedures used in putting it together.

> Press enter for the "Object" option.

AutoCAD will prompt you to select objects.

> Pick the union of the box and the wedge.

> Press enter to end object selection.

AutoCAD will switch to the text screen and show information similar to the following (the handles are arbitrarily assigned by AutoCAD and will be different).

Object type = UNION   Handle = 38
  Component handles: 15 and 23
  Area not computed   Material = MILD_STEEL
  Representation = WIREFRAME   Render type = CSG
Rigid motion:

     +1.000000   +0.000000   +0.000000   +0.000000
     +0.000000   +1.000000   +0.000000   +0.000000
     +0.000000   +0.000000   +1.000000   +0.000000
     +0.000000   +0.000000   +0.000000   +1.000000

From this you can see that our model has the handle 38 and was formed by the union of two components with handles 15 and 23. The area has not been computed yet. It will be when we use SOLMESH to create a mesh representation of the model, or when we execute SOLAREA specifically to find its area.

The current material is "MILD_STEEL", which is AME's default material. It will be used until you change materials with the SOLMAT command.

The representation is wireframe until we change to a mesh representation (SOLMESH), and the render type is CSG. CSG (Constructive Solid Geometry) rendering means that in producing a shaded representation of the model, AME will use the colors of components in the CSG tree (primitives and lesser composites), rather than using only the color of the composite itself. When only the composite color is used it is called a "uniform" rendering.

Finally, the Rigid motion table tracks information on the rotation and translation of the object. If you were to move or rotate the model before entering SOLLIST you would see that many of the numbers in the table change to represent the X, Y, and Z axis vectors involved in the motion.

Now let's look at the "tree" list.

> Press enter to repeat SOLLIST.

> Type "t".

AutoCAD will switch back to the graphics screen and prompt you to select objects.

> Type "p" (previous) or pick the box/wedge union again.

> Press enter to end selection.

What you see now will be similar to the last printout, but there will be three "paragraphs," and the rigid motion information will not be included.

```
Object type = UNION    Handle = 38
Component handles:                        15 and 23
Area not computed                         Material = MILD_STEEL
Representation = WIREFRAME                 Render type = CSG


Object type = BOX (4.000000,3.000000,1.5000000)    Handle=15
  Area not computed    Material = MILD_STEEL
  Representation = WIREFRAME   Render type = CSG
  Node level = 1


Object type = WEDGE (4.000000,3.000000,1.5000000)   Handle=23
  Area not computed    Material = MILD_STEEL
  Representation = WIREFRAME   Render type = CSG
  Node level = 1
```

This is the CSG tree for our solid model. Actually, if you want to think of this as a treelike structure, it is upside down, with the trunk at the top (the union) and the branches (box and wedge) following.

Most of the information is familiar, but the coordinates of the corner point have been added for the box and wedge primitives. The "node level" indicates how close the listed object or primitive is to the top composite level. To grasp this, imagine for a moment that you copied the box/wedge union, moved the copy, and then unioned the new copy with the original composite. You would have a new composite made from the union of two box/wedge unions. In this model, the new composite would be the trunk of the tree, the two box/wedge unions would be at node level 1, and the four box and wedge primitives would be at node level 2. This concept is illustrated in *Figure 14-6*.

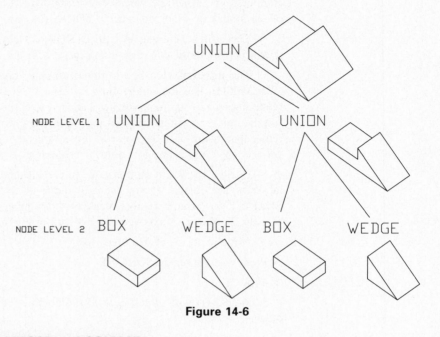

Figure 14-6

SOLMASSP and SOLMAT

As mentioned above, the most complete applications of AME are in design engineering in which computer models are used to design, simulate, test, and manufacture mechanical objects. When we begin to look inside our solid models to analyze or explore their physical properties, we are heading into the realm of materials science, among other disciplines. This takes us beyond the scope of our book. However, you should be aware that with the SOLMAT (solid materials) command you can define, change, and assign materials to a model. Then, based on the characteristics of the assigned material, the SOLMASSP command will compute the mass properties of the model, including mass, volume, bounding box, centroid, moments of inertia, products of inertia, radii of gyration, and principal moments about the centroid. The material characteristics definable in the SOLMAT command are: density, Young's modulus, Poisson's ratio, yield strength, ultimate strength, thermal conductivity coefficient, linear expansion coefficient, and specific heat. For further information see Autodesk's *Advanced Modeling Extension Reference Manual*.

Now, back to our drawing.

TASK 4: Creating Box and Cylinder Primitives Using the Baseplane Option and the Solid Primitives Dialogue Box

Procedure.

1. Pick "Model" and then "Primitives..." from the pull down menu, or type "ddsolprm".
2. Pick a primitive.
3. To initiate the baseplane option click the "On" button under "Baseplane".
4. Pick from the list of options to define a baseplane
5. Click on "Object Snap Modes..." to set a running object snap.
6. Define a baseplane.
7. Define a primitive from that baseplane.

Discussion. In this task we will draw two more solid primitives. The process will be similar to what you did in task 1, but we will use a dialogue box and some different options.

> To begin this task you should have the union of a wedge and a box on your screen, as shown previously in *Figure 14-5*.

We will begin by drawing a third box. This time we encourage you to try out the AME Primitives dialogue box.

> Pick "Model" and then "Primitives..." from the pull down menu.

This activates the "DDSOLPRM" command which calls the dialogue box illustrated in *Figure 14-7*. The six solid primitives are shown and may be selected by pointing.

> Pick the box at the upper left of the dialogue box.

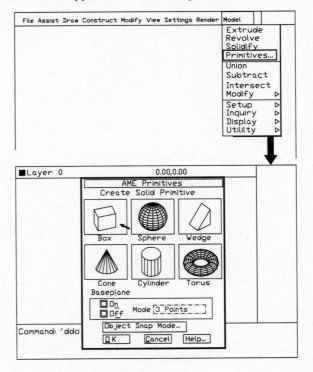

Figure 14-7

Remember that in the SOLBOX command there is an option to create a box in a baseplane different from the X-Y plane of the current UCS. In the dialogue box this option appears as a radio button below the word "Baseplane". Its default setting is "Off". We will turn it on to try out the baseplane option.

> Pick "On" to turn on the baseplane option.

As soon as you turn baseplane on you will have access to the "Mode" pop up list. Baseplanes are specified in the same ways as user coordinate systems. Clicking on "3 Points" or on the arrow to the right you will see a list of options for specifying planes. We will use the default 3 point option.

The dialogue box also has its own Object Snap Mode subdialogue. This will allow you to specify a running object snap mode, which is often convenient in specifying a base plane.

> Click inside the Object Snap Mode box.

You will see the Running Object Snap subdialogue.

> Select the Endpoint check box, then click "OK" to close the dialogue box.

> Click "OK" in the AME Primitives dialogue box.

We are now ready to define a third box primitive, but this time we will be prompted to define a new baseplane first. We will use this option to create the new box on top of the original box.

AutoCAD is prompting:

1st point on plane:

> Use the running end point object snap to pick the upper left front corner of the original box primitive, point 1 in *Figure 14-8*.

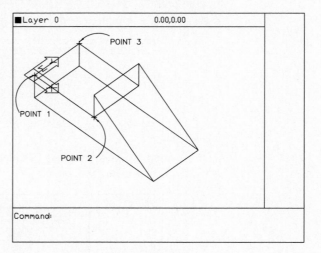

Figure 14-8

AutoCAD prompts:

2nd point on plane:

> Use the running end point object snap to pick the upper right front corner of the original box primitive, where the box and the wedge meet, point 2 in *Figure 14-8*.

AutoCAD needs one more point to define a baseplane.

> Use the running end point object snap to pick the upper back left corner of the original box primitive, point 3 in *Figure 14-8*.

AutoCAD temporarily moves the UCS icon to the origin of the baseplane you have just defined. If you watch closely you will see that the grid has also moved up into this plane.

From here on the prompts will be the same as those you have previously encountered in creating the box and the wedge.

We will place this box at the origin of the baseplane.

> Press enter to place the corner of the box at (0,0,0).

> Type "L" to initiate the "length" option.

> Type "4" or pick two points to show a length of 4 units.

If you are pointing, watch out for the running end point object snap, which is still on.

> Type ".5" or pick two points to show a width of 0.5 units.

> Type "2" or pick two points to show a height of 2 units.

When AutoCAD completes its calculations, your screen should resemble *Figure 14-9*.

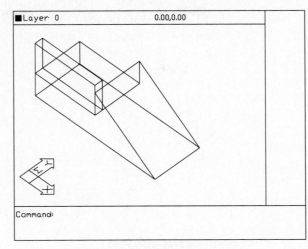

Figure 14-9

Now use the dialogue box to create a solid cylinder back in the X-Y plane of the current UCS.

> Press enter or click twice on "Model" to repeat DDSOLPRM and reopen the AME Primitives dialogue box.

> Pick the cylinder.

> Pick the "Off" radio button to turn the baseplane option off.

As soon as you turn off baseplane, the "Mode:" list should become inaccessible.

> Open the Object Snap Mode... dialogue box and turn off the running "Endpoint" osnap mode.

> Click on "OK" in the subdialogue and the dialogue box.

You are now ready to define a solid cylinder. AutoCAD prompts:

Baseplane/Elliptical/<Center point> <0,0,0>:

Note the option to create elliptically shaped cylinders.

We will pick the midpoint of the front edge of the wedge. This will require a midpoint object snap, but we did not set this as a running snap mode since we only need to use it for a single point.

> Type "mid" or select "Midpoint" from the screen menu or pop up osnap list.

> Point anywhere along the front edge of the wedge.

AutoCAD snaps to the midpoint. This will be the center of the circular base of the cylinder. Now AutoCAD needs a diameter or a radius for the circle.

> Type ".5" or show a point 0.5 units from the center of the cylinder base.

AutoCAD prompts:

Center of other end/<Height>:

Height, the default option, can be shown by typing or showing a distance in the X-Y plane. The other option, picking the center of the other end of the cylinder, can be used only if there is an object to snap to.

> Type "2" or pick two points to show a distance of 2.0 units.

Your screen should resemble *Figure 14-10*.

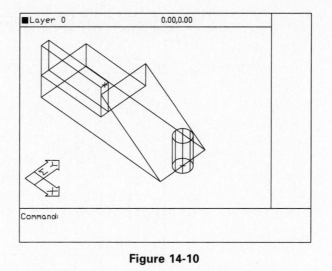

Figure 14-10

The Solwdens Variable

Your cylinder will probably be shown with only two vertical lines. The density of lines displayed by AutoCAD to represent solids in wireframe form is controlled by the variable "Solwdens". You can change this setting, if you wish, by typing or selecting "Solwdens" and then entering a number between one and twelve. If you see only two lines, SOLWDENS is set to the default value of 1. Ours is shown with a setting of 2. Changing SOLWDENS does not effect objects already drawn.

TASK 5: Creating Composite Solids with SOLSUB

Procedure.

1. Create source primitives and primitives to be subtracted.
2. Position primitives relative to each other.
3. Enter the SOLSUB command.
4. Select source primitives.
5. Select primitives to be subtracted from them.

Discussion. SOLSUB is the logical opposite of SOLUNION. In a union operation, all the points contained in one solid are added to the points contained in other solids to form a new composite solid. In a subtraction, all points in the solids to be subtracted are removed from the source solid. A new composite solid is defined by what is left.
> To begin this task, you should have one composite solid and two solid primitives on your screen, as shown in *Figure 14-10*.

Before subtracting, we will move the box to the position shown in *Figure 14-11*. Then we will use it to form a slot in the composite.

> Type "m" or select "move".
> Select the narrow box drawn in the last task.
> Press enter to end object selection.
> At the "Base point or displacement" prompt use a midpoint object snap to pick the midpoint of the top right edge of the box primitive.
> At the "Second point of displacement" prompt use another midpoint osnap to pick the top edge of the wedge, as shown in *Figure 14-11*.

This will move the narrow box over and down. Now let's do the subtraction.

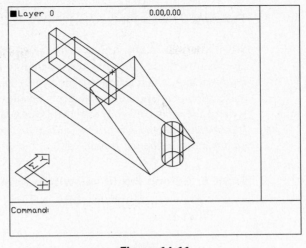

Figure 14-11

> Type or select "Solsub" (under "MODEL" on the screen menu) or pick "Subtraction" under "Model" on the pull down menu.

AutoCAD asks you to select source objects first:

Source objects...
Select objects:

Source objects are the solids to be subtracted from.
> Pick the composite of the box and the wedge.
> Press enter to end selection of source objects.

AutoCAD AME updates the source object in preparation for the subtraction operation and then prompts for objects to be subtracted:

Objects to subtract from them...
Select objects:

> Pick the narrow box and the cylinder.
> Press enter to end selection.

After AutoCAD has completed numerous calculations, your screen will resemble *Figure 14-12*.

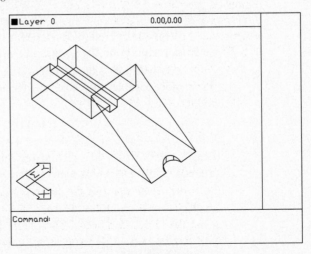

Figure 14-12

The AME_FRZ Layer

When you load AME, a new layer called "AME_FRZ" is created automatically. This layer is frozen and is used by the program to hold data that is not displayed in the model representation. This extended entity data includes the components and primitives that make up the composite model, their handles, and information about the representation style of the model. If you thaw this layer you will see all the graphic components there. *It is not advisable to execute any editing on the AME_FRZ layer, however, and in practice, the layer should be left frozen.*

TASK 6: Editing Primitives within Composite Solids with SOLCHP

Procedure.

1. Type or select "SOLCHP".
2. Select a region or composite solid. (Steps 1 and 2 can be reversed if noun/verb selection is enabled.)
3. Select a primitive that is part of the composite.
4. Specify a change option.
5. Follow the prompts.
6. Type "x" or select "eXit" to complete the command.

Discussion. Many standard edit commands can be carried out on solid primitives and composites in the usual ways. However, primitives that have become part of a composite can only be edited with SOLCHP, the change primitive command. Changes that can be made include changing color, deleting, copying, moving, replacing one primitive with another, and changing size.

Looking at *Figure 14-12*, you will see that we have created a slot only halfway along the length of the object. The slot stops where the box and the wedge meet. In this exercise we will change the size of the narrow box so that it creates a slot all the way through the wedge. You will notice that all the primitives used in the construction of our composite are still available, and that changes to them will update the composite as well.

> To begin this task you should have the composite solid shown in *Figure 14-12* on your screen.

> Type or select "SOLCHP", or select "Change Prim." under "Modify" on the "Model" pull down menu.

AutoCAD will prompt you to select a solid or region.

> Pick any point on the composite.

You will notice that AutoCAD needs to perform several updating and evaluation procedures as you make changes to a primitive. This can take time in larger models.

> When you see the "Select primitive:" prompt, pick any of the edges of the slot.

As soon as you have selected a primitive, AutoCAD makes it visible on your screen. In this case you should see the entire narrow box again, rather than just the edges of the slot that were left by the subtraction.

You will also see the following prompt:

Color/Delete/Evaluate/Instance/Move/Next/Pick/Replace/Size/eXit <N>:

We will try the "Size" option first to change the size of the narrow box. Later in this task we will use "Evaluate", "Instance", and "Next". "Evaluate" forces a reevaluation of the composite solid based on changes made since entering the SOLCHP command. This allows you to see the results of changes without leaving the command. "Instance" creates a copy of a primitive. "Next" allows you to switch from one primitive to another in sequence. "Pick" allows you to do the same thing by picking another primitive rather than cycling through until you get to the one you want.

In this task we want to change the size of the narrow box, so we will specify the "Size" option.

> Type "s" or select "Size".

AutoCAD prompts:

Length along X axis <4>:

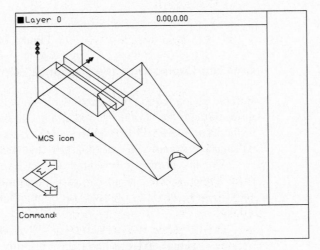

Figure 14-13

You will also see a new icon as illustrated in *Figure 14-13*. This is called the "Motion Coordinate System" or MCS icon. In this icon, one arrow (cone) is always on the X axis, two arrows on the Y axis, and three arrows on the Z axis. The same icon is used by the move option and the SOLMOVE command. In this case it is used to clarify changes in size along each axis.

We need to increase the size of our box primitive along the X axis so that it runs the length of the composite.

> Type "7" to change the X axis length.

AutoCAD prompts for a length along the Y axis. Looking at the MCS icon, you can see that a change here would affect the width of the primitive. We will leave ours at a width of 0.5.

> Press enter for no change along the Y axis.

Next AutoCAD prompts for a length along the Z axis. Changing this would affect the height of the primitive. We will leave ours at a height of 2.

> Press enter for no change along the Z axis.

AutoCAD will update the narrow box and lengthen it. Notice that while the size of the primitive has been changed, the change is not reflected in the composite yet. This will happen when we exit the command, or when we specify an evaluation.

> Type "e" or select "Evaluate".

AutoCAD computes a representation of the new composite model. When it is complete, your screen should resemble *Figure 14-14*.

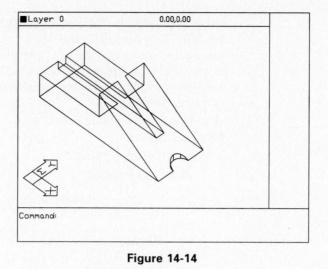

Figure 14-14

Creating Copies with the "Instance" Option

Before leaving the SOLCHP command we will make a copy of the cylinder. Copies are made through the "Instance" option and can be a little tricky. The copy will be created in the same place as the primitive and will have the color of the current layer, but you will not see it until you exit SOLCHP and REDRAW the screen.

The last primitive we edited was the narrow box, but because of the evaluation it is no longer visible. It appears as if no primitive is selected, but if we press enter or select "Next" another primitive will be highlighted.

> Press enter or select "Next". Repeat until the cylinder is highlighted.

AutoCAD will highlight a primitive. If it is not the cylinder, keep pressing enter until the cylinder is highlighted. Notice again that all the primitives are still available within the composite.

> With the cylinder highlighted, type "i" or select "Instance".

AutoCAD will create another instance of the cylinder primitive, separate from the original primitive but in the same space, so you will see no change. Before you can see it we will need to exit the command and perform a redraw.

> Type "x" or select "Exit".

> Type "r" or select "Redraw".

At this point you should see the new cylinder, as shown in *Figure 14-15*.

TASK 7: Moving Solids with the SOLMOVE Command

Procedure.

1. Type or select "SOLMOVE".
2. Select a solid entity. (Steps 1 and 2 can be reversed if noun/verb selection is enabled.)
3. Type a motion description.

Discussion. The SOLMOVE command offers another way to position solids and solid primitives in a drawing. It makes use of the Motion Coordinate System icon, introduced in the last task. It also uses a series of letter and number abbreviations to describe motion relative to the MCS axes. In this task we will move the cylinder you just created so that it can be subtracted from the composite to form a hole.

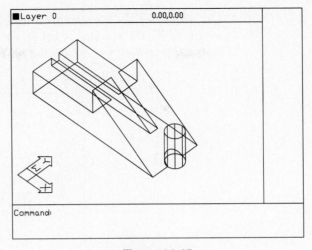

Figure 14-15

> To begin this task you should have the solid composite and the cylinder on your screen, as shown in *Figure 14-15*.

> Type or select "Solmove", or, on the pull down, select "Modify" and then "Move Object".

AutoCAD will prompt for object selection.

> Pick the cylinder.

> Press enter to end object selection.

AutoCAD now prompts:

?/<Motion description>:

Entering a question mark will get you a complete list of abbreviations for geometric descriptions of motion. Try it.

> Type or select "?".

AutoCAD will switch over to the graphics screen where you will see, among other things, the following list of motion descriptors.

a[efuw]—align with selected coordinate system

r[xyz]degrees—rotate about selected axis

t[xyz]distance—translate along selected axis

e—set axis to edge coordinate system

f—set axis to face coordinate system

u—set axis to use coordinate system

w—set axis to world coordinate system

o—restore motion to original position

What this all means is that you can align (a) the temporary motion coordinate system with an edge (e), a face (f), a UCS (u), or the WCS (w), and that you can move the selected object by translating (t) or rotating (r) around any of the three axes. For example, to align the MCS with a face, you could type "af" and then select a face to align with. To move 2 units along the X axis you could type "tx2". To accomplish both at once, you could type "af,tx2".

In our drawing we will move the cylinder two units back along the current x axis, so that it is positioned near the opening of the slot.

> Hit enter to continue and to return to the graphics display.

You may not have the MCS icon on your screen because it is located at the origin of the WCS, which is not on the screen. In *Figure 14-16*, We have shown our screen zoomed out, so that the MCS icon is visible.

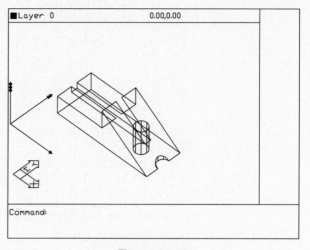

Figure 14-16

> Type "tx–2".

That is, "translate along the X axis two units in the negative direction."

> Press enter to exit SOLMOVE.

The cylinder will move two units to the left.

Finally, perform a subtraction to remove the volume of the new cylinder from the composite.

> Type or select "SOLSUB", or pick "Subtract" from the pull down.

> Select the composite as the source object.

> Press enter to end selection of source objects.

> Select the cylinder as the object to subtract.

> Press enter to end selection of objects to subtract.

The composite will be updated with the subtraction and your screen will resemble *Figure 14-17*.

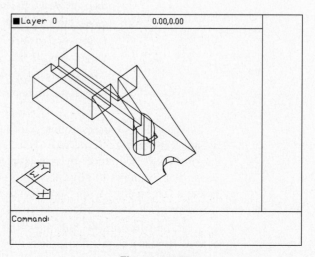

Figure 14-17

TASK 8: Creating Solid Chamfers and Fillets

Procedure.

1. Type or select "SOLCHAM".
2. Pick a base surface.
3. Press enter or type "n" to select the next surface.
4. Pick edges to be chamfered.
5. Press enter to end object selection.
6. Enter chamfer distances.

Discussion. Constructing chamfers and fillets on solids is simple, but the language of the prompts can cause confusion. Once you catch on you will have no difficulty.

Be aware that solid chamfers and fillets are created through subtraction. When the automated process is complete, the subtracted corner piece exists in the composite model as a primitive, just like the box and the cylinders we have subtracted from our model.

We will begin by putting a chamfer on the top left of the model.

> To begin this task you should have the solid model shown in *Figure 14-17* on your screen.

> Type or select "SOLCHAM" (under "Modify" on either the screen or pull down "Model" menus).

AutoCAD's first prompt is:

Pick base surface:

The confusion begins. What is a "base surface" in relation to a chamfered edge? Actually it refers to either of the two faces that meet at the edge where the chamfer will be. As long as you pick this edge you are bound to select one of these two surfaces, and either will do. Which of the two surfaces is the "base surface" and which the "adjacent surface" will not matter until you enter the chamfer distances.

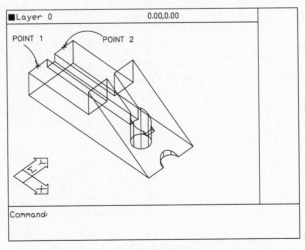

Figure 14-18

> Pick point 1 as shown in *Figure 14-18*.

AutoCAD now allows you to switch to the other surface that shares this edge, in case the first one was not right.

Next/<OK>:

It will not matter which of the two adjacent surfaces is selected unless you want to enter unequal chamfer distances.

> Press enter.

Now AutoCAD prompts:

Pick edges of this face to be chamfered (press ENTER when done):

You will have no difficulty here if you pick the edge you wish to chamfer again. The only difference is that you will need to pick twice, once on each side of the slot.

> Pick the top left edge of the model, to one side of the slot (point 1 in *Figure 14-18* again).

> Pick the same edge again, but on the other side of the slot, (point 2 in *Figure 14-18*).

> Press enter to end edge selection.

AutoCAD prompts:

Enter distance along base surface <0.00> :

> Type ".5".

AutoCAD prompts for a second distance:

Enter distance along adjacent surface <0.50> :

Now you can see the significance of "base surface." The chamfer will be created with the first distance on the base surface side and the second distance on the adjacent side. If the chamfer is symmetrical it will not matter which is which.

> Press enter.

After AutoCAD calculates, your screen will resemble *Figure 14-19*.

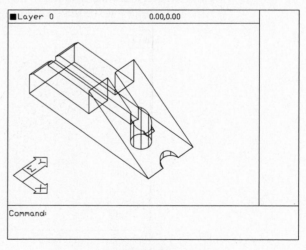

Figure 14-19

Creating Fillets with SOLFILL

The procedure for creating solid fillets is simpler. There is one less step since there is no need to differentiate between base and adjacent surfaces in a fillet.

> Type or select "SOLFILL" (under "Modify" on the screen and pull down "Model" menus).

AutoCAD prompts:

Pick edges of solids to be filleted (press ENTER when done):

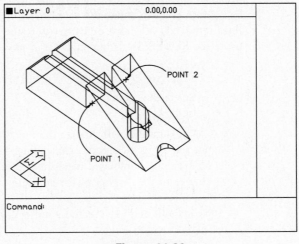

Figure 14-20

> Pick the lower edge where the box and the wedge meet, point 1 in *Figure 14-20*.

    You may have to wait a moment for AutoCAD to update and highlight the selected edge.

> Pick the lower edge on the other side of the slot, point 2 in *Figure 14-20*.

> Press enter to end selection of edges.

    AutoCAD will prompt for a diameter or radius of the fillet.

> Type ".5".

    After AutoCAD performs its calculations, your screen will resemble *Figure 14-21*.

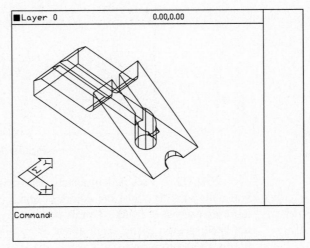

Figure 14-21

TASK 9: HIDEing and SHADEing Solid Models

Procedure.

1. Use SOLMESH to create a mesh representation of the model.
2. For shading, adjust layers or colors of primitives to create desired effects.

3. Enter "HIDE" for hidden line removal, or "SHADE" for shaded rendering.

Discussion. By default, all solids are drawn as wireframe models on the screen, because these require less memory and less generation time than surface (mesh) models. But before you can create representations of solid models with shaded surfaces or hidden lines removed, you must convert wireframe graphics to mesh. This is a simple process using the SOLMESH command. Try it now on your composite model.

> Type "mesh" or select "SOLMESH".
> Select the model.
> Press enter.

AutoCAD will update the model and create a mesh representation. You will not see a big difference. Depending on your current setting of "Solwdens", which controls the number of mesh lines used to display curved surfaces, you may see a change in the display of the cylindrical surfaces and the fillets.

Now that you have created a meshed model, you can perform hiding and shading.

> Type or select "Hide".

Hiding and shading both require some regeneration time, which can be quite significant in larger drawings. Release 12, however, accomplishes this much more rapidly than previous releases.

When the HIDE process is complete, your screen will resemble *Figure 14-22*.

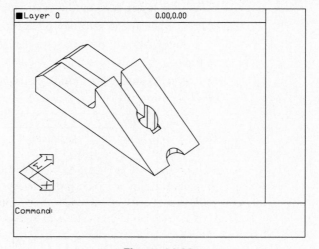

Figure 14-22

SHADE is executed in exactly the same manner, but takes longer. In addition, you may want to adjust the colors of some of the components of a model to create a more distinctive drawing. This is done easily using the SOLCHP command. We have not been specific to this point about layers and colors to use in constructing our model, but for this exercise we will create a shaded image with the outer surfaces in yellow and the slot and holes in green.

> Type or select "SOLCHP", or pick "Change Prim." from the pull down menu.
> Select the model.
> Select the original box portion of the composite model.
> Type "c" or select "Color".

AutoCAD will prompt for a new color.

> Type "2" for the color yellow.

> Press enter to move on to the next primitive.

Notice that when you first change a color it is reflected on the screen, but when you move on to the next primitive, the previous primitive reverts to its old color. This is only temporary. If you have made a color change it will show when you exit the command.

> Repeat these three steps for all primitives.

The procedure is as follows:

1. Type "c" or select "color".

2. Type a color number or name.

3. Press enter to move on to the next primitive.

The box, the wedge, the chamfers, and the fillets should be color 2, yellow. The interior narrow box, and the two cylinders should be color 3, green. Other color schemes are, of course, valid and would be carried out the same way.

> When all color changes have been made, type "x" or select "eXit" to exit the command.

> Type or select "Shade".

> Wait...

TASK 10: Creating Solid Objects with SOLEXT

Procedure.

1. Create a polyline, circle, or region shape in two dimensions.
2. Type "ext" or select "Solext" ("Extrude" on the pull down menu).
3. Select objects.
4. Specify an extrusion height.
5. Specify an extrusion taper angle.

Discussion. AME includes three additional ways to create solid objects other than through the primitive and constructive geometry commands. First, using the SOLEXT command, simple 2D polylines and regions can be "extruded." That is, the 2D shape can be built up or repeated along a linear path stretching up or down from the plane in which it is drawn. Second, using SOLREV, 2D polylines and regions can be revolved around an axis along a circular or semicircular path. The SOLREV command is very similar to REVSURF, but it creates a solid rather than a surface model. Finally, an object that has been given "thickness" using the CHPROP command can be made solid with SOLIDIFY.

In this task we will draw a simple polyline shape and extrude it to create a solid. In the next task we will begin working with regions.

> To begin this task, regenerate your screen and then clear it of all objects left from the previous task.

> Draw a 2.00 by 4.00 polyline rectangle as shown in *Figure 14-23*. Be sure to use PLINE to create a 2D polyline. 3DPOLY, which draws 3D polylines, will not work with SOLEXT.

> Type "ext" or select "Solext" (select "Extrude" under "Model" on the pull down menu).

AutoCAD will prompt you to select objects. Notice the message before the prompts. It tells you that only regions, polylines, and circles can be extruded.

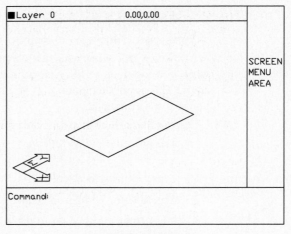

Figure 14-23

> Select the rectangle.

> Press enter to end object selection.

AutoCAD prompts:

Height of extrusion:

This will be measured in the Z direction, but you can show it with two points in the X-Y plane if you wish.

> Type "3" or show a distance of 3.00 units.

AutoCAD prompts:

Extrusion taper angle <0>:

This prompt gives you the opportunity to create a tapered extrusion by specifying an angle. This will be an angle between the Z axis and the edge of the extruded object.

> Type "10".

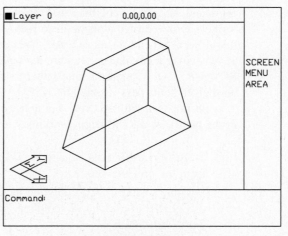

Figure 14-24

Your screen should resemble *Figure 14-24*. Be aware that if your taper angle is too flat (a large angle from the Z axis), edges will meet before the specified height is reached. In the case of an extrusion with a rectangular base, this would result in a prism, with a ridge at the top rather than a smaller rectangle.

The extruded solid you have just created will function exactly like the solid primitives created earlier. It can be used in union, subtraction, and intersection with other primitives to create complex solid objects.

In the next task we will explore solid regions.

TASK 11: Creating 2D Region Entities

Procedure.

1. Draw 2D polyline shapes.
2. SOLIDIFY or perform constructive geometry to convert to regions.

Discussion. Release 12 is the first AutoCAD version to include a region modeler. Regions are the 2D equivalent of 3D solids. They can be combined through union, subtraction, and intersection using the same commands used with solids. Regions are similar to faces in that they cover 2D spaces. Like polylines, they can be extruded to form 3D solids.

In this task we will create a simple composite region from two polyline rectangles. Individual regions may be created by SOLIDIFYing polylines (discussion following), but this step is performed automatically if the default setting of the "Solsolidify" variable is retained, as you will see.

> To begin this task, undo the last extrusion, so that you are left with the 2.00 × 4.00 polyline rectangle shown previously in *Figure 14-23*.

> Draw a second polyline rectangle, 1.00 × 2.00, centered on the midpoint of the edge of the first, as shown in *Figure 14-25*.

Next we will subtract the smaller rectangle from the larger to create a composite region.

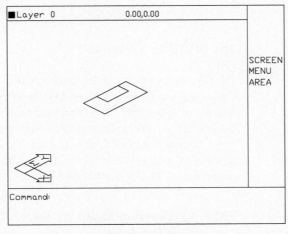

Figure 14-25

NOTE: This exercise assumes that the variable "solsolidify" is set to the default value of 3. With this setting, 2D polylines selected in AME solid modeling commands like SOLSUB are automatically converted to regions. If the variable is set to 1, polylines will not be converted, so the commands will not proceed. If the setting is 2, AME will ask first before converting.

> Type "sub" or select "Solsub" ("Subtract" on the pull down menu).

AME prompts for source objects.

> Pick the larger rectangle.

> Press enter to end selection of source objects.

      AME prompts for objects to subtract.

> Select the smaller rectangle.

> Press enter to end object selection.

      AME will convert the polylines to regions and perform the subtraction operation to produce the composite region shown in *Figure 14-26*.

NOTE: Regions are shown hatched according to the settings of the variables "solhpat" (solid hatch pattern), "solhangle" (solid hatch angle), and "solhsize" (solid hatch size). The default setting is a "user" pattern, with a 45 degree angle and a size of 1. You can change the variables one by one at the command line or call up a dialogue box through the DDSOLVAR command (pick "Setup" and then "Variables..." from the "Model" pull down menu, then pick "Hatch Parameters" from the dialogue box).

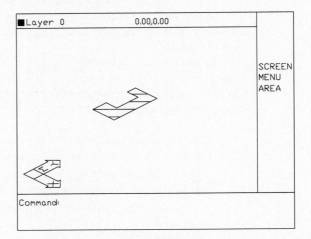

Figure 14-26

The SOLIDIFY Command

2D polyline entities, circles, traces, and 2D AutoCAD solids (created with the SOLID command, see Chapter 9), can also be converted to regions using the SOLIDIFY command. As noted previously, this operation is performed automatically when appropriate 2D entities are selected for use in AME commands, if the variable solsolidify is set to 3.

      To use SOLIDIFY, simply enter the command and select objects. Also note that SOLIDIFY will convert 2D entities that have been given thickness using the CHPROP command to 3D solids rather than 2D regions, giving you yet another way to create solids.

TASK 12: Creating Solids by Revolving 2D Entities Using SOLREV

Procedure.

1. Draw regions or 2D polyline shapes.
2. Type "rev" or select "Solrev" ("Revolve" on the pull down menu).
3. Select objects.
4. Specify an axis of revolution.
5. Specify an angle of revolution.

Discussion. SOLREV is a powerful solid modeling command which creates solid objects by revolving 2D shapes and regions around an axis. It functions in ways very similar to the REVSURF surface modeling command.

In this task we will create a spool-shaped 3D solid by revolving the composite region from the last task around an axis in the X-Y plane.

> To begin this task, you should have the composite region shown in *Figure 14–26* on your screen.

> Type "rev" or select "Solrev", or select "Model" from the pull down menu, and then "Revolve".

> Select the composite region.

> Press enter to end selection.

AME updates the display and prompts:

Axis of revolution - Entity/X/Y/<Start point of axis>:

"Entity" allows you to select a line or a one-segment polyline as the axis of revolution. "X" and "Y" allow you to specify one of the axes of the current UCS. We will specify an axis by pointing.

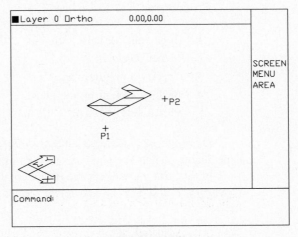

Figure 14-27

> Pick a start point 1.00 unit to the right of the region, as shown in *Figure 14-27*.

AME prompts for an end point of the axis.

> Pick an end point like point 2 in the figure.

AME prompts:

Angle of revolution <full circle>:

Like REVSURF, SOLREV gives you the option of creating only a portion of the circle of revolution. Unlike REVSURF, there is no option to begin the object somewhere other than in the plane of the region itself.

> Press enter to create the full circle.

In a few moments your screen will resemble *Figure 14-28*. This is a true 3D solid. It is currently drawn in wire frame and would have to be regenerated as a mesh (SOLMESH command) in order to HIDE or SHADE properly.

In the remaining tasks we will create a cutaway view, a section, a copied face, and a profile of this object.

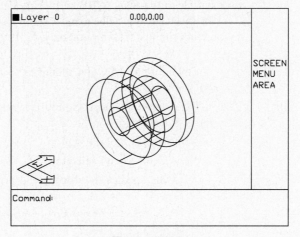

Figure 14-28

TASK 13: Creating Solid Cutaway Views with SOLCUT

Procedure.

1. Type "cut" or select "Solcut" ("Cut Solids" on the pull down).
2. Select objects.
3. Specify a cutting plane.
4. Specify a point on the plane.
5. Pick a side to retain.

Discussion. A single solid or set of solids may be cut along its intersection with a specifiable plane. The plane is specified in terms common to several AME commands.

In this task we will cut the object created in the last task along a plane parallel to the current Z and Y axes, and retain the left portion so that we can view the inside of the "spool."

> Type "cut" or select "Solcut" (on the pull down "Model" menu, select "Modify" and then "Cut Solids").

AME will prompt you to select objects.

> Select the spool.
> Press enter to end object selection.

AME now prompts for plane specification:

Cutting plane by Entity/Last/Zaxis/View/XY/YZ/ZX/<3points>:

This prompt is common to several AME operations, including the SOLSECT command which we will explore next. It is also used in defining "construction planes." A construction plane is a temporary coordinate system, which can be used like a point filter or an object snap any time a point is requested. Construction plane specification of a point is initiated by entering "cp" when a point is requested, and then specifying a plane just as we will do here.

Construction planes, or the cutting plane requested here, can be determined by an entity, an origin, and a point on the Z axis; by one of the current UCS planes; or by showing three points. In this task we will use a Y-Z plane.

Take a look at *Figure 14-29*. It should help you visualize the X-Y, Y-Z, and Z-X planes. The actual cutting plane will be parallel to a plane of origin in the current UCS. In other words, it does not have to have the same origin. Once you have determined which plane you want to use, the next step will be to specify a point on the plane.

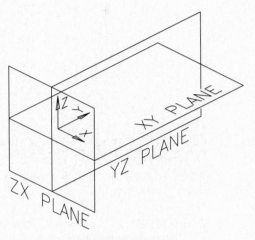

Figure 14-29

> Type or select "YZ".

AME will prompt for a point on the Y-Z plane. The default point is (0,0,0), which will specify the Y-Z plane of the current UCS. Any other point will specify a plane parallel to the current Y-Z plane.

> Pick a point so that the Y axis of the cross hairs runs through the center of the spool.

This will cause the spool to be cut along its centerline.

AME prompts:

Both sides/<Point on the desired side of the plane>:

> Pick any point to the left of the previous point.

This will show that you want to retain the portion of the spool that lies along the left side of the cutting plane.

When AME has completed its calculations, your screen should resemble *Figure 14-30*. Next we will create a cross section of the remaining half.

TASK 14: Creating Sections with SOLSECT

Procedure.

1. Type "sect" or select "Solsect" ("Section Solids" on the pull down menu).
2. Select objects.
3. Specify a sectioning plane.

Discussion. Sectioning works just like cutting, but the outcome is a region or a 2D block, depending on the setting of the "Solsectype" variable.

In this task we will create a region section of the spool by sectioning it along the X-Y plane. The result will be a U-shaped block with cross-hatching. It will look like the

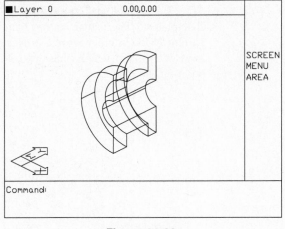

Figure 14-30

region we used to create the revolved solid in the first place, but it will not be a region unless "Solsectype" is set to 3.

> Type "sect" or select "Solsect", or select "Display" and then "Section Solids" from the pull down menu.
> Select the cut spool.
> Press enter to end object selection.

AME prompts:

> Sectioning plane by
> Entity/Last/Zaxis/View/XY/YZ/ZX/<3points>:

This is the same prompt as the cutting plane prompt, except for the first word. This time we will cut along the current X-Y plane.

> Type or select "XY".

AME will prompt for a point on the X-Y plane. Any point will do.

> Press enter for the point (0,0,0) or pick any point.

AME will create the section. To see it well you will need to move it, or move the spool. If you move the region, be aware there are two parts to move, the outer edge and the cross-hatching. When you are done your screen should resemble *Figure 14-31*.

NOTE: The default setting of the variable "Solsectype" is 1, which causes SOL-SECT to create a block containing 2D lines, arcs, and circles. If the variable is set to 2, sectioning with SOLSECT will create a block made up of polylines. If the setting is 3, the section will be a region. The three results will look the same.

TASK 15: Extracting Features with SOLFEAT

Procedure.

1. Type "feat" or select "Solfeat" ("Copy Feature" under "Display" on the pull down "Model" menu).
2. Specify edge or face.
3. Indicate whether you want all features or selected features.
4. Select features, if necessary.
5. Select more features or exit the command.

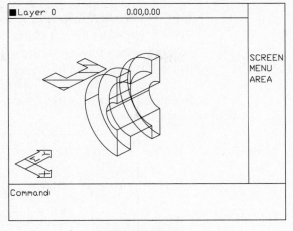

Figure 14-31

Discussion. SOLFEAT gives you the ability to extract faces and edges from 3D solids. Faces extracted in this manner are *not* 3D faces. They are not surfaces, but simple wireframe blocks made up of lines, arcs, polylines, and circles.

> To begin this task you should have the cut view of the spool on your screen.

> Type "feat" or select "Solfeat" (under "display" on both "Model" menus, look for "Copy Feature" on the pull down menu).

AME prompts:

Edge/<Face>:

> Press enter to specify "Face".

AME prompts:

All/<Select>:

> Press enter to indicate that you will select a face, rather than extract all faces.

AME prompts:

Pick a face:

> Pick the C-shaped face at the front of the object.

Often, faces will share an edge, so that your choice may be ambiguous. This is why you need the following prompt:

Next/<OK>:

If the highlighted face is not the one you want, you can switch to a face adjacent to the highlighted face by typing "n" or selecting "Next".

> If necessary, type "n" or select "Next".

> When the C-shaped face is highlighted, press enter.

At this point AME creates a block from the selected face. It also prompts for another face so that you can continue extracting faces.

> Press enter to exit the command.

The block is displayed directly on top of the face from which it was copied, so you will need to move the newly created block away from the spool in order to see it well.

> Type "m" or select "Move".
> Type "L" to select the last object drawn.
> Move the block forward so that your screen resembles *Figure 14-32*.
> REDRAW your screen.

Before going on, take a look at the new object. Be aware that it is a block made up of two arcs and two lines.

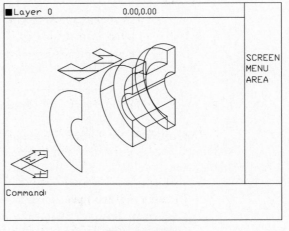

Figure 14-32

TASK 16: Creating Profile Images with SOLPROF

Procedure.

1. Change tilemode to 0, "off".
2. Use MVIEW to create at least one model space viewport.
3. Type "ms" to switch to model space.
4. Type "prof" or select "Solprof" ("Profile Solids" on the pull down "Model" menu, under "Display").
5. Select 3D solid objects.
6. Specify display parameters.
7. Wait...
8. Move the profile, or the object, or turn off the layer the object is drawn on.

Discussion.   The SOLPROF command is used to create a profile image of a 3D solid object. Profiles show only edges and silhouettes; they do not show lines created by meshing, and they may have hidden lines removed or not, depending on how you answer the prompts. They are created from a single viewpoint and will not display correctly if the viewpoint is changed.

Profiles can be created only in paper space. In this book we have kept the discussion of paper space and other plotting techniques clearly separated from our presentation of AutoCAD drawing techniques. Basic plotting, paper space, and plotting from multiple viewports have been given separate treatment in Chapter 15. In order to present SOL-PROF here, however, we must dip into paper space. If you have not explored Chapter 15 yet, this will serve as a brief introduction.

Tilemode

Before you can create a profile, you must turn the variable "tilemode" off. With tilemode on, you can create only tiled viewports. As discussed in Chapter 13, tiled viewports are non-overlapping and cannot be plotted simultaneously. They are useful for visualizing objects from multiple points of view, but are very limited when it is time to produce hard copy. Non-tiled viewports offer much more flexibility and can be plotted simultaneously. Non-tiled viewports must be created in paper space.

> Type or select "Tilemode" (under "View" on the pull down menu, "Mview" on the screen menu).
> Type "0", or select "Off".

Your screen will go blank, and you will see the paper space icon at the lower left of the screen in place of the UCS icon. When you change tilemode to off, AutoCAD automatically puts you into paper space and forces you to create at least one viewport before you can continue. This is done with the MVIEW command.

The MVIEW Command

The MVIEW command is used to create non-tiled viewports in paper space. It is similar to the VPORTS command, which creates tiled viewports in model space.

> Type or select "Mview" (under "View" on the pull down menu).
AutoCAD prompts:

ON/OFF/Hideplot/Fit/2/3/4/Restore/<First Point>:

We will discuss these options in Chapter 15. For now we will use the simplest option to create a single viewport which covers the drawing area.
> Type "f" or select "Fit" ("Fit Viewport" on the pull down menu).

Your screen will be redrawn as shown in *Figure 14-33*. Notice the paper space icon in the lower left corner. This indicates that you are still in paper space. The viewport you just created acts like a window from paper space into model space. But as long as you are in paper space, the window is closed. Any drawing or editing you do will be placed on the window pane, so to speak, and you will not have access to the objects inside the viewport.

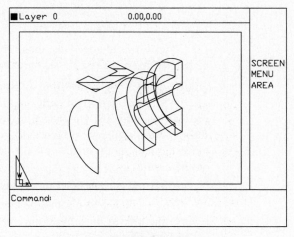

Figure 14-33

> Type "ms" or select "Model space" ("MSPACE" on the screen menu).

The paper space icon will be replaced by the familiar UCS icon. This indicates that you are now back in model space, within the window. At this point you are ready to create a profile.

> Type "prof" or select "Profile Solids" or "SOLPROF:" (under "Display" on both menus).

AME prompts for object selection.

> Select the half spool.

Notice that you can profile more than one object at a time.

> Press enter to end object selection.

AME updates the object and prompts:

Display hidden profile lines on separate layer? <Y>

Profiles are created in two parts by AME. One part includes the lines and edges visible in the current view. The other part includes hidden lines. If you answer yes (or press enter) at this prompt, the visible and hidden parts of the profile are created as separate blocks and placed on separate layers. The layers are created automatically and given names made from simple code letters followed by the handle of the viewport in which the profile is created. If the viewport handle is 3A, the visible line block goes on layer "PV-3A" and the hidden line block goes on layer "PH-3A". The hidden line block will be displayed with the "hidden" linetype.

If you answer no to the prompt, all lines are treated as visible lines and placed on layer PV–3A.

> Press enter to display hidden profile lines on a separate layer.

AME prompts:

Project profile lines onto a plane? <Y>

If the answer is yes, the profile blocks will be constructed with 2D entities and projected onto the plane of the current view. If the answer is no, the profile will be constructed with 3D entities.

> Press enter to project profile lines onto a plane.

The final prompt is:

Delete tangential edges? <Y>:

This refers to edges like those created at the end points of a fillet. These will be deleted from the profile if you answer yes.

> Press enter to delete tangential edges.

AME will perform a series of computations. When all phases are complete, you will see only a slight change in your screen image, because the profile will be sitting on top of the solid object. In order to see the profile itself you will need to move the half spool, or turn off the current layer (assuming the spool was drawn on the current layer).

> Turn off the current layer or the layer that the spool was drawn on.

Your screen will resemble *Figure 14-34*. Notice the hidden lines. You can remove the hidden lines by turning off the PH-layer. Using a wild card character (*) to turn off the hidden line layer may be useful, since you probably will not know the handle of the current viewport.

> Enter the LAYER command.

> Type or select "off".

> Type "PH-*".

This will turn off any layer beginning with "PH-".

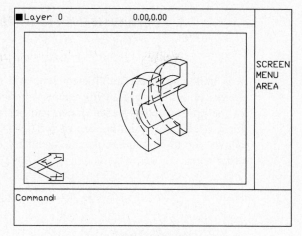

Figure 14-34

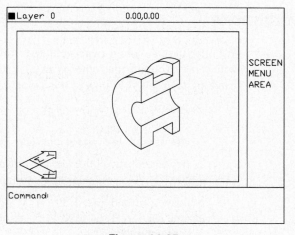

Figure 14-35

> Press enter to exit the command.

Your screen should resemble *Figure 14-35*.

TASKS 17, 18, 19, 20, and 21

The five drawings that follow will give you practice in the solid modeling techniques introduced in this chapter. The first is given with detailed drawing instructions, while the rest are left for you to explore on your own. As you look at the objects you will begin to view them as composites made from primitive building blocks. Look for opportunities to use SOLREV as well as union, subtraction, and intersection operations. In all cases, you can choose between hidden line images and profiled images of your composite solids.

If you would like further practice in solid modeling, any of the drawings in this book, 2D as well as wireframe and surface models, can be turned into full solid models.

DRAWING 14–1: BUSHING MOUNT

It is important to use an efficient sequence in the construction of composite solids. In general this will mean saving union, subtraction, and intersection operations until most of the primitives have been drawn and positioned. This approach has two advantages. First, it cuts down on the size of the CSG tree and takes up less memory. Second, it allows you to continue to use the geometry of the parts for snap points as you position other parts.

DRAWING SUGGESTIONS

We offer the following suggestions for Drawing 14-1. The principles demonstrated here will carry over into the other drawings, and we feel you should be quite capable of handling them on your own at this point.

> Use at least two views, one plan and one 3D, as you work.

> Begin with the bottom of the mount in the X-Y plane. This will mean drawing a 6.00 × 4.00 × .50 solid box sitting on the X-Y plane.

> Draw a second box, 1.50 × 4.00 × 3.50, in the X-Y plane. This will become the upright section at the middle of the mount. Move it so that its own midpoint is at the midpoint of the base.

> Draw a third box, 1.75 × 1.75 × .50, in the X-Y plane. This will be copied and become one of the two slots in the base. Move it so that the midpoint of its long side is at the midpoint of the short side of the base. Then use SOLMOVE to translate 1.25 along the X axis (positive if you are moving in from the left, negative moving in from the right).

> Add a .375 radius cylinder with .50 height at each end of the slot.

> Copy the box and cylinders 3.75 to the other side of the base to form the other slot.

> Create a new UCS 2.00 up in the Z direction. You can use the origin option and give (0,0,2) as the new origin. This puts the X-Y plane of the UCS directly at the middle of the upright block, where you can easily draw the bushing.

> Move out to the right of the mount and draw the polyline outline of the bushing as shown in the drawing. Use SOLREV to create the solid bushing.

> Copy the bushing over into the center of the mount, where it can be subtracted to create the hole in the mount upright.

> Union the first and second boxes.

> Subtract the boxes and cylinders to form the slots in the base and the copy of the bushing to form the hole in the mount.

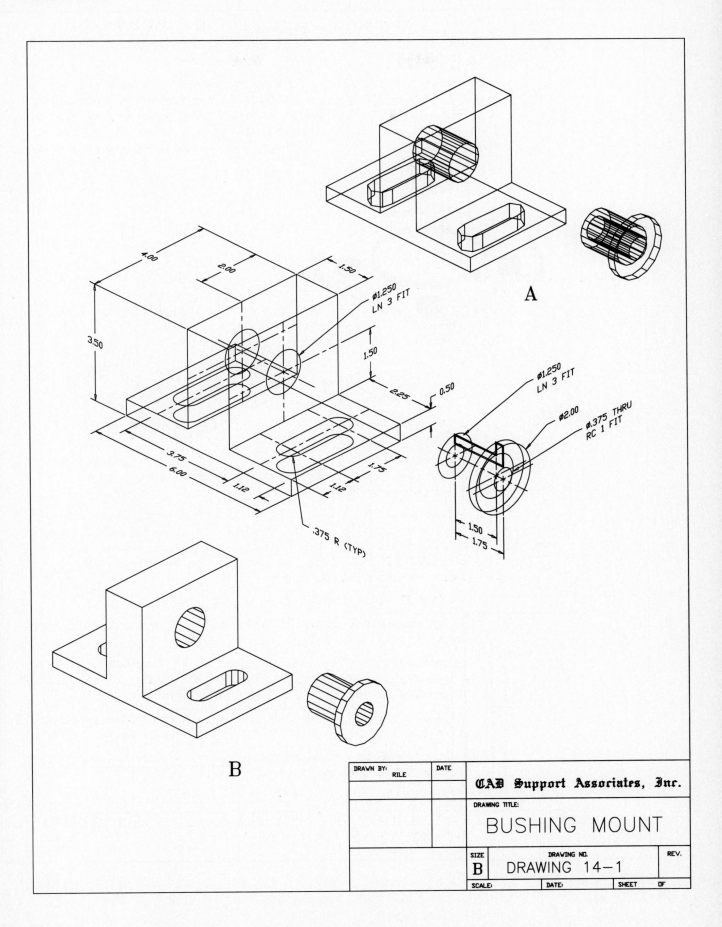

A

4.00
2.00
1.50
3.50
Ø1.250
LN 3 FIT
1.50
2.25
0.50
3.75
6.00
1.12
1.12
1.75
.375 R (TYP)

Ø1.250
LN 3 FIT
Ø2.00
Ø.375 THRU
RC 1 FIT
1.50
1.75

B

DRAWN BY:	DATE	CAD Support Associates, Inc.		
RILE				
		DRAWING TITLE:		
		BUSHING MOUNT		
		SIZE	DRAWING NO.	REV.
		B	DRAWING 14–1	
		SCALE:	DATE:	SHEET	OF

LINK MOUNT

Drawing 14−2

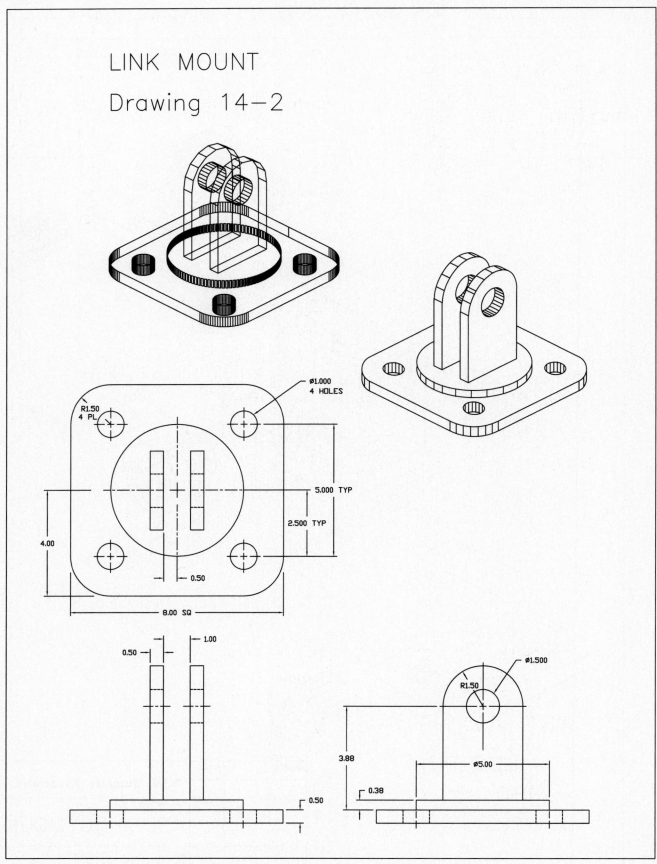

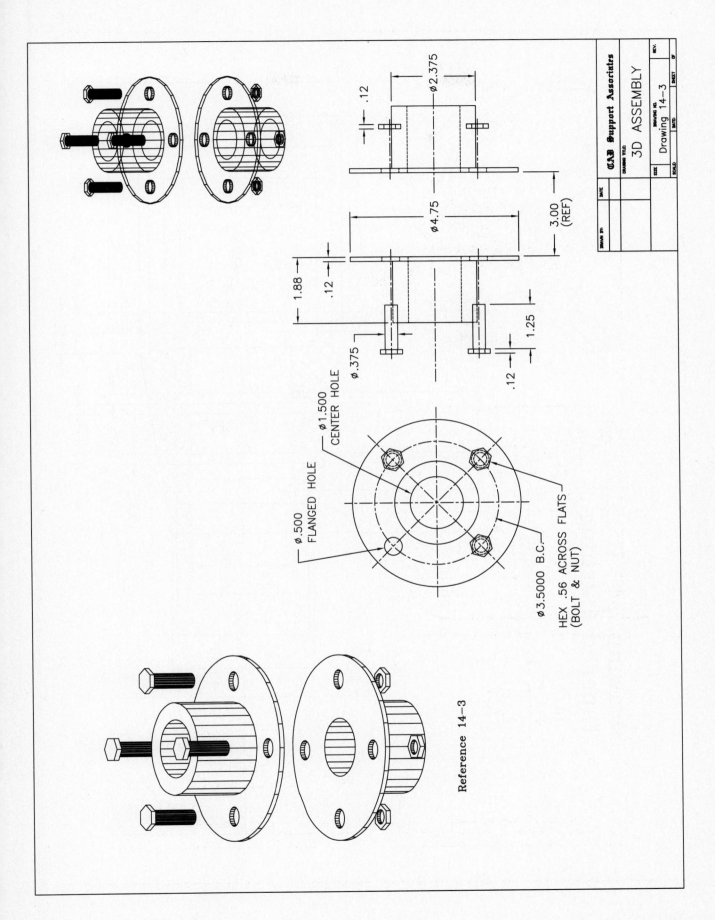

ø2.375

.12

ø4.75

3.00
(REF)

1.88

.12

ø.375

1.25

.12

ø1.500
CENTER HOLE

FLANGED HOLE

ø.500

ø3.5000 B.C.

HEX .56 ACROSS FLATS
(BOLT & NUT)

Reference 14-3

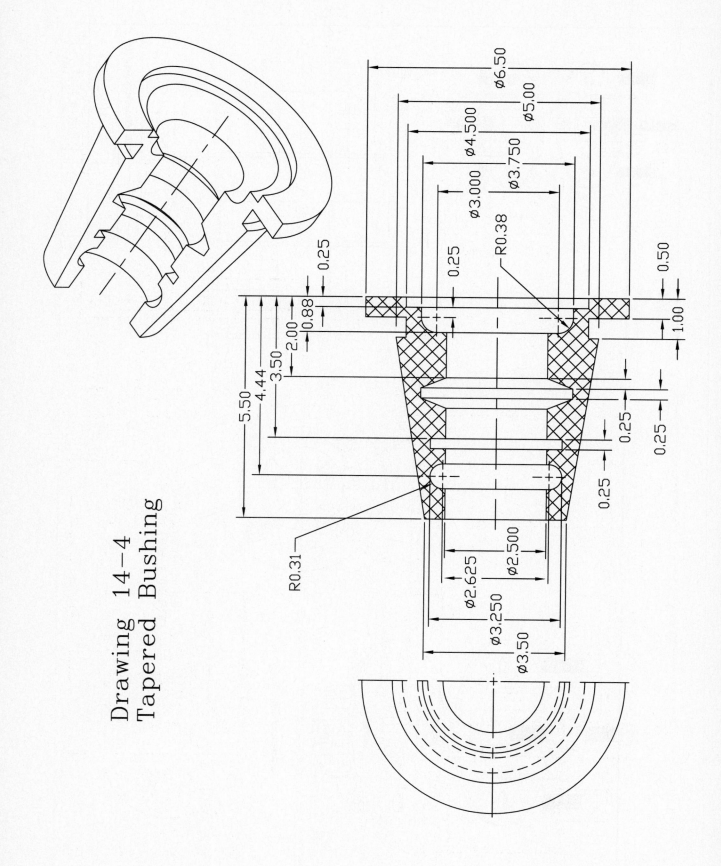

Drawing 14–4
Tapered Bushing

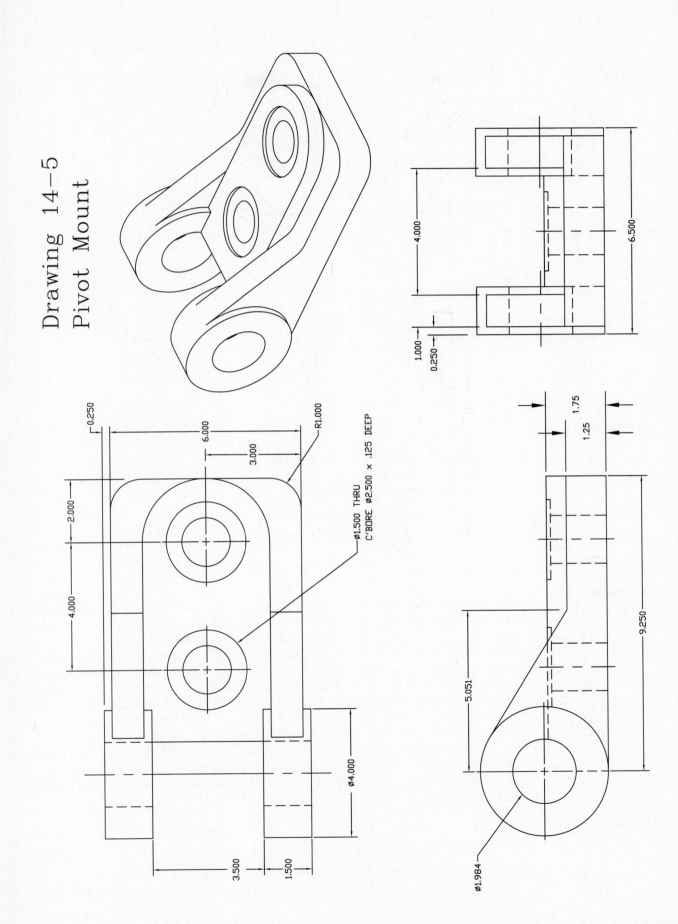

Drawing 14–5
Pivot Mount

0.250

6.000

3.000

R1.000

2.000

4.000

Ø1.500 THRU
C'BORE Ø2.500 x .125 DEEP

Ø4.000

3.500

1.500

4.000

1.000

0.250

6.500

1.75

1.25

9.250

5.051

Ø1.984

427

CHAPTER

15

COMMANDS

PLOT	MVIEW	DISPLAY
PLOT	MVIEW	DVIEW
	MSPACE	
	PSPACE	
	TILEMODE	
	VPLAYER	
	MVSETUP	

OVERVIEW

This chapter is intended to be accessible from various points in the progression through earlier chapters. The focus here is not on drawing techniques but on the information you need to get your drawings out on paper. Those who are in the early stages of drawing, Part I of this book, and wish to plot or print a drawing can do so by working through the first task, which covers basic plotting directly from the drawing editor in model space. Task 2 moves on to the use of paper space and multiple viewports but also should be accessible from the early chapters of this book. Task 3 introduces dimensioning and text size considerations when moving between model space and paper space. Task 4 covers issues of scaling and layer control in multiple paper space viewports. Tasks 3 and 4 are appropriate for those who have completed through Chapter 8. Task 5 introduces the MVSETUP program. Task 6 is an exercise on the use of DVIEW to create carefully prepared viewpoints and perspective views in three dimensions. Both of the last two tasks are intended for use after the completion of Chapter 13.

TASKS

1. Plot a 2D drawing from model space.
2. Plot a drawing from multiple viewports in paper space.
3. Control text and dimension size using different scales in model space and paper space.

4. Manipulate layer visibility in multiple viewports.
5. Use the MVSETUP program to create a four-view layout with title block.
6. Create perspective and clipped 3D views with DVIEW.

TASK 1: Plotting a 2D Drawing from Model Space

Procedure.

1. Type or select "Plot".
2. Set plot parameters.
3. Preview plot.
4. Click on "OK".
5. Prepare plotting device.
6. Press enter to plot.

Discussion. You can plot drawings on a pen plotter or a printer. In order for either to work, the plotting device needs to be correctly connected to your computer and AutoCAD must have a driver (software program) for that particular device. The AutoCAD software includes a large number of drivers, but the one you want must be correctly installed and located where AutoCAD can find it before plotting can be performed. If you need information on how to install a plotter or printer driver, see the *AutoCAD Interface, Installation, and Performance Guide* and the *AutoCAD Reference Manual*.

In this task we will take you through the options available in the Plot Configuration dialogue box and show you how to print or plot a drawing. The procedures discussed here will work for any drawing you have opened in the drawing editor in model space. If you have not previously read about model space and paper space, you will find these discussed in the next task. For now, all you need to know is that all the drawing exercises in this book have been done in model space. Paper space becomes most useful when you wish to plot from multiple viewports simultaneously.

> To begin this task, you should be in the drawing editor with a completed drawing on the screen. We have used Drawing 3-4, "Bushing" for purposes of illustration.

In Release 12, all plotting begins with the PLOT command, which calls the Plot Configuration dialogue box, illustrated in *Figure 15-1*. Your main goal in this exercise is to familiarize yourself with this dialogue box and its major subdialogues.

> Type or select "Plot" (under "File" on the pull down menu).

Take a look at the dialogue box. It is broken into six parts. "Device and Default Information" allows you to specify the printer or plotter you wish to use, along with some related information. "Pen Parameters" is only for plotting devices and allows you to relate pen colors to pen numbers on your plotter so that your drawing comes out looking the way you drew it on the screen. "Additional Parameters" include the portion of the drawing to be plotted and whether or not to remove hidden lines (for 3D drawings only). "Paper Size and Orientation" allows you to give AutoCAD information on the type of drawing sheet you are using. "Scale, Rotation, and Origin" is where you tell AutoCAD how to scale your drawing, which way to draw on the paper, and where to begin. Finally, "Plot Preview" is a Release 12 feature that lets you see how your drawing will look on paper before you actually execute the plot. We will look into these areas one at a time, using Plot Preview extensively along the way.

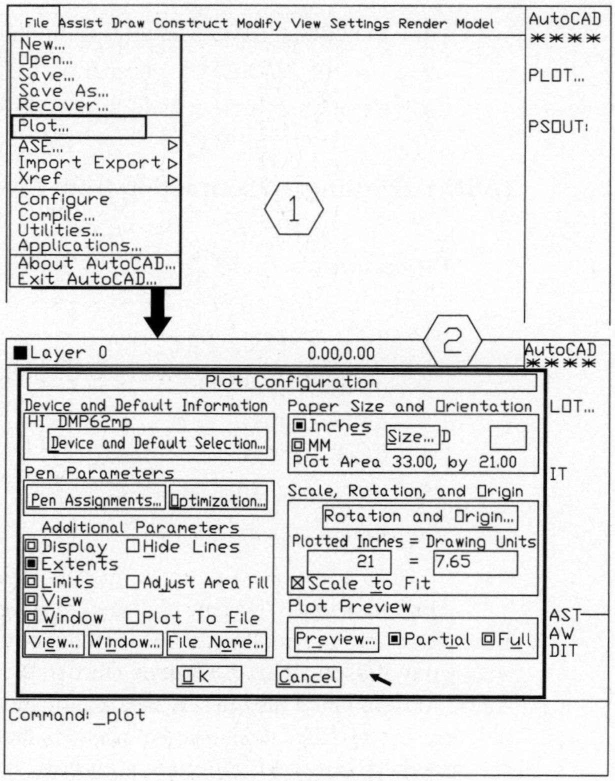

Figure 15-1

Plotting with No Changes in Parameters

If no changes in plotting parameters are needed, the plot sequence is extremely simple.

1. Type or select "Plot".
2. Click on "OK".
3. Prepare the plotter.
4. Press enter.

More often you will want to check a few things and make some changes before you commit your computer and printer to the time and material it takes to create hard copy. At the very least, you will want to preview your plot to make sure you get what you want. Release 12 has a plot preview feature which allows you to eliminate much of the guesswork from plotting. So, before doing anything else, learn how to preview plots.

Plot Preview

Plot preview is at the lower right of the Plot Configuration dialogue box. As you can see there are two types of preview, "Partial" and "Full". A partial preview will show you the effective plotting area in relation to the paper size. A full preview shows an image of your drawing as it will appear within the boundaries of the drawing sheet. Partial is quick to use, and should be accessed frequently as you set plot parameters that affect how paper will be used and oriented. Full previews take longer and should be saved for when you think you have got everything right.

We will look at a partial preview first.

> If the "Partial" radio button is not selected in your dialogue box, select it now.

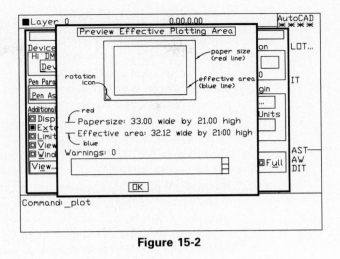

Figure 15-2

> Click on "Preview...".

You will see a preview image similar to the one shown in *Figure 15-2*. The exact image will depend on your plotting device, so it may be different from the one shown here. Notice the elements of the preview. The red rectangle represents your drawing paper. It may be oriented in landscape (horizontally) or portrait (vertically). Typically, printers are in portrait, and plotters in landscape.

The blue rectangle inside the red one illustrates the effective plotting area. This represents the size and shape of the area that AutoCAD can actually use given the shape of the drawing in relation to the paper. The effective area is dependent on many things, as you will see. We will leave it as is for now and return later when you begin to alter the plot configuration.

In one corner of the red rectangle you will see a small triangle. This is the rotation icon. It shows the corner of the plotting area where the plotter will begin plotting (the origin).

> Click on "OK" to exit the preview box.

> Click on the "Full" radio button to switch to a full preview.

> Click on "Preview...".

The dialogue box will disappear temporarily and you will see a preview similar to the one in *Figure 15-3*. We have used Drawing 3-4 to illustrate. You will see whatever drawing you are preparing to plot, with orientation and placement depending on your plotting device.

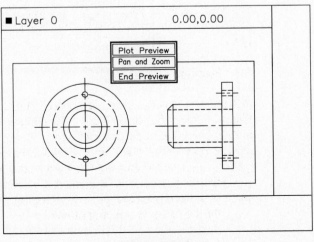

Figure 15-3

The Plot Preview dialogue box in the middle can be moved aside like any dialogue box. Just move the cursor to the gray title area, press the pick button, and hold it down as you move the box.

The pan and zoom feature allows you to look closely at small areas in the drawing, to check text or dimensions, for example. Panning and zooming in the preview has no effect on the plot parameters.

Selecting "Pan and Zoom" will cause the box to disappear and be replaced by a rectangle with an X in the middle. This feature functions like the pan and zoom box in the "dynamic" option of the ZOOM command (Chapter 11). The box shows the portion of the drawing that will be shown when the pan/zoom is executed. With the X showing you are in "pan" mode. You can move the box to any portion of the drawing you want to examine. If you press the pick button once, the X will be replaced by an arrow at the right side of the box. Then you will be able to shrink or stretch the box by moving the cursor left or right. This is the "zoom" mode which allows you to focus on smaller segments of the drawing. When you have moved and stretched the box to window the area you want to see, press the second button on your cursor, or press enter. This will execute the magnification and you will see an enlarged image.

> Click on "End Preview" to exit the full preview.

This will bring you back to the Plot Configuration dialogue.

This ends our initial preview of your drawing. In ordinary practice, if everything looked right in the preview you could move onto plot or print your drawing now by clicking on "OK". In the sections that follow, we will explore the rest of the dialogue box.

Device and Default Information

The device box should contain the name of the printer or plotter you are planning to use. If not, you can get a list of available options through the subdialogue illustrated in *Figure 15-4.*

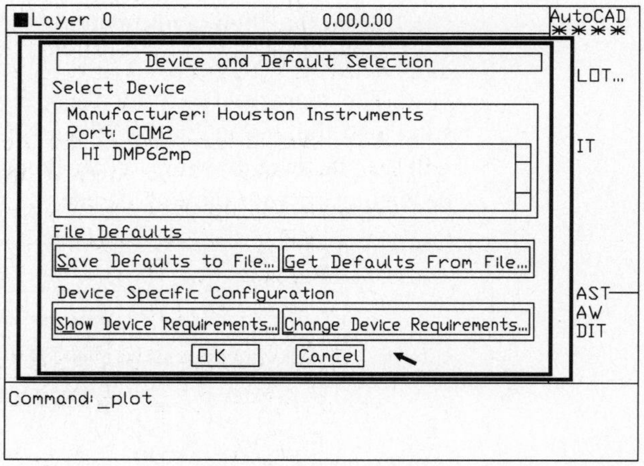

Figure 15-4

> Click on "Device and Default Selection..." or type "d" and press enter.

You should see a subdialogue box similar to the one shown in the figure. The list of devices will be your own, of course. If there is a need to change plotters or printers you can do so by selecting from the list. If the device you want is not on the list, you will need to make sure the device driver is properly installed and then use the CONFIG command to add it to the list. See the *AutoCAD Interface, Installation, and Performance Guide* for additional information.

Along with the list of available plotting devices, this dialogue box allows you to save plotting specifications to ASCII files and get them back later. AutoCAD automatically saves your most recent plot parameters in a file called ACAD.cfg. However, for a more permanent file, you can create a separate file. Such files are saved with a "pcp" extension ("Plot Configuration Parameters"). There are many parameters to deal with in plotting, including as many as 256 pen colors. So saving a set of default parameters to a file may be far more efficient than specifying them manually each time you plot. You may have one set of defaults for one device, and another set for a different device. Or you may have different setups for different types of drawings.

In addition, some plotting devices have special configuration requirements not needed or not available on other devices. If this is the case with your device, the boxes under "Device Specific Configuration" will be accessible. The specific parameters and options will be determined by the device driver for your plotter. See the *AutoCAD Interface, Installation, and Performance Guide* for more information.

> Click on "OK" or "Cancel" to exit the Device and Default Selection dialogue.

This will bring you back to the dialogue box shown in the first figure. Assuming the device named in the Device and Default Information box is the correct one, you are ready to move on. However, if you have made any changes, we recommend that you do another preview. Changing devices may bring about changes in paper size and orientation, for example, and you will see these changes reflected graphically in the partial and full previews.

Pen Parameters

If you are using a plotter with multiple pens, you can assign colors, linetypes, widths, and speeds to each pen individually. If you are using a printer, you may find that the Pen Assignments box is grayed out. If you do have access, we suggest you look at the subdialogue now, even though you may not want to make changes.

> Click on "Pen Assignments..." or type "p" and press enter.

This will call the dialogue box shown in *Figure 15-5*. If you select any pen, you will see its color, number, linetype, speed, and width displayed in the Modify Values box at the right. Changes can be made in these edit boxes in the usual manner.

The specifications made here are designed to relate pen numbers on your plotter to pen colors. If pen numbers are correctly related to pen colors, then layers will automatically be plotted in their assigned colors. The linetypes assigned to layers in AutoCAD are also plotted automatically and do not need to be assigned to pens at this point.

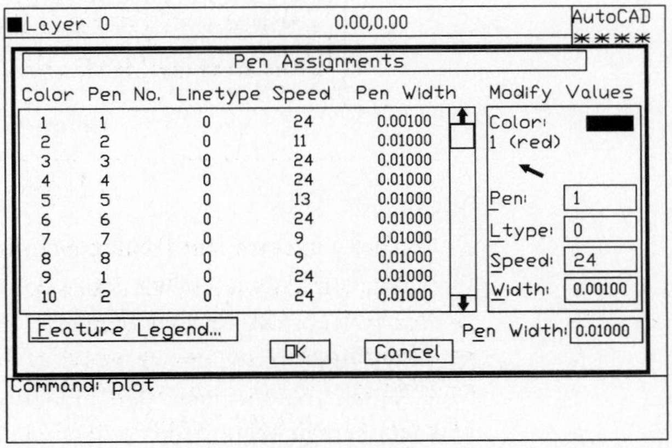

Figure 15-5

NOTE: If your plotter supports multiple linetypes, you will find a subdialogue showing numbered linetypes if you click on "Feature Legend...". These are not to be confused with the linetypes created within your AutoCAD drawing associated with layers. They should be used in special applications to vary the look of "continuous" AutoCAD lines only, otherwise you will get a confused mixture of linetypes when your plotter tries to break up lines that AutoCAD has already drawn broken.

> Click on "OK" or "Cancel" to exit the "Pen Assignments" subdialogue.

Additional Parameters

This area of the dialogue box allows you to specify the portion of your drawing to be plotted. This will have a significant impact on the effective plotting area.

Also available in this area are hidden line removal (for 3D drawings), fill area adjustment, which affects the way pen width is interpreted when drawing wide lines, and plotting to a file instead of to an actual plotter.

The radio buttons on the left show the options for plotting area. "Display" probably will be selected and "Extents" and "Limits" may be the only other options available initially. "View" will be accessible if you have defined views in the drawing using the VIEW command (Chapter 11). "Window" will not be accessible until you define a window. You should try this as an exercise.

> Pick "Window..." at the bottom of the box.

This will call a Window Selection dialogue box giving the coordinates of two corners of the current plotting area, as shown in *Figure 15-6*. By default, this will be the area currently displayed on your screen, and the actual numbers will depend on your drawing. You can change the numbers by typing, or you can click on the Pick box at the top and create a window by pointing.

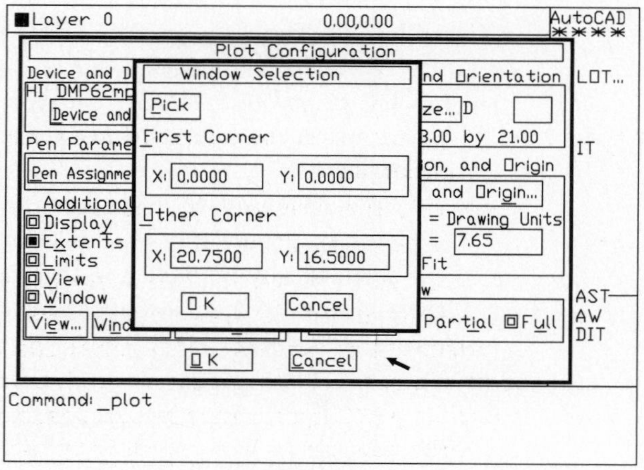

Figure 15-6

> Click on "Pick".

This will cause both dialogue boxes to disappear and give you access to your drawing. Now you can show two corners of a window in the usual manner.

> Pick two corners on your screen to include all the objects in your drawing that you want to plot.

When you are done, the Window Selection dialogue box will reappear with new numbers indicating the corners you have picked. Clicking on "OK" to approve the window as the new plotting area, or "Cancel", will take you back to the PLOT dialogue. In this exercise, your choice will depend on whether you want to proceed to plot the window or the previously shown "Display" area.

> Click on "OK" or "Cancel" to exit the subdialogue.

This will bring you back to the Plot Configuration dialogue box. If you have changed the plotting area, we suggest you do a partial preview to see the effect of the change on effective plotting area. If you do not like the change, click on "Display" to return to the former setting, or try "Extents" and "Limits" and preview these as well.

A few brief words about the other "Additional Parameters" options before moving on. "Hide Lines" is relevant only to 3D drawings. Lines that would be obstructed from the current point of view on a 3D surface or solid model can be removed from the display using the HIDE command. When it comes to plotting, however, they will not be removed unless the "Hide Lines" box is checked. Hidden line removal is discussed further in Chapter 13.

"Adjust Area Fill" is only relevant in drawings that must be precise to specifications less than a pen's width. In these cases, you can tell your plotter to compensate for pen width when it draws thick lines, such as wide polylines, solids, and traces (Chapter 9).

"Plot to File" saves the plot information so that it can be used later or sent to another site for plotting. This may be a more efficient way to plot if, for example, a number of files can be plotted at one time using a "plot spooler." Plot spoolers are software programs that plot a series of plot files one after another. Plots saved to a file are given the same name as the drawing but with a .plt extension.

Paper Size and Orientation

This box gives critical information and choices about the size and orientation of your drawing sheet. To begin with, you can see the information specified in inches or millimeters by choosing one of the two radio buttons. Inches is the default, as shown previously in *Figure 15-1*.

> Click on "MM".

You will see that both the plot area and the scale values are changed to reflect metric units.

> Click on "Inches".

On the right you will see a rectangle showing the orientation of the paper in the plotting device. It will be either landscape (horizontal) or portrait (vertical). This orientation is part of the device driver and cannot be changed directly. If you want to plot horizontally when your device is configured vertically, or vice-versa, you must rotate the plot using the Rotation and Origin subdialogue described in the next section.

The plot area is shown below the radio buttons and is also determined by the plotting device. The default size will be the maximum size available on your printer or plotter. If you are using a printer, for example, you will probably have the equivalent of an A-size sheet. In this case the plot area will be close to 8.00 × 11.00.

> Click on "Size...".

This will open the Paper Size subdialogue box shown in *Figure 15-7*. The standard sizes listed in the box on the left are device specific and will depend on your plotter. If you are using a printer, for example, you may see only the A size on the list. The "USER" boxes on the right allow you to define plotting areas of your own. This means, for example, that you can plot in a 5.00 × 5.00 area on an 8.00 × 11.00 or larger sheet of paper.

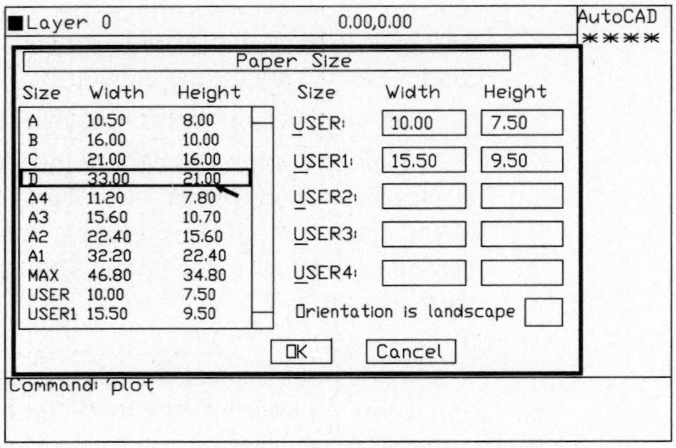

Figure 15-7

Paper size can be changed by picking any of the sizes on the list at the left.
> Change the paper size, if you wish, and then click on "OK" to exit the subdialogue.

If you have changed sizes, the new size will be named next to the Size box, and the new effective plot area will be listed below. The change also may be reflected in the scale box ("Plotted Inches = Drawing Units").

Once again, if you have changed paper sizes we suggest that you do a partial preview. Paper size is one of the important factors in determining effective plotting area.

Scale, Rotation, and Origin

Plots can be scaled to fit the available plot area, or given an explicit scale of paper units to drawing units. "Scaled to Fit" is the default, as shown by the "x" in the check box. With this setting, the area chosen for plotting in the Additional Parameters box (Display, Extents, Limits, etc.) will be plotted as large as possible within the plot area specified in the Paper Size and Orientation box. Fitting the chosen area to the available plot area will dictate the scale shown in the edit boxes. Plotted inches or millimeters are shown in relation to drawing units. If either the area to be plotted or the paper size is changed, the change will be reflected in the scale boxes.

If "Scaled to Fit" is not checked, the scale will default to 1 = 1. In this case drawing units will be considered equivalent to paper size units. 1 to 1 scale is preferred when paper space is in use (Task 2). Other scales can be specified explicitly by typing in the edit boxes. When you change the drawing scale, the area to be plotted may be affected. If the area is too large for the paper size given the scale, then only a portion of the chosen area will be plotted. If the area becomes smaller than the available paper, some blank space will be left. Changing scales should be followed by a partial preview.

The area of the paper that is actually used for plotting may also be affected by the rotation and origin of the plot. If your device is configured with paper oriented vertically (portrait style), and you want to plot horizontally (landscape), then you will need to rotate 90 degrees. This is done with the radio buttons in the Plot Rotation and Origin subdialogue box.

> Click in the Rotation and Origin box.

This will call the dialogue box shown in *Figure 15-8*. You can rotate to 0, 90, 180, or 270 degrees as shown. Rotating a plot by 90 degrees will have a very significant effect on the relationship between paper size and effective drawing area.

This box will also allow you to change the origin of the plot. Plots usually originate in the lower left-hand corner of the page. To use a previous example,

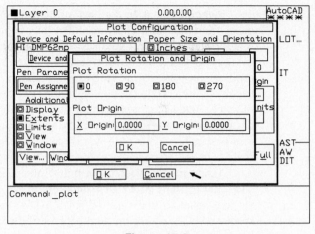

Figure 15-8

let's say you wanted to plot a 5 × 5 area in the upper right of an 8 × 11 sheet, landscape orientation. You could do this by creating a 5 × 5 "User" paper size as discussed previously and then moving the origin from (0,0) to (6,3).

> Change the plot rotation if you wish, and then Click on "OK" to exit the dialogue box.

At this point, you have been through all the major parameters of plot configuration. You should now preview your plot. If the effective drawing area or the full image do not appear the way you want relative to the drawing sheet, go back and make adjustments in the area of the drawing to be plotted (Additional Parameters), the paper size, the scale, rotation, or origin of the plot. When all is well, you are ready to carry out the plot.

> Click on "OK".

AutoCAD will pause and give you the following message:

Position paper in plotter.
Press RETURN to continue or S to Stop for hardware setup

This gives you the opportunity to prepare your plotter if you have not already done so.

> Press enter (RETURN) to proceed.

Now AutoCAD and your plotter will go through their plotting routine. You can cancel the plot by typing Ctrl-C. However, your plotter will not stop immediately, since it has a memory buffer, and will continue until it runs out of information.

TASK 2: Plotting from Multiple Viewports in Paper Space

Procedure.

1. Set "Tilemode" to 0 or "off".
2. Use MVIEW to create paper space layout.
3. Switch to model space to position or edit objects in the drawing.
4. Switch to paper space to plot.
5. Type or select "Plot".
6. Preview plot, change parameters, and execute plotting as usual.

Discussion. In the days of the drafting board, all drawings were conceived on paper from the start. This meant that people doing drafting were inevitably conscious of scale, paper size, and rotation from start to finish. When draftspeople first began using CAD systems, they still tended to think in terms of the final hard copy their plotter would produce even as they were creating lines on the screen. But as time goes on and we become more used to the powers of CAD systems, it is usually more efficient to conceive of screen images as representing objects at full scale, rather than as potential drawings on a piece of paper. After all, the units on a screen grid can just as easily represent miles as inches. This little world of the screen in which we can think and draw in full scale is called "model space" in AutoCAD lingo.

Using model space to its fullest potential, we can allow ourselves to ignore scale and other drawing paper issues entirely, if we wish, until it is time to plot. At that time, we may want to make use of AutoCAD's "paper space." Paper space overlays model space and allows us to create a paper-scale world on top of the full-scale world we have been drawing in.

This is the concept of paper space. However, in actual practice you may find paper space unnecessary for common two-dimensional plotting. As we have seen in Task 1, the PLOT command has a very efficient previewing system and scaling features of its own that will allow you to move very efficiently between 2D model space and the sheet of drawing paper waiting in your plotter.

Where paper space really begins to pay off is when you want to create multiple views of a single object and plot them all simultaneously. Without paper space and non-tiled viewports, you would have to create copies of the object and assemble them into one view. In this task we will create a plot of Drawing 6-4, the "Grooved Hub". The plotted drawing will include the original two views plus two close-up views. This will be done in paper space using three viewports. You should be able to generalize from the techniques demonstrated here to create a variety of multiple view drawings with whatever 2D or 3D drawing you may be working on.

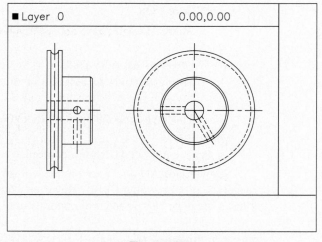

Figure 15-9

> To begin this exercise you should have a drawing on your screen which you want to plot showing some close-up views. We have used Drawing 6-4, shown in *Figure 15-9*, for purposes of illustration.

Before you can enter paper space you must change the value of the "Tile-mode" variable from 1 ("On") to 0 ("Off").

> Type or select "Tilemode" (under "View" on the pull down, "Mview" on the screen menu).

> Type "0" or select "Off (0)".

Your screen will go blank and AutoCAD will show the following message in the command area:

Entering Paper space.

Use MVIEW to insert Model space viewports.

Regenerating drawing.

If "Ucsicon" is "On", you will see the paper space icon in the left-hand corner of your screen, as shown in *Figure 15-10*. This icon appears in place of the UCS icon whenever you switch to paper space. For this reason it is a good idea to have the icon turned on when you are going back and forth between the two spaces.

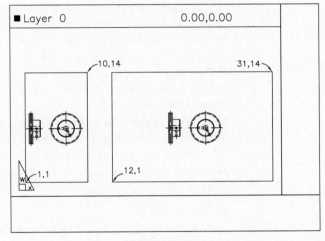

Figure 15-10

As the message suggests, we will need to create some viewports before we can see our drawing again. Viewports are like windows from paper space into model space. Until a window is opened, you cannot see what is behind.

But first, we need to think a moment about the paper our drawing is headed for. This, after all, is the whole point of paper space. Before opening viewports, we will set up limits and a grid in paper space to emulate the drawing sheet we are going to plot on. For purposes of illustration, let's say that we are going to plot on a D-size sheet of paper. If your plotter will take a D-size sheet you will be able to find the actual plotting area available by looking in the PLOT dialogue paper size list box.

> Type or select "Plot".

> Type "s" or select "Size...".

You will see the dialogue box illustrated previously in *Figure 15-7*. Ours shows us that the Houston Instruments plotter we are using plots in an area 33.00 by 21.00 on a D-size sheet. If yours is different, or if you have no D-size option, use a sheet size and plotting area from your list.

> Cancel the Paper Size subdialogue.

> Cancel the Plot Configuration dialogue.

This should bring you back to your blank paper space screen.

> Type or select "Limits".

> Set paper space limits to (0,0) and (33,21), or whatever is appropriate for your plotter.

> If your grid is off, turn it on.

> Zoom all.

> Reset your grid and snap to a 1.00 increment.

Your screen is now truly representative of a D-size drawing sheet. The plot will be made 1 to 1, with one paper space screen unit equaling 1 inch on the drawing sheet.

> Type or select "Mview" (select "Mview" under "View" and then "Create Viewport" on the pull down menu).

AutoCAD prompts:

ON/OFF/Hideplot/Fit/2/3/4/Restore/<First Point>:

We will deal only with the default option in this exercise.

> Pick a point at the lower left of your screen as shown in *Figure 15-10*. Our actual point is (1.00,1.00). All of the coordinate values in this exercise will need to be adjusted if you are using other than a D-size sheet of paper. Exact correspondence is not critical. As long as your viewports resemble our illustrations, you should be fine.

> Pick a second point up 9 and over 13 from point 1. The coordinate display will show (10.00,14.00).

Your screen will be redrawn with the drawing shown at small scale in the viewport you have just created. We will create a second viewport next.

Once you have viewports on your screen you may want to turn off your paper space grid. Otherwise you will see model space and paper space grids overlapping.

> Turn off the paper space grid.

> Repeat MVIEW.

> Pick point (12.00,1.00), as shown in the figure.

> Pick point (31.00,14.00), as shown.

You have now created a second viewport. Notice that the images in the two viewports are the same. Before we go on to create a third viewport we will enlarge and position these to create two different images inside the viewports. To do this we need to switch back to model space.

> Type "ms" or select "Model space".

The only change you will see is that the paper space icon will be gone and UCS icons will appear in the corners of the viewports.

If you have not used multiple viewports before, take a moment to explore the way the cursor works. You can have only one viewport active at a time. When the cursor is within that viewport, you will see the cross hairs. Otherwise you will see an arrow. To switch viewports, move the arrow into the desired viewport and press the pick button.

> Make the right viewport active.

We are going to zoom in on the two-view drawing so that it fills the viewport. We could do this by windowing, but we can maintain more precise scale relationships if we use the "Center" and "XP" options.

> Type "z" or select "zoom".

> Type "c" or select "Center".

AutoCAD prompts for a center point.

> Pick a point roughly halfway between the two views in the viewport.

AutoCAD will prompt for a magnification value. Accepting the default would simply center the image in the viewport. We will take an extra step by using the "XP" option here. "XP" means "times paper." It allows you to zoom relative to paper space units. If you zoom 1xp, then a model space unit will take on the size of a current paper space unit, which in turn equals one inch of drawing paper. We will zoom 2xp. This will mean that one unit in the viewport will equal 2 paper space units, or 2 inches on paper.

> Type "2xp".

Your right viewport will be redrawn to resemble the one in *Figure 15-11*. You may need to PAN slightly to the left or right to position the image in the viewport.

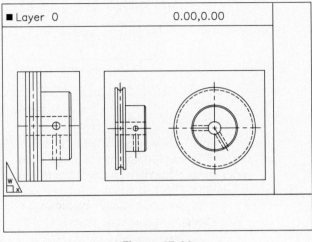

Figure 15-11

NOTE: If you are using a paper size other than D, you will have to adjust your zoom factors due to the difference in limit settings. On an A-size sheet, for example .75XP should be close to what you want.

Next, we will enlarge the image on the left so that we get a close-up of the left side view.

> Make the left viewport active.

> Type "z" or select "ZOOM".

> Type "c" or select "Center".

> Pick a center point in the middle of the left side view.

> Type "4xp".

This will create an enlarged image in which one model space unit equals 4 inches in the drawing sheet.

NOTE: If you are using A-size paper the zoom factor will be 1.5XP (double the .75 factor used previously).

> Pan left or right to position the enlargement in the viewport, as shown in *Figure 15-11*.

Now that you have the technique, we will create one more enlargement, focusing on the center of the hub.

> Type or select "Mview".

> Pick point (22.00,15.00).

> Pick point (31.00, 21.00).

Notice that the new viewport is created from the most recent viewport image.

> Use PAN in model space to bring the hub center into the new viewport.

> Zoom on the center of the hub at 6 times paper (2.25xp for an A sheet) in the new viewport.

> Type or select "Regenall" to regenerate the display and create truer circles.

Your screen should resemble *Figure 15-12*.

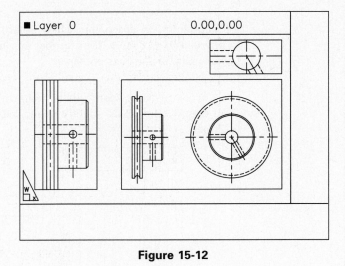

Figure 15-12

Great! Now we are ready to plot. Plotting a multiple viewport drawing is no different from plotting from a single view, but you have to make sure you plot from paper space. Otherwise AutoCAD will plot only the currently active viewport.

> Type "ps" or select "Paper space".
> Type or select "Plot".
> Click on "Limits" in the Additional Parameters box.
> Click on "Size" in the Paper Size and Orientation box.

We looked into this box for information before, but we cancelled the command. Now it is time to choose the paper size we have been preparing for.

> Select the D-size option, or whatever you have chosen for this exercise.
> Click on "OK".
> If the Scaled to Fit box is selected click on it so the X is removed.

When scaled to fit is deselected, the scale boxes should show 1 = 1. If not, you should edit them to show 1 = 1.

> Do a partial preview of the plot.

The effective area should match the paper size, because we are set to plot limits, and we have set our limits to match the effective drawing area of this paper size for this plotter.

> Do a full preview of the plot.

Your screen should resemble *Figure 15-13*. (We have moved the Plot Preview box to the upper left corner of the screen.)

Excellent. You are now ready to plot.

> Click on "End Preview".
> Click on "OK".
> Prepare your plotter. (Make sure you use the right size paper).
> Press enter and watch it go.

In the next task we will add some text and dimensions to this three-viewport layout in order to illustrate some important issues and techniques involved in the scaling of dimensions in multiple-viewport drawings. The presentation of this dimensioning exercise is designed for use after the completion of Chapters 7 and 8. If you have completed the current task but have not completed these two chapters, we suggest that you save your three-viewport drawing so that you can come back to it when you are ready to proceed.

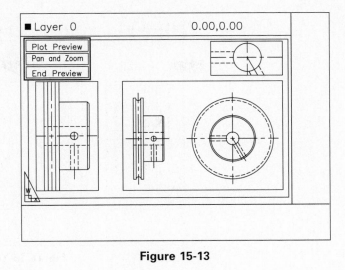

Figure 15-13

TASK 3: Scaling Dimensions Between Paper Space and Model Space

Procedure.

1. Use ZOOM XP to set scale in viewports.
2. Set Dimtxt to a desirable text size.
3. Set Dimscale to 0.
4. Create dimensions in model space.

Discussion.   There are numerous scaling problems that arise when you are working with viewports and paper space. The zoom xp feature introduced in the previous task allows you to create precise scale relationships between model space images and paper space units. Numerous other issues arise when you begin to use text and dimensions in paper space multiple-viewport drawings. We will begin by illustrating some of the problems.

> To begin this task, you should have the multiple-view layout of Drawing 6-4 on your screen, as shown in *Figure 15-12*. If this drawing is unavailable, any similar multiple-viewport drawing will do, though it may be more difficult to follow the steps given here if you are looking at a different drawing.

NOTE: This exercise assumes that the variable Dimscale is initially set to 1, and that Dimtxt is set to 0.18. These are default settings. If they have been changed in your drawing, you will not get the exact results shown here. Also, we assume that your current text style has a height setting of 0, meaning that it is variable. This is a default setting as well.

Draw Text in Paper Space

There are certain basic principles that are useful in adding text and dimensions to a multiple-view drawing in paper space. The first is that most text should be created in paper space. To see why, try entering some text in paper space and model space as follows.

> First, check to see that you are in paper space (look for the paper space icon). If you are not, type "ps".

> Type or select "Dtext".

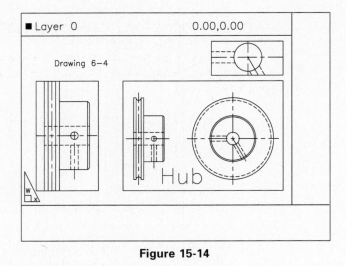

Figure 15-14

> Pick a start point outside any of the viewports. Our text begins about 3 units over the center of the left viewport, as shown in *Figure 15-14*.

> Type "1" for a text height of one unit. This assumes that you are using the D-size paper space limits from the previous task. If not, you will have to adjust for your own settings.

> Press enter for 0 rotation.

> Type "Drawing 6-4".

> Press enter twice.

Your screen should have text added as shown in *Figure 15-14*.

> Type "ms" to switch to model space.

> Make the largest viewport active.

> Type "Dtext".

> Pick a start point below the two views, as shown.

> Press enter to retain a height of 1.00 units.

> Press enter for 0 rotation.

> Type "Hub".

Your screen should resemble *Figure 15-14*.

What has happened here? Why is the "Hub" drawn twice as big as "Drawing 6-4" (or some other size, depending on your limit and zoom factor settings)? Do you remember the zoom xp scale factor we used in this viewport? You guessed it. This viewport is enlarged by two times paper space. So any text you draw inside it will be enlarged by a factor of two as well. If you want, try drawing text in either of the other two viewports. You will find that text in the left viewport is magnified four times the paper space size and text in the uppermost viewport is magnified six times.

You could compensate for these enlargements by dividing text height by factors of 2, 4, and 6, but that would be a bit cumbersome. Furthermore, if you decided to change the zoom factor at a later date, you would have to recreate any text drawn within the altered viewport. Otherwise, your text sizes in the overall drawing would be inconsistent.

For this reason, it is recommended that text be drawn in paper space.

Dimension Model Space Objects in Model Space

When it comes to dimensions, however, the rule is just the opposite. Dimensions should be kept in model space with the objects they refer to. The main reason is that dimensions in AutoCAD are associative. They will change when the objects they document are changed. This is true if they are in the same space. It will not be true if a model space object is dimensioned in paper space.

The rule is simple, but it requires some manipulation of variables to maintain consistency in dimension text size. As we proceed, we will also encounter some layering problems.

> Check to be sure that you are in model space before beginning. If not, type "ms".

> Make the "dim" layer current.

> Make the large, central viewport active.

> Type or select "Dim".

> Type "ver" or select "Vertical".

> Pick the top of the left side view for the first extension line origin.

> Pick the bottom of the same side for the second extension line origin.

> Pick a dimension line location about .25 to the left of the object. This may seem a little close, but it will help to illustrate an important point.

> Press enter to accept the dimension text (4.00).

   Your screen should resemble *Figure 15-15*.

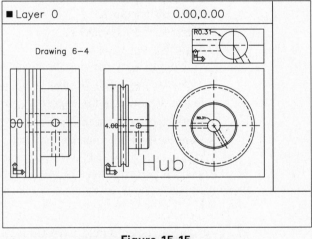

Figure 15-15

Two things to notice: The dimension looks fine in the active viewport, but it is duplicated in the enlargement on the left at twice the size and may be cut off. This illustrates our two main problems. We want all our dimensions to appear the same size, and we do not want dimensions intended for one viewport to appear in others. The first problem is a scaling issue, while the second involves layering. We will pursue scaling in this task and leave layer control for the next exercise.

To get more of a flavor of what's going on, try one more dimension.

> Make the upper viewport active.

> Assuming you are still at the "Dim:" prompt, type "rad" or select "Radius".

> Select the circle in the upper viewport.

> Press enter to accept the dimension text "0.31".

> Look at the size of the dimension.

   Obviously it is way too big.

NOTE: If the variable dimsho is not set to 1 in your drawing, you will not be able to see the dimension until it is drawn. In this case, go ahead and draw the dimension so that you can see it, and then undo it afterwards.

> Cancel or Undo the radial dimension so that it is not drawn.

In fact, the dimension shown in the upper viewport was three times as big as the dimension in the central viewport and twice as big as the duplicate dimension in the left viewport. As you may have guessed, the dimensions in each viewport are being magnified just as the text was previously. The default dimension text size, set to .18 by the dimtxt variable, is being doubled (2 times paper size) to .36 in the central viewport. So the text "4.00" has a height of .36 paper space units in that viewport. But in the left viewport it has a height of .72 units (4 times paper space). The radial dimension in the upper viewport had a height of 1.08 units, or 6 times the dimtxt setting.

AutoCAD has a simple fix for this problem. When the variable dimscale is set to 0 instead of the default value of 1 or some other explicit scaling factor, dimension text in viewports is adjusted according to the model space to paper space zoom factor. With this setting, dimensions in all viewports can be maintained at the same desirable size.

For our purposes, let's say we are satisfied with the .36 size we see in the central viewport. In order to achieve this size in all viewports simultaneously, we will need to set dimscale to 0 and dimtxt to .36.

> Type or select "dimtxt" (under "dimvars" on the screen menu).
AutoCAD shows you the current value and asks for a new value.
> Type ".36".
> Type or select "dimscale".
> Type "0".
Now let's try drawing the radial dimension in the upper viewport again.
> Type "rad" or select "Radial".
> Select the circle in the upper viewport.
> Press enter to retain the dimension text.
> Position the leader outside the circle, as shown in *Figure 15-15*.

Wonderful, except that now we have a tiny duplicate of the radial dimension showing in the central viewport. This is another example of the layering problem, which we will explore in the next task.

TASK 4: Manipulating Layer Visibility in Multiple Viewports

Procedure.

1. Create viewport specific layers for entities whose visibility should be controlled between viewports.
2. Freeze and thaw layers in different viewports to create the desired images.

Discussion. The duplicate dimensions that appeared in the last task are just one example of the need to control layer visibility separately in different viewports. In Release 12 this can be done using either the VPLAYER command or the current viewport thaw and freeze features of the Layer Control dialogue box. We will demonstrate using the VPLAYER method, since it allows you to make changes in more than one viewport at a time.

> To begin this task you should have the multiple viewport layout of Drawing 6-4 on your screen, with dimensions as shown in *Figure 15-15*. Other similar drawings may be used as well.
> You should be in model space to begin. If you're not, type "ms".

Our goal will be to make dimensions intended for the central viewport invisible in other viewports and vice-versa. In order to accomplish this, we need at least two dimension layers. If you wanted independent dimensions in all three viewports, you would need three layers.

> Make the upper viewport active.
> Open the Layer Control dialogue box, under "Settings" on the Release 12 pull down menu.
> Type "Dim-u" (for dimensions in the upper viewport) in the edit box.
> Click on "New".
> Select the new "DIM-U" layer from the layer list.
> Use the Set Color subdialogue to give it color number 4, cyan.
   This should be the same color as your regular DIM layer.
> Click on "OK" to return to the main dialogue.
> Click on "OK" to exit the dialogue box.

Now that we have two dimension layers we can freeze dimensions in the viewports where they are not wanted. But first we must move some of the previously drawn dimensions to the newly created layer.

> If necessary, cancel the DIM command.
> Type or select "Chprop".
> Select the radial dimension.
> Press enter to end object selection.
> Type "La" or select "LAyer".
> Type "Dim-u" for the new layer.
> Press enter to exit the CHPROP command.

Now the 4.00 vertical dimension and the 0.31 radial dimension are on different layers, although they appear the same. We need to freeze DIM in the top and left viewports, and freeze DIM-U in the central viewport.

> Type or select "Vplayer" (under "Mview" on the pull down and screen menus).
   AutoCAD will prompt as follows:

              ?/Freeze/Thaw/Reset/Newfrz/Vpvisdflt:

The "?" option will give you a list of layers currently frozen in a selected viewport. "Freeze" and "Thaw" will allow you to freeze and thaw layers in selected viewports. "Reset" sets layers in selected viewports to default visibility settings. These defaults are established using the "Vpvisdflt" option. The "Newfrz" option provides an efficient sequence for controlling layers in multiple viewports. With "Newfrz" you create a new layer which is frozen in all viewports. Then you can thaw the new layer in selected viewports where visibility is desired.
   For our purposes we only need the freeze option.
> Type "f" or select "Freeze".
> Type "Dim".
> Type "s" or select "Select".
   AutoCAD temporarily switches to paper space so that you can select viewport entities.
> Pick any point on the border of the left viewport.
> Pick any point on the border of the top viewport.
> Press enter to end object selection.

We also need to freeze DIM-U in the central viewport.

> Type "f" or select "Freeze".

> Type "dim-u".

> Type "s" or select "Select".

> Select any point on the border of the central viewport.

> Press enter to end object selection.

> Press enter to exit the VPLAYER command.

Your screen will be regenerated to resemble *Figure 15-16*. In the next section we will plot a 3D object in multiple viewports and demonstrate the MVSETUP program (multiple viewport setup) which automates some of the techniques you have already learned, and contains additional useful features. But first, a word about viewport borders.

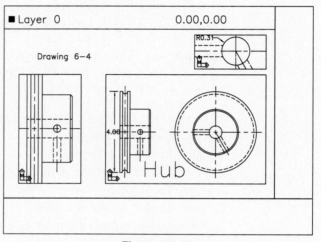

Figure 15-16

Turning Viewport Borders Off

We have used the borders of our viewports as part of our plotted drawing in this drawing layout. Frequently, you will want to turn them off. In a typical three-view drawing, for example, you do not draw borders around the three views.

In multiple-viewport paper space drawings the visibility of viewport borders is easily controlled by putting the viewports on a separate layer and then turning the layer off before plotting. You can make a "border" layer, for example, and make it current while you create viewports. Or you can use CHPROP to place viewports on the border layer later.

TASK 5: Using the MVSETUP Program

Procedure.

1. Create objects in model space.
2. Type or select "Mvsetup".
3. Insert a title block.
4. Create viewports.
5. Scale viewports.
6. Align viewports.
7. Set paper space limits to extents.
8. Plot.

Discussion. MVSETUP is one of a number of AutoLISP and ADS programs (see appendix B) included with the Release 12 software. Like AME and region modeling, the MVSETUP program will be initialized when it is first entered. MVSETUP has a number of useful features, as evidenced by items 2 through 7 on the procedure list above.

In this task we will create a simple 3D object and then go through the steps involved in using MVSETUP to plot a multiple-view layout of the object in paper space.

> To begin this task you should be in model space with a blank screen.

> For demonstration purposes, draw a 3D surface model of a wine glass, about 6.00 units high, using the following procedure.

1. Draw a 2D polyline outline and axis of revolution as shown in *Figure 15-17*.

2. Type or select "Revsurf".

3. Select the outline as the path curve.

4. Select the line segment as the axis of revolution.

5. Press enter twice to accept the defaults and create a complete revolution.

6. ERASE the axis.

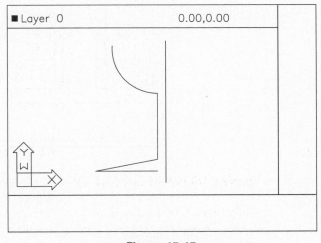

Figure 15-17

> Type or select "Mvsetup" (under "View" and then "Layout" on the pull down menu).

Assuming tilemode is set to on, AutoCAD will initialize (load) the MVSETUP program and then prompt:

```
Paperspace/Modelspace is disabled. The pre-R11 setup will be
invoked unless it is enabled. Enable Paper/Modelspace? <Y>
```

All this really means is that tilemode must be set to off so that non-tiled viewports and paper space are available.

> Press enter to enable paper space.

Your screen will go blank and the paper space icon will appear, as in the MVIEW command.

You will see the following prompt, along with Autodesk's copyright notice:

```
Align/Create/Scale viewports/Options/Title block/Undo:
```

We will be using all of these options together to create a drawing layout of the wine glass, but keep in mind that many of the options work just as well independently with any multiple-view drawing. You do not, for example, have to use the MVSETUP title block feature in order to use the alignment feature.

First, we will insert a title block and set up paper space to reflect a B-size drawing sheet.

> Type "t", for the "Title block" option.

    MVSETUP prompts:

Delete objects/Origin/Undo/<Insert title block>:

> Press enter to insert a title block at the current origin.

    MVSETUP switches to the text screen and shows a list of paper sizes. An ANSI-B sheet is designated by the number 8.

> Type "8".

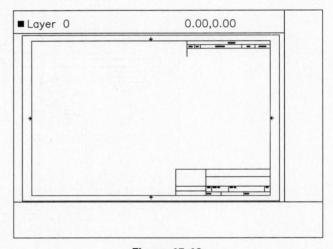

Figure 15-18

In a moment your screen will resemble *Figure 15-18* and MVSETUP will prompt:

Create a drawing named ansi–b.dwg? <Y>:

This prompt is encountered the first time you load a given sheet size title block. Once the title block is created it will remain on file and you will not be prompted the next time.

> Press enter to create the B-size title block and border.

    Now we need to create some viewports.

> Type "c" for the "Create" option.

    MVSETUP prompts:

Delete objects/Undo/<Create Viewports>:

> Press enter to create viewports.

    The text screen returns again, showing a list of available viewport layout options. We will use a standard four-view engineering layout.

> Type "2".

The graphics screen returns and MVSETUP prompts with two options for specifying the boundary area of the viewports:

Bounding area for viewports. Default/<First point>:

The first point option will allow you to create a window within which the four viewports will be drawn. The default option will choose an area based on your title block. In some cases you will not be offered a default. If this happens, window the area where you want the viewports to be drawn.
> Type "d" for the default option.

MVSETUP prompts for a distance between viewports in the X direction. This is similar to defining an array.
> Type "1".
> Press enter to create the same distance in the Y direction.

Be prepared for some fireworks. MVSETUP will draw four viewports and then create three 2D projections and a 3D view within them. When this is done your screen should resemble *Figure 15-19*, though the size of objects may be different.

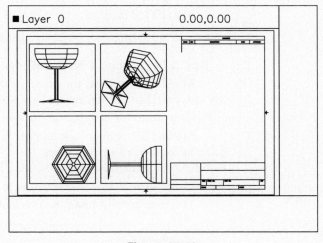

Figure 15-19

MVSETUP also has its own scaling option which sets zoom scale factors between paper space and viewports. We will use this feature to scale down the three orthographic views and leave the 3D view as is.
> Type "s" for the "Scale viewports" option.

MVSETUP puts you into paper space, regardless of where you were before, so that you can select viewports.
> Select the three projections (top left, bottom left, and bottom right viewports) one at a time, by pointing to the borders.
> Press enter to end object selection.

MVSETUP prompts:

Set zoom scale factors for viewports.
Interactively/<Uniform>:

The interactive mode lets you establish different zoom factors in each selected viewport independently. The Uniform option will set them all to the same factor. Notice that this feature could have been used in the previous task in place of zoom xp.

> Press enter for a uniform zoom factor.

The next options will allow you to specify a ratio of paper space units to model space units. We will use a ratio of one paper space unit to two model space units.

> Press enter to specify one paper space unit.

> Type "2" to specify two model space units.

Your screen will be redrawn as shown in *Figure 15-19*.

We have one more layout operation to perform before we are ready to plot. You will notice that the three projections are not lined up with each other. This can be readily fixed using the align option.

> If the image in your lower left viewport does not appear to be centered, first exit the MVSETUP program, go into model space, and PAN in this viewport to center the image.

> If necessary, reenter the MVSETUP program.

> Type "a" for the "Align" option.

MVSETUP prompts:

Angled/Horizontal/Vertical alignment/Rotate view/Undo?

> Type "h" to perform a horizontal alignment.

MVSETUP prompts for a base point. This should be a point of alignment in the viewport that will remain unchanged by the alignment.

> Pick the center of the glass in the lower left viewport.

MVSETUP prompts for another point. This should be the corresponding point in another viewport. When the operation is complete this point will align with the base point selected in the first viewport.

> Pick any point along the center line of the glass in the bottom right viewport.

The program will bring the two views in line, as shown in *Figure 15-20*.

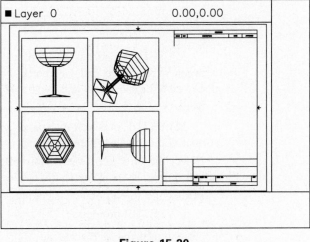

Figure 15-20

Now do a vertical alignment on the remaining view.

> Type "v".

> Pick the same base point at the center of the glass in the lower left viewport.

> Pick any point along the center line of the glass in the top left viewport for the other point.

At this point the three views should align and your drawing should resemble *Figure 15-20*.

Before you proceed to a plot preview, set limits equal to extents in your drawing. This will make the plot configuration easier to manage.

> Type "o" for the "Options" option.

MVSETUP prompts:

Set Layer/LImits/Units/Xref:

> Type "Li" for "Limits".

> Type "y" to set drawing limits equal to drawing extents.

> Press enter twice to exit the MVSETUP program.

> Check to be sure that you are in paper space.

> Turn off the "border" layer.

> Type or select "Plot".

We are, of course, ignoring the step of adding documentation to the title block.

> Select either "Extents" or "Limits" from "Additional Parameters".

> Assuming you are actually using B-size paper, make this selection from the Size subdialogue box.

> If "Scaled to Fit" is not checked, click in the box to check it.

> Click on "Full" and then "Preview".

If you like what you see, then you are ready to plot.

TASK 6: Creating Perspective and Clipped 3D Views with DVIEW

Procedure.

1. Type or select "DVIEW".
2. Select objects to view.
3. Specify a DVIEW option.
4. Specify a view.
5. Specify another option or exit the command.
6. Use VIEW to save 3D views.

Discussion.   For most drawing purposes, using the VPOINT command or preset views from the pull down menu is adequate and efficient for creating 3D views of objects. However, the DVIEW ("Dynamic View") command has several capabilities that do not exist in VPOINT. DVIEW allows you to "drag" the object or portions of it as you define the view. In addition, it has the capability of creating perspective views and allows you to "clip" the object at specified planes to temporarily remove all objects in front of or behind a specified plane.

Within the DVIEW command there are also options to zoom, pan, and rotate ("Twist") to achieve the exact display you want, and to remove hidden lines to better visualize the view you are creating. As a general rule, DVIEW is best used when your drawing is complete and you want to create a plot or display that shows it to best advantage. Perspective views, for example, are strictly for presentation. Many draw and edit commands will not work at all in a perspective view.

In this task we will test some of the DVIEW options on a simple mesh in one plane. In particular, this mesh will demonstrate clearly the effect of the perspective view feature.

> To begin this task, you should be in the drawing editor with a blank screen.

First, create a 3D mesh from the pull down menu. If you need assistance beyond the instructions that follow, see Chapter 13, Task 5.

> Select "3D Surfaces" and then "3D Objects..." from the pull down menu.

> Select the word "Mesh" from the list, or the image on the third line.

> Click on "OK".

> Pick the four corners of a rectangle, approximately 6.00 × 6.00, as illustrated in *Figure 15-21*. Exact size and location are insignificant.

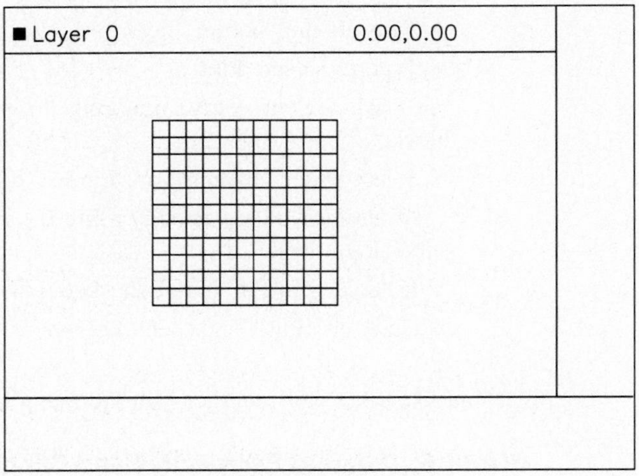

Figure 15-21

> Type "12" for the "M size".

> Type "12" for the "N size".

These two prompts establish the number of vertices in each direction of the mesh.

Before entering DVIEW it will be useful to have a smaller snap increment. This will become apparent when we use the "Camera" option to establish a view-point dynamically.

> Set your Snap to .05.

> Type or select "dview".

AutoCAD prompts for object selection:

Select objects:

One of the advantages of DVIEW is that it lets you adjust your view of objects in 3D space dynamically. In order to do this effectively, however, the number of objects on the screen may need to be limited. If you have ever tried to drag a complex object across the screen, you are familiar with the problem. The object is drawn and redrawn so slowly as you move your pointing device that the dragging process becomes too cumbersome to be useful. In the DVIEW command, you select a portion of your drawing to serve as a "preview image" for the process of dynamic view adjustment. The rest of the drawing is temporarily invisible and ignored. When you have defined the view you want by manipulating the preview image, exit DVIEW and the complete drawing will be restored in the newly defined view.

For our purposes, there is only the mesh to select.

NOTE: AutoCAD also provides a default preview image. If you press enter at the "Select objects:" prompt, DVIEW will show a simple wire frame house for your preview image. Or if you prefer, you can even create your own default image. (See the *AutoCAD Reference Manual*.) For most purposes, however, you will want to see at least a portion of the drawing you are working on.

> Select the mesh.

> Press enter to end object selection.

AutoCAD will prompt with the following DVIEW options:

CAmera/TArget/Distance/POints/PAn/Zoom/TWist/CLip/Hide/Off/Undo/<eXit>:

These options vary considerably in their effect and ease of use. We will begin with a "Zoom".

NOTE: To avoid confusion, AutoCAD switches to the WCS whenever you enter DVIEW. DVIEW proceeds with the WCS in effect and then returns you to your UCS when you exit the command. We are working in the WCS in this exercise anyway, so this will not be noticeable.

"Pan" and "Zoom"

Panning in the DVIEW command is very easy. After specifying a base point, you can drag objects around the screen in any direction.

> Type "Pa" or select "Pan".

> Pick a point near the middle of the mesh for a base point.

> Move the cursor slowly and observe the preview image moving along with it.

> Center the image on the display.

Zooming in DVIEW is a little different from the regular ZOOM command.

> Type "z" or select "Zoom".

AutoCAD places a "slider bar" at the top of the screen, as shown in *Figure 15-22*, and prompts:

Adjust zoom scale factor <1>:

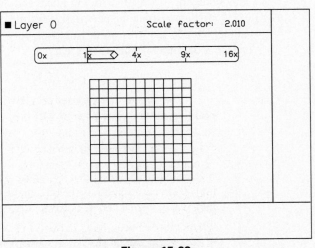

Figure 15-22

The slider bar consists of a scale with numbered divisions (0X, 1X, 4X, 9X, 16X), a diamond-shaped "cursor" that is controlled by your pointing device, and two rubber bands that connect you to a short line marking the current magnification. The current value is always "1X." If you move the cursor to the right, objects on the screen will be enlarged by the factors shown on the scale; if you move to the left, they will be reduced by fractional factors.

> Move the cursor so that the diamond is on the short vertical line at the "1X."

"1X" is the current magnification, so the preview image will appear as it did before you entered the zoom option, except that any color will be gone.

> Now stretch the rubber bands to the right and left and watch the mesh expand and shrink.

Notice that it doesn't take much movement to produce a significant change. Also, pay close attention to the coordinate display. It will show you your zoom scale factor to three decimal places.

If snap is on you may want to turn it off to see the full range of magnification.

> Pick a zoom factor of about 2.00.

Your mesh will be enlarged by the scale factor shown, and AutoCAD will return to the DVIEW options prompt:

CAmera/TArget/Distance/POints/PAn/Zoom/TWist/CLip/Hide/Off/Undo/<eXit>:

"Camera" and "Target"

Next we will change our view of the image using the "CAmera" option. "Camera" and "Target" refer to two aspects of a point of view relative to a 3D object. "Distance" is a third we will discuss shortly.

The photographic metaphor was originally introduced in AutoSHADE, an Autodesk software package used in creating the effect of light and shadow on modeled surfaces. When you sight through an actual camera, what you see is dependent on the location of the camera and the direction its lens is pointed. In the metaphor, "Camera" refers to your point of view in space, and "Target" refers to the point at which the camera is aimed. In the DVIEW command you change views by moving the point of view (Camera), by aiming towards a new point (Target), or both.

In practice, setting the "Camera" placement is very similar to using the rotation option of the VPOINT command (the option used by the Preset dialogue box). If you recall, in using "VPOINT Rotate" you define an angle of rotation within the X-Y plane and a viewing angle above or below the plane. Viewpoints we have used typically in this book are 315 degrees in the plane and 30 or 45 degrees up from the plane.

To demonstrate the perspective feature, we are going to use a longer, flatter viewing angle. Notice that this view would be very impractical for drawing purposes, but will create a dramatic perspective effect.

> Type "ca" or select "Camera".

The appearance of your preview image will depend on the placement of your pointing device. The prompt will be:

Toggle Angle in/Enter angle from XY plane <90>:

You can enter angles by typing or by picking a point on the screen. Picking may seem easier and has the advantage of allowing you to drag the preview image into place. However, it is difficult to conceptualize exactly what the cursor and image are doing.

> Move the cursor slowly and watch how the preview image and the coordinate display react.

The behavior of the cursor, image, and coordinate display will be unfamiliar. In effect, vertical movement of the cursor controls the angle from the X-Y plane, while horizontal movement controls the angle in the X-Y plane. If you move the cursor freely, you are seeing both angles adjusted simultaneously. The coordinate display, on the other hand, can only show one angle at a time. You can toggle from one to the other by typing "t" and pressing enter. The prompt line refers to these as "angle in" and "angle from".

You will have a better sense of how it all works if snap is on. This is where a small snap increment is useful in this exercise.

> If snap is off, turn it on.

> Move several snap points horizontally, and then several vertically.

If you watch the coordinate display you will see that it changes only when you move vertically.

> Type "t" and press enter.

> Now move horizontally and watch the angle display change. There will be no change when you move vertically.

Continue moving horizontally and vertically to get a feel for the camera position system. As the camera moves up and down from the plane, the preview image appears to tip forward and back. It may be difficult to visualize what is happening as you pass below 0 degrees. As you pass zero, the front of the object begins to tip away from you so that you are looking up from underneath.

If you move the camera back and forth in the plane, the image will appear to turn.

Also notice that with snap on the angle moves in 9 degree increments from the X-Y plane. This is a translation of the .05 snap increment into a degree measure. The range of angles from the X-Y plane is −90 to 90, a total of 180 degrees, and .05 X 180 is 9.

For a good perspective view, we want an angle of about 9 degrees from the X-Y plane, and 0 degrees in the X-Y plane. To ensure that you get the results presented here, we suggest that you type in the angles.

> Type "9" for the angle from X-Y and then "0" for the angle in X-Y.

Your screen will resemble *Figure 15-23*. Though it appears that your mesh has been flattened, in fact this is a three-dimensional parallel projection. The flattening is a result of foreshortening. When we switch to a perspective view, the appearance will be quite different. Notice that it would be extremely difficult to draw in this foreshortened image.

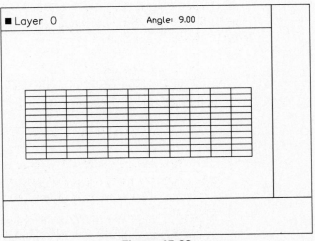

Figure 15-23

NOTE: If you find that your mesh has turned into a horizontal line on the screen it is because you have reversed angles. With 0 as the angle from the X-Y plane, you will be looking edge on and the mesh will appear as a line regardless of what angle in the X-Y plane is specified.

We will not use the TArget option in this exercise. The process is exactly the same. Vertical and horizontal motion controls the rotation of the target point from and in the X-Y plane. The camera location does not change. Instead, we change the direction in which the camera is aimed. It is like panning with a movie camera. The camera pans up and down with the vertical motion of the cursor, left and right with horizontal motion. You will notice that the image on the screen shifts more radically than in the Camera option and that it is easy to "pan" away from the image so that it flies off the screen entirely.

"Distance" and Perspective

Another aspect of any camera-to-target relationship is the distance between the two. The "Distance" option moves the camera position in or out along the line of sight. It differs from "Zoom" in that it automatically creates a perspective view.

> Type "d" or select "Distance".

The distance option uses a slider bar just like the zoom option. However, since "Distance" turns perspective on and distances are interpreted differently in perspective viewing, your preview image may look very different from the way it appeared before you entered the option.

> Move the cursor back and forth and watch the image move along the lines of perspective.

> Move the slider to about 1.5X and press the pick button.

Your screen will resemble *Figure 15-24*. Notice the perspective effect and the perspective icon that replaces the UCS icon.

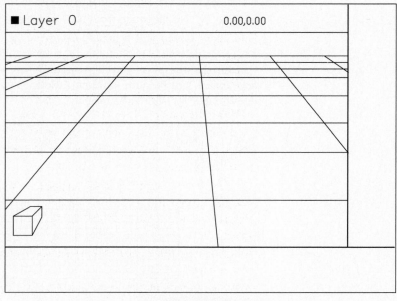

Figure 15-24

NOTE: If you enter the "Zoom" option while in a perspective view, you will see AutoCAD prompt for a "Lens length" rather than a zoom factor. In perspective, "DVIEW Zoom" operates like changing lenses on a camera to enlarge or reduce the field of vision. This is consistent with the photographic metaphor. We suggest you try it.

Saving 3D Views with VIEW

Once you are in perspective, you will find that your drawing capabilities are severely limited. Many commands will not work at all. Perspective is a presentation feature, not an editing or drawing feature. If you wish to do more drawing and editing, you will need to leave the perspective view and go back to the usual parallel projection. However, by using the VIEW command you can save all the view adjustment work you have done so that you can come back to it at any time without going through DVIEW again. When you do, any editing or drawing done in the meantime will be included. For reference, here is the procedure for saving a view:

1. Type or select "view".

2. Type "s" or select "Save".

3. Type a name for the view.

Clipping Planes

Next we will explore one last feature of the DVIEW command. By using a "clipping" plane, we will temporarily remove part of the drawing.

> Type "cl" or select "CLip".

This option allows you to temporarily remove everything in front of or behind a specified plane. In a full 3D model of a house, for example, you can use this option to remove a wall and display the inside of a room.

AutoCAD prompts:

Back/Front/<Off>:

If "back" is chosen, everything behind the specified plane will be removed; if "front" is chosen, objects in front will be removed. We will use a front clipping plane.

> Type "f" or select "front".

AutoCAD places a horizontal slider bar at the top of the screen.

> Move the cursor all the way to the right.

This places the clipping plane completely behind the mesh, so that the entire image is clipped, leaving nothing but the horizon.

> Move the cursor slowly to the left.

Watch the image gradually appear as the clipping plane covers up less and less. Keep moving to the left until the whole image is visible. Notice that the clipping plane is perpendicular to the line of sight, parallel to the plane of the screen.

> Now move the cursor back to the right until you have an image similar to the one in *Figure 15-25*.

> Press the pick button to register the clipping plane position.

> Press enter to exit the DVIEW command.

Your screen will be redrawn as shown in the figure.

Clipped images, like perspective views, can be saved using the VIEW command.

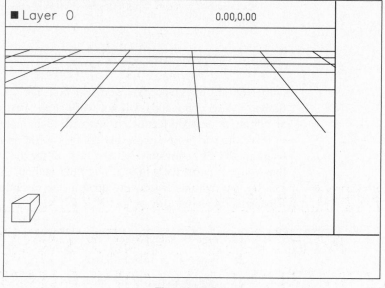

Figure 15-25

The Dview Hide Option

There is a "Hide" option within the DVIEW command that allows you to hide your preview image. This can help in visualizing the 3D object and as a preview of the HIDE command itself. Hidden lines are only removed temporarily. They will return as soon as you exit DVIEW.

Turning Off Perspective and Clipping Planes

It is extremely important to turn off perspective and clipping when you are through with them. With perspective on, you will be unable to execute most drawing functions. Try zooming, for example, and you will get a standard message:

**   ** This command may not be invoked in a perspective view **

Clipping planes are somewhat less inhibiting, but remain in effect even as you change viewpoints. When you switch viewpoints the line of sight and viewing angle may change dramatically. However, the clipping plane will remain parallel to the plane of the screen and at the same "distance". This can yield some pretty strange results.

Both effects may be turned off by reentering the DVIEW command. The "Off" option of the first prompt will turn perspective off, while "CLip" has its own "Off" option. In either case, you can speed up the process by pressing enter at the "Select objects:" prompt and ignoring AutoCAD's default preview image.

There are quicker methods, however. For example, usually you will leave a perspective view in order to work in another 3D view or a plan view. You can go directly into these by entering the VPOINT or PLAN commands and specifying a new view.

VPOINT and PLAN will turn perspective off but not clipping planes. However if you have saved any views, you can restore them using the VIEW command. VIEW will remove clipping planes.

In summary, you can use VIEW or DVIEW to remove clipping planes and perspective, VPOINT or PLAN to remove perspective only.

APPENDIX

A
RELEASE 12 PULL DOWN MENUS AND PRIMARY SCREEN MENU HIERARCHY

On the next two pages you will find charts to help you find your way around in the AutoCAD standard menu system. The first shows you what is available in the pull down menus and the second shows you where to find commands and subcommands in the screen system.

AutoCAD®Release 12

Menu Bar and Pull Down Menus

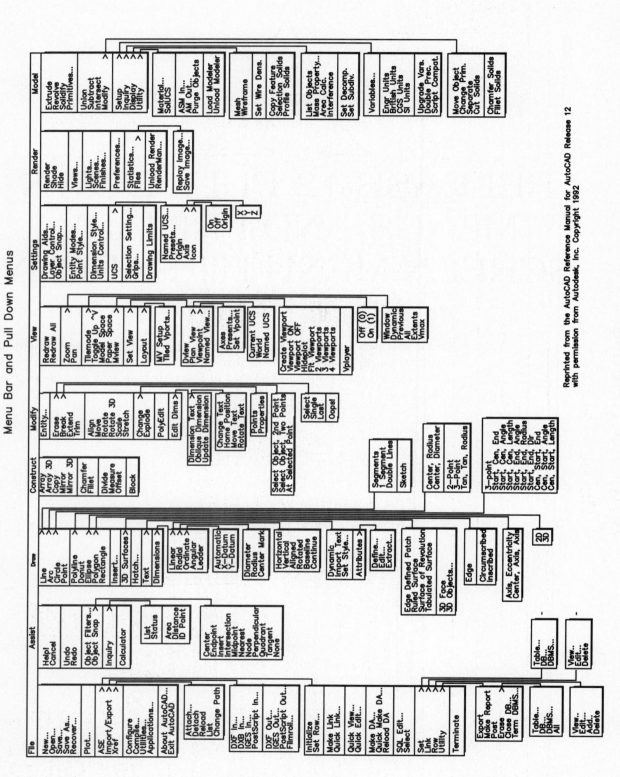

Reprinted from the AutoCAD Reference Manual for AutoCAD Release 12 with permission from Autodesk, Inc. Copyright 1992

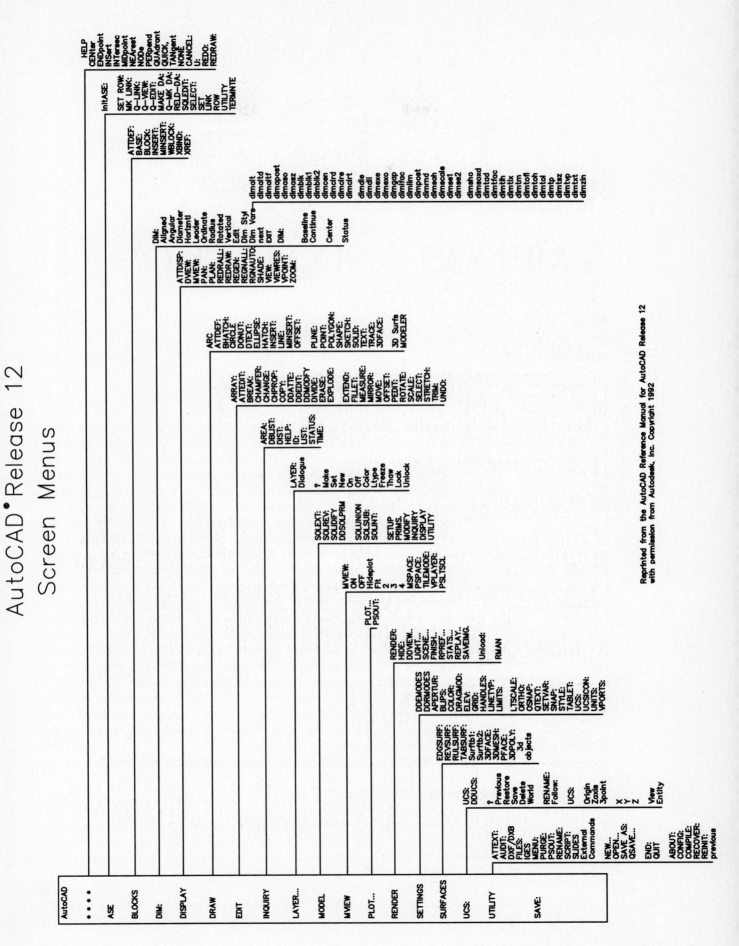

AutoCAD® Release 12
Screen Menus

Reprinted from the AutoCAD Reference Manual for AutoCAD Release 12 with permission from Autodesk, Inc. Copyright 1992

APPENDIX

B

MENUS AND MACROS

When you begin to look below the surface of AutoCAD as it is configured straight out of the box, you will find a whole world of customization possibilities. This "open architecture," which allows you to create your own menus, commands, and automated routines, is one of the reasons for AutoCAD's success. It is characteristic of all AutoCAD releases and has made room for a vast network of third party developers to create custom software products tailoring AutoCAD to the particular needs of various industries.

Over time, the options for customizing AutoCAD have grown and become more powerful. Many of the basics of menu structure, however, have not changed. The intention of this discussion is not to make you an AutoCAD developer, but to give you a taste of what is going on in the menu system. After reading this, you should have a sense of what an AutoCAD menu is and how it works. You should also understand that menu development is a complex subject. Before you attempt any menu development of your own, you should make a thorough study of the *AutoCAD Customization Manual*.

True to form, AutoCAD Release 12 provides several different ways to accomplish most customization tasks. A customized command sequence, for example, may result from a simple keyboard macro, an AutoLISP routine, a line of DIESEL string expression language, or a C language program connected to AutoCAD through ADS (AutoCAD Development System). We will confine our discussion to the organization of a menu file and the language of macros. These are easy to learn and require little programming background. AutoLISP, DIESEL, and C, on the other hand, are topics requiring a good deal of explanation and a knowledge of programming.

The following discussion also assumes a basic knowledge of MS-DOS.

What Is an AutoCAD Menu?

Most likely, every time you have begun a drawing in AutoCAD you have used either the AutoCAD standard menu or some other menu that is available on your system. This menu is what makes it possible for you to select commands off the screen or tablet. Without a menu, you are limited to typing commands.

Menu files have a standard format that AutoCAD can read, and standard extensions so that AutoCAD can recognize them. The extensions include .mnx, .mnu, and .mnl files. For example, the AutoCAD standard menu is contained in a file called ACAD.mnx. This file is loaded when you begin a new drawing using the ACAD.dwg prototype or any other prototype drawing that was created using ACAD.mnx. The .mnx file is an executable file written in machine language. But there is also an ASCII version of ACAD.mnx called ACAD.mnu. ACAD.mnx was created by compiling ACAD.mnu into machine code. The importance of ACAD.mnu is that you can look at it with a word processor and revise it if you wish. Then you can compile it again with your changes included. .mnu files can be created in any word processing program or text editor and are easy to read and understand once you know the syntax.

There is also a file called ACAD.mnl which is loaded along with ACAD.mnx. This file contains AutoLISP expressions that are referred to in ACAD.mnx.

Once you know the language, you can create your own menu, completely separate from the ACAD file. You would create the file in any word processor or text editor with an ASCII format and give it a name with a .mnu extension. Then when you wanted to load it into a drawing you would follow this procedure:

1.   At the "Command:" prompt, type "menu".

2.   Type your menu's name with no extension.

3.   Wait... AutoCAD will create the .mnx file and then load it. (Once the .mnx file is created, it will not have to be recompiled the next time you load it.)

What Does a Menu Look Like?

If you go into whatever word processor or text editor you have available on your system and load the file ACAD.mnu (it usually will be located in a directory called Acad\Support) you will see the first page of the menu. Menu files are quite large and you will see only a small portion on your screen. The complete menu will be about 120 pages long. A good way to learn about menus is to print out a copy and study it, using the list of characters at the end of this appendix, and the *AutoCAD Customization Manual*.

How Is a Menu Organized?

Take a look at this section from ACAD.mnu, which creates the familiar main screen menu:

```
***SCREEN
**S
[AutoCAD]^C^C^P(ai_rootmenus) ^P
[* * * *]$S=OSNAPB
[ASE]^C^C^P(ai_aseinit_chk) ^P
[BLOCKS]$S=X  $S=BL
[DIM:]^C^C_DIM
[DISPLAY]$S=X  $S=DS
[DRAW]$S=X  $S=DR
[EDIT]$S=X  $S=ED
[INQUIRY]$S=X  $S=INQ
[LAYER...]$S=LAYER  '_DDLMODES
[MODEL]$S=X  $S=SOLIDS
[MVIEW]$S=MVIEW
[PLOT...]^C^C_PLOT
[RENDER]$S=X  $S=RENDER
[SETTINGS]$S=X  $S=SET
[SURFACES]$S=X  $S=3D
[UCS:]^C^C_UCS
[UTILITY]$S=X  $S=UT

[SAVE:]^C^C_QSAVE
```

If you look closely at the words in brackets beginning on the third line, you will recognize the items from the main screen menu.

Using this as an example we can make the following general points about organization:

1. Menus are organized into lines. Each line is associated with a single item on a screen menu, an item on a pull down menu, or a box on a tablet menu. The only exceptions to this are those lines that begin with asterisks. These serve organizational purposes.

2. Lines that begin with asterisks are called section headers. These lines serve only organizational purposes.
   - "3 star headers" such as "***SCREEN" identify major sections including the button functions, the pull down menus, the screen menu, and the four tablet areas.
   - "2 star headers" such as "**S" identify individual menus and submenus.

3. Menus and submenus are called using the format $S=S (notice that the asterisks are dropped in the call).

4. Words written in brackets, such as [AutoCAD] are labels. They do not perform functions but are simply written on the screen as identifiers.

What Is a "Macro"?

Macros are available in many software packages and have the function of storing lengthy and frequently used sequences of keystrokes in a reduced shorthand form. Much of AutoCAD's menu system depends on macros. In order to understand and create macros in this system there are a few items of syntax that you need to know.

Let's look at a very simple item from the LINE command submenu of the screen menu system. It looks like this:

[LINE:]^C^C_LINE

[LINE:]   You will see brackets in items on the screen menu or the pull down system but never in the tablet area. These entries simply write text to the screen to identify the function that the line is to perform. This is the way all text is written for the screen and pull down menus.

^C^C   This appears frequently. The """ character is read by AutoCAD as the equivalent of the Ctrl key on your keyboard. So, what you see here is the menu equivalent of typing Ctrl-C (Cancel) twice. This ensures that any command in process is cancelled before another one is entered. Often two cancels are required to bring you all the way out of one command before you enter another.

_LINE   This is the LINE command. Commands on the menu are typed exactly as they would be on the keyboard except that the _ is added as a flag identifying this as the English language command. This allows foreign language versions of AutoCAD to use menus developed in English.

Taken as a whole, then, this line does three things:

1. [LINE:] writes "LINE:" on the screen menu.
2. ^C^C cancels any command in progress.
3. _LINE initiates the LINE command.

With this basic understanding, you should be able to make use of the list of macro characters included at the end of this appendix.

What Other Languages Can Be Used in Menu Development?

AutoCAD Release 12 allows you to create customized routines in three other languages in addition to the macro language presented here. AutoLISP is a programming language based on LISP. LISP is a "list processing" language. You will see AutoLISP statements in ACAD.mnu enclosed in parentheses.

DIESEL (Direct Interpretatively Evaluated String Expression Language) is a language that evaluates strings and returns string results. DIESEL borrows many of its terms from AutoLISP, and DIESEL expressions are also enclosed in parentheses. DIESEL expressions, however, are always proceeded by $M=. DIESEL is useful for such simple procedures as toggling the values of AutoCAD variables.

C language programs can be written and linked to AutoCAD through ADS, the AutoCAD Development System. ADS programs are read by the AutoLISP interpreter and then passed to AutoCAD as if they were AutoLISP. C is a high level programming language. It has more power and is also significantly faster than AutoLISP. Programs written in C and run through ADS will run faster than AutoLISP programs.

In addition to these three languages, AutoCAD also includes a language for interface with database programs such as PARADOX or dBASE IV. This is called the AutoCAD SQL Extension (ASE). SQL stands for Structured Query Language.

How Is a Tablet Configured to Match a Menu?

AutoCAD reads the tablet sections of a menu file in a particular way that must correspond to the configuration of the physical tablet overlay that is attached to the digitizer. In ACAD.mnu there are four tablet sections, each corresponding to an area on the tablet overlay. Each line of the menu file corresponds to a box on the overlay, and boxes are read from left to right, top to bottom, area by area. This means that there must be a way to tell AutoCAD how many rows and columns are contained in each tablet area. This is done using the TABLET command and the following procedure (the tablet overlay must be securely in place on your digitizer before you begin):

1. Type or select "TABLET".
2. Type or select "CFG" (configure).
3. Enter the number of tablet areas on your overlay.
4. Type "y" to indicate that you want to realign the tablet menu areas.
5. In response to AutoCAD's prompts, point to the upper left, lower right, and lower left corners of each tablet menu area. Be sure that you do this in the same order as the tablets are named in the .mnu file.
6. After the outline of each area is specified, also specify the number of columns and rows in that area.

For additional information on tablets, see the *AutoCAD Customization Manual*.

The following table lists all the macro characters you will find in any AutoCAD menu, along with their functions.

Most Common AutoCAD Macro Characters
(in order of appearance in ACAD.mnu)

***	Major section header.
;	Same as pressing enter while typing.
$	Begins any screen or pull down menu call.
$pn=*	Pulls down the menu called for pull down area n.
^	Ctrl
^C	Ctrl-C
^C^C	Double cancel, cancels any command, ensures a return to the "Command:" prompt before a new command is issued.
***POPn	Section header, where n is a number between 10 and 16, identifying one of the 16 possible pull down menu areas. POP0 refers to the cursor menu.
[ ]	Brackets enclose text to be written directly to the screen or pull down menu area. Eight characters are printed on the screen menu. The size of names on the pull down menu varies.
->	Indicates the first item in a cascading menu.
<-	Indicates the last item in a cascading menu.
'	Transparent command modifier.
_	English language flag.
[--]	Writes a blank line on a pull down menu.
^P	Toggles menu echo off and on so that macro characters do not appear on the command line as they are being entered via the menu.
( )	Parentheses enclose AutoLISP and DIESEL expressions.
$S=	Calls a menu. If there is no menu name following the equal sign, the previous menu is called.
$M=	Introduces a DIESEL expression.
\	Pause for user input. Allows for keyboard entry, point selection, and object selection. Terminated by press of enter or pick button.
~	Begins a pull down menu label that is "grayed out." May be used to indicate a function not presently in use.
*^C^C	This set of characters will cause the menu item to repeat.
space	A single blank space in the middle of a line is treated as a press of the enter key.
$i=*name*	Calls an icon menu.
$i=*	Displays an icon menu.
+	Used at the end of a line to indicate that the menu item continues on the next line.

APPENDIX

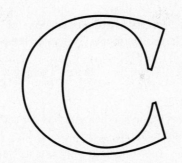

ADDITIONAL AUTOCAD COMMANDS

In order to make this text as clear, concise, and useful as possible, we have had to set some priorities about what to include. The following is a glossary of commands we have not discussed. Some are obsolete or seldom used, while some are very useful but only for a limited range of applications.

All commands that are marked with an apostrophe (') can be used transparently. That is, they can be executed while other commands are in process.

'ABOUT. Displays a dialogue box with the version of AutoCAD, the serial number, and other information.

AREA. Computes the area of a polygon, circle, or closed polyline entity.

AUDIT. Locates and diagnoses errors in the current drawing.

'BASE. Allows specification of a base insertion point for a complete drawing. If a base point has not been specified, (0,0,0) will be used.

BLIPMODE. When set to "off," blips are not shown.

COLOR. Sets color for subsequently drawn objects. Setting may be BYBLOCK or BYLAYER.

COMPILE. Compiles shape and font files so that they will load faster.

CONFIG. Allows configuration of video display, digitizer, plotter, and operating parameters.

'DDGRIPS. Displays a dialogue box for enabling or disabling grips, and setting their colors.

'DDEMODES. When "on," makes a dialogue box available for setting current layer, color, linetype, elevation, and thickness.

'DDLMODES.   When "on," makes a dialogue box available for defining properties of individual layers.

DDRENAME.   Displays a dialogue box for renaming text styles, layers, linetypes, blocks, views, User Coordinate Systems, viewport configurations, and dimension styles.

'DDRMODES.   When "on," makes a dialogue box available for setting snap, grid, and axis.

'DDSELECT.   Displays a dialogue box for setting entity selection modes, pickbox size, and entity sorting method.

DDUCS.   Displays a dialogue box for defining, saving, and selecting User Coordinate Systems.

'DELAY.   Used in script files to pause for a specified period of time.

DIVIDE.   Draws marker points at evenly spaced intervals along an object, dividing it into a specified number of parts. These points can be used as "nodes" for object snap.

DRAGMODE.   When set to "A," allows dragging to occur automatically, without request, whenever possible. When "on," allows dragging by request only. When "off," inhibits all dragging.

DXBIN.   Inserts a DXB format, binary coded, file into a drawing.

DXFIN.   Loads a DXF format, drawing interchange file, into a drawing. DXF files are standard ASCII text files that can easily be processed by other programs.

DXFOUT.   Creates a drawing file in DXF format.

ELEV.   Sets elevation and thickness for subsequently drawn objects.

FILES.   Allows access to the "File utility" menu from within the drawing editor.

FILMROLL.   Writes a file for use with AutoShade.

'GRAPHSCR.   Switches to the graphics screen. Used in script files in conjunction with TEXTSCR to switch between text and graphics.

HANDLES.   Assigns a unique identification number to every entity in a drawing.

'ID.   Displays x,y, and z coordinates of a selected point in the command area.

IGESIN.   Loads an IGES, Initial Graphics Exchange Format, drawing file.

IGESOUT.   Writes a drawing file in IGES format.

LOAD.   Loads a file of shapes to be used by the SHAPE command.

MEASURE.   Draws marker points at specified intervals along an object. These points can be used as "nodes" for object snap.

OPEN.   Displays a standard dialogue box file list of existing drawings. Selected drawing will be opened.

PFACE.   Allows vertex by vertex construction of a 3D polygon mesh.

PSDRAG.   When set to 0, only the bounding box of a postscript image file being brought into AutoCAD using the PSIN command is shown. When set to 0, the actual image is visible for dragging into place.

PSFILL.   Fills 2D polyline outlines with patterns contained in the postscript support file ACAD.psf.

PSIN.   Allows importation of Encapsulated Postscript Files (.eps extension).

PSOUT.   Allows exportation of the current drawing and view as an Encapsulated Postscript File.

PURGE.   Deletes unused blocks, layers, text styles, linetypes, and dimension styles from the current drawing. Must be the first command executed when a drawing is opened.

QTEXT.   When "on," allows text to be written without displaying actual characters on the screen. Instead, the text area is outlined for faster regeneration. When desired, turn QTEXT "off" and perform a REGEN to replace outlined areas with actual text.

RECOVER.   Attempts to recover damaged drawings.

REINIT.   Allows reinitializing of ports, digitizer, display, plotter, and PCP file.

REDEFINE.   Restores the definition of built-in AutoCAD commands that have been temporarily deleted using UNDEFINE.

REGENAUTO.   When "off," inhibits automatic regenerations that occur as the result of certain commands.

RENAME.   Allows user to change the names of layers, linetypes, blocks, views, text styles, User Coordinate Systems, viewport configurations, and dimension styles.

'RESUME.   Used in script files to resume execution of a script that has been interrupted.

RSCRIPT.   Used in script files to repeat the script. Allows for continuous running of slide show presentations.

SCRIPT.   Loads and executes a script file.

SELECT.   Allows object selection to occur before entering other commands. Options are the same as those in most edit commands.

SH.   Allows access to MS-DOS/PC-DOS commands while running AutoCAD. Requires less memory than SHELL.

SHAPE.   Draws shapes that have been defined in the drawing database using the LOAD command.

SHELL.   Allows access to operating system and utility programs while running Auto-CAD. Available memory may restrict what programs can be run. Requires more memory than SH.

'STATUS. Displays statistics and information about the current drawing on the text screen.

TABLET. Aligns tablet with paper for digitizing a drawing. Also allows tablet to be configured correctly for a tablet menu overlay.

'TEXTSCR. Switches to the text screen. Used in script files in conjunction with GRAPHSCR to switch between text and graphics.

'TIME. Displays current time and date, time and date current drawing was created, time and date of last update, time of current session in drawing editor, and elapsed time. Elapsed time is a timer function. To begin timing, it must first be set to "on."

UNDEFINE. Temporarily deletes the definition of a built-in AutoCAD command. This allows the command name to be used for an alternate function defined in an AutoLISP program. See REDEFINE.

UNDO. Undoes multiple commands. UNDO is similar to "U", but it contains options to define a series of commands as a "group" that can be undone at once.

VIEWRES. Controls the precision with which arcs and circles are displayed prior to regeneration. The higher the resolution, the longer it takes to display objects. Resolution is based on the number of sides displayed in a "circle."

3DPOLY. Creates a 3D polyline with straight line segments only. There are no arc options in the 3DPOLY command.

INDEX